Basic Concepts and Models for Interpreter and Translator Training

Benjamins Translation Library (BTL)

The BTL aims to stimulate research and training in translation and interpreting studies. The Library provides a forum for a variety of approaches (which may sometimes be conflicting) in a socio-cultural, historical, theoretical, applied and pedagogical context. The Library includes scholarly works, reference books, post-graduate text books and readers in the English language.

EST Subseries

The European Society for Translation Studies (EST) Subseries is a publication channel within the Library to optimize EST's function as a forum for the translation and interpreting research community. It promotes new trends in research, gives more visibility to young scholars' work, publicizes new research methods, makes available documents from EST, and reissues classical works in translation studies which do not exist in English or which are now out of print.

Volume 8

Basic Concepts and Models for Interpreter and Translator Training.
Revised edition
by Daniel Gile

Basic Concepts and Models for Interpreter and Translator Training

Revised edition

Daniel Gile
Université Paris 3 - Sorbonne Nouvelle

John Benjamins Publishing Company

Amsterdam / Philadelphia

^{TM} The paper used in this publication meets the minimum requirements of American National Standard for Information Sciences – Permanence of Paper for Printed Library Materials, ANSI z39.48-1984.

Library of Congress Cataloging-in-Publication Data

Gile, Daniel.
  Basic concepts and models for interpreter and translator training / Daniel Gile. -- Rev. ed.
      p. cm. (Benjamins Translation Library, ISSN 0929-7316 ; v. 8)
  Includes bibliographical references and index.
  1. Translators--Training of. 2. Translating and interpreting. I. Title.
P306.5.G55   2009
418'.02071--dc22   2009035932
ISBN 978 90 272 2433 0   (Hb ; alk. paper)
ISBN 978 90 272 2432 3   (Pb ; alk. paper)

John Benjamins Publishing Co. · P.O. Box 36224 · 1020 ME Amsterdam · The Netherlands
John Benjamins North America · P.O. Box 27519 · Philadelphia PA 19118-0519 · USA

Table of contents

Preface to the revised edition

Acknowledgments

Before anything else, I should like to acknowledge the time and effort Miriam Shlesinger and Gideon Toury devoted to the manuscript of the first edition of *Basic Concepts and Models* back in 1994 and thank them for their comments and suggestions. For this revised edition, I am grateful to Carol Patrie and María Teresa Bajo Molina for their input on signed language interpreting and psycholinguistic issues respectively. All these contributions have been very valuable.

∽

In 1995, John Benjamins kindly published my textbook for the interpreter and translator training classroom entitled *Basic Concepts and Models for Interpreter and Translator Training*. The book turned out to be successful, perhaps because it met a need. Meanwhile, I have continued to experiment and learn in various training environments and to read (increasingly interesting) publications from the literature. This has provided me with useful input to correct and hopefully improve my ideas, models and methods. Nearly a decade after the publication of *Basic Concepts and Models*, I completed a new book focusing on the translator training component, which was published by Presses Universitaires de France (Gile 2005); it was translated and published in Chinese in 2008 and is being translated to be published shortly in Arabic as well. Such encouraging reactions and the need to update *Basic Concepts and Models* prompted me to work on this new text, which incorporates further corrections and improvements for the interpreting component as well.

My initial idea was to write a new book which would replace *Basic Concepts and Models*. Reading it critically again and again, I found that while many clarifications, corrections and references were necessary, the overall structure and content of *Basic Concepts and Models* were still the best I could offer. Another question was whether the content was still relevant after 15 years in view of developments in the field. My subjective answer to some soul-searching was that it was, as I have not found in the literature other concepts and models of the same type to replace them. A somewhat less subjective and perhaps more reliable answer is suggested by citation evidence: *Basic Concepts and Models* is cited often in the literature, including recent papers, which suggests it is still viewed as useful.

I therefore opted for a revision of the previous edition, keeping its general structure except for the last chapter. In the first edition, Chapter 10 was devoted to an analysis of the literature on training. Over the past decade, training-centred and training-related publications have come out in large numbers and are still being produced at a high rate, dozens or more each year, including research papers, theses, dissertations, monographs and collective volumes. Writing a review of the literature, while useful in a paper, would probably not make much sense in a book. It was replaced with a new chapter devoted to a conceptual framework designed to help introduce students to Translation *theory* beyond basic concepts and models – painlessly, or so I hope.

Corrections and improvements have been introduced in all chapters. Some references to public service interpreting and to signed language interpreting have been incorporated for awareness raising. Terminology has been revised. *Inter alia*, 'interpreting' has replaced 'interpretation' systematically when referring to oral translation, 'Translation competence' has replaced 'Translation expertise' to avoid ambiguity associated with current interest in the psychological concept of expertise. 'Short-term memory' has been kept, but 'working memory' has been added, with explanations about the similarities and differences between the two concepts.

The following are a few changes introduced in various chapters:

In Chapter 2, a distinction has been introduced between macro-level and micro-level aims in language communication, as well as a discussion of behavioural components of Translation quality. In Chapter 3, the Cultural component has been added to 'Linguistically Induced Information', turning the term LII into LCII; the discussion of fidelity in relation to the Message and Secondary Information has been fine-tuned, and a second appendix showing data from another replication of the fidelity experiment has been added. In Chapter 5, an analysis of decision-making, with associated gains and risks of losses, has been added. In Chapter 6, the overall analysis has been tightened up, and the important role of the Web in ad hoc Knowledge Acquisition is discussed.

Note that this book, which is devoted to concepts and models, addresses the *fundamentals* of human Translation and does not cover Translation technology, including Translation memories.

Chapter 7, on the Effort Models, has been rewritten extensively, with reference to working memory, to the Tightrope Hypothesis, and explanations about how these Efforts stand with respect to cognitive psychology and about their status as didactic models as opposed to falsifiable theories. In Chapter 8, a substantial analysis of conditions and reasons for online problems in interpreting has been added, including a discussion of potential language-specific difficulties, and in Chapter 9, references to relevant studies from cognitive science have been added. The discussion of language availability and the presentation of the Gravitational Model have been extended with some changes and further considerations, and a section on directionality has been added. Overall, for Chapters 7 to 9, relevant studies from cognitive science have been cited to show its relevance to comprehension of interpreting and translation processes, but I have tried to keep the text simple.

A glossary has been placed at the end of the book for convenience, and a name index has been added. The bibliographical reference list has been updated, with more than 150 new entries.

I hope that this revised version of *Basic Concept and Models* will continue to be useful as a conceptual companion to practical exercises in the classroom.

Introduction

Over the last few decades, there has been a dramatic increase in the number of publications on interpreting and translation. Whereas in the past most were 'philosophical' and dealt with notions such as translatability, questions of fidelity and the role of translation in literature and culture, an increasing proportion of texts on interpreting and translation (*Translation* with a capital T) are becoming technical and specific and focus on linguistic, psycholinguistic, terminological and professional issues.

One very central topic in writings about Translation is training. It is increasingly recognized that formal training in Translation schools is the most practical way to teach and test abilities to provide the market with reliable professionals, and the number of translator and interpreter training programmes has been increasing sharply over the past two to three decades in many parts of the world. Caminade and Pym (1995) list more than 250 university programmes in more than 60 countries, but since the 1990s, many more programmes were set up, in particular in China where the government has recently decided to set up MTIs, Masters in Translation and Interpreting.

Research on the nature and components of Translation competence and on its acquisition has also been developing, and research on training methods is starting to gain momentum as well. And yet, the diversity of situations, needs and relevant variables and parameters is huge, meaning that it may take a long time before empirical research findings can claim to be able to discriminate between excellent, good and sub-optimal methods on a solid basis. This is why at this point the training of professional translators and interpreters is still based essentially on professional experience, introspection, intuition and negotiations between trainers on methods and modalities rather than on research.

Such a situation does not preclude conceptual, theoretical or philosophical grounding for Translator training, especially in programmes training professionals (as opposed to language departments where translation is essentially part of language instruction). In fact, communication-based approaches such as functionalist theories or Interpretive Theory have been a strong conceptual basis for training methods in major programmes in Europe and beyond for several decades.

The concepts and models presented here were developed initially to meet a personal need. Like other colleagues, having had the good fortune of learning a couple of languages early in life, I started my career as a self-taught translator. About ten years later, I had the opportunity to undergo formal training in conference interpreting and became fascinated by the debates around Translation which Translation practice generated. Some answers were suggested at classroom sessions during initial training, and others in a doctoral programme which I attended in the late 1970s. I was not always happy with those answers. Inter alia, I felt the need for some justification of the claim that fidelity is maintained even when words are changed during interlinguistic transfer, and wanted to understand why interpreting was such a difficult exercise and what evidence there was to demonstrate that the learning and interpreting strategies advocated by teachers were the best. Many of the teachers' answers were initially attractive because they were short, clear and gave a positive image of the Translator's work, but I felt that some were overstated, and that the rationale and evidence to back them were weak. As a self-taught translator who had learned his trade while working, I also felt, while undergoing formal training in one school, and later, when learning about the situation in other schools, that the potential advantages of the classroom environment over self-training and on-the-job training were not always leveraged as they could be, and that training methods could be improved. I therefore set out to seek my own answers.

My search for answers to fundamental questions in the literature began in 1978. I started developing personal training principles and methods in 1979, when I was entrusted with a course in scientific and technical translation from Japanese into French, and then with interpreting courses as well. As time went by, a set of basic concepts, models and methods gradually crystallized. My doctoral dissertation on the training of interpreters and translators between Japanese and French (Gile 1984a) already included many of the ideas presented here – in various states of development. Since then, I have gained more experience and conducted classroom experiments, held more discussions on training practices with colleagues in various parts of the world, read more texts in Translation Studies and related subjects, attended more conferences and seminars. As a result, I have continued to develop and improve my conceptual framework. In 1989, I wrote a short monograph on basic concepts and models for interpreter training which I distributed to colleagues, asking for comments and criticism. There were many requests for copies of the monograph, including several requests for permission to use it as a textbook for Translation courses. This suggested that, imperfect as the work was, its approach apparently met a need, and it could possibly be turned into a useful publication. The present book is the much expanded and (it is hoped) significantly improved product that evolved from the initial 1989 monograph.

The concepts and models presented here are the result of much research, including naturalistic studies (the systematic observation of phenomena as they occur in the field), experimental studies (the study of controlled situations generated by the researcher), and theoretical studies, both from Translation Studies and from other disciplines, in particular *cognitive psychology* and *psycholinguistics*. However, this text is not a presentation of research: first, the book reports on results more than on the processes that led to them; second, it ventures beyond research results into some speculation, when evidence points strongly in certain directions but does not provide a solid enough basis for 'scientific' assertions. Moreover, because of their didactic nature, the contents of this book are often prescriptive. Their prescriptions are to my knowledge shared by a majority of trainers in professional schools of interpreting and translation world-wide. I have attempted to spell them out explicitly, along with some justification, but it is up to the reader to accept or reject them.

This book is written primarily for practitioners of conference interpreting and/or translation who teach one or both disciplines. Colleagues who are not engaged in training may also be interested in the basic concepts and models presented here as *explanations* of phenomena they encounter. Readers are presumed to be familiar with most of the practical Translation problems referred to in the text. Examples and detailed explanations are therefore given primarily for concepts which may be new to them. The bibliographical references vary in number according to the topic. Few references are given for questions which I thought of as posing no particular comprehension problems and as more or less generally accepted, and many more when discussing concepts from the cognitive sciences.

As explained in Chapter 1, this book is constructed around concepts and models designed as building blocks for training in conference interpreting and general non-literary translation. They cannot include *all* the questions and problems which crop up during courses, but they do attempt to respond to the most fundamental. They are designed to be integrated directly into classroom practice, as shown in the examples and appendixes. This is probably the most characteristic feature of this book as opposed to other books on Translator training. However, the explanations accompanying the concepts and models aim to give teachers some useful background beyond what will eventually be taught to the students. A summary, under the heading "What students need to remember," is provided at the end of each chapter as a checklist reminding instructors of the main points of the main points it seeks to make.

Another distinguishing feature of this book is that it deals with both interpreting and translation. Over the years, I have become convinced that the differences between these two activities are essentially associated with the cognitive stress interpreters face under the pressure of time (with far-reaching implications on strategies and online tactics), but that the similarities are fundamental and deserve to be highlighted for the benefit of all. I believe the contrast between interpreting and translation has been somewhat exaggerated in many schools, often by interpreters rather than translators, and often for sociological reasons rather than for reasons having to do with truly operational parameters. I also feel it is useful for translators to know something about interpreting and vice versa. All the chapters in the book except possibly Chapter 7, which deals specifically with cognitive pressure and its implications for interpreting, are to at least some extent relevant to both interpreting and translation.

The concepts and models presented in this book are intended for wide use and should be suitable for most learning situations in interpreting and translation. They have been designed as quasi-autonomous modules, which can be taught individually during short working sessions. Depending on the time available and on the trainees' needs, each component can be presented to them in less than one hour or up to several hours, as has been done many times in the past twenty-five years.

When conducting short seminars for Translation teachers, the modules can be used in lectures more or less as they are presented in the book because, as stated above, they are designed around and refer to phenomena and ideas already known to the participants. In initial training of students with no professional Translation experience, they are a methodological aid which introduces and supports the primary ingredient of training, namely hands-on practice. In continuing education seminars for professional interpreters and translators, they should at least be combined with a few examples so that their application becomes clear to trainees. In research seminars, they can provide a conceptual framework for a general overview of the problems at hand, but have to be supplemented with wider and more specific considerations and references, using material from Translation Studies and from the relevant cognate disciplines.

This book is designed for teachers of 'high-level' interpreting and translation, that is, interpreting and translation defined as the production of ready-to-use, accurate and well-written or well-prepared target-language texts or speeches respectively. Accordingly, it has been written primarily *for teachers in higher education*. Most of the principles it expounds can also be used in other types of courses, but students who do not have sufficient linguistic competence and/or taste for intellectual exercise may not be able to apply them to the same extent.

It may also be worth noting that this book deals with non-literary interpreting and translation, which are concerned mostly with messages *centred on information* rather than emotions. I have been told by literary translators that its concepts and models also apply to literary translation (my personal view it that they only do so to a limited extent – because they tend to deal with texts where communicational objectives are information-oriented)., but I do not feel qualified to tackle the problem of literary translation, with its intricate relationship between content and 'linguistic packaging' and the various aesthetic and other emotional dimensions it is associated with.

It is hoped that the basic concepts and models presented here will provide useful material to the reader: a reordering and clarification of familiar experience and ideas, suggestions for the optimization of Translator training, some new facts and ideas about the processes underlying interpreting and translation. Clearly, these concepts and models cannot be considered final: they have been evolving continuously, and can and must be improved with new input from experience and research. In keeping with the spirit in which they have been developed, I should be most grateful for comments on and criticism of the book's content and presentation.

Chapter 1

Theoretical components
in interpreter and translator training

1. The role of training in interpreting and translation

Interpreting and translation ('Translation' with an upper-case T) are practiced under a wide variety of conditions. Many interpreters and translators work full-time. Others such as housewives, students, medical practitioners, engineers and journalists work part-time for supplementary income (see for instance Katan 2009). Interpreting and translation work can also be assigned occasionally or regularly to employees whose official duties bear no relationship to such tasks but who happen to speak one or more foreign languages.

Translators can be required to perform highly creative work, as when they translate poems or other literary texts. At times, their work involves the acquisition and some deep processing of specialized information, in particular – but not exclusively – in scientific and technical translation. In other circumstances, it involves rewriting into a target language business letters, road signs, directions for hotel guests, information for tourists, etc. Translators may have to accept much responsibility, for instance when translating or interpreting important political speeches and legal texts. In other cases, they have a modest role, for instance when translating the menu for a cafeteria in a small town. Their educational level varies from top academic qualifications to a modest primary school level. Some enjoy high social prestige as 'creators' in their own right or highly skilled language mediators, while others are viewed as minor clerical staff. Their work may be intended to serve a single person, for instance a foreign guest at a specialized conference, or be subject to much exposure, for instance when they interpret for television or translate a best-selling book. Some earn a great deal of money, and others have very low salaries. In other words, although their activity is given the same name – 'interpreting' or 'translating'– intellectually, technically, socially, economically, it is far from homogeneous and perhaps these two words could be seen as hypernyms covering a rather wide range of distinct occupations.

Socially and economically, this situation is not favourable to top-level professionals: their status and working conditions tend to be dragged down by the existence of interpreters and translators at 'lower' levels rather than the other way around. Because there are so many self-proclaimed interpreters and translators whose level of performance is very low and so many 'bilinguals' who engage in translation without any training, many a layperson is not in a position to (and does not necessarily wish to) see and acknowledge the difference between them and high-level professionals. Titles such as 'conference interpreter', 'court interpreter', 'community interpreter', 'scientific translator', 'technical translator', or 'legal translator', which, incidentally, are not protected by law or regulations in most countries, may afford some defence against this phenomenon by discriminating between specialties and levels of expertise, but with insufficient effectiveness in most cases. Many laypersons, and even regular users of conference interpreting services, do not even have a clear idea of the difference between translation and interpreting.

In spite of the diversity of performance levels and conditions, interpreting and translation can be defined as performing essentially the same function, namely re-expressing in one language what has been expressed in another for communication or other purposes. At the lowest levels of performance requirements, this function can be fulfilled by persons having a minimum knowledge of the languages involved and no specific training. As quality requirements become more stringent, performance problems arise in connection with comprehension of the source Text, linguistic reformulation in the target language, behavioural issues (including compliance with norms of appropriate professional conduct), technical issues, ethical issues, psychological issues (in particular in public service interpreting)… Some of these are solved naturally: Translators (translators and interpreters) extend and deepen their knowledge of the languages and the subjects they deal with while Translating and by seeking to learn more through books, newspapers, other periodicals, lectures, workshops etc. Their technical and other skills also improve with practice.

Some, perhaps many, actually reach top-level performance through experience and self-instruction. Others encounter obstacles which halt their progression. I have been told by some experienced translators that they somehow never manage to free themselves from the source-language structure when writing target-language sentences, and by several experienced conference interpreters that they feel they do not perform well enough in consecutive interpreting because they have had no formal training in note-taking techniques. Other colleagues reach a certain level of proficiency with which they are comfortable but do not know how to move up, from instance from general translation to specialized translation, from sentence-by-sentence interpreting to 'true' consecutive interpreting, from consecutive to simultaneous interpreting.

This is by no means an absolute rule. I have had the opportunity to meet and sometimes work with self-taught interpreters and translators who have developed bad habits, but my experience does not match that of Wilhelm Weber, former dean of the Translation and Interpreting Division of the Monterey Institute for International Studies, who writes:

> Only exceptionally gifted people (of whom I have only met one or two during my professional career) can hope to accede to these professions on their own without developing serious bad habits and making mistakes that will tarnish their professional performance for the rest of their careers. (1984: 2)

In this context, the sometimes heated debate on whether "translators are born, not made" (Nida 1981) or "made, not born" (Healey 1978) seems rather pointless, at least if taken literally. While certain 'natural' aptitudes are prerequisites to high-quality translation – especially literary translation – or to simultaneous interpreting, it makes little sense to challenge the idea that guidance into Translation *can* be useful, be it for the purpose of helping natural talents unfold and develop or for instruction in technical procedures (see for instance Tetrault 1988; Viaggio 1988) and in the acquisition of linguistic and extralinguistic knowledge.

Interpreter and translator training can usefully be considered against this background. Formal training is not mandatory, but it can perform at least two important functions. One is to help individuals who wish to become professional interpreters or translators enhance their performance *to the full realization of their potential*. The other is to help them develop their Translation skills *more rapidly* than through field experience and self-instruction, which may involve much groping in the dark and learning by trial-and-error.

Formal training programmes also have other functions, more social or professional in nature. In particular, they can help raise general professional standards in the marketplace by selecting the best candidates at admission and the truly skilled at graduation. This in turn may help raise the social status of Translators, especially if standards are set at postgraduate academic level. Through the professional circles they are connected to, training programmes can also help beginning interpreters and translators start their professional careers by introducing them to professional organizations and clients. This is a particularly important function in conference interpreting, as interpreting schools maintain close links with major international organizations and other institutional clients, and invite their representatives to take part in graduation examinations. Training programmes may also help standardize working methods (which may or may not be desirable), give Translators the comforting feeling they belong to a genuine profession, and provide good observation opportunities for research into interpreting and translation. Indeed, the vast majority of research projects on Translation are planned and carried out by academics who teach translation or interpreting (see Pöchhacker 1995 for interpreting), and a considerable amount of research uses the training environment for reflection, observation and experimenting.

All these social functions are important. However, they are to a large extent context-dependent and vary considerably from one country to the next and from one market to the next. In contrast, the didactic function of formal training is essentially invariant, although the *application* of common principles is also context-dependent, as operational aims vary according to the nature, duration, resources and baseline status of the relevant training programmes.

This book targets a relatively wide audience and focuses on the principles underlying the didactic function of training for high-level non-literary translation and conference interpreting.

Principles which apply to general, non-specialized translation, to technical and scientific translation, to conference interpreting and broadcast interpreting are presented and discussed; the book does not address systematically the specific needs and circumstances of dubbing, subtitling, localization, public service interpreting and of various signed language interpreting contexts. While I believe that students and practitioners studying and/or working in these areas can also benefit from the concepts and models presented in this book, and references to them can be found in works on signed language interpreting (see for instance Bélanger 1995, papers in Janzen 2005, books by Carol Patrie) and on public service interpreting (see for example Collados Aís & Fernández Sánchez 2001), each of these Translation sectors and modalities has technical, sociological and other idiosyncrasies, in particular with respect to the role of the translator or interpreter, and deserves additional teaching materials which are found in sector-specific literature.

2.   The components of Translation competence

In order to plan a syllabus and/or assess the value of a training programme, it is necessary to analyze what knowledge and technical skills are required for interpreting and translation (interesting practical suggestions on how to go about it are found in Kelly 2005). Over the years, authors have attempted to describe the components of Translation competence in many ways (see inter alia Roberts 1984; Nord 1991: 235; Kiraly 1995; Hansen 1997; Schäffner & Adab 2000; Hansen 2006b). Each individual analysis has its merits, but for the sake of simplicity and for the purposes of this book, I will stick to a presentation similar to Jean Maillot's (1981). More detailed discussions of the points made here can be found in other chapters in this book:

a.   Interpreters and translators need to have good passive knowledge of their passive working languages.

At first sight, the ability to understand texts/speeches in the languages translators and interpreters work from seems to be an obvious and therefore trivial prerequisite. It is less clear to the layperson how good this passive knowledge must be. For the 'lowest' levels of interpreting and translation work as referred to above, high-school knowledge of the foreign language can be enough, but as one moves up toward top-level translation and conference interpreting, requirements also increase. In conference interpreting, professionals must be able to respond *very rapidly* (see Chapters 7 to 9) to spoken language, a skill which is not acquired in foreign language studies as such. Moreover, they must understand specific language registers used in international organizations, in law, in politics, in science, in various realms of technology, as well as in literary, musical and other artistic and cultural circles. Literary translators must be able to grasp not only the basic informational meaning of texts, but also fine shades of meaning as expressed by subtle choices of words and expressions, as well as by their rhythm, music, and images – and be highly aware of cultural facts, norms, trends and atmospheres.

b. Interpreters and translators need to have good command of their active working languages.

In top-level interpreting and translation, this requirement is set at a very demanding standard. Basically, technical translators are required to be able to write *publishable* texts, that is, to have *professional writing/editorial skills* besides their trans-linguistic communication competence. As for literary translators, their writing skills must indeed be of the same nature as those of literary writers. Likewise, conference interpreters are required to be able to make speeches at a language quality level expected from the personalities they interpret, be they diplomats, scientists, politicians, artists or intellectuals, and appropriate for the relevant circumstances: press conferences, political speeches, scientific presentations, intellectual discussions etc. This requirement goes much beyond the 'natural' command one acquires over childhood and adolescence in one's native language.

c. Interpreters and translators need to have sufficient knowledge of the themes and subject-matters addressed by the texts or speeches they Translate.

This third requirement is formulated above in general and somewhat vague terms. Indeed, needs are highly variable, depending on the level of translation required, the subject-matter at hand and working conditions – hence the less than explicit "sufficient knowledge" qualification. Depending on their existing thematic knowledge and on the availability of documents and of human help, Translators can tackle more or less specialized subjects. 'Extralinguistic Knowledge' or 'World Knowledge' issues are discussed in Chapters 4 and 6, respectively on the Translator's comprehension of specialized discourse and on ad hoc Knowledge Acquisition.

d. Translators must have both declarative and procedural knowledge about Translation

'Declarative knowledge' is the kind of knowledge which can be described in words (see Chapter 8 in Anderson 1980); the Translator's declarative knowledge *about Translation* includes knowledge about the marketplace, about clients, about behavioural norms governing relations between Translators and clients and between Translators and other Translators, knowledge about information sources, about tools used in Translation, about the clients' specific expectations for each assignment etc. 'Procedural knowledge' is the ability to actually perform actions; the Translator's relevant procedural knowledge refers to 'technical skills' such as the ability to follow in one's decision-making the principles governing fidelity norms, to use techniques for ad hoc Knowledge Acquisition, for language enhancement and maintenance, for problem-solving, for decision-making, for note-taking in consecutive, for simultaneous interpreting, as well as, increasingly so, to mastery of modern translation technology and of technical skills required for specialized forms of translation, in particular localization, web translation and audiovisual translation. Chapters 3, 5, 6, 7, and 8 address the most fundamental of these technical skills, though, as mentioned in the introductory section to this chapter, they do not cover translation technology or the specifics of public service interpreting, audiovisual translation and interpreting, signed-language interpreting and localization.

Beyond translation competence, interpreters and translators need to meet some intellectual criteria and apparently to have some personality features. These have been listed and discussed intuitively by translator and interpreter trainers (see for instance Herbert 1952; Nilski 1967; Keiser 1978; Bossé Andrieu 1981), but have not yet been determined scientifically, notwithstanding a small number of research endeavours (see for example Campagne 1981; Henderson 1987; Suzuki 1988; Kurz 2000; Montani 2003; Schweda-Nicholson 2005). They are sometimes seen as prerequisites for admission into Translation schools, but are not directly addressed by training, although training should improve the subjects' capacity to use them more fully.

3. The diversity of training requirements

Of the components of knowledge and skills listed above, only the fourth is specific to Translation. Knowing foreign languages, being able to write texts of good editorial quality in one's own language and having general and specialized knowledge in one or several subjects are qualifications that can be found in many individuals, inter alia among international civil servants, international lawyers and journalists as well as expatriates working in many fields.

It also seems clear that journalists, scientists, international civil servants, international lawyers, engineers or scientists wishing to become interpreters or translators would not require the same training as language teachers who do not have much general and specialized knowledge, and requirements would differ for experts in a field of human activity who have good thematic and linguistic knowledge but lack editorial skills on one hand, and first-year university students in any discipline on the other. All such candidates to Translation could benefit from training in translation and interpreting techniques, but their needs in terms of language skills, editorial skills and knowledge build-up would differ greatly.

For the sake of optimization, variability in these parameters would call for a variety of training programmes, both short and long, full-time and part-time, student-oriented and professional-oriented, but basically two prototypes of formal training programmes can be defined.

3.1   Initial training programmes for newcomers to Translation

These are designed for regular (young) students who wish to become interpreters or translators through a formal training programme. Although some of them may already have some professional experience, they accept both beginner status in the course and the idea of a considerable time investment – several years. In most of the major schools of interpreting and translation in the 'West', which, incidentally, are part of or associated with universities, programmes last 2 to 4 years of full-time studies (generally 2 years at graduate level or 3 to 4 years at undergraduate level). There are or have been some shorter programmes as well, such as an intensive 6-month syllabus in conference interpreting at the University of Ottawa, 6-month in-house training programmes in conference interpreting at the United Nations and at the Commission of the European Community, and one-year programmes in some universities such as ETI (Geneva), but the vast majority of programmes with a solid reputation extend over two to four years.

In such programmes, students are involved full-time in training over a relatively long period and are therefore in a position to devote thousands of hours and considerable effort to all four components of Translation competence.

3.2   Conversion courses/further training/continuing education for practicing Translators

In spite of the fact that an increasing number of professional interpreters and translators are graduates of Translation schools, many have come and still come to the profession from other fields and activities. There is no reason for this to stop as long as interpreting and translation are not legally restricted to professionals holding official qualification. On the other hand, many self-taught professionals feel they would benefit from further training in some basic technical skills, and even Translation professionals who have been through formal training often wish to strengthen such skills and increase their familiarity with one or several specialized fields, or even improve their passive or active proficiency in one of their working languages for Translation purposes. This leads to some demand for additional training as well, as suggested by high attendance in workshops and seminars designed for professionals by Translation schools and professional associations in many countries.

Long programmes like those designed for ordinary students over one or several years full-time are not suited to the needs of professionals, who can ill afford to stop working for such a length of time to go over ground they have already covered during their previous studies and/or in the course of their professional experience and only pick up some useful elements here and there. This is why courses and workshops for practicing professionals are often short (one to several days), or held in the form of evening classes.

Regarding the syllabus of conversion/further training/continuing education courses: much of what is taught to beginning students is already known to professionals; moreover, practitioners with field experience can grasp easily some concepts which may seem abstract to beginning students and require more explanations and more class time. It follows that course design should differ in both content and approach depending on whether training aims at introducing beginning students to Translation or at strengthening a practicing professional's expertise. In the latter case, training may consist of customized efforts focused on particular sub-components of Translation competence as opposed to full coverage of the whole range of knowledge and skill components: for instance, individual courses and workshops may focus on note-taking in consecutive, on fundamental concepts and principles in legal interpreting, on translation in computer science, on patent translation, etc.

4.   The need for optimization in formal Translator training

In very short programmes designed for professionals, optimization is desirable as it can be for any endeavour which costs time and money, but it is perhaps not essential. If a bit of time is lost, it is not critical time, and professionals who feel they are not gaining much from the programme can stop attending it. In initial training programmes, the situation can be viewed differently in view of their duration and of the fact that *formal training* is but one way to access the Translation professions, two other choices being the *no-training option* and the *in-house on-the-job training option*; by the latter I mean learning by Translating for a company under the supervision or guidance of experienced colleagues.

The no-training option is probably weaker than the other two because it provides no outside guidance to the beginner who may thus be deprived of good advice and fall into bad habits. However, it is by no means clear that formal training is necessarily a better option than the in-house alternative. Some factors may make the latter more desirable than the former:

–   Both options involve progress under supervision. Theoretically, formal training provides closer supervision by qualified training experts (the teachers). In real life, the quality of supervision is not always better in formal training. When Translation teachers are professionals who teach part-time, which is the case of many instructors in many schools that train professional interpreters and translators, their (more lucrative) professional Translation work does not necessarily leave them much time to devote to supervision. Moreover, such professional Translators have generally not been trained for teaching and do not necessarily have pedagogical skills. When trainers are full-time academic instructors rather than professional Translators, they may be out of touch with professional reality and their guidance may become less relevant or even misleading (see for instance Bouderradji's 2004 survey on the relevance to the marketplace of translator training in certain French training institutions). In the in-house option, supervisors are generally not trained teachers either, but they are familiar with the market as it is and as it evolves. Moreover, they supervise the trainee's translation of texts which are to be handed over to *clients* as a *professional service*. They are therefore likely to have a stronger sense of professional responsibility toward such texts and to supervise translators-in-training more closely, the more so in view of the fact that they will only have to supervise each assignment once rather than several times as in a classroom exercise. Last but not least, they may be assigned to one or two beginners, while in formal training, Translation instructors have a whole class to teach. The supervisor-to-trainee ratio is clearly better in the in-house option in most cases. Of course, in-house supervisors can be more or less conscientious and have more or less time for their supervisees depending on their other tasks, so that these potential advantages of in-house training may be set off by other parameters, but they deserve to be considered nevertheless.

– Translation exercises in the framework of formal training are by definition *artificial* insofar as they are performed not for a client and against remuneration, but 'for' instructors for learning purposes (with the exception of translations done for authentic clients as part of the curriculum in some training programmes, as recommended by some authors such as Kiraly (2005)). As a consequence, although texts and speeches used for training are sometimes taken from actual Translation practice, Translation exercises in the classroom as such can be less relevant and less efficient as pedagogical tools than the translation of texts assigned to trainees or interpreting speeches in a mute booth (in which the interpreter 'works', but without his/her output being heard by the delegates) as is done in on-the-job training. Similarly, knowledge acquired in-house is by definition totally relevant, while knowledge acquired in Translation schools may be less so. Overall, the average amount of *relevant* work done per unit of training time is smaller in formal training than in the in-house option. Over a period of two to four years, the difference may become far from negligible.

– Formal training is *paid for* by students or their family, whereas in the in-house option, beginning Translators are often paid while learning, although their wages may be low. This means that would-be Translators who choose the formal training option may have to find money to pay for tuition and living expenses for 2 to 4 years, while those who are trained on the job can start earning money while learning their trade. This may make a big difference, especially for adult candidates who are already engaged in another professional activity and who may have a family to support and other financial commitments.

Note that these are only general considerations based on informal exchanges with colleagues and field observation, not claims based on systematic empirical studies. It should also be pointed out that when properly designed and implemented, formal training programmes take advantage of the 'artificial' environment they create in order to increase the efficiency of the students' progression beyond that of unplanned, market-dependent in-house progression. Helping instructors make such efficient use of time in the classroom is indeed one of the main objectives of this book. I hope the points made above show convincingly that optimization of formal training programmes is of some importance if the potential advantages of this option are to be realized. Ideally, for maximum efficiency, formal training should be streamlined into 'lean' programmes, meaning maximum relevance of the knowledge and skills gained.

5.   The process-oriented approach in Translator training

The desirability of optimization is one good reason for adopting a *process-oriented approach* in at least the first part of Translator training. The idea is that in the classroom, trainers should focus on the Translation process, not on the end product. More specifically, rather than giving students texts to translate or speeches to interpret, commenting on the Translations produced by saying what is 'right' and what is 'wrong', suggesting appropriate solutions and counting on the accumulation of such indications to guide trainees up the learning curve, in the process-oriented approach, trainers attempt to identify problems in the process followed by the students, raise their awareness of problems and suggest good Translation *principles*, *methods*, and *procedures*:

- Along with Translation exercises, methodological guidance is given on how to go about Translating so as to achieve quality. As explained later in this chapter, I believe that such guidance is most efficient if it is associated with basic concepts and models. This book is essentially devoted to the presentation of and explanations about such concepts and models.
- When annotating and marking students' exercises, rather than commenting on the end-product arising from their choice of particular target-language words or linguistic structures to construct their Target Text, instructors analyze and react to the *processes* involved by offering diagnoses and advice pertaining to these processes, including the general sequence of Translation actions completed by the students and their handling of difficulties.

I believe the process-oriented approach has a number of advantages over the traditional product-oriented method in the early stages of Translation training (the first few weeks or months of training, depending on the total length of the programme and its specific objectives):

- Students are likely to learn to select and implement Translation strategies (overall action plans) and tactics (decisions made when encountering difficulties) faster if these are explained to them than if progression is left to trial-and-error experience or if strategies and tactics are recommended on a case-by-case basis.

– By concentrating on the *reasons* for errors or good choices in Translation rather than on the specific words or language structures selected/produced by the students, teachers devote most of their effective teaching time to Translation *strategies*, *tactics* and *skills* which can be generalized, and lose little time dealing with Translation solutions to specific words and structures in the source Text from which extrapolations can be more problematic.

– By focusing on the process, teachers can be more flexible as regards linguistic acceptability and standards of fidelity than when they have to comment on the product, that is, on the features of the Target Texts produced by the students. They do not have to lose valuable time trying to convince students that *their* solutions are better, and there is a lesser risk of antagonizing students by *imposing* one's own standards and thus reducing their receptiveness. In the process-oriented approach, the teacher verifies that the student has indeed followed certain principles, an approach or a process, and comments on problems which may have arisen along the student's course of action, but does not insist that specific words or phrases are the only correct solution or the best solution to Translation problems – this can be done at a later stage as explained below (for further details, see Gile 1994, 2005).

The process-oriented approach should improve the Translation product as well. In some cases, for instance if the course is designed to train medical practitioners in medical translation or to train engineers who wish to become translators in their field, process-oriented training may be sufficient to achieve the objective of raising the trainees' level to professional proficiency. In many other cases, and in particular in initial training for university students, depending on their declarative knowledge at baseline, improvements resulting from process correction are not sufficient to fine-tune the product, and the acquisition of more extensive and precise linguistic and extra-linguistic knowledge is required. Generally, the process-oriented approach is suited to the beginning of a course (as mentioned earlier, perhaps a few weeks to a few months, depending on the total length of the programme), but must be followed by a rather long period of product-oriented guidance for fine-tuning, with instructors commenting on the trainees' choice of words and structures as well as on their strategies and tactics and suggesting specific solutions.

This book focuses on concepts and models for the initial, process-oriented guidance.

It does not attempt to formulate recommendations for the complementary Translation practice 'mileage' which should follow, and which in my opinion is best left to the initiative of individual instructors who will implement their personal norms.

6. Potential benefits of theoretical components in interpreter and Translator training

Most professional interpreter and translator training programmes worldwide consist essentially of practical interpreting and translation exercises: a source-language text or speech is selected, students are invited to interpret or translate it, and the result is commented on and corrected by or under the guidance of the instructor. Judging by the literature, there does not seem to be any disagreement between teachers, practitioners, or students as to the principle that training should consist essentially of such exercises, although there are differing opinions as to implementation with respect to duration, progression, types of materials used, admission standards, graduation standards, etc. (see for instance Delisle 1981; Reiss 1986; Seleskovitch & Lederer 1989; Dollerup & Loddegaard 1992; Dollerup & Lindegaard 1994; Hung 2002; Pym et al. 2003; Kelly 2005; Tennent 2005).

While interpreting and translation exercises always make up the core of the curriculum, a number of other subject-matters and activities revolve around them. Besides language enhancement and thematic courses in economics, political science, technical and scientific subjects, etc., skills *around* Translation are also taught in many programmes. Public speaking, documentary and terminological work, précis writing and technical writing are some examples. Theoretical courses on linguistics or interpreting and translation theory are also found in an increasing number of syllabi. However, the usefulness of such theoretical courses is often challenged on the grounds that they are too abstract or remote from actual Translation practice and are therefore not useful to students. This idea is discussed further below (see also Chapter 10).

Courses in Translation *theory* can serve functions other than the purely pedagogical purpose of helping future interpreters and translators advance faster and better toward mastery of their professional skills. Some theoretical courses are a necessary part of academic programmes leading to BA or higher degrees. Incidentally, some research may also be part of the requirements. Such functions are legitimate in the academic context and may also serve useful purposes in enriching the future Translators' conceptual frames of reference and knowledge – and in raising the social status of the Translation professions. However, as mentioned in Section 1 of this chapter, this book deals basically with the *pedagogical function* of training. Therefore, only the pedagogical function of theory will be considered here.

Many authors have written on the pedagogical value of theory in Translation training. According to Komissarov (1985: 208), "It cannot be denied … that translation theory is supposed, in the final analysis, to serve as a guide to translation practice." A similar view is expressed by other authors (Kade & Cartellieri 1971; Delisle 1980: 57, 96, 1981: 136; Vinay 1983; Gémar 1983; Juhel 1985; Larose 1985; Gentile 1991; Pöchhacker 1992; Viaggio 1988, 1992; Sawyer 2004). Also note that Hansen (2009) and Katan (2009) found that after a number of years in professional practice, in retrospect, translators considered theory useful to them.

I believe the main positive effects of theoretical components in a training programme should be sought in their *explanatory power* and in the reassurance it can provide to students who experience doubts and difficulties. Whatever theory is taught to students, trainees or seminar participants, its contribution is greatest if it can help them gain better understanding of Translation, particularly with regard to the following:

–   Understanding *phenomena*: Why do authors write the way they do? Why do speakers make ungrammatical sentences? What does it mean to 'understand' a verbal statement? How are written or oral statements perceived and processed by the human mind?
–   Understanding *Translation difficulties*: Why is it difficult to re-express the same message in a different language? Why is there linguistic interference between two working languages during translation or interpreting? Why do interpreters in the booth sometimes fail to understand very simple source-speech segments?
–   Understanding *Translation strategies and tactics* recommended by instructors: Why is it acceptable for translators to change some information elements when going from source language to target language? Why should interpreters spend as little time and effort as possible on note-taking in consecutive? Why do many translators and interpreters say one should only translate into one's native tongue, and why do others challenge this view?

From such understanding, training programme participants may expect the following advantages:

–   They may be able to advance *faster* and *further*, as mentioned above. In particular, by providing them with an appropriate explanatory framework, theoretical concepts and models can help them prevent or do away with *strategic* and *tactical errors* in translation. For instance, if they understand the basic dynamics of language availability, Translators can avoid the waste involved in the use of inappropriate material for enhancement of linguistic skills in their working languages (see Chapter 9). They can also discriminate between good and less desirable advice given to them by colleagues or even by instructors who, in some schools, are not qualified interpreters or translators themselves.
–   Theoretical concepts and models can help them *choose appropriate strategies and tactics* when they are faced with *new situations* not met during the training programme, by providing them with tools for analysis of possible actions and their probable or possible consequences.

- Finally, theoretical concepts and models can also help them *maintain appropriate strategies and tactics* rather than drift over time into less professional and less efficient practices under market forces such as financial needs, client demands, or misperception of their work by third parties. For instance, clients may insist that they work into their non-native languages without understanding the limitations associated with such Translation, or neglect to provide them with necessary information for preparation and decision-making, and it sometimes takes Translators considerable efforts to convince them that such information is necessary. Again, a conceptual framework which explains phenomena, their causes and their possible consequences is easier to keep in mind as a reference than isolated rules of behaviour dictated by a teacher.

7.   Potential criteria and rules for theoretical components for training

I believe the criteria explained further down are useful in helping design and use theoretical components for programmes training professional Translators. They should also be useful in training programmes having wider academic objectives insofar as they can initiate beginners to *introductory* theoretical modules. Simple theoretical components with obvious links to everyday practice can be taught during the first semester of training without further elaboration, as an introduction to practical strategies and tactics on one hand, and to a theoretical approach of interpreting and translation on the other, to be followed, if the syllabus calls for more extensive theoretical explanations, by more abstract, wider components, which would be easier for students to accept and understand on the basis of the concepts acquired during the initial stage. If such deeper exploration of theoretical issues is part of the syllabus, an introductory conceptual framework as presented in Chapter 10 (the IDRC platform) could also be useful.

More generally, the following rules for the design and implementation of theoretical components in interpreter and translator training can help optimize their efficiency in syllabi which follow a highly profession-oriented philosophy in a lean-programme approach:

Design rule 1:
Theoretical components should be designed so as to be *directly relevant* to the students' needs.

They should provide answers to questions and problems actually faced or liable to be encountered by students and graduates, and should not contain many more concepts than can reasonably be considered *practically* useful to the trainees.

Under this rationale, historical descriptions of language-related research, terminological comparisons between authors and between theories, linguistic taxonomies, etc. have low priority. Not that such elements are devoid of general interest, but their direct contribution to the students' progress is small, and they ought to be the first to be abandoned under a streamlining scheme.

Design rule 2:
Theoretical components should be designed so that they are *easy to grasp*.

Theoretical components developed for training purposes should have a simple logical structure and require little acquisition of theoretical concepts and technical terms. In designing them, the proper balance will have to be found between the ideal of exhaustiveness and accuracy in explaining phenomena on one hand, and simplicity on the other. Such theoretical components are taught for *pedagogical* purposes. As stressed earlier, models taught under this approach primarily seek to offer representations of reality to students for the purpose of helping them understand certain phenomena they will encounter so that they can take appropriate *action* when translating or interpreting. In such a context, simplification becomes an end in itself. This is perhaps a central reason which explains the popularity of ESIT's Interpretive Theory, of *skopos* theory, of Chernov's probabilistic prognosis model (Chernov 2004), of the concepts and models developed in this book's 1995 version as opposed to more advanced and more sophisticated models proposed by Moser (1978) or Setton (1999) for interpreting.

Implementation rule 1:
Theoretical components should preferably be taught *after student sensitization*.

Theoretical components should preferably be taught after trainees have been made aware of phenomena they address, and preferably of their implications. Many students are not aware of issues such as linguistic interference, reliability problems in lexical 'equivalences' offered by dictionaries or conflicting interests between clients, authors/speakers, and readers/listeners; many fail to identify the real issue when facing a translation or interpreting problem. For instance, they may not be aware of the role of processing capacity limitations and therefore fail to recognize the risks involved in taking notes too exhaustively in consecutive interpreting. Enlisting their participation in an experiment which shows that their listening efficiency deteriorates when they start taking notes (see Chapter 7) is one way of sensitizing them to the issue. Sensitization should increase the students' receptiveness by showing that the theoretical components taught to them are relevant to their daily experience and can help them understand and act in the best way.

Implementation rule 2:
Theoretical components should be *referred to repeatedly* throughout the course when discussing the students' achievements and weaknesses.

The practical implications of theoretical components should be evident to students, but they should also be stressed repeatedly during the correction of practical Translation exercises so that their impact is made deeper and more enduring. This does not mean that models should be explained over and over during the course, but they should be referred to whenever they are relevant to a strategy or tactic being explained or to comments on a student's performance. For instance, if a student is found to have written a sentence which does not make logical sense in the context of a text s/he has translated, instead of telling him/her that the sentence makes no sense, it may be best to ask whether s/he has conducted a plausibility test (see Chapter 5). This should both help convince the students of the components' relevance and strengthen their imprint in their minds. It goes without saying that such references should only be made when useful, which means that components should be designed in such a way as to be *simple* to recall and *powerful* as explanatory and/or guiding tools. One major weakness of some theories taught in Translator training programmes with respect to didactic effectiveness is that they are neither directly applicable to concrete action in Translation nor designed in such a way as to be recalled relevantly when discussing practical exercises. As a result, students learn them initially and store them in some memory compartment where they are seldom if ever accessed. Eventually, they are forgotten without having had much effect on the learning process.

8. Where and how to find theoretical components for Translator training

Basically, there are three ways of finding theoretical components suitable for optimized or 'lean' training programmes. The first is to *adopt* those which have been developed by other Translation instructors or researchers. The second is to *adapt* existing components developed by others in a form which was not directly usable in the framework of 'lean' programmes. The third is to *develop* such components on one's own.

Ready-made theoretical components that can be presented directly to students and meet the criteria explained above are difficult to find in the literature. Two exceptions are the basics of ESIT's Interpretive Theory and of *skopos* theory, which are explained clearly and simply in many books and papers by authors such as Danica Seleskovitch and Marianne Lederer for the former and Christiane Nord for the latter. There have been many studies of interpreting and translation phenomena as such, but most of these are either highly theoretical or research-oriented rather than teaching-oriented, even though their aim, as formulated by those who conceived them, is often to help draw inferences applicable to Translation and Translation teaching.

There are also many books offering practical ideas on teaching interpreting and translation with at least some theoretical references. Vinay and Darbelnet's *Stylistique comparée de l'anglais et du français* (1958/1995) is a classical example, with its definitions of categories for translation tactics – though these are probably more accurately defined as descriptions of types of post-translation correspondences rather than actual tactics. Seleskovitch and Lederer's books, and in particular *Pédagogie raisonnée de l'interprétation* (1989), explain theoretical concepts from ESIT's Interpretive Theory.

Other examples are Delisle's *L'enseignement de l'interprétation et de la traduction* (1981) and *Handbuch Translation* by Snell-Hornby, Hönig, Kussmaul & Schmitt (1999 for the second, revised edition), Čeňková, Ivana a kolektiv (2001) for the Czech Republic, Komatsu (2005) for Japan, etc. Note that these are only a few examples among scores of other works which keep coming out at a steady pace in English, French, German, Spanish, Italian, Russian, Chinese, Japanese and Korean, each time with some new facts, ideas and methods. No literature review will be attempted here, as it would probably become obsolete very rapidly. What should be highlighted, though, is the existence of numerous papers on Translation didactics in journals such as *Meta, Babel, Multilingua*, the University of Granada's *Sendebar*, the University of Trieste's *The Interpreter's Newsletter*, etc. Interestingly, Translation training has been deemed important enough to launch journals devoted specifically to the subject. One is St Jerome's *The Interpreter and Translator Trainer*, and the other the US-based Conference of Interpreter Trainers' *International Journal of Interpreter Education*.

However, by the beginning of the 1990s, I was not aware of the existence of packages of theoretical components as toolkits for direct use in the classroom. I therefore decided to develop my own. It soon became apparent that while some such components, including important ones, could be developed on the basis of observation without much theoretical background (see for example the *Sequential Model of translation* in chapter 5 or the Informational composition of informative sentences in Chapter 3), explanations of some phenomena had to be sought in linguistics, psycholinguistics and cognitive psychology. In particular, highly relevant information came from psycholinguistic research on speech production and comprehension and from cognitive psychology studies on shared attention and more generally on memory, including working memory. However, these elements also had to be adapted to the students' needs so as not to require too much time and effort in learning terminology and concepts. The models presented in this book are therefore at an intermediate position. They are indeed 'theoretical' rather than plain practical (and often prescriptive) suggestions, but they are far less abstract and complex (and comprehensive) than theories developed within psychology or linguistics. In spite of these limitations, reactions from students and instructors over the past 15 years or so and comments published in the literature suggest that they are cohesive and powerful enough (and sufficiently stable in spite of advances in research in cognitive science, in linguistics and in Translation theory) to be of use to teachers and students of interpreting and translation.

9. The models

In trying to develop theoretical components for easy assimilation and use by students, I naturally turned to the idea of models, i.e. simplified representations of phenomena or ideas, constructed with the most important entities and inter-entity links which could explain their operation. The models introduced in this book have been developed over 30 years. As explained in the introduction, they were first conceived as a package for my interpreting and translation students at the department for Korean and Japanese of *Institut National des Langues et Civilisations Orientales* in Paris. Since then, they have been under continuous fine-tuning on the basis of new information acquired from the literature and of reactions to presentations in many lectures at universities, in Translation conferences and in training seminars and workshops, including professional workshops for professional translators and interpreters and a number of training seminars for Translation teachers.

The main models I use in interpreting and translation programmes are the following:

-   A Communication model of Translation (Chapter 2)
-   The informational structure of informative sentences (Chapter 3)
-   The Effort Models for interpreting and sight translation (Chapter 7)
-   The Gravitational Model of Language Availability (Chapter 9)
-   The Comprehension of technical speeches and texts (Chapter 4)
-   The Sequential Model of Translation (Chapter 5)

These models are fairly autonomous and can be taught individually. However, when taught in a programmatic sequence, the following progression generally works well:

1. *Communication issues* (Chapter 2): If interpreters and translators are to make the right decisions for optimum quality, they first have to be made aware of the fact that Translation is a *service* provided to particular persons in a particular communication situation. Quality is usefully judged against criteria based on this idea of Translation as a *communication service*.
2. *Fidelity* (Chapter 3): Because of differences between languages and cultures in terms of information given or implicit, lexical units and linguistic structures, interpreting and translation practitioners inevitably have to make choices which imply some informational differences between source-language statement and target-language statement. This leads to the well-known dilemma of *content fidelity* versus *linguistic/ cultural acceptability*, which has to be dealt with early on in training in order to optimize the students' progress thereafter.
3a. *For interpreting students:* The Effort Models (Chapter 7) and the Gravitational Model of Language Availability (Chapter 9). Both are based on the concept of the human mind's limited processing capacity and explain many of the problems encountered regularly by students and practitioners while interpreting. Both help understand and assess the strategies and tactics suggested by teachers to deal with these difficulties (Chapter 8).

b. *For translation students:* The Sequential Model of translation (Chapter 5): A model of written translation stressing methodological principles such as the separation between comprehension and reformulation into two phases, the need for tests at each phase, the importance of decision-making in translation. I have found this model very useful in explaining the precise location of sources of weaknesses in students' translations.

4. *The comprehension of technical speeches and texts* (Chapter 4): Once the basic methodological elements have been presented and practiced in non-specialized interpreting and translation, the difficulties of specialized texts and discourse can be addressed. This component is a discussion of the comprehension of technical speeches and texts by non-specialists, highlighting the requirements and problems associated with the interpreting (and translation) of such prose.

I believe that there is room for further models more specifically designed to address the needs of public-service interpreters in various sectors, for signed-language interpreting, for dubbing, subtitling, surtitling, for web translation, for localization and for audio description, but should like to leave the task to experts in these specific environments.

10. This chapter's main ideas

1. Formal Translator training is not an absolute necessity, but it can help beginning interpreters and translators improve their performance and/or improve it faster.

2. Interpreters and translators must have:

    –   good passive knowledge of their passive working language(s)
    –   good command of their active working language(s)
    –   adequate World Knowledge
    –   good command of the principles and techniques of Translation

3. Training needs vary depending on the trainees' pre-existing knowledge and skills. In order to optimize programmes, a distinction between *initial training programmes* and *further training programmes* is useful.

4. Formal training needs to be optimized in order to be a truly better option than on-the-job training, which has distinct advantages in terms of relevance, finances, and actual translation practice.

5. The *process-oriented approach* focuses on principles, methods and procedures rather than on the Translation product. It can be assumed to be a more powerful teaching tool during the initial part of training, but must be complemented by more traditional, result-oriented correction for fine-tuning.

6.   Theoretical components in interpreter and translation training can contribute to better understanding of phenomena, difficulties, and strategies and tactics, thus helping students advance further and faster and maintain appropriate strategies even after they have left school.

7.   Ideally, theoretical components should be:

   –   directly relevant to the students' needs
   –   easy to grasp
   –   taught after sensitization
   –   recalled repeatedly during comments on hands-on Translation work.

Chapter 2

Communication and quality
in interpreting and translation

1. Introduction

When enrolling in a translation course, most students are only aware of linguistic aspects of translation, and even this is generally limited to the school-translation approach, the one they have been taught for language acquisition purposes throughout their years at school. When given a text to translate, they use 'translinguistic equivalences' they have learned, supplement them with lexical 'equivalences' they find in dictionaries, and seek target-language syntactic structures approximating those found in the source text without being aware of or taking into account the fact that texts are translated to serve some purpose, or giving a thought to the possibility that this could have some implications on how they should be translated.

In other words, they do not know what professional Translation is about and have no framework for self-evaluation and 'navigation' toward good quality as it is conceptualized and assessed in professional settings. According to my experience, until they are provided with an appropriate conceptual framework, they do not *understand* their instructors' corrections and suggestions, which guide them toward optimum quality through analysis and decisions which often deviate from linguistic correspondences. If students do not understand the reasons underlying such instructions and advice, they cannot analyze them rationally. In some cases, depending on their cultural background and personal inclinations, they may consider that the instructors' word carries the ultimate authority and must be obeyed blindly. In other cases, they may be frustrated by the fact that in their new training environment, they are being told to act in a way different from what they have always been told was right during their school years. They may also resent and/or dislike and/or distrust the instructor, perhaps because they disagree with some of his/her corrections. Even when they accept their instructors' authority, as soon as the advice of two instructors clash, they find themselves in a difficult situation.

For all these reasons, relying on the instructors' sole authority to guide students towards maximum quality in professional Translation may not be the smoothest way to ensure progression.

It is therefore important to help students understand the fundamental philosophy underlying their instructors' comments and suggestions by explaining to them very early on, perhaps as early as the very first classroom sessions or lectures, that professional Translation is essentially a *service activity with a communication function*, performed in a professional setting with a professional aim in mind and constrained by this setting. Quality in professional Translation is necessarily linked to its function and its environment, and can therefore be perceived in the professional world (in the 'marketplace') in a manner quite different from the way it is perceived in a traditional classroom situation. A few simple models and ideas presented in the following pages have been found helpful as awareness-raising tools for students.

2.   Professional Translation: An act of communication

2.1   School Translation vs. Professional Translation

Translation activity (interpreting and translation) takes place in several types of environments and can be categorized into several types including the following:

-   *School translation* is the most widespread and best known type of translation – virtually everyone experiences it in school when learning a foreign language.
-   *Translation for one's private practical purposes* is another case. For instance, one may wish to translate certain parts of a user's manual into one's own language if it is written in a language one does not read easily and if one expects to have to consult the relevant passages often.
-   *Translation* can be done *for pleasure in a non-professional context*. The pleasure can be associated with the idea of working on a text by an author one admires or on a text which one appreciates, with the fact that translation involves a careful study of the text, with the creativity which is part of the process and with its challenges etc., without there being any communication operation in the usual sense of the word.
-   *Interpreting* is often done *in a non-professional context* to help friends, relatives or tourists during visits, sightseeing, shopping, etc.

As explained earlier, when students are admitted into a professional Translator training programme, their ideas on quality are most strongly associated with language comprehension, with grammatically correct writing in the foreign language and with translinguistic equivalences which they have learned at school and practiced systematically for several years under the guidance of foreign-language teachers. In order for them to understand the parameters of quality in professional Translation, they need to be made aware of fundamental differences that distinguish it from such school translation.

School translation is designed to help students acquire foreign languages, and translation exercises at school serve mostly as drills for the acquisition of foreign-language vocabulary and grammar structures and as foreign-language proficiency tests. It is therefore intended to serve the students themselves, in a closed system the participants

of which are a teacher and language learners. In contrast, the main purpose of professional Translation is to help people who speak different languages communicate in specific situations. Translators are enablers or facilitators. They are only ancillary albeit
sometimes indispensable agents because the principals need them to communicate,
but theirs is a service role only.

2.2   The actors' configuration in professional Translation

The actors' configuration in Translation is often represented as follows (see for instance
Dollerup 2007: 3)

Sender → Translator → Receiver

As is shown later in this section, this model depicts adequately some situations, but it
is not a very good representation of the more general case, if only because two important aspects of the communication configuration in the professional context are missing:
firstly, the fact that generally, the Translator acts at the request of a Client who, more
often than not, is neither the Sender nor the Receiver, and secondly the fact that the
Sender's intended receivers are generally not the Translator's receivers. A more relevant general model to present to students is the following:

Sender → Source Language Receiver(s)

Client   Translator → Target Language Receiver(s)

The principals in professional Translation are a Sender (author, speaker/signer),
the Target Language Receiver(s) and the Client (or 'Commissioner' of the Translation).
Note that Senders and Receivers are generally 'natural persons' (people), whereas the
Client is most often an organization (a business, an international organization, a research
body, a department within a company etc.), though contacts between the Client and the
Translator will be managed by persons. Students are generally not aware of the paramount
importance of the Client. A speaker or author may wish to send messages to a foreign-
language audience or readership (Receivers) and Receivers may wish to understand
what an author or speaker is saying, but in professional Translation, nothing happens
until someone asks the Translator to do the job. Sometimes, the Client and the Sender
are the same, but generally they are not, if only because Translation is relatively expensive and more likely to be paid for by organizations than by individuals.

   This general pattern collapses into different configurations in specific cases. For
instance, if the Sender is only speaking to Receivers who do not understand his/her
language, as is the case of a foreign speaker who has come to talk to a local audience
and needs an interpreter to get his/her message across, the configuration turns into

Client   Sender → Translator → Receiver(s)

and if the Client happens to be the Sender, into:

Sender → Translator → Receiver(s)

But, as explained above, the most general case is the one involving a Client and two separate but inter-related acts of communication, one going from the Sender to his/her Receiver(s) and one from the Translator to his/her Receiver(s). These differences between the communication configurations are not just formal. As will be shown later, they have considerable implications on how quality is defined and on how it is perceived.

2.3   Awareness of Translation and its effects

In all cases, the Client is by definition aware of the existence of the Translation task, but this does not necessarily apply to the Senders or to the Receivers. Senders do not necessarily know that their texts have been translated. More importantly perhaps, readers of translated technical document are not necessarily aware of the fact that they are reading translations. In interpreting, the interpreter's listeners realize they are not listening to the original speaker, and speakers are generally aware of the fact they are being interpreted, but not necessarily – for instance when making political or other official statements on television in front of national audiences which happen to be picked up by other television stations and interpreted into other languages for foreign audiences.

When they do know that they are being or will be translated or interpreted, Senders may want to adapt the content of their Text (written, spoken or signed) and/or its presentation to suit their communication purposes knowing that the Receivers of the Translated version may have relevant knowledge, values and/or expectations which differ markedly from those of intended Receivers of their original Text.

In interpreting, when all parties are aware of the communication situation, including possible difficulties associated with the inter-lingual and sometimes intercultural transfer, assuming that generally the principals wish to communicate, more cooperation can be expected from them than in translation, where clients and readers may be more aware of a *text* than of a communication situation. Speakers may try to speak/sign more slowly, pronounce words more clearly, choose certain terms and structures and avoid others, and clarify terms and concepts that they would not otherwise bother to explain (incidentally, in spite of what would seem reasonable and contrary to Newmark's assumption as formulated in 1983: 13, this is not a pattern observed consistently in the field). Cooperation may also be forthcoming from listeners/viewers, especially in consecutive, where they can help the interpreter with word equivalents and generally listen sympathetically, though again, this is not always the case, and they may resent the time taken by interpreting. In other words, although the interpreter essentially works alone, s/he may be helped through on-line interaction with both Sender and Receiver, while in translation online interaction is less frequent. Note however that if the proportion of target-language listeners in the audience is very small, the interpreter may suffer from interference instead of benefiting from cooperation, especially in consecutive. The reason is that source-language listeners often perceive interpreting as a nuisance; when the delegates who actually need interpreting are not numerous and if they are unimportant for the others, the extra costs, time and inconvenient technical constraints associated with interpreting (reduced speed of delivery, seating arrangements, the mandatory use of a microphone, etc.) may trigger annoyance. Delegates may therefore put pressure on the interpreter to be brief or summarize, and refuse to cooperate in other ways.

3.   Aims and intentions

3.1   Fundamental aims and intentions

An overwhelming majority of texts and utterances which are translated or interpreted professionally can be viewed as representing their Senders' *aims* or *intentions* to provide information or explanations to their intended Receivers, or more generally, to have some sort of influence on them. There are some exceptions. For instance, people may take notes for their own purposes (ideas for possible films to see, an inventory of objects left somewhere, addresses of restaurants with comments on the quality of food and service as a reference for later visits, general ideas for a paper to be written, important points to remember when operating a complex device etc.), and a third party may want these notes to be translated later – this could be a historian, a biographer, a lawyer etc. The case of Senders writing for themselves can also be viewed as a particular case of communication, in which the Sender and the Receiver are the same person, but when professional translation comes in, the intended Receiver is almost by definition someone else. Sometimes, Senders of Texts have no 'significant' personal communication aim, and only speak or write because it is their duty to do so, for instance when being asked to declare a meeting open or closed.

When authors of literary texts write for their readers, the effect they seek to have on them often has aesthetic and affective components. This book is about non-literary Translation, and the focus will be on 'informational Texts' (scientific, technical, legal, administrative, commercial, press articles etc.), where affective and aesthetic aims are marginal. While some of the concepts and models, as well as Translation strategies and tactics, can be applied to the two types of Texts, literary aspects of Texts and of their Translation will not be addressed here.

Informing the Receiver is a very common aim in a Sender's verbal statements. *Explaining* something, *convincing* someone, *making someone do something* (vote for a particular candidate or action, buy a product, take on administrative duties) are other common aims. Actually, underlying a single Text or statement, there are often many aims which are intended to support each other. For instance, a Sender may wish to inform Receivers for the purpose of convincing them and/or making them do something, but also to impress them with his/her wit or wisdom. Communication theoreticians often speak of a *phatic* layer, consisting to a large extent of chit-chat or small talk to help build a personal relationship; of a *cathartic* layer, that is, communication aimed at releasing emotions; and of an *informational* layer (for a more extensive discussion of human communication through language, see for instance Hörmann 1972; Cherry 1978; or Schramm & Porter 1982, among many good books on the subject).

Not all layers are equally powerful in shaping the message which is eventually verbalized. Nor are they equally visible to an outside observer, to the Receiver or even to the Sender him/herself. Some may be hidden in the subconscious or unconscious part of his/her mind, and would be sincerely disavowed if s/he became aware of them – incidentally, psychoanalysis, and in particular the Lacanian school, claims that such deep-lying forces shape much of our linguistic output, but we will not deal with such claims here. For convenience, our discussion will be restricted to the following types of aims underlying informational Texts:

- *Informing*: the aim underlying the production of a Text may be limited to providing information such as an address, a name, dimensions of an object, properties of an object, the programme of events due to take place etc.
- *Explaining*: the aim of a Text or a segment thereof may be to clarify or explain through information, as is the case of the explanation of symbols and abbreviations in a scientific paper.
- *Persuading*: a Text may be produced for the purpose of convincing the reader or listener that an opinion or option is correct, morally right, appropriate or best for the circumstances, etc. For instance, figures may be given as evidence, or an authoritative personality supporting an opinion may be quoted.
- *Making the receivers do something – or refrain from doing something*. Again, a Sender may attempt to achieve this aim by informing, explaining and/or seeking to persuade, but also by instructing or ordering the Reader to engage in some action of refrain from acting in a particular way. Such Texts can be considered informational insofar as they *inform* the Receivers of what the Sender wishes them to do – or not to do.

3.2   Macro-level and micro-level aims

As explained earlier, in informational discourse such as is generally Translated in non-literary interpreting and translation, some or all of these components may be active in the Sender's mind, albeit not necessarily at the same level of awareness and intensity and with possible variations at local levels (a paragraph, a sentence, etc.): an economist may prepare a speech (at macro-level) to convince his/her listeners that a particular economic strategy is the best for his/her country, but in a specific sentence (micro-level), s/he may be focusing on providing information. The information is there to serve a persuasion intention, but the focus in that part of the text is just on getting it across to the readers. To take the example a bit further, this economist may be running for a high position in a political organization, and the whole Text in favour of a particular economic strategy may be part of his/her electoral campaign. In that case, the sentence has an informational aim within a speech aiming to persuade with an underlying political aim. When translating or interpreting a Text, Translators proceed sequentially, most often sentence by sentence and paragraph by paragraph (see Chapter 5). When Translating at micro-level, they analyze the micro-level aim of the local unit, but are also aware of and orient their decisions by macro-level aims of the Text. The co-existence of various layers of micro- to macro- level aims is relevant when deciding how to deal with specific Text segments. Incidentally, the findings of process research into written translation so far seem to suggest that one of the main differences between novices such as students and experienced translators is the ability of the latter to take on board the wider context and communication situation, including aims, to a significantly larger extent than the former, who tend to focus on local problems (see for instance Krings 1986; Tirkkonen-Condit 1990; Lörscher 1993; Jääskeläinen 1999).

3.3   The communication actors' aims and professional loyalty

3.3.1   *Convergence and divergence of aims*

As stressed by Edmond Cary (1985: 85), professional Translation exists only as a service to be provided to people who require it to serve certain aims. Serving these people by serving their aims, as opposed to serving a Text or 'serving a language', is paramount, though indeed Translation of a Text can also serve the Text *per se* (by making it available to a larger potential population of readers), or the target language (for instance by contributing to make more texts available to readers in that language and lower their dependence on foreign languages).

A common and somewhat naïve view of Translation sees Clients as helping Senders and Receivers communicate through Translation in a common cooperation effort around the same communication aims. In such a configuration, which is indeed not rare, the Translator can be seen as serving the aims of the Sender *and* the Receivers. Reality is often a bit more complicated.

First of all, the Sender and Receivers may not have the same aims. For instance, in a political debate between two personalities defending opposite views, the statement of one may be made in order to convince the other and the public if any, but the other will listen to it with a view not to be convinced but to detect its flaws so as to be in a better position to fight it.

Moving on to an example from a non-confrontational situation, the manufacturer of a piece of equipment may write a description of a machine with the aim of convincing readers to buy it, while a reader may scrutinize it for the sole purpose of gaining information about the machine without any intention of purchasing it. Incidentally, professional Translators read many texts for the sole purpose of gaining familiarity with the subject matter they deal with or for the purpose of picking up specialized terminology and phraseology irrespective of the authors' aims.

While Graham's (1983: 99) idea that "with very few exceptions, the principal definitive indicator [of the translator's orientation] is the reason, purpose, or intention accorded to the translation" is not fundamentally incorrect, it therefore deserves some elaboration.

The Sender's aims were listed earlier: informing, explaining, convincing, making the Receivers do something, etc. The Receiver's aims may match the Sender's aims – or not. Receivers may seek to be informed or to understand, they may want to be convinced, but they may equally resist the Sender's efforts to persuade them. Nevertheless, in most cases, both the Sender and the Receiver have what might be called 'communicational' aims closely associated with the sending and/or receiving of information. The Client's motivation and interests can be different. In particular, a translation company's interests are essentially commercial: making money by offering translation and interpreting services. The fact that these services have to do with communication is incidental.

These differences between the aims and interests of the principals can lead to contradictions. Quoting L. Castellano:

> It would be proper for the client commissioning a translator to judge the work by its intellectual quality. He does not. He is likely to be more concerned with the speed at which it arrives on his desk, its plausibility and its presentation. (1983: 47)

When such contradictions materialize, they are not without practical consequences: a client such as a translation agency may want speedy translation service in spite of the loss of readability or terminological accuracy of the output that the required speed of delivery can cause. As stated by Sager (1983: 121): "The initiator of the translation … determines the time available for the work of the translator, and, through the price he is willing to pay, the type and quality of the translation required." In interpreting, a listener or chairperson in a negotiation may want the interpreter to summarize or skip some speech segments because they do not want to hear them even though the speaker clearly intends them to be part of the message. In such cases, the Translator is caught between conflicting interests and pressures.

An eloquent example is given in a paper by D. Mellen (1988: 274); she quotes the following letter from an investment company:

Many educators have expressed their concern of their tax liability as well as planning for their short and long term goals. Maybe it's been a while since your current programme has been reviewed or you feel satisfied.

Mellen comments that "these sentences include obvious and serious grammatical errors, and they were included in a letter that was generally poorly written." Supposing the readers of the translator are Spanish-speaking prospective customers of the investment company, if the person doing the translation merely summarized the letter or did not take the pains to reproduce the poor quality of the writing, the Spanish (customers) would not learn everything the letter had to tell about the company. Indeed, they would lose potentially critical information.

3.3.2 *Professional loyalty*

The question of *professional loyalty* is therefore a very real one: to whom is it due? To the Client? To the Sender? To the Receiver? The question is not only ethical or 'philosophical' issue; as will be shown later, it has practical implications.

One fundamental determinant of a professional activity involving an employer and an employee are the employee's duties towards the employer. In the case of an independent service provider, his/her duties are determined by the service contract signed with the client. This also applies to professional Translators – see Gouadec 1989, 2002, Robinson 1997. Incidentally, the Translator's livelihood depends on the Client, not on the Sender or Receiver. This is one of the reasons why conference interpreters, who are often recruited by colleagues (who therefore become 'Clients' in a way even though they are not the ones who pay them), may attach more weight to their reputation in the profession than to feedback from conference delegates.

As a professional, the Translator owes his/her loyalty to the Client first and foremost.

There are of course limits to what any employee or service provider will accept, and if the Client's brief is strongly objectionable on legal or moral grounds, Translators can refuse it, but such cases seem to be rare. Moreover, in the field, the Client's brief and interests are generally compatible with the Sender's and the Receiver's aims. This does not mean that they are necessarily convergent. Problems do occur, but they involve mostly prioritization of resources and optimization rather than opposing interests. If the Client is a translation company, translations which satisfy Senders and receivers are also satisfactory for him/her because they are liable to help generate good business. On the other hand, as mentioned above, in order to gain a larger market share, translation companies may wish to offer faster and cheaper translation services than their competitors. This is no longer necessarily in line with the aims or interests of Senders or Receivers, because optimizing the commissioned translation requires time, and having to work at cheap rates will not necessarily encourage translators to give their very best to the job.

The Client's brief can be considered an *environmental constraint*: the Translator needs to meet the requirements of the Senders and/or Receivers subject to certain constraints of time, remuneration and perhaps access (translation companies, in particular, may worry about losing their own clients, that is, the Senders or Receivers, to the Translator if s/he is given direct access to them).

Once this environmental constraint is taken on board, whose aims and interest should the Translator serve? The Sender's or the Receiver's? The prevailing position is probably that in most circumstances, the Translator functions as an *alter ego* of the author or speaker. In written translation, this position is morally 'natural' because setting aside literary texts, readers tend to perceive the text they are reading as the author's, not the translator's. The translator thus *represents* the author and intuitively, it would seem wrong to betray him/her by serving another party's interest without indicating so explicitly. In simultaneous conference interpreting, the same position is standard and is reflected in a norm: interpreters use the first person generally, and they tell listeners explicitly when speaking on their own behalf ("the interpreter cannot hear because the microphone is off", "the interpreter missed the name", etc.). The fact that they sometimes depart from this position (see a case study in Diriker 2004) does not change this Sender loyalty principle. The situation can be different in court interpreting, where the principals' interests can be strongly divergent and even confrontational and interpreters may need to observe specific rules which impose strong adherence to the form of statements they interpret.

The Translator's position as representing the Sender, and therefore his/her aims and interests, does not mean that the Receivers' interests are not heeded, at least as long as they are compatible with the Client's and with the Sender's. This is most often the case in informational Texts aimed at informing or explaining, insofar as it is in the Receivers' interests to be informed and to understand.

In interpreter training programmes for spoken languages, the Translator's position is often defined as 'neutral' with a role sometimes referred to as a transparent 'conduit role'. In Translation Studies, this role is now being challenged (see for example Angelelli 2004 for interpreting). In signed-language interpreting circles, it does not seem to prevail at all – as can be seen clearly in several papers in Janzen 2005 and as discussed extensively in Metzger 2002. More generally, in public service interpreting, expectations from interpreters sometimes deviate markedly from 'transparent' neutrality.

As will be shown in Chapter 3, even technically, the need to make choices when Translating is incompatible with transparent neutrality as implicitly taught in school translation, and Sender-loyalty has concrete implications. In interactive meetings with interpreting, the main communication actors alternate as Senders and Receivers in the course of the exchange; since the Sender loyalty principle applies equally to each in turn, the Translator's position is perhaps best summarized as *rotating side-taking*. This means that if decisions must be made in the course of Translation, the Translator is 'biased' in favour of the author's or speaker's interests as long as this is compatible with the Client's brief and interests – and with applicable norms of professional ethics and practice.

Note that in signed language interpreting, the Client's brief often defines the deaf Receiver rather than the Sender as the main beneficiary of the interpreter's work, for instance when interpreting for a deaf student in a class of hearing students.

In written translation, Sender-loyalty as a principle generally poses few practical problems; in interpreting, interference can come in during interpreting (especially, hostile reactions and interruptions from listeners). In public service interpreting (this term will be used here for what is also known as 'community interpreting' and 'dialogue interpreting'), this becomes a key issue, as some clients and parties to the interaction having the same ethnic or religious background as the interpreters fail to understand the *rotating side-taking* principle and expect single-sided loyalty from them. In some cases, rotating side-taking may also be psychologically difficult to achieve: interpreters do belong to social groups and have their own moral, political, and religious convictions as well as personal interests against which it may be difficult for them to speak. In such a case, it may be better for each side to have its own interpreter, even though this can be expensive and technically unnecessary. Conference interpreters tend to have no similar problems stemming from their personal moral or political positions; they generally implement the rotating side-taking principle without difficulty and without feeling uneasy about the conflicting economic or political interests of the parties for which they are interpreting alternately by translating their statements. Exceptions include war-crimes trials, a sensitive assignment which some interpreters have refused; it seems that those who do accept them in spite of their moral convictions do manage to perform adequately.

In the present (didactically oriented). analysis, the important point is that differing principles of loyalty can affect quality criteria with respect to both content and packaging. The following discussions, including that of fidelity (Chapter 3), are based on the Sender-loyalty choice. In cases where a different loyalty principle applies, it should be easy for the reader to extrapolate to the relevant environment.

4.   Content and packaging

In most verbal communication acts, in order to achieve an aim, the Sender issues a verbal signal, written, spoken or signed, which can be viewed as consisting of informational content and its *packaging*. In spoken speeches, the 'packaging' is made up of the words and linguistic structures of the speech and of features of the voice and of delivery (sometimes, especially in poetry, specific combinations of word sounds and rhythm are part of the 'packaging'), plus non-verbal signals and information, including body language, diagrams on paper or on screen etc. In signed speech, 'signs' are the main vector of the content. In written texts, the signal is composed of letters, characters, words, linguistic structures, fonts, page layout, graphics, etc. In other words, the term 'packaging' refers to the linguistic and peri-linguistic choices made by the Sender and to the physical medium through which they are instantiated.

Distinguishing the content from the 'packaging' can be tricky. For instance, by using deliberately technical terms to express ideas for which there are also less specialized synonyms, in other words, by modulating form without informational changes, a speaker or writer can send the message to Receivers that s/he is a specialist; by using familiar style or slang in a type of discourse where more formal language is generally used, Senders may aim at presenting an image of themselves as 'cool' people not bound by formal conventions; by copying or imitating someone's linguistic or gestural mannerisms, they may wish to express a message about their attitude towards him/her (respect or affection in some cases, the opposite in other cases). Much information is also transmitted unintentionally by Senders in the 'packaging': mistakes may show a Sender's low level of education, an accent can indicate the country or part of a country s/he comes from, certain features of delivery can betray a speaker's nervousness, and much information is carried by a writer's handwriting (see the discussion of 'Personal Information' in Chapter 3).

In the present context of *basic* concepts and models *for training* as opposed to a scientific exploration of communication acts, for the sake of convenience and efficiency, the discussion will focus on the *Message* as defined in the following restrictive way, which I believe is adequate for the discussion of Translation of informational Texts but insufficient for the discussion of literary translation:

The Message in a Text or in a Text segment is the information the Sender wishes to convey to the Receiver through it.

This includes factual information, information about the Sender's opinion about something, or about the Sender's wish to have the Receiver do something or refrain from doing something.

One important point for the discussion of quality is that Senders select and adapt both the content and the 'packaging' of their texts or utterances to their intended Receivers. They do so to a varying extent, depending inter alia on how strongly they wish their Message to be received and accepted and on their skills as communicators. Such adaptation can include varying degrees of explanation and explicitation, selecting certain registers of language, certain delivery features in speeches etc., and is determined by what they know and what they imagine about the knowledge, language skills, intelligence, attitudes and values of the intended Receivers. As will be shown later in this chapter, this often has considerable implications on Translation.

5.   Quality

5.1   The criteria

Considering that in everyday life, Senders formulate statements with an aim – or several – in mind, it is reasonable to assume that from their point of view, at the level of each Text segment, communication is successful if their aim(s) is/are achieved or at least reasonably well served by the relevant segment. From the Receivers' point of view, communication is successful if they understand the Sender's message, regardless of the fulfilment of the Sender's aims: in translation and interpreting, they may be satisfied with the communication service offered by the Translator even if they challenge the Sender's information and/or explanation and even if they fail to be convinced by the message.

Generally, as explained earlier in this chapter, Translators regard themselves as serving primarily the Sender or the Client – with the exception of signed language interpreting, where interpreters may view themselves as serving primarily their deaf Receivers. They can therefore consider their task to have been successfully performed if they provide satisfactory communication service according to the criteria of the Sender or the Client (or the deaf Receivers) respectively.

Note that the correlation between satisfactory quality as perceived by a given communication actor and the level of fidelity, linguistic acceptability, clarity, or terminological accuracy of the Translator's output can be weak: setting aside issues of assessment competence which will be taken up later in this chapter, interpreters sometimes serve mainly the purpose of adding prestige to conferences where their linguistic mediation is not really necessary; at other times, they have a useful albeit painful role as scapegoats in diplomatic negotiations, allowing participants to withdraw or change positions without admitting it, by claiming they have been mistranslated; they can also serve tactical purposes by giving one of the parties in negotiations, who has understood the original statement, more time to think before reacting. Translators have also been known to fulfil legal or administrative translation requirements rather than actually transfer information, for instance in bilingual countries where readers understand both languages. In such cases, Translation 'quality' as expected and as perceived may have little to do with getting the message across in a genuine act of communication.

Such situations exist, but they cannot serve as a basis for general Translation strategies and tactics, especially in a training environment. For students, the goal should be presented as serving *communication interests* efficiently and in compliance with applicable norms.

Another point is that the Translator can be required to *help* achieve the Sender's aims but cannot be expected to *guarantee* their fulfilment: the Sender's statement may be psychologically, socially, culturally and/or informationally inadequate or less than optimal. Receivers may also lack the necessary background knowledge, intellectual aptitudes or motivation to understand the message and its implications, or, as mentioned earlier, they may not wish to act or react upon it as the Sender would like them to.

Translators are also hampered by their position as 'outsiders' who know less – generally *much* less in most technical and scientific Translation settings – about the subject at hand than the Senders and Receivers they serve. Furthermore, on the communication configuration side, the Translator may know little about the Sender and the Receiver, especially when working for a Client such as a translation company who is neither; the interests of the company lie in keeping its own clients (who may be Senders or Receivers), and it often refuses to give Translators access to them for fear of being by-passed in ulterior assignments. This is a specific and frequent case where the communication interests of the Sender clash with the commercial interests of the Client.

Success or failure of Translated communication can therefore not be taken as the sole criterion or even as the main criterion for Translation quality, though decisions made by the Translator have to be compatible with the aims of the communication actor the Translation is serving primarily, generally the Sender.

5.2   Discourse and quality components

As indicated above, Texts Translated in a communication setting can be analyzed as consisting of content and 'packaging' (form) which interact and produce effects. While 'accurate' rendition of information or Messages (see Chapter 3) is essential, it is also important to make students aware of the weight of the packaging. A third type of quality component covers the Translator's behaviour (see later in this chapter).

Good voice and pleasant delivery, pleasant style and good layout of a printed page can occasionally do more toward convincing a listener or reader than the quality of the idea that is formulated or the information that is delivered. Conversely, good content is weakened by poor style in writing, unusual or inaccurate terminology, a poor voice or poor delivery of a speech. This applies to any Sender, including the translator or interpreter. Translation readers sometimes complain about inaccurate use of terminology which makes comprehension of translated texts difficult in spite of a faithful rendering of the content. It can also impede communication by lowering the credibility of the Translator, who is thus identified in the eyes of the Receiver as an outsider to the field. Similarly, conference delegates sometimes complain about the monotonous delivery of interpreting which makes listening tiresome and hinders communication.

The 'packaging' can have much weight in the assessment of interpreting quality, more so than in the assessment of translation quality. In the field, one often hears delegates assess an interpreter's performance as "very good" in spite of the fact that the interpreter sitting adjacent in the booth could detect numerous and sometimes major errors of content. It appears that the interpreter's voice and self-assured delivery have a confidence-inspiring effect, especially when interpreting for radio and TV. Conversely, beginning interpreters with a somewhat hesitant voice are often mistrusted by delegates notwithstanding the faithful, clear and terminologically correct content of their speech.

Interesting research work on quality perception of conference interpreting performance has been done (inter alia) in Spain under the leadership of Ángela Collados Aís of the University of Granada. It is perhaps best represented by a collective volume edited by Collados Aís *et al.* (2007). The studies involved manipulating single parameters such as accent, voice, intonation, style, grammar etc. in the interpreter's performance and having the manipulated recordings assessed by listeners. Findings suggest strongly that in simultaneous interpreting, weaknesses in one parameter of form can have extensive negative effects on the users' perception of the quality of other packaging parameters, as well as on their overall assessment of the quality of the interpreter's output.

5.3 The perception of quality: Positions

The perception of quality in Translation depends to no small extent on the viewpoint of each participant in communication: a passionate speech interpreted convincingly can be highly appreciated by the Sender but resented by Receivers, and fast completion of a rather coarse (written) translation may result in reactions of satisfaction by a translation company which pays for the work as long as their client does not complain, while readers of the target-language text may find the translation mediocre or poor. Such phenomena are observed frequently in the field. In interpreting, where quality is often assessed by Clients *and* participants, general behaviour and outward appearance are important quality components, especially in high-level diplomatic and political meetings and conferences. Price considerations also come into play: a low-priced Translation service and a higher-priced Translation service may be judged differently because of the different price-to-performance ratio (see Pinchuk 1977: 206 and Sager 1983: 121–22). Since professional Translation is generated in and constrained by the social and economic context, such factors in quality assessment cannot be disregarded.

Basically, however, there is a consensus on some quality criteria which are more or less independent of the context: ideational clarity, linguistic acceptability and terminological accuracy as well as fidelity on one side, and appropriate professional behaviour on the other all contribute to high-quality Translation, although the relative weights given to them by individual raters can vary (see for example Bühler 1986; Kurz 1989 for conference interpreting).

Note also that some authors, in particular Toury (1991), who has been investigating translation norms, stress that acceptability criteria are not necessarily the same for translated texts and for 'authentic' texts (written directly in the target language). In literary translation, this is easy to understand: literary texts are essentially vehicles for much more than information, including emotional and aesthetic components, and readers may be aware of and wish to retain in the target text linguistic traces of some features of the source language and culture and of the author's literary personality even if this means informational shifts from the Source Text (see Berman 1984 and Chapter 10). As regards translation of primarily informational texts, translation instructors seem to hold the unanimous view that the sole applicable criteria of acceptability are those of the target language. According to J. Sykes (1983: 42), "The translation is to read like a composition originally written in the target-language." Graham (1983: 103) goes further: "In the revision stage, the translation is a text in its own right and must be able to stand up to scrutiny as a finished item, divorced from its original Source Text." In this book, which deals with primarily informational texts in a didactic and therefore normative approach, the same view will be adopted.

When applying universal quality criteria such as ideational clarity, linguistic acceptability and terminological accuracy, competent assessors of non-literary Translations should theoretically arrive at similar assessments of Translation quality. In the field, some actors in the communication situation may be dissatisfied with the results of Translation because they are not compatible with their interests or not positive enough from their viewpoint, but they will probably acknowledge that a Translation is good even if it does not serve their aims. For instance, in a TV interview with interpreting, the journalist may express dissatisfaction with the end result because the interviewee's answers were too long or not to the point, but nevertheless acknowledge that nothing was wrong with the interpreter's output as such.

Translation assessments do tend to fluctuate greatly, especially in interpreting (Bertone 1989). This can be due inter alia to variability in individual sensitivity to deviations from 'acceptable' spoken language and in individual norms of language acceptability. In a study by Gile (1985b), the number of deviations from linguistic acceptability detected in a short interpreted speech by a sociolinguistically homogeneous sample of 10 informants varied from 5 to 28. Differences in fidelity norms (as to what information should be kept in a Translation and what can be changed) also contribute. In an experimental study, Gile (1999b) found differences in the assessment of fidelity between assessor groups (professional conference interpreters, translation and interpreting students, translation teachers, academics not engaged in translation or interpreting) and between assessment modalities (assessment of transcripts of speeches versus listening to the interpreters).

Assessment variability can also be ascribed to the various actors' positions in the communication configuration, and to limitations with which these positions are associated:

The Sender
Senders may understand the target language well enough to assess the fidelity of written translations of their texts insofar as they understand the content and can pick up inaccuracies. However, without an understanding of the principles of Translation, they may not understand certain linguistic transformations which involve some apparent 'loss' or 'gain' of information (see Chapter 3). Moreover, their assessment capacity can be strongly influenced by their subjective feelings, and they may attribute weaknesses

to a Translation which fails to produce the expected results while in fact the inadequacy of their own Text is the cause of the lack of success.

In interpreting, in the consecutive mode, speakers can listen to the target-language speech and at first sight, it would appear that if they understand the source language, they have all it requires to assess the interpreter's output. It turns out that their assessments are not necessarily reliable, perhaps due to attention fluctuations. In a classroom experiment reported in Gile 1995, one of the students made a short speech (1 minute and 54 seconds) which was interpreted by another student; the speaker failed to notice two errors the interpreter made but reported three 'false' omissions in the interpreter's rendering (omissions which the interpreter had not made). In the simultaneous mode, Senders cannot hear the target-language speech, and can therefore only check it to a limited extent through the reaction of the Receivers (the *delegates*) – if any.

The Receiver of the target-language text
Receivers are at the opposite end of the communication line. In translation, they generally see only the target-language text. They can judge the clarity, linguistic acceptability, terminological accuracy and logical consistency of the translation. They have no way of checking directly its fidelity, though they may be able to identify inaccuracies if the translator's output contains inconsistencies or gross errors which they believe are not likely to have originated in the Sender's text.

In simultaneous interpreting, the situation is similar insofar as delegates can listen only to either the original or the interpreter's speech. Spot-checking of words or groups of words can be done by listening to isolated sentences or to sentence endings in the source speech and then checking on the interpreter's rendering of them, but it is extremely difficult to listen to the whole target-language speech and to the whole source-language speech while it is being interpreted. Moreover, while the reader of a written translation can often get hold of the source-language text for verification purposes, doing the same thing for an interpreted statement is difficult unless both the original and the target-language speech have been recorded and/or transcripts are available, which is not standard practice – with some exceptions such as important speeches broadcast on television or made available to the media, or multilingual events which are posted on the World Wide Web. Even if such recordings are available, the comparison process is lengthy and tedious. A delegate listening to simultaneous interpreting can therefore assess the packaging, but is not in a good position to assess content fidelity. Besides, usually delegates listen to speakers because they are interested in what they have to say, not for the purpose of assessing the interpreter's rendering of the speeches, and it does not make much sense for them to devote much attention to spot-checking the interpreter's target speech instead of concentrating on the content of the speech.

In consecutive interpreting, the situation is somewhat different: if the delegates' understanding of both languages is good enough, they are in a relatively good position to assess the quality of interpreting regarding the accuracy of individual segments, though they may not be able to note all the omissions because of the large amount of information involved and the fact that they do not take notes as the interpreter does. In the classroom experiment mentioned above (Gile 1995), no error made by the interpreter was noticed by all students, only 2 errors out of 10 were noticed by close to half the students, half of the errors were noticed by less than a fifth of the 10 students, and some 'false' errors and omissions were reported. If student interpreters, who know both languages very well and are trained to listen carefully, are unreliable, it seems safe to assume that so are delegates.

The Client

When the Client is neither the Sender nor the Receiver, chances are that s/he does not read the translation or listen to the interpreter's output and does not know much about the subject. S/he is therefore not in a good position to assess the quality of the Translation, and relies mostly on feedback from the Receivers or from other Translators. Experience shows that with some exceptions such as demanding TV viewers, reactions from Receivers are a rather blunt instrument to judge quality. In some cases, the Client does have Translation competence and does check Translation quality as a service to the other actors. In such a case, s/he can be a good quality assessor.

The Translator

The Translator is a Receiver *and* a Sender, has a good understanding of the source language and a good command of the target language, but, as mentioned previously, generally knows less about the subject, the motivations, the aims and the respective interests of the principals and is less familiar with the appropriate terminology and phraseology than the Sender and the Receiver. Another constraint applies specifically to interpreters: because they are engrossed in complex cognitive operations under severe time pressure (see Chapter 7), their processing capacity is busy if not overloaded, and they are not in a position to monitor fully the quality of their output while interpreting. They can be (painfully) aware of some of the shortcomings of their target speech when they fail to understand certain parts of the source speech, when they find themselves unable to render them, when making errors or formulating clumsy sentences in the target language, but probably have a limited capacity to view their speech as a whole and assess its overall quality. After interpreting, part of the material for comparison is no longer there, as words have disappeared from their minds. In contrast, translators have the material at hand and can scrutinize it in both the source language and the target language at any time.

To sum up, the Translator is in a better position to assess quality than either the Sender or the Receiver in some respects, but also has a limited assessment capacity.

Revisors

In the case of written translation, experienced revisors with appropriate extralinguistic knowledge in the relevant speciality field are perhaps in the best position to assess translation quality. In interpreting, interpreters are sometimes hired to check on other interpreters (for instance during interpreted depositions, when one party's lawyer wants to make sure not to miss any relevant information in a witness statement) and are in a similar position when the deposition is taken in consecutive.

5.4   The perception of quality: Motivation and attention

The preceding analysis indicates the basic positions and possibilities for quality assessment. In actual practice, assessment also depends on the motivation of the actors and on the attention they wish to devote and can devote to quality evaluation.

As explained earlier, receivers of informational discourse may not be equally interested in all the information offered in the Source Text or in the overall quality of Translation. They may be interested in particular pieces of information which are found in a fraction of the Text and disregard the rest, in which case their perception of quality depends to a large extent on one or several Translation segments that are scrutinized carefully while the rest of the target-language statement goes virtually unnoticed.

This is particularly salient in conference interpreting: delegates tend to listen to only part of the presentations given at conferences, both because they feel that many are not relevant or not interesting enough and because the concentration required to listen carefully to all of them is taxing. They therefore tend to judge quality without the necessary control of informational content, which often leads to a favourable assessment of quality in conferences in which interpreters feel they have done a poor job. Carroll noted in 1978 the absence of any "thoroughgoing study" on interpreting quality. The situation has improved dramatically over the past decade or so – see for example Collados Aís *et al.* 2003a, 2003b, 2007 and many master's theses and papers reported in the *CIRIN Bulletin* at www.cirinandgile.com), but in spite of all this work, the delegates' reactions are difficult to predict.

An anecdote from my own experience may be enlightening: at a sports conference, a rather poor speaker from a manufacturing company presented his company's device for measuring an athletic performance variable. The audience consisted of administrators of athletic events and two representatives of another firm which manufactured a similar machine. The organizer was worried about the poor quality of the source-language speech and asked the participants whether everything was clear; all delegates said they were fine – except the two representatives of the speaker's competitor, who complained they "had not understood anything" listening to the interpreters. This anecdote illustrates the fact that the actual assessment of quality depends inter alia on the specific needs of the assessor, and suggests that although common quality criteria do exist, actual overall quality assessment can vary markedly in any given context for this very reason.

Another point which may be worth noting is that Translation readers and listeners tend to keep their reactions to themselves. While some, who are particularly happy or unhappy about a translation or interpreting service, may make a laudatory comment or complain respectively, most do not bother. In the absence of reactions from Receivers, clients tend to assume that Translation quality is good, but this is clearly an unreliable inference.

5.5 Behavioural components of quality

Professional Translation is a professional *service* activity. As such, its quality is judged not only by Text-related parameters (fidelity, language quality, Text clarity etc.), but also by other aspects of the service. While Translator training tends to focus on technical issues revolving around fidelity and output quality, it is important for students to understand that their professional future will depend to no small extent on other aspects as well.

Besides rules best classified under professional ethics, which can be taught separately toward the end of the training curriculum, professionalism, responsible behaviour, dignity without arrogance, and even cleanliness and appropriate clothing style (rarely mentioned in the literature in the West, but discussed in a Japanese publication – Kunihiro, Nishiyama, & Kanayama 1969), can strongly influence the Clients' and delegates' perception of quality. Being on time is obviously crucial. In written translation, observing deadlines is also important in the perception of quality by Clients. Good relations with colleagues are particularly relevant in conference interpreting, which is most often practiced in teams, at least in the simultaneous mode. Solidarity and active cooperation in the booth and with technicians enhance not only the quality of interpreting *as it sounds*, but also the *image* of interpreting in the eyes of the Client. Booth manners are also an important quality component, often ignored by practitioners. The following rules inter alia deserve to be taught:

- use the *cough* (or *mute*) button rather than the *microphone off* button when coughing, clearing one's throat, asking a question or making other noises; the mute button cuts the delegates' earphones from the noise, but the 'microphone off' button immediately replaces the interpreter's voice by the speaker's voice, often at a different volume, and seems to disturb delegates markedly.
- avoid excessive movements in the booth, which cause fluctuations in the volume of the target-language speech in the delegates' headset;
- avoid rustling papers in front of the microphone;

  These principles were not taught in the programme where I was enrolled in the 1970s, and I suspect mine was not the only interpreting school where they were neglected. In the field, I continued being unaware of their relevance until at a multilingual IBM conference where quality was monitored systematically, little slips of paper from delegates started coming to the booths complaining about the noise of rustling paper and about variations in the volume of the interpreters' voices.

- keep your booth tidy and arrange working documents so as to make them easy to find and retrieve when required. This quality component matters to other team members more than to the delegates, who may only be affected indirectly by the untidiness of the booth which prevents interpreters from finding the required documents rapidly enough to retrieve information, but quality as perceived by colleagues can make a difference with respect to the chances of obtaining further assignments from the Client.

Students should be made aware of these aspects of quality from the start of training. Relevant principles which can be implemented in the classroom should be stressed throughout training. Those which cannot should at least be recalled at the end of the curriculum.

6. Social status and quality

One recurrent theme in Translators' meetings and in statements published in Translation journals is the low social status of the profession. As explained in Chapter 1, this phenomenon can be explained partly by the existing diversity in interpreters' and translators' tasks and qualifications. The marketplace does indeed comprise all kinds of 'interpreters' and 'translators', from the low-end non-professional linguistic mediators barely acquainted with the languages they use to the highly professional, highly qualified experts who take responsibility for processing important and complex documents and speeches. Since the layperson sees more of the former than of the latter, it is understandable that the general social status of the profession tends to be below top level.

All of the existing forms of translation and interpreting are socially legitimate, as all make contributions to society, and it is natural that remuneration should vary depending on various quality criteria associated with the service provided. However, it is also natural that top-level practitioners should wish to raise the general status of the profession, and it is also in the interest of lower-level practitioners to upgrade their qualifications and accede to a higher status. The status question is not only a matter of social prestige, which is marginal in the present discussion although its importance should not be denied in the practitioners' individual feelings of satisfaction or lack thereof about their job. The point is that higher social status means a stronger position for negotiating better working conditions, both in terms of wages or fees and in terms of access to information. This is salient in conference interpreting, where speakers and listeners being served by the interpreter often hold high positions in society. When interpreters are seen as low-level linguistic or secretarial staff, they are sometimes refused direct access to the speaker and to documents ("I am not going to bother the minister/President to get you documents"). When their status is higher, such access is easier, and they are in a better position to do a good job. The difference is particularly striking when going from environments where conference interpreters' access to ministers and other important personalities is considered natural to other environments where it seems that protecting the individual status of civil servants in a ministry somehow involves raising barriers between interpreters and the upper echelons of the hierarchy, which makes the interpreting task more difficult.

One important point that can be stressed in the classroom is that, because people know so little about interpreting and translation, the practitioners' status is determined to a significant extent by their behaviour. Whatever status their vis-à-vis grants them at first contact, if they behave like responsible professionals, the attitude of people around them will tend to shift toward more respect. This is why I disagree with Pinchuk's view that

> ... [an] adequate translation will always be one that has been produced with just enough expenditure of time and energy to meet the needs of the customer. It should not be of a higher quality than he requires if this will introduce a higher cost. (1977: 206)

I believe such an attitude is bound to have a detrimental effect on Translation quality and working conditions, and that it should be proscribed from Translator training.

Some difficulties may arise because of psychological or sociological factors. Much of the hiring or commissioning and negotiating may be done by lower-level or clerical staff that resent the Translation practitioners' claim to a higher status – and their relatively high remuneration for their services. In any case, it is useful if instructors stress to the students that dignity and seriousness should be key elements in the practitioner's behaviour. Losing one's temper, showing off, acting irresponsibly will tend to undermine this professional status.

7.   Teaching suggestions

As mentioned at the beginning of this chapter, I believe that explaining quality around *communication* as is attempted above can be helpful to students whose experience with Translation is confined to school translation exercises and who only rely on linguistic decisions when translating.

In this awareness-raising chapter, there is not much theory in the abstract sense of the word. Ideas are simple and can be formulated in a straightforward way. *Skopos* theory and other functional theories – which revolve around ideas in line with the principle that Translators serve people and aims as opposed to Texts – can be used as a general framework, but I believe plain explanations are more efficient at early stages of training than abstract terms and concepts.

One sensible way to teach Translation quality is to start with examples which will raise the students' awareness (see the appendix to this chapter). However, the principles also need to be recalled and strengthened throughout the course.

One way of doing this consists in analyzing systematically with the students the (sometimes authentic, sometimes fictitious) communication situation around any Translation exercise before starting it, at least during the first months of Translator training. Some obvious questions are: Who are the speakers/authors (identity, field of expertise, function, status, etc.)? Who are their listeners/readers, or who does the

Translator assume them to be? Who are the Translator's listeners/readers? On the basis of available information (on the nature and function of the text, on the conference), what is the likely message the speaker or author wishes to send across to the listeners or readers? Are there pragmatic, psychological, social, or cultural factors which may interfere? Sometimes this information is explicit in the context surrounding the translation task itself – translator trainers include a brief in translation tasks, and interpreter trainers explain who the speaker is supposed to be and at what type of meeting s/he is speaking. Sometimes this information is not explicit and students have to make assumptions. Students should be told that professional translators need such task-related information or assumptions to guide their decision-making throughout (see for instance Jääskeläinen & Tirkkonen-Condit 1991).

Once the communication context has been established, the instructor can refer to it repeatedly. In particular, when monitoring or correcting students' interpreting and translation exercises, comments should be made not only on linguistic or informational questions, but also, whenever possible, on communication-related issues: students should be made aware of the relative merits of their general decisions and choices of words and structures with respect not only to general stylistic criteria, but also to the aim of serving the Sender (or the Receiver or Client) in achieving the desired effect in the specific communication situation.

For instance, instructors explain that when interpreting for an American audience, it is better to refrain from using purely British idioms and figures of speech. When interpreting for an audience a sizable proportion of which does not have very good comprehension of English, it may be better to use simple English rather than very elegant language. When translating for American readers, spelling should follow American rather than English usage. When translating into French for someone known for his/her purist attitude toward the French language, it may be better to avoid words imported from English if French synonyms exist, even when such English imports are more generally used in the field than the French counterparts (a good case in point is the vocabulary of computer science, with *le driver* vs. *le pilote, le CASE* vs. *l'AGL – Atelier de Génie Logiciel, le repository* vs. *le référentiel*, etc).

In the spirit of process-oriented teaching, when a student makes an inappropriate choice, rather than simply indicate a preferable alternative, it is better to *question* the choice in the particular communication situation: "How do you think the reader will react to that?" "Do you not think that term X will be easier to understand than term Y?" "Do you feel the speaker would recognize the idea as you have interpreted it, with the particular connotation contributed by term Z?"

A caveat: I believe that at the beginning of the course, it is somewhat risky to highlight to student interpreters the limitations of participants in interpreted communication events as regards the perception of Translation quality. If they are told that it is impossible for listeners to check their output in the simultaneous mode and that their clients' appreciation of quality can to a large extent be unrelated to what *they* consider good-quality interpreting, they may feel demotivated and fail to try as hard as during training to do *good* work. It may therefore be wiser to wait until they have been socialized into demanding standards. However, at least towards the end of their formal training, when they are about to start working in the marketplace, it is a good idea to prepare them for the way quality is actually perceived in the field. I believe that when doing that, instructors should stress that whatever the reaction of delegates, interpreters in the same team listen to each other with an often critical ear. Since most interpreters are hired more frequently by their colleagues than directly by Clients, this tends to keep them on their toes.

The case of translation is different. Sometimes translation work is reviewed by colleagues (revisors) whose work it is to do just that. This is the optimal case. At other times, a translation is read critically by the Client or by readers who give some feedback to the translator. This also provides motivation for quality, although their criteria may not be identical to the translator's, depending on the Client's or translation reader's philosophy. Problems occur mostly when there is no systematic quality control and when no feedback is offered to the translator, as is often the case when translating for a translation company or for a big organization without direct contact between the translator and the readers of the work. In this case, efforts toward quality will depend on the translator's professional pride and ethics, which should be built up during training.

8.   What students need to remember

Translation serves people and aims
In order for students to be best equipped for decision-making, it is paramount for them to understand that when Translating, they will be serving people and their aims, and that Source Texts and their Translations are essentially tools to achieve these aims.

Loyalty
In non-literary translation and conference interpreting, loyalty is due first and foremost to the Client, and secondly to the Sender, if the Sender's aims do not clash with the Client's. In other forms of interpreting interpreters may feel their loyalty is due to one party (for instance deaf persons) more than to another irrespective of their status as speakers or listeners.

Quality optimization and conflicting loyalty interests
When the Client is a Translation company with essentially commercial interests, the working environment associated with the Translation task often involves severe time pressure and no access to the Sender for documents. Both of these cause limitations and interference in the communication process. At other times, the Client is a facilitator and actually provides

documents and other resources. When the Client is a Translation company, it is generally difficult to change the working environment and most often the Translator will have to live with it. When the Client is an in-house Translation department and is interested in satisfying its own clients, namely persons from other departments, some improvements may be achieved through discussion and negotiations.

Quality will depend on the Translator's skills and attitude, but also on prevailing norms, on the Client's brief and on limitations associated with the working environment, including time available for the task and availability of documentary and other information sources. Translators will have to do their best under existing conditions, which may be far from ideal.

Behavioural quality components
Quality is measured by Textual parameters, but also by behavioural aspects of the service, which may be important in the Translator's career.

Quality assessment
Quality assessment done in the field is not necessarily reliable. This is due to several factors, including the assessors' cognitive limitations and the variability of their needs, which makes them attribute different weights to various quality components. Regardless of the Client's assessments, constant striving for maximum quality is an important prerequisite for each Translator's long-term job satisfaction.

Appendix – A demonstration in the classroom for written translation

The following describes a demonstration conducted with the aim of illustrating to students several points on quality assessment as explained in this chapter. The material reproduced here was used at the University of Montreal in September 1993. The text is now old and its content is technologically obsolete, but the principle of the demonstration remains valid and I assume that translation instructors can find their own texts in the relevant fields and languages for demonstrations in their classrooms without difficulty.

The Source Text, in English, was taken from an issue of the magazine *PC Laptop*. Four successive segments were translated into French by the instructor. In the first, deviations from linguistic acceptability were introduced. In the second, there are errors in substance. In the third, terminological usage is incorrect. The fourth was meant to be an acceptable translation.

Students were given the French text only and told that it was the translation of an English text. They were first asked to read segment A (with deviations from linguistic acceptability) and comment on it. When they reported the deviations, the point was made that they were able to judge this aspect of quality on the basis of their knowledge of the target language without knowing much about the subject and without looking at the source-language text.

Next, they were asked to read segment B (with errors in substance) and make comments on it. It turned out that those who knew something about microcomputers spotted translation errors. Those who did not could not identify them. The point can be made that these errors in substance could have serious consequences for the Sender and for the magazine which was to publish the translation if it remained uncorrected.

Again, in segment C (in which there were instances of incorrect terminological usage), only participants familiar with computers found fault with the text. It was pointed out that in spite of the errors, the paragraph was understandable. Implications of such errors with respect to the transmission of the Message to Receivers and with respect to the loss of impact due to the loss of credibility of the text were discussed.

The fourth segment contained no errors. Nevertheless, some participants did find fault with it stylistically. This was a good opportunity to demonstrate to students variability in norms of linguistic acceptability, which is also found among Clients and target-language Receivers, as well as translation revisors.

French translation

A   *Le premier ordinateur Quaderno d'Olivetti avait montré qu'il était possible d'offrir a un prix raisonable des très petits sub-notebooks avec une excellente qualité.*

Deviations from linguistic acceptability:
- "a un prix raisonable" should read *"à un prix raisonnable"*
- "des très petits" should read *"de très petits"*
- "avec une excellente qualité" should read *"d'excellente qualité".*

B   *Le nouveau Quaderno 33 d'Olivetti est un sub-notebook à base de 686 capable d'intégrer Windows. Il est équipé d'un écran rétroéclairé et ne pèse que 3,9 kg.*

Errors:
- there is no such thing as a 686 processor
- 3.9 kg was very heavy for a state-of-the-art subnotebook

C   *Le Quaderno 33 a un écran VGA de 7 pouces de 640 x 400 pixels et offre 16 ombres de gris. Son clavier à 93 touches comporte un pad numérique distinct, et sa batterie au Nickel-Cadmium lui donnerait une autonomie de 4 à 6 heures. Il est équipé en standard d'un disque dur de 60 Mégaoctets et de 4 Mégaoctets de mémoire à accès aléatoire (extensible à 12 Mo). Il est livré prêt à l'emploi, configuré avec Windows 3.1, Works for Windows et Lotus Organizer, auxquels s'ajoute un programme de transfert de fiches (cordon fourni).*

Deviations from standard terminological usage:

-   *"ombres de gris"* should read *"nuances de gris"*
-   *"pad numérique"* should read *"pavé numérique"*
-   *"mémoire à accès aléatoire"* should read *"mémoire vive"* or *"RAM"*
-   *"cordon"* should read *"câble"*
-   *"fiches"* should read *"fichier"*

D   *Pour permettre une extension de la mémoire et pour pouvoir connecter des périphériques, il a été équipé d'un slot pour carte PCMCIA de type II. Le Quaderno comporte également un port parallèle, un port série, un port pour moniteur VGA externe, ainsi qu'un port PS/2, un slot pour modem interne et un connecteur pour un lecteur de disquette externe en option (145$).*

Source-language text

A   The original Olivetti Quaderno showed that extremely small, high-quality subnotebooks could be offered at affordable prices.

B   Olivetti's new Quaderno 33 is a Windows-capable 386 subnotebook with a bright backlit screen – that weighs just 2.97 pounds.

C   The Quaderno 33 sports a seven-inch backlit VGA display with 640 x 400 resolution and 16 shades of gray. Its 93-key keyboard houses a separate numeric keypad, while a NiCd battery is said to power it for four to six hours. A 60-megabyte hard drive and four megabytes of RAM (expandable to 12) come standard. Windows 3.1, Works for Windows, and Lotus Organizer, plus a file-transfer programme (with cable), are preloaded for full plug-and-play capabilities.

D   For more storage and peripheral connectivity, a PCMCIA Type II Card slot is built in. The Quaderno 33 also features serial, parallel, external VGA display, and PS/2 ports, an internal modem slot, and a connector for the optional external floppy drive ($145).

Chapter 3

Fidelity in interpreting and translation

1. Introduction

Fidelity may be the most fundamental and is probably the most widely discussed component of Translation quality. It is a central part of reflection on 'translatability' in the literature; it is linked to the concept of equivalence and to theories about equivalence; it is virtually unavoidable in research measuring shifts between Source Texts and Target Texts, errors and omissions; it is relevant to reflection about the respective status of the author and the translator, about the literary status of translators, about creativity in Translation.

The most salient problem that arises when considering fidelity in Translation stems from the obvious and well-known fact that languages – in the context of the respective cultures where they operate – are not isomorphic. Firstly, there are obvious differences in the lexicons and grammars of different languages, for instance with 'missing' words in some and an 'abundance' of words around the same referents in others (see for instance Chapter 6 of Georges Mounin's *Les problèmes théoriques de la traduction*, 1963). Secondly, while many lexical units and rules of grammar in two languages look similar at first glance and may even be described as having the same functions in dictionaries and grammar textbooks, there are often subtle differences in their use in context. Thus, at first glance, it would seem that one of the main problems Translators face is not being able to re-express 'exactly' in a target-language Text what has been expressed in the source-language Text; since they need to write their translation or utter their interpreted rendering of the source speech in acceptable language, their Texts, especially literary texts, look 'nice' but are 'unfaithful'. Hence the idea, defended inter alia by Georges Mounin (1963), that translation is an approximation at best.

A theoretical or philosophical discussion of the subject is beyond the scope of this chapter. Some basic communication-oriented ideas, and in particular the concepts of 'formal equivalence' and 'dynamic equivalence' are explained in Nida's now classic *Towards a Science of Translating* (1964) and in Nida and Taber's *The Theory and Practice of Translation* (1969). For interesting reflections on fidelity in conference interpreting, see Donovan-Cagigos 1990. I believe an extensive analysis of the issue is not very time-efficient in a professional translator or interpreter training course, in which *practical* skills must be learned and in which fidelity is analyzed for every exercise on a case-by-case basis. However, a simple conceptual framework providing students with some guidelines and criteria can be usefully integrated into the training programme.

The reason is that due to their experience at primary and secondary school where 'translation' meant matching words and linguistic constructions in their native and foreign languages, when they reach university and translation school, they often find it difficult to accept the idea that changing a construction or 'adding' or 'deleting' words while translating does *not* necessarily amount to a breach of fidelity. They tend to be very conservative in their decision-making and fail to use their full analytical and creative potential to optimize their translations.

Prescriptive statements and explanations alone are not necessarily efficient didactic tools; advice and rules should be supported whenever possible by convincing evidence. The experiment described below provides evidence that justifies some degree of freedom in the translation process. In my experience over the years, the experiment and the model derived from its results have clearly helped students make more daring decisions and more effective use of their analytical intelligence and writing skills when translating.

In view of its contribution to the understanding of the nature of fidelity and in view of the very central position of the question of fidelity in Translation strategies and tactics, I believe that the experiment and the informational model of informative sentences explained in this chapter should be introduced at a very early stage in the syllabus, preferably immediately after the module on communication and quality.

Before going into the actual analysis, I should like to recall that fidelity principles as outlined here are those which are generally considered to apply in technical and scientific translation and in conference interpreting, in which the Translator's role is basically taken to be a 'neutral', 'transparent' or 'conduit' role. As explained in Chapter 2 (Section 3.3.2), authors from Translation Studies have been raising doubts about such neutrality over the past few years, and in some Translation settings, in particular in health interpreting including psychological counselling situations, in asylum hearings, in signed language interpreting, expectations about the Translator's role can deviate markedly from that of the conduit. Nevertheless, in most technical and scientific translation and conference interpreting situations, they still follow this somewhat idealized concept, and I believe it still deserves to be taught in Translator training programmes as a basis for fidelity strategies and tactics. Instructors who train Translators for other settings can probably find the concepts and models presented in this chapter useful, but will need to adapt them to their needs.

2. An experiment in fidelity

The experiment reported below was designed initially in the late 1970s. It was intended to investigate empirically aspects of the process leading up from an idea selected for verbalization through its verbalization in one language to its translation into other languages in an attempt to examine the assertion that translators should translate from meaning, not from words (a strong claim which I encountered at ESIT, Paris, found attractive and sought to investigate and validate). The experiment proved interesting and fruitful in a number of ways. I have replicated it dozens of times (more than once a year) in Translation classes over close to 30 years, in various countries and with languages as different as Arabic, Chinese, Danish, English, Finnish, French, German, Hebrew, Igbo, Italian, Japanese, Spanish, Swedish, Tahitian and Yoruba, with consistent results as outlined below, demonstrating wide applicability across languages and cultures. What follows is the description of typical replications.

2.1   Phase one: Verbalizing a simple idea

Half the students are asked to leave the room. A simple drawing suggesting an elementary informational Message is presented on a whiteboard to the remaining participants, who are told what situation is simulated and are asked to formulate the Message in their own words in their native tongue. The sentences thus obtained are then read aloud.

At this point, it may be appropriate to recall and stress that in this book, which deals essentially with the Translation of Informational Texts, the word *Message* is used to mean not the statement produced, i.e. the verbal materialization of a communicative intention, but *the information that the Sender wants to get across to the Receiver* and around which the verbal statement will be constructed (Section 4 of Chapter 2). This is not the only definition of the term found in the literature, but it serves our purposes here and should be kept in mind when reading the following pages.

In the example discussed here, the drawing shown to participants depicted a road as seen from inside a car, with a road sign showing "Paris 50 km" (Figure 3.1).

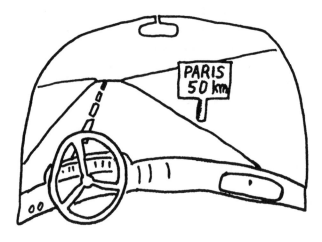

Figure 3.1

The participants were told the following:

> "You are sitting in the car next to the driver. At a certain point during the trip you see the road sign. Please write down exactly what you would say (in your mother tongue) to the driver to tell him/her what the sign says."

In numerous replications using different Messages as expressed by different drawings (see Gile 2005 as well as the appendices for further examples), only rarely have two or more participants written identical sentences in the same language during the same experiment. This is a non-trivial finding, considering that the Message is very simple and that most groups were large, from a few dozen to more than a hundred people, often with more than twenty having the same mother tongue.

Thus, the first consistent empirical result from the experiment is the following:

Given the same simple informational Message presented under identical conditions, individuals sharing the same mother tongue tend to write different sentences to express it.

This result was partly due to differences in the way the subjects understood the Message as presented to them, as retrospective analysis and questions to the students showed. In other cases, the statements did seem to reflect essentially the same Message, as is the case of the six sentences listed below, a subset of those collected from native English speakers in one replication of the experiment performed in Seattle in October 1988, at the 29th convention of the American Translators' Association.

1. Fifty kilometres to Paris.
2. Still fifty kilometres to go.
3. We'll be in Paris in fifty kilometres.
4. Fifty kilometres longer.
5. We'll be there in fifty kilometres.
6. Paris is fifty kilometres from here.

The first question one may ask is whether the Message given in the road sign is actually conveyed in all the sentences despite the differences between them. In this particular replication of the experiment and in this sample of statements produced, the question only arises with respect to sentences 2, 4 and 5 in which Paris is not mentioned, as the other three sentences explicitly mention both Paris and the distance.

Taking into account the situation (being in the car heading toward Paris) and the context (the information explicitly given by these sentences), the answer can only be that for the driver to whom the speaker is addressing the sentence, the Message is conveyed fully in all sentences, as s/he presumably knows where s/he is heading. This answer is based on a particular communication situation in which the Sender and the Receiver share some knowledge. If this were not the case, the Message might not be fully conveyed in sentences 2, 4, and 5, which could be interpreted as referring to another destination ("there") or possibly to a destinationless situation, in which a car (or another vehicle) is driven in circles for testing or some other purpose.

In fact, while all the sentences express the same Message in this situation, they could also express different Messages if they were formulated in different circumstances, which is a good illustration of the idea that there is generally no one-to-one relation between statements and Messages.

In the classroom, in replications of this experiment, when asked whether the different sentences express the same Message, some students initially say they do not and point out differences in their information content. When reminded that in the context of the experience, the term 'Message' refers to the content (in this case the information) that a Sender *wishes* to get across to a Receiver and when asked whether all the sentences express this content, they generally agree that they do.

The finding that the same Message as defined here is verbalized in different ways has a corollary:

If different sentences in the same language can express the same Message, then in Translation, different sentences in the target language may also reflect the same Message as the one initially generated in the source language.

The next step is to look at what else is found in these sentences.

Differences between sentences
In our experiment, it turned out that sentences expressing the same Message could be strikingly different. Although the basic information about the distance being fifty kilometres is found in all six sentences reproduced above, Paris is not mentioned in sentences 2, 4 and 5. Furthermore, sentences 2, 3, 4 and 5 indicate that the speaker is moving toward a place located fifty kilometres from his/her position at the time the utterance is made; through the personal pronoun "we," sentences 3 and 5 indicate that at least one person besides the speaker is also moving toward the same destination. Sentences 2 and 4 also indicate that the speaker has already been moving for some time, i.e. that s/he is not starting at the time the utterance is made. Finally, sentences 3, 4 and 5 indicate that reaching Paris is a future event with respect to the utterance, sentence 2 that the speaker still has to "go" a certain distance before something happens, while sentences 1 and 6 give no indication of time with respect to an action.

The differences in information content between any sentence and the drawing and between any two sentences can be described as:

– *Information 'gains'*: Information given in one sentence which is not found in another or in the drawing, such as the arrival in Paris being a future event, or the presence of at least one more person besides the speaker who is concerned by the statement;
– *Information 'loss'*: Information not given in the sentence under consideration although it is present in a sentence it is being compared to or in the drawing, such as the explicit mention of Paris.

In a communication situation and in context, there may be no actual informational 'gain' if information made explicit in a statement by the Sender is already known to the Receiver or is also made available in another part of the same Text. The absence of a piece of information in a statement may not amount to any informational 'deficit' if the information is known to the Receiver or provided elsewhere. Redundant informational explicitation can serve rhetorical purposes and may compensate for attentional lapses on the part of Receivers who may have missed a piece of information in its first occurrence, but in terms of informational presence/absence in the Text, it makes no difference.

This leads to another question: why is information added to the Message in a large proportion of the sentences? (in four of the six in this case – only sentences 1 and 6 do not carry information beyond that given by the road sign). A partial answer to the question is proposed below.

2.1.1 *Framing Information*

One reason for adding information to the Message becomes clear when considering two possible situations in which the speaker would have attempted to convey the road-sign information to the driver:

– In one scenario, the driver could have asked the speaker, "How many more kilo-metres to Paris?" The answer could have been the single word "Fifty," which would have conveyed the full Message.
– In another scenario, the initiative could have come from the speaker, who had noticed the road sign while the driver's mind was elsewhere. In this case, if the speaker had only said "Fifty", the driver would probably have failed to understand and asked for clarification. A more explicit utterance, perhaps something simi-lar to one of sentences 1 to 6 as reproduced above would have been required to convey the Message successfully. In other words, the speaker would have had to provide a *frame* for the Message so that the listener could understand what was being referred to.

After conducting the experiment a number of times and having become aware of the existence of such a framing component, I observed authentic utterances made in the field and found that very simple sentences generally contain *Framing Information* (FI), which serves as a guide and facilitator to help the Receiver (listener or reader) interpret correctly and more easily the part of the utterance conveying the Message proper. In the case of the experiment reported here, it is present even in sentence 1, as the mini-mum utterance that could have conveyed the Message would have been "Fifty" as in the first scenario. The references to Paris and to kilometres in the examples presented above are Framing Information, although the speaker was probably not aware of this when composing his/her statement.

Note that the road sign itself also contains Framing Information, insofar as it indicates the distance unit "km." In France, road distances are almost always expressed in kilometres (and in meters when they are very small, which would not be the case here). This Framing Information is required because, since conventionally, "km" is indicated on road signs indicating distances, if this sign did not have it, drivers could be puzzled as to the actual meaning of the sign. The abbreviation does not provide new information, but helps drivers interpret the information correctly. Note that speed limitation signs in France do not indicate the units (km/h).

Actually, in this experiment, the entire drawing presented to students around the sign, including the lines indicating the road, the landscape on both sides and the interior of the car are Framing Information designed to help students understand the situation and the Message.

2.1.2   *Linguistically/Culturally Induced Information*

Framing Information is selected by the Sender (speaker or writer), consciously or not, to help the Receiver grasp the Message from the words. Another type of information can be identified which is not part of the Message and is not introduced by the Sender by choice. This can be seen in sentences 3 and 5: in both, the future of the verb (abbreviated as "'ll' for 'shall' or 'will') indicates that the arrival in Paris is a future event – as opposed to a present or past event. The Sender had no 'communicational' need to specify this information, which was *induced by linguistic rules*: in this sentence structure, a choice between a past, present, or future tense of the verb was mandatory. Note that time-related information in the utterance was not mandatory, as demonstrated by the very existence of sentences 1 and 4 where no such information can be detected, but once a verb was introduced, it became unavoidable.

According to Jakobson (1959), "Languages differ essentially in what they *must* convey and not in what they *can* convey". This statement is perhaps too strong, but rules of language (and of associated culture) do tend to induce the presence of some information in utterances beyond what is strictly necessary for comprehension of the Message.

Similarly, in all probability, the pronoun "we" in sentences 3 and 5 was not deliberately chosen by the Sender in order to 'frame' the Message, as the driver presumably knows who is in the car and will be arriving in Paris. The personal pronoun which provides this information was made mandatory for the same reasons as the future of the verb by the particular linguistic construction used and by the rules of English. In Japanese, this information would not have been made explicit in the statement.

Linguistically/Culturally Induced Information (LCII) can be mandatory (as is generally the case in the choice that must be made between the singular and plural of nouns in English, French, German, Spanish and most other European languages and cultures); it can also be strongly induced without being totally unavoidable, for example as regards titles when addressing people or naming them to a third party (Mr/Mrs/Miss, doctor, professor etc.).

2.1.3   *Personal Information*

Finally, some information found in utterances beyond the Message is neither chosen by the Sender for framing purposes nor induced by linguistic or cultural rules, but is associated with personal habits or with the personal 'style' or other features of the Sender.

There is no clear-cut example of such *Personal Information* (PI) in the replication of the experiment reported here, but there were in other replications. For instance, participants made spelling mistakes which showed their weak mastery of the language, and some wrote sentences which sounded unnatural and in which the influence of a foreign language could be detected. These sentences gave the reader some information about their authors – as was indeed the case of the investment company's text as presented and discussed by Mellen in Section 3.3 of Chapter 2. In oral utterances, regional or foreign accent, certain errors in grammar, or certain stylistic and lexical choices often carry information about a speaker's personal background (native tongue, level of education, social class, etc.) and personality which are not connected to the Message s/he is trying to get across (see examples in Appendix B).

Summary of the findings of phase one of the experiment

The first phase of the experiment as replicated many times shows consistently that:

1.   The same Message, verbalized under identical conditions by different Senders, tends to be expressed differently by each individual.

In fact, the same Message may also be expressed differently by the same Sender under quasi-identical conditions at two different points in time. This is suggested by findings from a slightly different version of the experiment which is explained later in this chapter.

2.   In most statements produced, the Message (which can also be referred to as 'Primary Information') is accompanied by 'Secondary Information', which can be of three types:

   –   *Framing Information* (FI), which is introduced by the Sender, consciously or not, for the purpose of facilitating comprehension of the Message by the Receiver.
   –   *Linguistically/Culturally Induced Information* (LCII), which is not selected deliberately by the Sender but is made mandatory or is induced by the rules of the language used and the associated culture.
   –   *Personal Information* (PI), which is neither selected by the Sender nor induced by linguistic constraints, but is associated with personal characteristics of the Sender.

Informative sentences can thus be represented informationally using the following Model:

Sentence information = Message + (FI + LCII + PI)

2.2   Phase two, version 1: Translating a simple statement

In the version of the experiment presented here, once the original sentences have been collected, the drawing is removed from the whiteboard and replaced by three or more of the collected sentences written in a language shared by the largest number of participants. Participants who have been waiting outside are called back into the classroom, and all are asked to translate the sentences into their native language or into the same common language (depending on the working languages of the participants – the aim of the operation is not to produce high-quality translations but to make a point as outlined below).

It turns out that participants tend to translate each sentence separately, more or less word-for-word and keeping the structure and information content of their translations very close to the original. Out of more than a thousand people who have taken part in the experiment between 1979 and 2009, only a handful have produced a single translation for all the sentences.

When asked for explanations, participants single out differences in information content between the sentences, which, some say, differ in their 'viewpoint' or 'emphasis.' When asked specifically whether they consider the *Messages* in the sentences to be different, some say they are the same, and others consider they are not. Interestingly, almost invariably, even those who say the Message is the same in all sentences translate each of them differently. Still more interesting, this same pattern was found not only with student-participants, but also in replications with experienced interpreters and translators.

One explanation could be that given a text to translate, the translator, who is generally not familiar with the precise circumstances under which it was generated, is not in a position to discriminate between the Message and Secondary Information. Translating all the information ensures that no relevant component of the Message is missed.

Another explanation could be that the artificial nature of the experimental setup induces behaviour somewhat different from that which would occur in an authentic translation context in the field. In this second part of the experiment, participants, who were not in a communication situation, did not know what the purpose of the exercise was and may have assumed that since there were three distinct sentences on the whiteboard, there was some kind of difference between them which should not be 'neutralized' in the translation.

This however does not account for the fact that even participants who were present throughout the first phase and knew precisely what the Message was and under what circumstances it generated the three sentences translated each differently.

Yet another explanation could be the existence of an implicit operational rule internalized even by professional translators that translation should preferably render *all* the information contained in the source-language text. This could be due to the fact that translators do not really become aware of the distinction between Primary and Secondary Information unless translation poses problems and forces them to make choices. From field observation, it seems that conference interpreters take a wider margin of freedom, possibly because of cognitive constraints in the processing of spoken language which make them forget rapidly at least part of the form (the 'packaging') of utterances they hear and replace them with mental representations of their content (what has been theorized as 'deverbalization' in ESIT's interpretive theory – see for example Lederer 2005). These important cognitive aspects of language comprehension and production in Translation are discussed in later chapters, especially Chapters 7 and 9.

2.3   Phase two, version 2: Immediate replication

In another version of this classroom experiment, the graphic representation of a simple idea is shown to students, they are asked to verbalize it in writing in their native language on a piece of paper and turn it over, and the instructor turns to another topic. After a short while (perhaps twenty minutes or so), the same graphic representation of the same idea is shown to students again and they are asked to verbalize it again after the instructor assures them there is no 'trap' in the exercise. Once all participants have finished writing their sentences, they are asked to answer two questions in writing:

1.   Was your second statement identical to the first?
2.   If it was not, why not?

In about 10 replications of the experiment carried out so far, many participants said their second utterance was different from the first. A few students explained that they wrote a different second statement "just for the sake of changing", but the majority said they thought their initial sentence was clumsy, incomplete, ambiguous or too explicit. In other words, they found it preferable, when given a chance, to improve upon it. This is a good opportunity to point out to students that authors of Source Texts could feel the same way about what they write even after revising their texts, and that they do not necessarily consider that the texts they produced are the best to serve their intentions and interests. I have often asked students whether in their personal experience, they had not felt sometimes, after writing texts which were important to them and sending them off to their destination, that some of their sentences or choices of words were clumsy. There are always students who acknowledge this emphatically, which helps make the point in class.

Interestingly, in each replication conducted so far, a few participants wrote that their first and second utterances were identical whereas when this was checked, it turned out they were different (the data for one replication are presented in Appendix B). A few also said their two utterances were different whereas it turned out they were identical. While intentional variability as described in the previous paragraph is due to the fact that authors do not necessarily consider their linguistic choices optimal, this second finding suggests that in addition, they do not necessarily remember the exact wording of their own statements.

3.   Principles of fidelity

The principle, apparently taken for granted by all beginning students and even by some professionals, that basically, all the information carried by the source-language text should be kept in the target-language, calls for a discussion of fidelity using the findings of the experiment.

In determining principles of fidelity for interpreting and translation, it seems appropriate to start not with the finished linguistic product, but with the communication setting. As a reminder, as explained in Chapter 2, in informative communication such as is found in conference interpreting and in technical and scientific translation settings, Senders produce Texts to carry Messages for the purpose of achieving aims such as informing, explaining, persuading or making Receivers do something or refrain from doing something (the *skopos* of the Source Text). As is also explained in Chapter 2, for Senders, communication is successful if this aim is achieved. Generally, the Translator 'represents' the Sender and the Sender's interests, and therefore 'does a good job' if the Translation contributes to the success of the Sender's endeavour. Translators should therefore take this principle as an essential reference to guide their decisions.

Secondly, there seems to be a universal or quasi-universal social consensus that *Translators* who are merely asked to 'Translate' should not rewrite or reformulate the speech *as they wish* in a way which *they* believe will achieve the Sender's objective more efficiently than the Sender's words – unless they have a specific mandate to do that. That is, the Translator must contribute toward successful communication while following what is essentially the same 'route' as the one the Sender chose in the source Text to lead the Receiver along.

Translators thus have to serve the Translation's *skopos*, but in compliance with the relevant social norms of Translation. The following analysis is an attempt to help students learn to navigate in the waters of Translation using the concepts of informational components identified above.

3.1   The message

It is probably safe to say that a *minimum fidelity principle* applies 'universally' or quasi-universally as regards conservation of information in the Target Text in Translation under normal circumstances. From field observation, from the analysis of Translation literature and from discussions with fellow Translators, it appears that there is general agreement that in the Sender-loyalty option (see Chapter 2), *the Message or Information which the Sender is trying to convey in an utterance or text should be re-expressed in the target-language Text.*

Note that this rule is not absolute. For instance, when the Message expressed in a small Text segment such as a sentence is factually incorrect and there is good reason to believe that the mistake is only a slip of the tongue or a minor unintentional misrepresentation of reality (for instance associating the wrong day of the week with a particular date) and if the error does not carry over into the rest of the text or speech, many translators and interpreters consider that it should be corrected.

Sometimes, the correction is very important if the Sender's aims are to be achieved: in a diplomatic encounter, a small factual mistake due to a speaker's ignorance of the other party's culture could have serious detrimental effects on the outcome of the meeting; this provides a strong case in favour of correction. From observation and discussions with colleagues, they will tend to correct errors in single names more easily than mistaken ideas reflected in full sentences. In other circumstances such as a trial where the translator works for a party who is attempting to discredit the author of a text, errors can be useful tools for the Client and must be reflected in the Target Text even if the translation thus produced does not represent the author's Message (but in such a case, the Translator is no longer in the Sender-loyalty scenario).

In written translation, when errors are encountered, there may be time for the translator to consult with the Client and/or author of the text before deciding whether to correct or not. In the case of interpreting, there is often no time or opportunity to consult with anyone, and the interpreter will have to make the decision him/herself on the spot.

3.2   Framing Information

As explained earlier, Framing Information is introduced in the statement by the Sender for the purpose of facilitating the reception of the Message by the Receiver. But as pointed out in Chapter 2, Receivers of the original speech or text may not have the same pre-existing knowledge and values as Receivers of its Translated version. Framing Information which is appropriate for the original Receivers may not be suitable for target-language Receivers, in which case rendering it in the target language as it stands in the Source Text can be counterproductive.

For instance, when translating an American's statement about "Cairo, Egypt" (as opposed to "Cairo, Illinois") into 'Le Caire, en Egypte', the French translator working for French readers makes an awkward statement to the detriment of the real Message: most French readers only think of "Cairo, Egypt" and are totally unaware of the existence of "Cairo, Illinois"; the explicit mention of Egypt may distract their attention from the actual Message. Conversely, when translating an Australian text quoting prices in "dollars," it may be useful to add Framing Information by specifying *dollars australiens* so that these are not mistaken for U.S. dollars.

Fidelity to the Sender's interests may thus require deleting some of the original FI and adding some FI for the benefit of the target-language Receiver.

The selection of Framing Information is not strictly determined by objective circumstances. Depending on the Sender's *style*, FI may vary, as illustrated by its diversity in the experiment reported above. The selection of FI can also be said to reflect the *personality* of the Sender – to a varying extent. From discussions with Translators, teachers of Translation and users of Translation services, it would seem that there is also a general consensus that *Translation should also reflect the Sender's personality*. This view, which is only seldom made explicit in writings about non-literary Translation, is consistent with the general principle of fidelity; after all, the Sender's Message and interests also reflect personal choices, and therefore 'personality.' However, the consensus regarding the Translation of non-literary texts also seems to incorporate a *low-priority* rating of fidelity to the author's 'personality' as opposed to informational fidelity. Therefore, if the Sender's original FI does not seem appropriate for the Receivers of the target-language product, there is some justification for changing it.

3.3 Linguistically/Culturally Induced Information

The case of Linguistically/Culturally Induced Information is different, in that LCII is never selected by Senders of their own free will. They are often free to choose one out of several linguistic options, but *must* choose one. In the Source Text, LCII, which may include redundant and some non-relevant information, is by definition 'natural' and well integrated into the discourse. In contrast, in the Target Text, the conservation of such LCII can be awkward, or even distort the Message.

Incidentally, LCII requirements of the target language, plus the fact that Translators cannot always discriminate between the Message and Secondary Information and tend to translate the latter in order to be sure not to leave any part of the Message untranslated, often combine and generate target-language Texts which contain not only information induced by the target language and culture, but also LCII from the Source Text which does not meet any need in the Target Text and which can distract the attention of the Receiver from the Message and be counterproductive in terms of communication.

For instance, in Japanese, when referring to somebody's brother, there is a mandatory lexical choice between a word representing an elder brother (*ani*) and a word referring to a younger brother (*otooto*). If the Sender's intent is only to indicate that there is a brotherhood link between two men, depending on the context, the best solution when translating the text into English could be to write "his brother", as opposed to "his elder brother". Otherwise, depending on the context, the Receiver may consider that the age difference between the two brothers has some kind of meaning in the text, which it does not (see an anecdote in Torikai 2009: 167).

The translator's tendency to add Secondary Information from the Source Text in the Target Text, combined with the Secondary Information required in the latter, could be part of the explanation of the so-called 'explicitation hypothesis' (Blum-Kulka 1986), according to which Target Texts tend to be more explicit than Source Texts. This hypothesis has been a candidate for "Universal" status, a "universal" in Translation being a rule which tends to apply to all types of Translation and all language pairs (see for instance Mauranen & Kujamäki 2004). The same tendency to add unnecessary Secondary Information from the Source Text also explains partly the trend of some Target Texts to be longer than Source Texts (although this is not always warranted, as stressed in Durieux 1990a).

It is the source language and culture and not the Sender which basically determine the LCII in the Source Text. This would imply that there is no reason to try to reproduce said LCII in the target language and culture, which are different by definition. On the other hand, as mentioned above, Senders may be free to choose from two or more options, and their 'linguistic style' (individual preferences for certain sentence structures and words) does determine partly the LCII which will ultimately be carried in the source-language Text. LCII therefore does reflect individual personalities to some extent, which provides some reason to try to reproduce it in the target-language Text. However, contrary to Framing Information, it is not aimed at optimizing communication efficiency, and therefore can be taken to rank even lower on the priority list of information to reproduce in the Target Text – if there is no counter-indication (see Section 3.5).

3.4 Personal Information

Recalling that Personal Information is by definition a reflection of the Sender's personality or other personal features, Translators may choose to attempt to keep it in the Target Text because it reflects something about the Sender for the same reason which would make them consider rendering LCII, but most of the time, this is difficult to do. Moreover, PI is often counterproductive from the Sender's viewpoint: it can indicate through an accent or regionalisms where the Sender comes from, which is generally irrelevant to the communication aim and can distract the Receiver's attention from the Message, or highlight his/her social circumstances, which can have a similar effect, or show through grammatical errors or a foreign accent that the Sender is using a language which s/he has not mastered fully or that s/he is a state of stress etc. In these cases, reflecting this information in the Target Text is contrary to the principle of Sender loyalty, though it may be relevant when another professional loyalty principle is adopted.

3.5 Conclusion

The verbalization experiment suggests that when asked to put an informative Message into words, individual Senders tend to produce statements which differ in their information content. Analysis, supported by the finding that when formulating the same message twice they often write two different sentences, reveals that part of the packaging and part of the information it carries are not fully under their control, at least at an initial formulation stage (this may change after revision). This, by the way, is true not only of information content, but also of syntactic choices (although the experiment does not address this aspect): later in this book, Chapter 7 explains that speech and text production are complex and demanding tasks, which in part explains why authors and speakers are not necessarily in full control of or happy with the words and structures they produce when expressing a thought or information. Neither the authors nor readers/listeners of texts/speeches are conscious of all the choices made or all the information provided in the sentences. Moreover, because Secondary Information is by definition ancillary, they generally have no strong feelings about it and do not view it as 'intellectual property' to be handled respectfully: in short experiments which I conduct regularly, speakers presented with several TL versions similar to their own SL utterances but not quite identical to them with respect to Secondary Information and structure tend to accept all of them as legitimate translations and to prefer the TL version which they consider most efficient in terms of communication – whenever they understand the target language well enough.

Admittedly, this evidence alone cannot be considered conclusive, because of both the artificial experimental setup and the ever-present possibility of an active *experimenter effect* (experimenters tend to be biased toward facts that strengthen their hypotheses and views and may unwittingly induce in their subjects behaviour going in the same direction). Further evidence which can be brought into the discussion are field observations which show that authors of informational texts, and especially speakers in conferences who understand the target language, regard Translations as faithful even when their information content differs with respect to Secondary Information, and sometimes even with respect to Primary Information – though this may be due to the fact they forgot the exact words and informational content of their utterances rather than to particular fidelity norms.

The discussion in the preceding paragraphs provides justification for some shifts in the information content and linguistic structure of informational texts and speeches when translating or interpreting them, and suggests hierarchical rules that can help make the right decisions while Translating:

- In informational texts and speeches, whenever conservation of the original Secondary Information is believed to be counterproductive with respect to the intended impact of the Message (inform, explain, persuade, make the Receiver do something or refrain from doing something), it is the latter which takes precedence over 'fidelity' to Secondary Information.
- Conservation priority in Secondary Information is highest for Framing Information, which can be partially chosen deliberately by the Sender; it is second highest for Personal Information, which may be considered to represent partially the Sender's 'personality' but is not controlled by him/her. Linguistically/Culturally Induced

Information should only be rendered without change in the target language when this is believed to have no adverse effect on the communication impact of the statement.
- Conversely, Translators should have no qualms about introducing whatever Linguistically/Culturally Induced Information is necessary for their Text to be linguistically acceptable and to optimize its impact. Nevertheless, Framing Information should be introduced with caution, lest it change the Sender's 'style'. As for Translator-generated Personal Information, since it is the product of the Translator's personal style rather than the Sender's, it should be avoided whenever possible.

This model provides qualitative suggestions, but no quantitative guidelines. It tells students that they can add or delete *some* information during Translation according to some priority rules, but it does not tell them how far they can go in that direction. Because of the virtually unlimited number of possible situations and speech segments that are or could be Translated, it is difficult to give practical 'recipes' for fidelity, even supposing the various informational components (the Message, FI, LCII, and PI) can be clearly identified by the Translator. It is difficult to say how far Translators can or should go in changing the information content of the text or speech, since from a given point on, depending on prevailing norms, they may be seen as *adapting* the Text rather than Translating it. However, the following rules of thumb for the Translation of informational Texts, based on the most widely accepted concept of Translation (though not the only one to exist – some bold ideas about translation can be found in Gouadec 1989) and on the Sender-loyalty principle (see Chapter 2), can be useful:

1. The order of ideas identified as part of the Message in the Source Text should be followed in the Target Text: For instance, if the Sender starts a source-language Text by presenting idea A, then illustrates it with examples B, C and D and ends with a conclusion E, Translators should not start with examples B, C, and D and follow with the presentation of idea A and with conclusion E – unless there is a strong norm in the target culture that this should be the order in the relevant type of text.
2. In translation, within a sentence, structural changes necessary for linguistic acceptability are generally accepted by all parties concerned and are therefore legitimate. Moreover, in the interest of communication efficiency, long sentences can be segmented into shorter ones, and sentences that follow each other in the source-language text can be merged in the target language. For instance, "*Les essais ont été une réussite. Toutefois ils ont coûté très cher*" (Tests were successful. However, they cost a lot) can be merged into "Tests were successful, but very expensive." However, in compliance with rule 1, the order of sentences in a group of several consecutive sentences should generally not be changed in the target-language text.

In interpreting, more extensive stylistic and informational changes may be acceptable. One justification for this difference in norms is that in a written text, authors are supposed to have had the time to review and correct their prose until it reflects their thought as they want it to. In oral discourse this is not the case, and more elements may be escaping the speaker's control. S/he may therefore be better served if the interpreter focuses more than in written translation on the Message as the interpreter feels the speaker would word it if s/he had full control of the linguistic choices. For instance, sentences that speakers do not complete because of speech-production difficulties tend to be completed in the target language, and sentences that the speaker repeats because s/he has lost his/her train of thought tend not to be repeated. In special circumstances, however, for instance if interpreters feel they serve listeners rather than speakers, when interpreting for a lawyer in the courtroom (see Morris 1989), when the Client is the listener and his/her interests clash with those of the speaker (as illustrated in Section 4 of Chapter 2), when certain moral issues are at stake, such latitude is no longer justified.

3.   If the Translator feels that a particular choice of words or linguistic structures may have been made deliberately by the speaker/author for impact (and therefore becomes part of the Message), this choice should be followed whenever possible. This is frequently the case with word repetitions, humorous distortion of words or grammar, etc.

4.   Secondary Information: An obstacle and a help

Secondary Information is a major source of fidelity problems and decision-making requirements in the Translation of informational Texts. The questions that arise regularly are whether to preserve in the target-language Text information that might be detrimental to communication and whether to introduce new Secondary Information to help communication be more effective.

From experience, in the field, many of these questions are answered spontaneously by Translators without any conscious decision-making. For example, when Translating from English into Japanese, the English singular/plural LCII is most often suppressed spontaneously if the information is irrelevant, because Translators are aware of the fact that trying to keep it can make the Japanese Text clumsy or even distort the Message. Similarly, in a speech made in English by a female speaker, interpreters working into Hebrew will not hesitate to introduce the LCII indicating the gender of the speaker not found in the English speech (in Hebrew, forms of verbs in the present tense are not the same for male and female speakers).

Problems arise when information required because of target-language rules is not *known* to the Translator and is not given in the source-language Text. For example, in a conference, a French speaker may refer to somebody as "*Monsieur Martin*," giving the interpreter working into English Linguistically/Culturally Induced Information relating to the gender of X but failing to indicate whether he should be referred to as "Dr. X," "Prof. X," etc. as may be appropriate in English in the context at hand. An American speaker may refer to another person by his/her first name without indicating the last name, whereas norms in the target language and culture might call for the use of a title followed by the last name. Failure on the part of the interpreter to refer to X by the proper title can affect communication. Similarly, since the singular/plural discrimination in Western languages is generally difficult to escape, Translation from Japanese into a Western language poses problems when the Translator needs to know whether in a sentence, the Japanese Sender is referring to something in the singular or in the plural. The Translator is forced to make a decision and take a chance on the possibility of an erroneous decision. Decision-making and risk-taking are discussed further in Chapter 5.

Secondary Information is often important to the Translator while being of little value to the Receiver. For the latter, part of it is already known (Receivers may be familiar with the academic qualifications of people referred to in an utterance, with their first and last names, with their gender). The Translator, being to an often large extent an outsider to the field and to the relationship between Sender and source-language Receivers, suffers from informational deficit. Secondary Information can provide him/her with useful indications for a correct interpretation of the source-language statement and for adequate reformulation in the target language.

4.1   The language-specificity of LCII-generated problems

As will have become clear, the most difficult problems with respect to fidelity and the resolution of ambiguity arise when target-language rules require information not provided by the source-language Text. Experience shows that the frequency of such problems depends to a marked extent on the specific language pair involved (some factors which will be discussed in this book are actually *language-pair specific* rather than language-specific, but for the sake of simplicity, the term 'language-specific' will be used throughout). In the translation of informational texts and speeches between English and French, they are relatively rare: occasional forms of address as illustrated above, the use of the passive form in English, which cannot always be replicated in French and which poses problems to the Translator who does not know the agent of the verb, etc. In translation between Japanese and Western languages, problems associated with LCII are more numerous, in particular because of the following two differences, already mentioned several times in this book:

– Western languages generally discriminate between singular and plural and between various points in the past, present, and future, whereas Japanese does not necessarily do so. This does not cause difficulties when Translating *into* Japanese because such Linguistically Induced Information simply disappears in the target-language product; but when translating *from* Japanese, when they lack background information, Translators may have to make hazardous decisions or try to bypass the problem somehow.

– Western languages tend to indicate explicitly the subject and object of verbs, which is not necessarily the case in Japanese. When translating from Japanese into a Western language, problems sometimes arise because the target language requires information about the subject and/or object of the verb and the Translator does not have access to it.

Interestingly, the lack of such 'objective' LCII in Japanese sometimes results in comprehension problems among the Japanese themselves (see Hara 1988; Ito-Bergerot 2006; Kondo 2008). This fact does not lessen the burden on the Translator working into a Western language, as his/her readers/listeners will feel frustrated by what they may perceive as 'lack of clarity' in the Text they read or hear regardless of the possibility that the ambiguity could be 'natural' for a Japanese. In literary translation, problems become more frequent and difficult. For example, Japanese sentences most often contain some linguistic and culturally induced information on the social relationship between protagonists (through suffixes, honorific words etc.). The fact that the information is not necessarily given in French or English Texts (or in many other Western languages, for that matter) forces Japanese Translators to take the risk of making guesses about it. Sometimes the context helps, and sometimes it is insufficient (for a more extensive discussion of the subject, see Gile 1984a).

4.2   Interpreting vs. translation from the Secondary Information perspective

In written translation, numerous difficult decisions regarding fidelity have to be made, which can lead to iterative corrections of the target-language text (see Chapter 5). The question naturally arises as to whether it is possible for interpreting, with its practically instantaneous and virtually correctionless production process (but see Petite 2005), to be reasonably effective in producing faithful *and* linguistically acceptable target-language speeches.

Several fundamental facilitating factors can be identified in the conference interpreting environment as opposed to the translation environment:

In international conferences, speakers and listeners are assembled in the same place at the same time, and speakers know they are talking not only to listeners who understand their language, but also to people who will have to listen to them through interpreters. Generally, they also know more about the target-language listeners than authors do about their target-language readers' at the time they will read their translated texts. Therefore, on the whole, though situations vary, one could say that speakers at conferences are more likely to select Framing Information suitable for their target-language Receivers than authors for readers of translations of their texts. Moreover, the diagrams and slides shown during speeches, as well as the speakers' body language, provide cues beyond those included in the linguistic part of the interpreters' speech and help them achieve more effective communication.

As regards cognitive processing, in international conferences, the Receivers (*delegates*) process the speaker's words by ear. The often-mentioned evanescence of the spoken word is probably associated with less 'word-bound' processing of speech: while both readers and listeners seem to process incoming language signals into general propositions (that is, into a 'logical', semantic representation of the content of the speech – see for example Kintsch 1970, 1974; Kintsch & Van Dijk 1975), readers have the possibility of lingering on words and single clauses, whereas this is seldom possible when listening to a speech due to the speed of delivery and to limitations in working memory (see Chapters 7 and 9). As a general rule, processing capacity limitations make it reasonable to assume that listeners tend to focus on the essential parts of the Message more than readers, and the effect of changes introduced by interpreters in Secondary Information becomes less of an issue than in written translation.

When reading *rapidly*, for the same reason, readers also tend to concentrate on Primary Information. Nevertheless, they retain the possibility of focusing on a particular word for a longer time or rereading a text segment after going through it a first time, and their perception of the Message may be more word-bound than in speech processing because of this non-linearity. This may result in a greater impact of Secondary Information.

It is perhaps necessary to recall at this point that this analysis is speculative. I am not aware of empirical research on such a difference between word-boundedness in reading versus listening, and am only offering a potential explanation for phenomena observed in the field in terms of user reactions and Translator strategies and tactics.

One further point is that in *extempore* speeches, formulation is less carefully thought out and is not corrected iteratively as can be the case in written texts. Speakers are less in control of Secondary Information (see Chapter 7), which arguably loosens the constraints on fidelity in the reproduction of Secondary Information by interpreters. This may explain partly why delegates who speak both the source and the target languages, and even speakers themselves, often come up to interpreters after consecutive interpreting and ask them how they manage to do such a perfect "word for word translation" of speeches – when the interpreter has in fact made many changes in Secondary Information.

5.   Teaching suggestions

5.1   The experiment

-    As explained in the introductory section of this chapter, students have much to gain from some input that will free them from their linguistic code-switching habits right at the beginning of their training curriculum. The experiment described here, combined with the presentation of Translation quality from the communication angle as discussed in Chapter 2, has been found to help.

However, depending on available time, not all of the experiment can be carried out or needs to be carried out. The main expected effect is awareness of natural variability in the verbalization of simple messages, which helps do away with the illusion that there is a fixed one-to-one correspondence between specific words and structures and specific messages. This effect can be achieved with the first part of the experiment, the most spectacular one, which can be conducted in a quarter of an hour or so, by presenting a simple idea graphically and asking students/participants to write down how they would express it verbally in a given situation (it is important to describe a specific communication situation), and then asking them to read aloud what they wrote and starting a discussion in the classroom. Other parts of the experiment can be helpful but they need not be carried out in class, while the first part is more convincing if it is experienced by the participants live.

– During the experiment, some participants may misunderstand the Message, and some may express a different Message in their sentences. For instance, one student wrote: "There are only 50 kilometres to Paris." In this sentence, "only" changes the Message. Another wrote: "In Paris, the speed limit is 50 km/h." In such cases, even though the reason for the misunderstanding or modification may be an interesting object for study in itself, deviant sentences should be disregarded in the analysis in the classroom because they do not contribute to fidelity analysis, and spending much time on them would not be very helpful with regard to the pedagogical goal of the experiment.

– After the experiment has been carried out in class and the three components of Secondary Information are discussed, students sometimes object that they can be difficult to identify in a given text (as is indeed shown in the second phase of the experiment); as a consequence, they wonder about the practical applicability of the rules of fidelity explained to them. Indeed, in the comprehension phase of the Translation process (see Chapter 5), informational components cannot always be identified as FI, LCII, or PI. However, when they are, the rules can be applied. Moreover, when Translators *produce* their own Target Text, they are aware of the need that sometimes arises to introduce additional Framing Information and of the fact that linguistic rules in the target language may force some Linguistically/ Culturally Induced Information into their Text – they are especially aware of it when the required information is not available from their knowledge of the subject, from the context or the situation. Knowing that some information in the source Text has not been deliberately selected by the Sender and why it is part of the Text is mainly useful for the purpose of understanding why some shifts are legitimate.

In this respect, judging by my students' reactions over the years, the experiment is a convincing one. In fact, its impact is sometimes so strong that it drives them overboard: after its presentation and discussion in class, some of them tend to make decisions in excess of what is generally considered reasonable leeway in translation, and move into what could be viewed as *adaptation* (no precise definition of the boundaries between the two is given here, but the idea should be clear to readers of these lines as it is for students when instructors make comments to this effect). This does require remedial action, but I believe it is easier to restrain such excesses in a student translator who understands that it is the Message, not words, which must be kept in the Target Text, than to struggle for months with word-for-word school translation habits in a long war of attrition.

5.2   A road-map metaphor

A metaphor may leave a lasting imprint in the students' minds and help them explain to others in simple terms why some leeway is justified in translation: using language is *not* similar to drawing a detailed and precise map of reality in which each 'real' object has one conventional representation; rather, it is like using a set of road signs to *point* toward a destination. It is up to the Receiver to reach that particular destination by interpreting the signs. Each language and its associated culture can be likened to a set of available road signs. When producing a source-speech or text, Senders use the signs available in the relevant language and place them along the roads on a particular route. Translators use signs available in the target language and place them along the same general route. Their main task is to lead the Receivers to the same destination as the Senders. As far as possible, they try to place their signs in a way similar to the way Senders use their own signs. By definition, the signs in the two languages are different in types, shapes and sizes, which implies different natural uses. In the translation of non-literary, essentially informational texts, the Translator's mind is on the *destination*, and the exact use of individual signs is of lesser importance, especially in view of the fact, shown by the experiment discussed in this chapter, that Senders generally do not have full control of the way they use their road signs in the Source Text.

As for the difference between oral and written communication: when writing a text, Senders have some time to select the signs and place them carefully along the route, then add signs, remove signs, switch signs, change their positions in different sequences until they are satisfied. When making speeches, Senders focus on the destination and tend to grab whatever signs are available at the time they believe they are necessary. When reading a translation, Receivers have time to stop and look at the signs along the way, and perhaps note a particular selection or arrangement of signs, approve or disapprove. When listening to a speech, including the interpreter's speech, listeners travel at high speed and have less time to do so. This is why it is important for translators to be able to select and place their target-language signs carefully so as to lead Receivers to the destination in a way closely resembling the one selected for them by the Sender, while for *interpreters*, it is more important to be able to drive rapidly to their destination, following speakers at an imposed speed. In the simultaneous mode, at the same time they are following the speaker's signs, they are also selecting and placing their own signs – which is not an easy task, as discussed in Chapter 7.

6.   What students need to remember

1.   Given the same elementary informational Message in non-verbal form, people tend to give it different verbal expressions. Moreover, when asked to re-verbalize the same Message after even a short time, each individual tends to give it a different second verbal expression.
2.   These differences do not result solely from the Sender's deliberate choices, and Senders do not necessarily realize what information they have added to the Message and why. Some of it is made mandatory by linguistic/cultural rules in the relevant language.
3.   As a result, neither the specific wording in a statement nor all the information it carries can be automatically viewed as reflecting a Sender's intentions and linguistic or informational choices. This means that adjusting the language structure and *some* information content of the target-language version of the statement is not tantamount to breaching the Sender-loyalty principle, provided the Message the Sender wanted to get across is rendered in a way which is compatible with the Sender's intended aims.
4.   More specifically, when Translating informational Texts, in most cases, the Message should be kept in the Target Text. As for Secondary Information, when it is identified, it should only be kept in the target Text without any changes if this does not interfere too severely with its impact on the Receiver. Otherwise, changes are legitimate and sometimes desirable or even necessary.
5.   These fidelity rules apply to the traditional 'conduit role' of Translators. In specific settings, in particular in public service interpreting, somewhat different fidelity rules may apply.

Appendix A

The following are data from one administration of the experiment performed at the end of September 1993 at the University of Montreal. The drawing was similar to Figure 3.1, with the difference that it was the town Trois-Rivières and not Paris that was indicated, and the road sign announced the distance as 40 km and not 50 km.

The instructor took advantage of the fact that he had the same group of students for two periods of 90 minutes to check formulation variability over time: students were asked to do the formulation task a first time before the first lecture, which was not on fidelity, and sentences produced (on paper) were picked up by the instructor (but not shown to the participants). Ninety minutes later, at the beginning of the second period, which was devoted to the fidelity issue, the drawing was presented again and the participants were asked to perform the formulation task once more. Only then did the instructor actually present and discuss the results. In this replication of the experiment, only the first phase was performed: no translation of the original sentences was done. Sentences elicited from each subject are marked by a number (1 to 14); the first formulation is marked "a" and the second "b."

The sentences produced were the following:

French

1a. *40 km avant Trois-Rivières.*
  b. *Trois-Rivières est à 40 km.*
2a. *Encore 40 km avant d'arriver à T-R.*
  b. *Encore 40 km avant T-R.*
3a. *Encore 40 km avant d'arriver.*
  b. *Il reste encore 40 km avant d'arriver.*
4a. *On arrive à Trois-Rivières dans 40 kilomètres.*
  b. *On arrive à Trois-Rivières dans 40 kilomètres.*
5a. *Encore 40 km et on arrive à Trois-Rivières.*
  b. not available
6a. *Il reste 40 km avant d'arriver à Trois-Rivières.*
  b. *Il ne reste plus que 40 km avant l'arrivée.*
7a. *Le panneau indique qu'il y a 40 km à parcourir avant d'arriver à Trois-Rivières.*
  b. *Le panneau indique qu'il y a 40 km à parcourir pour arriver à Trois-Rivières.*
8a. *Trois-Rivières est à 40 km.*
  b. *Trois-Rivières se trouve à 40 km de route.*
9a. *Trois-Rivières est à 40 km.*
  b. *Il nous reste 40 km.*
10a. *Trois-Rivières est dans 40 kilomètres.*
  b. *Trois-Rivières est dans 40 kilomètres.*
11a. *Trois-Rivières dans 40 km.*
  b. *Trois-Rivières dans 40 km.*
12a. *Il reste 40 km pour arriver à Trois-Rivières.*
  b. *Ça n'a pas de bon sens ! On est toujours à 40 km de Trois-Rivières.*

English

13a. Another 40 to go.
  b. Still 40 to go.

Portuguese

14a. *Trois-Rivières a 40 km.*

   b. *Faltam 40 km para Trois-Rivières.*

In this replication of the experiment, inter-subject variability was clearly demonstrated in French: only 2 sentences out of the 12 produced the first time are identical (sentences 8a and 9a). As for intra-individual variability over time, it was also demonstrated by the fact that out of 12 available sets of two sentences (Subject 5 left after the first period, and subject 12 made a mistake the first time and replied facetiously the second time), 9 sets (75% of the total) show such variability.

The presence of Linguistically/Culturally Induced Information and of Framing Information could also be demonstrated. No example of Personal Information was identified.

Appendix B

This replication was carried out in 2000, a week after a referendum in France on a change in the duration of the Presidential term of office from 7 to 5 years. At the beginning of the class the 27 students who attended were requested to answer the following question, on the purpose of the referendum:

> « *Sur quoi portait le référendum d'il y a 8 jours?* »
> [English gloss: "What was the referendum held 8 days ago about?"]

No time limit was imposed; the experimenter waited until everyone had finished and then collected the sheets of paper with the students' responses. The same assignment was given again about half an hour later. Students, who were surprised (as they always are), were reassured that the exercise was the same as at the beginning of the class, and that this was an experiment, with no 'right' or 'wrong' answers and no 'traps'. When they finished writing their second formulation, they were asked to write down whether it was strictly identical to the first, and if not, why.

The following are 7 examples of sentences produced, with the first and the second sentence for each subject marked respectively n/1 and n/2, n being the identifier of the student.

1/1. *Le référendum de dimanche dernier se portait sur le quinquennat*
1/2. *Le référendum, qui a eu lieu le dimanche 24 septembre se portait sur la question du quinquennat*

2/1.   *Le referendum portait sur le quinquénat - pour ou contre le quinquénat*
2/2. *Il y a une semaine, il fallait voter pour ou contre le quinquénat*

3/1. *Quinquennat ou septennat pour les présidentielles?*

3/2.   *Septennat ou quinquennat pour les présidentielles*

4/1.   *Le quinquennat*
4/2.   *Le quinquennat*

5/1.   *Le réferendum portait sur la réduction du mandat du président de la République (de 7 à 5 ans)*
5/2.   *Le réferendum portait sur la réduction du mandat présidentiel (de 7 à 5 ans)*

6/1.   *Le référendum portait sur la réduction de la durée du mandat présidentiel. S'il faut adopter le quinquennat ou conserver le septennat*
6/2.   *Le référendum portait sur la réduction de la durée du mandat présidentiel. S'il faut adopter le quinquennat ou conserver le septennat*

7/1.   *Référendum sur le quinquennat*
7/2.   *Référendum portait sur le quinquennat.*

Note high inter-subject variability and some intra-subject variability. Also note spelling errors and grammatical errors in some of the sentences (1/1, 1/2, 2/1, 2/2, 7/2). They are part of the information available from the statements. They do not say explicitly that the authors have a low level of education or are writing in a non-native language or have not checked carefully what they wrote, but the inference is immediate. This implicit information is clearly not part of the Message, and can be classified as Personal Information.

In 16 out of the 26 valid pairs of sentences (more than 60% of them), there were differences between the first and the second sentence. Out of the 16 authors, 7 (44%), explained the reasons for the differences: one student claimed that the question was put differently the second time, two students said they wanted to improve their first wording, 2 wanted to avoid simply repeating the first sentence, one student said he did not have time to write the first sentence as he wished initially, and one student said he "likes to change". It is clear that in this experiment, more than half of the students did not value highly their first wording and took advantage of the second opportunity that was given to them to change it.

This fact was then used in the classroom to argue against the idea that the particular choice of words and syntactic structures in a text produced by an author is necessarily a faithful reflection of his/her style and should therefore be reproduced 'faithfully' with respect to form.

Even more striking to the students was the fact that 5 out of the 16 authors who had written a different sentence the second time thought it was identical to the first. Interestingly, one of the students who wrote a second sentence identical to the first thought it was different. It seems that in this type of exercise, not only do authors not feel a strong attachment to the words and sentence structures they use, but they do not necessarily remember what precise words and structures they used in a statement written very recently.

As a final observation, note that the numbers and proportions measured in this replication are not necessarily representative of all replications: there is some variability in the proportion of identical pairs vs. different pairs, in the reasons given for the differences, in the proportion of participants who incorrectly believe they wrote identical utterances; in some replications, there were participants who answered that they did not know whether their second utterance was identical to the first. Nevertheless, the fundamental phenomena as reported here have always been observed so far.

Chapter 4

Comprehension of specialized discourse in interpreting and translation

1. Introduction

It is now well established among Translation instructors and theoreticians on the one hand, and practitioners on the other, that Translation involves at least some degree of non-trivial *comprehension* of the source-language discourse – that is, that such comprehension goes beyond the simple recognition of words and linguistic structures.

This idea is probably as old as translation itself. Nevertheless, it is underscored time and again in the literature on interpreting and translation as a starting point to explanations about the nature of Translation and about Translation competence. However, other than statements stressing the central role of comprehension in Translation, there have been few efforts to investigate systematically its *nature* and extent (a doctoral dissertation by Dillinger (1989) analyzing the types of inferences made during simultaneous interpreting is one exception).

The main reason for the comprehension requirement in Translation lies in the fact, already mentioned in Chapter 3, that languages (in cultures) are not isomorphic: since they are not modelled on exactly the same lexical and structural patterns, there is no one-to-one correspondence between all the words and structures of any two languages. Even the layperson knows about gross differences such as words existing in one language and not having 'exact equivalents' in another, or elements of grammar that differ from one language to the next: declensions, verb tenses, articles and other function words are salient examples which learners of foreign languages encounter early on. What the layperson often fails to perceive are more subtle differences that relate to stylistics or pragmatics: a particular word or linguistic structure may mean something in one language and seemingly corresponding words and structures mean something else in a cognate language, and/or and be associated with different social contexts and rules of behaviour.

Obvious examples are found in everyday language. For instance, even though French, German and Spanish have basically what seems to be the same choice between *tu* and *vous*, *Du* and *Sie*, *tu* and *Usted* respectively, the circumstances where people use one or the other are not the same. Neither do they use first names in the same way, or in the same way as English-speaking Americans. In more formal language, which is more relevant to written translation, the use of academic titles (Prof., Dr. Dr. Habil) may be unmarked ('normal') in Austrian documents whereas it would be perceived as emphatic in similar French documents. Many sentences produced in a language under the influence of another language sound unnatural and lose some of their impact because of that, while their informational content may be correct.

It follows logically that *transcoding* ('automatic' word-for-word translation), even if it is linguistically possible, may result in a target-language text or utterance that is clumsy, erroneous, or even nonsensical. Again, this is obvious to the layperson when differences are gross, but the rule extends to subtle levels that are more difficult to detect. If a sentence in a translation looks grammatically and logically correct, readers may not even suspect its information content or message differ from those conveyed by the source-language text.

The extent of the potential damage caused by translation without comprehension became very salient with the first machine translation experiments in the 1950s. Readers will find examples of amusing mistranslations in many accounts of the early days when 'automatic translation' through lexical and syntactic substitution was thought possible. One such example, often quoted, is the automatic translation of the English sentence "the spirit is willing but the flesh is weak" into a Russian statement about the wine (or vodka in one variation of the story) that was good and the meat that was rotten. Similar examples can be found in automatic translation now offered on the World Wide Web. Human translators can avoid such gross errors but are nevertheless frequently at a loss when translating or interpreting statements which are lexically or syntactically ambiguous.

For instance, in texts on computer technology, it is often difficult to discriminate between a function and the name of a product: "Network Manager" could be the name of a product, not to be translated, or an executive position that can and should be re-expressed in the target language using the relevant terminology. Also in computer science, "User Models" might mean 'Models for the user' or 'Models made up by the user' and may require a different translation in each case, depending on the target language. As explained in Chapter 3, comprehension of more than linguistic structures is also necessary when linguistic or cultural rules in the target language require the Translator to express explicitly information which is not given in the source-language text.

This chapter analyzes discourse comprehension by describing components of comprehension and their interaction. It stresses in particular the importance of extra-linguistic knowledge (or 'World Knowledge') and analysis. The first part of the chapter is a general presentation of the components of comprehension from this viewpoint. The second part shows how sentences in specialized texts and speeches can be represented mentally as logical and functional networks, thus making it possible to translate them with limited background knowledge. I should like to stress once again (see the Introduction to this book) that the discussion of comprehension in this chapter is limited to Translation-teaching requirements. The issue of comprehension as such is wide and complex, and clearly no attempt to cover it exhaustively or in depth can be made here – neither would it be very time-efficient. For readers interested in a more extensive discussion, psycholinguistics offers a large body of studies on the comprehension of natural languages (see for instance Clark and Clark 1977, Costermans 1980, Noizet 1980, Matthei and Roeper 1985, and many more recent publications are easy to locate). Artificial Intelligence investigators have also been working on the subject (see for instance Winston 1984, Bonnet 1984, Sabah 1988).

2. The comprehension 'equation'

2.1 A basic 'equation'

In the classroom, when native speakers of English are asked whether they understand the sentence

> "This car is very powerful"

they almost invariably say they do, as I have found dozens of times during lectures and workshops. Their comprehension is based on two major resources. One is their knowledge of the words and grammar of the English language. This is not enough. In different contexts and in different situations, the word *powerful* may mean different things: a 'powerful' car in an advertisement does not refer to exactly the same property as a 'powerful method' for solving a problem or as a 'powerful man' who is described felling trees, though the three '*powerful*' do have something in common. Similarly, the word *car* can mean not only an automobile, but also, according to *Webster's New World Dictionary of the American Language* (1974 edition), a streetcar, an elevator cage, or the part of a balloon which carries people and equipment. 'Understanding' the above sentence about the "powerful car" means that those hearing or reading it can imagine an automobile (this was my intended meaning), with a strong engine, which can accelerate rapidly even when it is full of passengers and luggage and going uphill. This is where the second element of comprehension comes in: besides knowledge of the language, comprehension implies knowledge of the *outside world*, also called in the literature *extralinguistic knowledge, world knowledge* or *encyclopaedic knowledge*.

In an American novel one of the characters says: "If you don't look, you step in it. It's as true in medicine as in the streets of New York" (Harold L. Klawans, *Sins of Commission*, London, Headline Book Publishing PLC, 1982, p. 79). What you step in in the streets of New York if you do not look will not be indicated as one possible meaning of "it" in any dictionary, but knowledge of the streets of New York (and of Paris) makes interpretation of the sentence possible.

The relationship can be expressed in the following way (the mathematical symbols are borrowed for convenience, but their meaning is not the conventional one):

(1)   C = KL + ELK

      C   stands for comprehension
      KL   stands for 'knowledge of the language', hereafter 'linguistic knowledge'
      ELK stands for 'extralinguistic knowledge'

The mathematical signs in the 'equation' should be interpreted in the following way:

= indicates that the term on the left (comprehension) is the *result* of the interaction of the two terms on the right;
+ indicates *some additive effect* of interaction, not arithmetic addition as we understand it in everyday life.

Comprehension is not a binary variable that takes on one of two values, namely 'comprehension' or 'non-comprehension'; it should be viewed as taking on values along a continuum going from non-comprehension to what might be called 'full comprehension' – in practice, neither of these poles is absolute in any way. A later section of this chapter discusses this idea in more detail, but note at this stage that:

–   When people say they 'understand' a sentence, generally their comprehension can be considered incomplete, because they do not know and understand *all* it actually says in its context. In the 'powerful car' example, they may not know which car the author is referring to or what level of power is meant by "powerful". Putting it differently, their comprehension would be more complete if they knew who is talking, what car is in the speaker's mind, and in what context.
–   In spite of such incomplete comprehension, it is possible to translate this sentence into at least some other languages without any further information on the situation and the context with a low risk of writing an inadequate translation. This is not necessarily true for all languages. For instance, in Japanese and some other languages, more information about the social context is necessary for the purpose of choosing the right level of politeness/formality. However, in French,

      Cette voiture est puissante

is probably an acceptable translation of "This car is powerful" in most contexts. Of course, one may imagine a situation where 'car' means something else than an automobile, in which case the French translation given above is no longer valid, but as long as the word does refer to a motorized vehicle on four wheels as is commonly found on our roads, it is likely that the French sentence *cette voiture est puissante* will do the job. In fact, in spite of the theoretical possibility of ambiguity in any discourse segment, in practical terms, it is probably true that, as claimed by Newmark (1983: 7), "… more words in a text are either relatively context-free or more conventionalized than is often assumed."

Complementarity between linguistic knowledge and extralinguistic knowledge is another fundamental point which deserves to be highlighted: the higher the level of each of these two components of comprehension, the better the resulting comprehension. If one component is weak, the other may compensate to some extent. Depending on the Text, it may be possible to achieve a relatively high level of comprehension even with a relatively low level of linguistic knowledge provided the level of extralinguistic knowledge is high and vice versa. Such complementarity is particularly important in interpreting and translation because of the Translator's deficit in extralinguistic knowledge as compared to the principals'.

Sometimes, the distinction between linguistic knowledge and extralinguistic knowledge becomes blurred, in particular as regards sociolinguistic and other cultural aspects of the language used in the relevant communities. Clearly, in order to use appropriate forms of politeness in a given situation, one needs to know not only linguistic rules, but also cultural rules, as well as something about the particular communication situation at hand. One could also argue philosophically that there is no knowledge of a language without knowledge of what words refer to in extralinguistic reality. Nevertheless, regardless of whether such knowledge is considered 'linguistic' or 'extralinguistic', the fundamental relation represented by the comprehension 'equation' remains valid.

2.2   Analysis

Spontaneous, subconscious use of linguistic knowledge and extralinguistic knowledge may not be enough to ensure comprehension, either because the Receiver's combined level of both is not high enough or because the text or speech itself has a complex content or deviates from generally accepted linguistic or cultural standards. This happens frequently with speakers and authors who use languages other than their own and have strong accents, make lexical or syntactic errors, employ unusual metaphors or rationales, use inappropriate register etc. In such cases, it is necessary to engage in a more intense analysis than the one associated with discourse comprehension in everyday life.

At an international school I attended many decades ago where English was the language of habitual use, a Spanish teacher whose English was poor used to come into the classroom and ask:

"Every people at home?"

It took some thinking before students realized, on the basis of both the words used and the specific situation, that he was asking whether all the enrolled students were present in the classroom. Many examples of similar sentences, difficult to understand because of their faulty grammar or lexical usage rather than because of their technical or complex nature, are part of any conference interpreter's or translator's experience. Actually, they are also part of the experience of any reader of *poor translations*. Newmark (1983: 6) quotes several such translations from materials for guests in a hotel in Germany, including the following sentence:

> "Our social rooms are at your disposal for the most different occasions."

Many other amusing examples can be found in *Løst in Tränšlatioπ*, a recent book which lists announcements, warnings and other notices in English from all over the world (Croker 2006).

In order to account more fully for comprehension, the basic comprehension 'equation' requires another element besides knowledge of language and extralinguistic knowledge, namely *deliberate analysis*:

(2)   C = KL + ELK + A

2.3   More about the relations in the comprehension 'equation'

'Equation' (2) is a very simple representation of the components of Text comprehension and their complementarity in comprehension, but does not say it all.

2.3.1   *Subjective aspects of comprehension*

It was pointed out above that comprehension is a variable which can take on different values, intuitively from 'non-comprehension' to 'full comprehension'. 'Total' non-comprehension of verbal statements is extremely rare, since the situation and/or the context almost always indicate *something* about their meaning – though this 'something' may not be sufficient for Translation purposes. In particular, it is shown in the second half of this chapter that 'total' non-comprehension of natural language Texts produced in a communication context does not occur even when they are highly specialized.

The question of 'full comprehension' is more complex. To discuss it efficiently, it is necessary to elaborate on the concept of comprehension and decide whether it refers only to the semantic content of the Text, or also to the connotations and to the role of the Text in the social interplay between the participants in the specific communication context at hand.

In Translation, the issue of 'full comprehension' is not really relevant, since Translation requirements are relative to the need to reformulate the source-language message in the target language. The question is therefore not whether 'full comprehension' has been achieved, but what comprehension level is necessary for interpreting and translation purposes and how it can be achieved.

An important point to be made in the classroom is that the subjective *feeling* of comprehension that may arise in a reader's or listener's mind is not necessarily a reliable indicator of the *actual* level of comprehension achieved. A good illustration of this fact is found in a typical phenomenon encountered frequently in the translation profession: when first reading a text before agreeing to translate it, practitioners may feel it poses no comprehension problems, but difficulties crop up when they start working on it (as documented in a recent empirical study on professional translation – see Lagarde 2009). The feeling of comprehension that arises when listening to a speech or reading a text seems to be related not only to the amount of information one actually grasps from processing it, but also to:

–   The Receiver's *familiarity with the linguistic structures* and *vocabulary* of the Text. Receivers are thrown off by unfamiliar words and sentence structures and may feel at ease with a Text formulated in familiar words and in a familiar style even if its information content or the rationale on which it is constructed are far from clear. Hence the occasional unpleasant surprise when they later have to analyze the Text more closely in order to translate it and find out it contains segments they do not understand. It is interesting in this respect to read a Japanese journalist's comments about speeches interpreted at international conferences: while listening to the Japanese renderings, delegates (journalists in this particular case) feel they are understandable, but when listening to their recordings, they find that many are full of errors and omissions or make no sense (Fujimura 1983: 30).
–   The number of *technical terms* in the Text in proportion to its length. The more specialized terms a Text contains, the more it is perceived as 'difficult to understand' by laypersons.
–   The *length* and *complexity* of sentences: the longer and the more complex they are, the more likely Receivers are to feel they do not quite understand them. Conversely, short sentences tend to generate the feeling that the Text is easy to understand, which may turn out to be wrong when the Text's *content* must be used for operational purposes.
–   The *functional requirements* of the Receiver from the Text: Does it contain precise instructions that will have to be followed? Does it contain important information required for some kind of action or decision-making? Does it only provide irrelevant or unimportant information? Depending on the Receivers' needs, some may feel that they have understood the Text to a satisfactory extent and others that they have not. Precise testing might reveal little difference in the information they have actually extracted from it.

In non-literary interpreting and translation, the need to reformulate the information content of the original Text in the target language means that its logical infrastructure, information content and *skopos* must be understood to the point where:

–   it can be disambiguated to a sufficient extent to be meaningfully reworded in the target language
–   appropriate terms and phrases in the target language can be selected by the Translator if they exist in comparable documents, or be created by him/her if they do not.

–   The *comfort threshold*, a subjective factor which depends on functional requirements, but also on psychological parameters such as the Receiver's personality and various adjustment mechanisms. During a stay in Japan, I observed that Western residents had developed a comfort threshold which gave them the feeling they understood local radio and TV broadcasts 'perfectly' (this is based on an unpublished questionnaire-based survey I conducted in Tokyo in 1986). When required to answer questions on specific words and sentences in recorded extracts from radio programmes, they realized they did not understand many of them. I believe this reflects one type of psychological adjustment to life in a foreign-language environment. Similarly, a medical practitioner's or lawyer's secretary may feel s/he 'understands' some texts, whereas close scrutiny shows s/he *recognizes* words and phrases without having much more than a vague idea of the concepts or actions they refer to or of their implications.

2.3.2   *Linguistic knowledge*

The contribution of this component of the comprehension 'equation' increases as knowledge of the language increases, but it levels off at a certain point where knowing more words, more idioms, more grammatical, stylistic and pragmatic rules will not contribute anything. The maximum contribution of linguistic knowledge is reached rapidly in many non-literary sentences. An extreme case is that of mathematical papers published in specialized journals, which can be read and understood by mathematicians with a limited command of the language used which would not enable them to interact with native speakers in daily conversations.

In the case of simple sentences such as "We found a significant correlation between A and B", "The agreement was ratified by 75 countries", "We agree to the terms and conditions in the contract", having a good command of rare literary words and poetic style will not enhance comprehension. Incidentally, this implies that spending two or three years at university doing an M.A. or Ph.D. in literature is probably not as profitable for future translators of technical or scientific texts as spending the same time reading such texts or attending lectures in technical and scientific disciplines in their foreign language(s). In literary, diplomatic and political Texts, the contribution of good linguistic knowledge (including knowledge of relevant cultural environments) to comprehension can be very important; hence the need for Translators dealing with such Texts to have an extensive knowledge of the source language in its general, cultural part, but perhaps a lesser need to be familiar with technological and scientific terms, though many literary works have non-negligible specialized components – think of novels describing medical, legal, financial and other settings (these issues are discussed further in Chapter 9). The vast majority of speeches made in technical and scientific conferences and most scientific and technical texts probably do not require an extensive knowledge of stylistic and cultural aspects of the source language.

In interpreting, since speeches are not heard in advance and since the unexpected is always to be expected (except when speeches are read from written texts and interpreters have them in advance), comprehension in a wide range of registers and styles in the source language must be very good. Incidentally, beginning interpreters as well as interpreters who are fluent in languages which are not part of their official language combination can be tempted when listening to 'easy' speakers to accept working from such languages. The problem is precisely the uncertainty factor: speeches may be easy to understand most of the time, but professional ethics require that the interpreter be able to handle difficulties adequately when they do arise even if they only occur once every 2,000, 3,000, or 10,000 words, that is, only a few times during a day's work. In conference interpreting, having a sufficient comprehension of the source language 'most of the time' is just not enough.

This may be compared to the situation of beginning mountain-climbers embarking on a difficult climb. As long as they are not too tired and the rock is dry, they will have no particular problem, but in case of a sudden drop in temperature, a snowstorm or an unexpected technical difficulty, their expertise may not be sufficient to ensure survival, whereas more experienced mountaineers with a higher level of technical expertise can overcome the obstacles successfully.

In any case, *relevant* elements of vocabulary, grammar, and style in the source language should be well mastered by the Translator. In conference interpreting in particular, relevant language elements should be mastered well enough to require little time and processing capacity to be understood (see Chapters 7 and 9 on the concept of processing capacity and its implications). The situation is somewhat different in translation work, in which at least some time is generally available for research and consultation of native speakers in case some words or structures are not understood (see the discussion in Chapter 6).

A secondary but interesting point is that in Translation and especially in interpreting, it can be very useful to have some knowledge not only of the language used in the Text to be translated, but also of the Sender's mother tongue when it is different, as interference between those two languages can lead to faulty word usage and syntax as well as unnatural pronunciation which make comprehension more difficult. Knowing the Sender's mother tongue provides the Translator with more elements for analysis of lexical, grammatical and pronunciation errors (for instance the way the Japanese pronounce some English vowels and the consonants 'r' and 'l', the way the Spanish and Latin Americans pronounce the 'z' sound as an 's' or the way native speakers of Arabic pronounce 'p' as 'b'). Translators cannot be expected to master all languages – a preposterous requirement – but knowledge of the speaker's native language is a natural extension of 'linguistic knowledge' as defined earlier in this chapter. In interpreting, where time pressure makes each element of the comprehension 'equation' more important, knowledge of the speaker's mother tongue is often an important factor in assigning speeches to specific interpreters in an interpreting team.

2.3.3 Extralinguistic knowledge
The contribution of extralinguistic knowledge to comprehension does not level off more or less abruptly at a certain point as is the case of linguistic knowledge. The more one

knows about the situation, including the interests of the participants in communication, their lines of reasoning, positions, wishes, weaknesses, interaction, etc., the better the chances of understanding the Sender's discourse more accurately. Again, such knowledge is useful in that it facilitates anticipation and Text comprehension not only as regards linguistic disambiguation, but also when reading between the lines. Such deeper and wider comprehension is an immense advantage when tackling Translation production difficulties, as it makes it possible to overcome or bypass many linguistic obstacles.

In any given Translation situation, currently available extralinguistic knowledge (as opposed to extralinguistic knowledge which will have to be acquired ad hoc, as explained in Chapter 5) can be broken down into two subcategories:

–   pre-existing ELK
–   contextually derived knowledge acquired from the Text and the situation.

A minimum level of pre-existing ELK is necessary in order to disambiguate the source-language Text and select the appropriate target-language equivalents, but the contribution of contextually derived knowledge, which is also *situational* or *environmental* in the case of interpreting (in the majority of cases, the interpreter is in the relevant physical environment at the time communication takes place), is generally considerable. This is another reason why, beyond language comprehension requirements, it is important for the Translator to maintain a high level of attention throughout his/her work on the Text so as to incorporate new information into the existing Knowledge Base (Chapter 6 discusses in greater detail ad hoc acquisition of knowledge in Translation).

2.3.4   *Analysis*

In Translation, analysis must go beyond the minimum required to deal with the most obvious ambiguities in the source-language Text and to reach a comfort threshold. It must help the Translator meet the requirements of the task, namely the acquisition of a sufficiently deep and wide understanding of the source-language Text to enable him/her to reword in a clear, editorially and socially/culturally acceptable target-language Text all the relevant information it contains.

Experience shows that this calls for a *deliberate* and *sustained* analysis effort at least during initial training, as demonstrated regularly in the classroom by the fact that Translations made by students contain many errors which could have been avoided by plain common-sense analysis. When such errors occur, if instructors ask the students whether their rendition of the relevant segments makes sense, the very question triggers an analysis process at the end of which the students generally identify their errors and correct them without even having to acquire new information in the process. This issue is discussed in greater detail and illustrated in Chapter 5.

An important point is that this analysis takes *time*. Assuming a speech contains no particular difficulty associated with incorrect language or facts or unclear thinking, the

time required to process single words in order to 'understand' them in context is a fraction of a second. Understanding full sentences may require a bit more time, but the order
of magnitude will not change dramatically. In translation, this is generally not problematic; even the mechanical act of typing a word on a keyboard takes longer, and the time
required for analysis of simple, well-formed sentences is not even perceived consciously.
In contrast, in interpreting, as explained in Chapters 7 and 9, cognitive pressure and the
limitations of short-term memory make even such short processing times sufficient to generate serious difficulties and to actually jeopardize the feasibility of the interpreting task.

3. Translation and the comprehension of specialized texts

Among laypersons, one often finds two extreme positions: some believe that Translating is simple for the bilingual and that even highly technical or scientific texts can be
translated without difficulty provided one 'knows the words.' Others as well as some
beginning Translators and non-specialized Translators tend to be overawed by the 'difficulty' of texts in fields they are not familiar with. In fact, many Clients, and even some
professional Translators, feel that Translators can only perform a decent job in fields
they know as well – or nearly as well – as specialists. This is also the impression that may
be generated by statements in the literature on translation such as "The technical translator's stock in trade is an in-depth understanding of the referent" (Folkart 1984: 229);
"Only by understanding the author's meaning thoroughly can the translator be sure
to choose the best available words and to present them in the best possible structure"
(Mellen 1988: 272); "The basic principle is that an interpreter cannot interpret what he
does not understand" (Kurz 1988: 424); or "*Nous savons depuis longtemps … que l'on ne
traduit bien que ce que l'on comprend – ou ressent, parfaitement*" [we have known for a long
time… that you only translate well what you understand or perceive perfectly well (my
translation)] (Gémar 1990: 665). Such statements can be misleading when read out of
context. Actually, they are made in texts that stress the importance of analysis and knowledge acquisition in Translation as opposed to 'automatic' word-for-word translation.

As explained in detail in Chapter 5, Translation can be modelled as a recurrent two-
phase process operating on successive Text segments: the first phase is comprehension, and
the second is reformulation in the target language. The next part of this chapter attempts to
show that even in the case of highly specialized texts or speeches in fields Translators are not
very familiar with, they can do a good job in the comprehension component by relying on
their linguistic knowledge, their extralinguistic knowledge and analysis (though such comprehension may not be enough to construct a good Translation of the Source Text – but
this is another matter). By adopting an appropriate attitude and choosing the right strategies, they can go beyond mere 'knowledge of the words' and gain non-trivial understanding
of the text or speech in spite of their lack of specialized knowledge. Chapter 6 discusses
principles of knowledge acquisition required for reformulation in the target language.

3.1   An example

In the classroom, the explanation of the Translator's comprehension of specialized Texts can be usefully started with an example. The following is a sentence taken from a medical textbook, which I have used in lectures to English-speakers.

> Hematogenous tuberculosis may appear in various morphologic forms: classical miliary tubercles, sizable nodules, necrotic foci simulating abscesses, massive tuberculomas simulating neoplasms and even caseous pneumonia not at all suggestive of a hematogenous origin. (Rubin 1948: 194)

At first sight – and this is the reaction of many non-medical readers – this highly technical sentence is 'totally incomprehensible' to the layperson. Once the initial reaction of awe is overcome, a reasonably educated and intelligent reader will realize that from its structure and on the basis of common general knowledge, it can be interpreted as meaning:

> A certain type of disease which may have something to do with tuberculosis ("hematogenous tuberculosis") may appear in various forms called "miliary tubercles," which are the classical or most widely found form, *something* ("necrotic foci") that looks like abscesses, *something* very large ("tuberculomas") that looks like *something* else ("neoplasms"), and even symptoms that suggest some kind of pneumonia ("caseous pneumonia") that apparently would not normally suggest that the origin of the condition is of the *something* ("hematogenous") type.

The fact that some symptoms suggest pneumonia tends to strengthen the hypothesis that "hematogenous tuberculosis" has something to do with tuberculosis, as the layperson knows that both pneumonia and TB affect the lungs.

It is also found that general English language dictionaries explain most of these 'somethings' in terms understandable to the layperson. According to *Webster's New World Dictionary of the American Language*, 1974 edition:

–   "Hematogenous" means "forming blood" or "spread by the bloodstream".
–   "Miliary" is something "characterized or accompanied by lesions about the size of millet seeds: said specifically of a form of tuberculosis which spreads from a primary focus of infection to other parts of the body, forming minute tubercles". This explains the "foci" in the sentence and strengthens further the hypothesis that "hematogenous tuberculosis" is a certain type of tuberculosis.
–   A "tubercle" is "any abnormal hard nodule or swelling, specifically the typical nodular lesion of tuberculosis".
–   "Nodules" are "small nodes", and "nodes" are "localized swellings".
–   "Necrotic" is the adjective formed from the noun indicating the "death or decay of tissue in a particular part of the body".
–   "Neoplasms" are "abnormal growths of tissue such as tumors".

Only two words were not explained in the general language dictionaries I consulted and had to be looked up in medical dictionaries. One is "tuberculoma," which, according to *Butterworth's Medical Dictionary* (second edition), is a "well-defined tumour-like mass of tuberculous tissue", and the other is "caseous pneumonia," a term which is not found in all medical dictionaries. However, the term "caseous" is listed in general dictionaries, where it is explained as meaning 'cheeselike'.

It thus appears that following the retrieval of information from a general language dictionary and with the help of some analysis, the meaning of the sentence becomes clearer, in that it is confirmed that it refers to a certain type of tuberculosis and to various types of swellings which are its clinical signs, some of which are misleading in that they suggest other conditions.

With the exception of the term "caseous pneumonia," which can be imagined as referring to a type of pneumonia in which lung tissue becomes *similar* to cheese in some respect (possibly in its texture), the sentence can be 'understood' to a large extent by a non-specialist reader. Such a reader will not know exactly what the various types of swellings referred to look like, or comprehend the bacteriological background, evolution, and treatment of the condition, but will grasp the logic of the sentence and have a not too vague idea of what each of the technical terms it contains refers to.

Actually, intelligent readers gain significant information from the sentence, in that they learn a number of nontrivial bits of information about the disease.

3.2 The layperson's comprehension

When comparing this 'comprehension' to the medical doctor's comprehension of the same sentence, one finds that doctors grasp the logic of the sentence much as the layperson does, but that their idea of what each technical term in the sentence means is more accurate, and that they can relate the terms and the information to more bits of information they already possess: they probably have at least some pre-existing knowledge about hematogenous tuberculosis, are to some extent familiar with caseous pneumonia, may be able to discriminate between abscesses and tuberculomas (but not necessarily, depending on their medical specialty and experience), and are in a position to establish many links between the information given in the sentence and their previous knowledge and experience regarding the pathology, the treatment, and other aspects of respiratory and other diseases.

These basic aspects of comprehension can lead to a didactically useful model when they are formalized as follows:

Sentences in informative Texts can be represented as network-like structures consisting of three types of components:

–   Nouns and noun-phrases that indicate persons, objects, ideas, actions, etc. These will be referred to here as *Nominal Entities* (NE's).
–   Adjectives, adjective-like words, and clauses that *describe* these persons, objects, etc. (big, small, expensive, resistant), as well as statements of existence,

disappearance, growth, etc., about them ("X exists," "Y has grown," "Z prolif-
erates"). This type of component will be referred to as an *Attribute* (A).

–   Sentence structures and rules of grammar (declensions, word order, etc.)
which indicate logical or functional links between these persons, objects, or
concepts (A is compared to B, A acts on B, etc.). This third type of component
will be referred to here as a *Link* (L).

Figures 4.1 shows graphic representations of sentences (a), (b), and (c) as *semantic
networks* (this concept as used here is slightly different from the one used in the field
of Artificial Intelligence, in which it is defined more formally and in greater detail – see
for instance Winston 1984).

a.   The machine (Nominal Entity) is large/small/blue, etc. (Attribute).

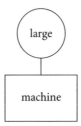

b.   A good (A) methodology (NE) results in (Link) powerful (A) algorithms (NE).

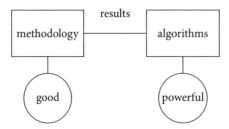

c.   A comparison was carried out (L) between X (NE) and Y (NE).

Figure 4.1 Examples of simple semantic network representations

Note that sentence (c) could be reformulated as: "X (NE) and Y (NE) were compared (L)". This is why "A comparison was carried out" is represented as a link in spite
of the fact that "comparison" is a noun. For many sentences, there are several possible
formal representations with different L, NE and A allocations. While the basic logical
and functional message is the same, languages make it possible to refer to an action by

a verb *or* a noun, which changes the Entity composition of the sentences as was just shown with respect to sentence (c), and therefore their representation as a network.

Long and complex sentences can be represented in many ways, depending on how they are decomposed into sub-assemblies. Consider the following sentence, in which a much-debated opinion in interpreting research is reported:

"According to some interpreting theoreticians, a stage occurs between comprehension and reformulation during which a *pure message* without any trace of its linguistic envelope is extracted from the statement, but this *deverbalization* principle has not been demonstrated to be true by proper testing procedures."

This sentence can be modelled as:

"Some	interpreting	theoreticians	believe	that	X,	but	Y"
A		Noun Entity		Link	NE		NE

Where X is:

"a stage occurs between comprehension and reformulation during which a *pure message* without any trace of its linguistic envelope is extracted from the statement"

And Y is:

"this *deverbalization* principle has not been demonstrated to be true by proper testing procedures"

X can be decomposed as follows:

- "a stage occurs between comprehension and reformulation"
- "during this stage, a *pure message* is extracted from the statement"
- "this message is without any trace of its linguistic envelope"

The process can go on until elementary-level segments are reached. Such segments are often called *propositions*. Psycholinguistic research makes much use of them; formal analysis of sentences into propositions is of interest to researchers working on the comprehension and production of natural languages. In this book, suffice it to say that it is generally possible for readers or listeners to find at least one network-like representation of even highly technical and highly complex sentences that will enable them to understand the logical structure of the ideas represented by the sentence (for a more extensive psycholinguistic discussion, see for example Costermans 1980, Noizet 1980).

Interestingly, even in the most highly specialized texts, the Attributes and Links are to an overwhelming majority the same as those found in non-technical informative Texts: As explained earlier, Attributes may assert the existence of something, describe it in terms of shape, texture, and dimensions and assess it qualitatively; and Links can be causal relations, comparisons, agent relationships ("A is used to produce B"), time relationships, etc. It is also noteworthy that Attributes and Links are generally expressed by words and structures that belong to non-specialized language. This is why the *logic* of highly specialized sentences can generally be understood by non-specialists, although some ambiguities may remain.

It appears that, seen from this angle, comprehension difficulties in the Translation of specialized discourse arise mostly from insufficient thematic knowledge regarding the Nominal Entities and their referents – nouns are the grammatical category of words most generally used to denote technical referents (Rey 1979), and by definition, they are not well known to laypeople.

This point needs further elaboration. If words appearing in specialized Texts were to be classified as 'completely clear', 'partly clear', or 'totally obscure' to a given reader, even in the most specialized Texts, words in the last category would be rare: in the medical example given earlier, not even "caseous pneumonia" can be counted as one, since both the context (the source-language Text environment) and the term's morphology, suggesting that it is some kind of pneumonia, say something about the pathological condition it refers to.

At first sight, this three-category classification, with two extremes ('completely clear' and 'totally obscure') on the one hand, and the whole range of the continuum between them on the other, may seem trivial and pointless. Indeed, its descriptive value is questionable. In the classroom, it has psychological value in that it stresses that in context, almost any word can be understood to some extent, thus helping to make highly technical texts look less formidable in the eyes of students.

Intelligent readers can generally model a technical sentence in a field they are not familiar with as a semantic network having the same structure – or an equivalent structure – as the network that will be constructed mentally by specialists. The main difference lies in the fact that Nominal Entities in the non-specialists' networks are *fuzzy* rather than neatly contoured, as laypersons have a less precise idea than specialists of what their referents are. Actually, in many cases, the latter's comprehension of specialized terms is also fuzzy, sometimes as much so as the layperson's, as interpreters and translators who consult specialists find out regularly. A medical doctor's knowledge of caseous pneumonia may be good, but it may also be superficial or even nonexistent. Dentists attending a conference on laser applications in medicine may have fuzzy understanding of terms used in a presentation on the use of lasers in gynaecology, and cardiologists having one subspecialty may have little knowledge of another.

It should be pointed out that although most comprehension problems occur for Nominal Entities, sometimes they extend to the actual *network structure* of the sentence, that is, to the underlying configuration of Nominal Entities, Attributes and Links. For instance, in overhead transparencies, statements are often made in *telegraphic style*, without many of the function words of everyday grammar that make the logical or functional infrastructure of sentences explicit. One classical example of ambiguity in the *scope* of Links as defined above can be found in a line of text such as:

"Query and error handling"

taken from a transparency designed for a presentation at an Information Technology meeting.

This line could refer to 'query handling' *and* 'error handling', to 'query' and 'the handling of errors', or to the handling of something called 'query and error'. The semantic structures underlying the same linguistic structure can be quite different, and so would the translations be, depending on the target language. This is a case in which the lack of extralinguistic knowledge does make it difficult for the Translator to understand specialized discourse (the context provided by the transparency and by other transparencies in the presentation was not sufficient to allow disambiguation).

4.   The Translator's comprehension requirements

For the Translator, it is important to understand the functional and logical infrastructure underlying sentences sufficiently well to be able to reproduce it in the target text, because it is not always possible to transcribe a source-language structure (i.e. its surface form) into a similar linguistic structure, and when it is, the result is more often than not clumsy or even linguistically unacceptable – as can be seen in word-for-word translations that are sometimes published in conference proceedings and even in scientific journals, let alone advertisements in tourist sites. At the entrance of a beach on the French Riviera, a French and English sign warns tourists that they are about to enter a "not watched beach" – "*plage non surveillée*" in French.

When the functional and logical infrastructure of a sentence is understood, it may be enough for the Translator to know the appropriate terminological equivalents of nouns or noun groups, and sometimes verbs, to produce a good Translation in a field s/he does not know very well. Many practical problems in technical and scientific Translation are indeed terminological. Glossaries and dictionaries are never exhaustive, never totally reliable, and seldom precise enough to provide non-specialized Translators with the definitive solutions to their terminological problems: the problematic source-language term may be missing in the glossary, or several possible target-language 'equivalents' may be listed without sufficient indications to allow the Translator to determine which is the right one in the Translation context at hand, or an 'equivalent' is given but is erroneous or inappropriate for the particular Target Text (see Chapter 6 for a discussion of the limitations of 'terminological' sources). Note that terminology may not be sufficient, as specific phraseology is also part of the relevant sociolect.

In written translation, the non-availability of editorially appropriate terminological 'equivalents' is problematic insofar as the translators' brief is to produce an editorially acceptable text which can be read repeatedly by many readers, and often over a long period. Interpreting is made for real-time oral communication, and accuracy in terminological usage is often less critical than in translation (but not always – it is especially critical in legal meetings). Moreover, participants in on-site verbal exchanges can react and ask for clarification if they detect a terminological problem that hampers communication. Nevertheless, the terminological dimension of quality perception by users of interpreting services should not be underestimated, if only because correct terminology inspires confidence and incorrect terminology breeds distrust in the interpreter's expertise and reliability – see for instance Collados Aís *et al.* 2007.

Summing up, in order to Translate a sentence in specialized discourse, interpreters and translators have to understand its functional and logical infrastructure (the *semantic network structure* of the sentence) and to have available the appropriate 'equivalents' or other terms or paraphrases to express the same message in the target language. Translators can look for the necessary information in various written sources, and interpreters are helped by the conference context, including conference texts and speeches written or made in the relevant source and target languages and written information on the screen. Both interpreters and translators use the context provided by the texts and speeches to gain more knowledge about the subject by analyzing available clues and thus improve their comprehension of subsequent speeches or later text segments. While processing the texts or speeches, they familiarize themselves with the subject and gain a better understanding of the authors' and speakers' statements to an extent which sometimes approximates that of experts and has surprised more than one translation reader or delegate at an interpreted conference.

5.   The Translators' acquired specialized knowledge

It turns out that Translators without training in a specialized field may come to understand quite well Texts or speeches which they Translate in that field, especially if they are composed of a succession of fairly common types of propositions such as:

> "Because of A and B, C seems to be better than D, in spite of E and F. G was also attempted, but obstacle H made this solution less efficient than expected..."

in which only the Nominal Entities are specialized. This is far from uncommon. In such a case, 'understanding' the Message means essentially understanding the logical steps from the initial premises to the conclusion. When such understanding occurs repeatedly, Translators end up with a certain familiarity with the reasoning mode of experts and sometimes with considerable information acquisition in the relevant field. This knowledge remains superficial and, in terms of semantic networks, does not form sufficiently dense and cohesive networks in their (long-term) memory to allow them to interpret phenomena and act upon them as specialists could.

Interestingly, when asked how much they understand of what they translate, Translation practitioners vary greatly in their answers. One of the reasons may be found not in actual comprehension differences, but in differing awareness and attitudes: some tend to answer on the basis of the *logic* of the speech or text they were able to follow, some are more (painfully) aware of the fact that they know little about the actual objects, concepts, etc. that terms refer to even when they are familiar with the words; some take an optimistic view and some are more pessimistic or frustrated about the relatively superficial understanding and knowledge they gain when compared to that of the experts who write or read the texts.

A more optimistic view of one's comprehension of specialized Texts probably has a positive effect on one's motivation and general satisfaction, and instructors could perhaps guide students gently towards this attitude by pointing out how much they learn whenever they Translate a new specialized Text.

6. Teaching the principles of comprehension

6.1   I believe that the most important model in this chapter is that of semantic networks representing the comprehension of specialized discourse, which, according to comments by students, makes technical interpreting and translation appear less formidable to beginners. For some students and in some classes, the terms 'semantic networks', 'Noun-Entities' etc. may sound abstract and forbidding. It is also possible to teach the model without them, through examples and diagrams.

6.2   The two parts of this chapter, dealing respectively with general comprehension and comprehension of specialized discourse, have been grouped together for the sake of convenience and logic. In the classroom, they can be separated:

–   The part on general comprehension can be taught at the beginning of the syllabus. It does not serve an autonomous objective, but helps reinforce concepts that are stressed later in the programme, in particular the role and importance of analysis, which is the focus of much attention throughout training in interpreting and translation exercises, and the idea that comprehension sometimes has to be *forced out* of a text or speech segment rather than just 'happen'. The part of this module devoted to general comprehension also underscores the importance of general and thematic knowledge besides knowledge of the working languages, and helps prepare students for later knowledge acquisition work (see Chapter 6).
–   The part on specialized texts and speeches can wait until students start tackling such assignments, at a more advanced stage of training, after several weeks or months depending on the total duration of the curriculum.

6.3   The discussion of general comprehension does not warrant any particular teaching method. A simple lecture with a few illustrations will do. The discussion of comprehension of specialized texts and speeches is more sensitive due to the students' preconceptions and has an important psychological role in trying to show them that scientific and technical interpreting and translation are within reach of practitioners who have had no training as experts in the relevant disciplines. According to my personal experience, a demonstration-type classroom session can be effective for both translator and interpreter training.

One procedure I use is the following:

–   A rather short technical text (up to several sentences) is presented to students, who are then asked to rate their comprehension of the text, for instance on a 1 to 5 scale ("no comprehension at all" to "very good comprehension").

–   The students' ratings are written down by the instructor, who then asks participants *what* they do not understand in the text they have read. It generally turns out that problems relate only to specialized terms, something which the instructor can make the students aware of with 'leading' questions. At the same time, s/he can point out that linguistic structures in the Text are simple and that the Links and Attributes which they represent can be understood and re-expressed in the target language without particular difficulties.

–   Students can then be asked to indicate the terms that they do not understand 'at all.' If there are any, the instructor shows them that using the context and morphological analysis (looking at their components such as Greek or Latin roots, characters in the case of Chinese or Japanese etc.), nontrivial information can be inferred about their meaning. General dictionaries can be used to learn more. Specialized dictionaries can also be consulted if the need arises.

–   In the case of interpreting, the instructor can use a transcript from a conference in which sentences, non-technical words, and technical terms have previously been counted. On the basis of the students' responses, s/he can show them that problematic sentences and terms represent only a small fraction of the speech (12% on average according to Newmark (1983: 6), who does not indicate the source of this figure). S/he can also show how much of the speech can be understood by using the information provided by the Links and Attributes as well as by the context and by the morphology of the terms as illustrated in the medical example analyzed in Section 3.

Speeches from disciplines in the natural sciences and from medicine are particularly suited to the demonstration, especially when they present clinical trials, a discussion of hypotheses or a comparison between products in which logic plays a large part and in which specialized concepts refer to objects or actions that can be related to the student's general experience: pharmaceutical drugs, illnesses, parts of the anatomy, efficiency, speed, power, energy, microscopic living organisms, etc. Speeches which refer mostly to abstract concepts (mathematics, theoretical physics, psychoanalysis, etc.), or lists containing many product names with little logical reasoning (such as can be found in many conferences on computer technology) are often more difficult to use in such demonstrations. It is also preferable to avoid using texts requiring particular phraseology. Such texts can be understood through analysis, but without solid research into comparable target-language texts, they cannot be translated appropriately; this introduces a further requirement which is not the focus of attention in this exercise. Legal texts are more difficult to use for this kind of awareness-raising exercise, both because they often contain and require specific phraseology and because many legal terms look like words from everyday language whereas in the legal context, they have specific meanings which make it difficult to understand what they really say without specialized knowledge in law.

- The instructor then sums up the information acquired from the sentence or speech on the basis of the analysis performed in class and points out to students the new knowledge they have gained.
- Finally, students are asked to rate their comprehension of the sentence or speech once again, and results are compared with the first ratings. In my experience, the students' evaluations generally rise by an average of about 2 points, suggesting a possible reduction in the level of anxiety when they face later similar specialized texts and speeches. In personal conversations, students and former students now engaged in professional activity as interpreters and translators have made comments to the same effect a number of times.

It is only fair to note that the experiment does not provide answers to all the questions. Knowing the proper terms and understanding the logic is not necessarily enough, as there may be many reformulation problems (see Chapters 5 and 6). However, the effect sought here is psychological, and in my experience, in that respect, the method has proved rather effective.

6.4   Even more than their ability to comprehend specialized texts and speeches, the *attitude* of professional interpreters and translators toward such discourse should be discussed with students. With a few exceptions such as journalists, interpreters and translators are possibly the only professionals who systematically process in some depth the full informational content of texts and speeches in fields they do not specialize in. If they perceive this as a burden, a difficult and tedious task, they are deprived of much of the pleasure of interpreting and translation which comes from learning and acquiring new knowledge. If they perceive it as a challenge which non-specialists can tackle successfully and which provides learning opportunities, they may find their profession far more gratifying. I believe it is a useful attitude for students to adopt, as it encourages and motivates them.

7.   What students need to remember

1. Comprehension of verbal statements relies on knowledge of the language used, on extralinguistic knowledge, both pre-existing and acquired from the context and the communication situation, and on analysis.

2. Comprehension is relative and subjective. A statement is to a large extent perceived as having been understood or not depending on its linguistic complexity, on the Receiver's familiarity with its linguistic components, on the Receiver's functional requirements from the text and more generally on a subjective 'comfort threshold.'

3. Even the most specialized Texts are generally made up of sentences with a logical structure identical or very similar to logical structures found in everyday language. Most comprehension problems are associated with specialized nouns which refer to concepts and objects with which laypersons are not familiar.

4. In nearly all cases, these concepts and objects can be understood to some non-trivial extent on the basis of the morphology of the relevant specialized terms, of general knowledge and of the context.

5. Thus, an educated layperson *can* achieve a significant understanding of highly specialized Texts, and thereby also learn something about the subject. This is one of the attractive aspects of Translation. However, this newly acquired knowledge remains rather isolated; it is not strongly integrated into a wide and well-structured Knowledge Base as is the case when a specialist hears or reads the same Text. The specialist's understanding of specialized Texts is more precise, but not necessarily 'total' either.

6. As long as there are no specific stylistic and phraseological requirements, on the basis of a solid analysis of the source-language Text, Translators can Translate specialized Texts in fields they are not familiar with if they find appropriate equivalents for specialized terms in the target language.

Chapter 5

A Sequential Model of translation

1. Introduction

As recalled repeatedly in this book, students generally come to translation school after many years of 'school translation' in which they essentially learn how to find linguistic correspondences to words and sentence structures with little room for analysis and communication-oriented writing. The communication models and the discussion of fidelity offered in Chapters 2 and 3 can help sensitize them to the primarily communicational nature of professional Translation, but do not show them how to use their newly gained awareness in actual translation work. The Sequential Model of translation presented here is designed to do just that: it describes and explains a path in the (written) translation process which takes the translator from the source-language text to a target-language text (Figure 5.1). It is a streamlined, idealized guidance tool rather than a descriptive process model such as Krings's (1982/1986) or Hönig's (1995: 51).

The Model is primarily targeted at translation students, although, as explained later in this chapter, it also has some use in interpreting. Since it can be applied at a very fundamental and practical level in the teaching process, and in particular in error analysis, I recommend that it be presented to students at an early stage of training, for instance immediately after the discussion of communication, quality, fidelity, and basic comprehension (of non-specialized Texts).

2. The model

The model proposed in this chapter (Fig. 5.1) describes translation as consisting of a succession of two-phase processing operations. Each 'Translation Unit' in the Source Text goes through a comprehension phase and a reformulation phase, and the 7-component structure of the model highlights knowledge as a resource, and decision-making as a necessary optimization tool.

2.1 The comprehension phase

The translator reads a source-language *Translation Unit*; that is, a text segment which s/he will deal with as a single unit. The Translation Unit can vary in length from a single word ("Yes") to a whole sentence ("Results were excellent indeed") or more than one sentence, depending on the source-language text and on the translator. There has been much theoretical discussion in the literature on the definition and size of such Translation Units (see for instance Larose 1989). In this discussion, I define them as *processing units* (which is also de Beaugrande's definition as in de Beaugrande 1980). As pointed out by Dancette (1989: 96), this implies subjective variability, but in a didactic context such as this one, such variability should not pose practical problems. Also note that such Translation Units, or 'speech segments' in other parts of this book which deal with interpreting, are conceptually similar to 'chunks' in the psycholinguistics literature.

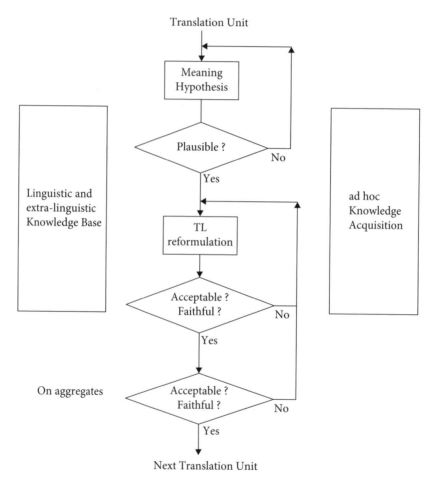

Figure 5.1 A Sequential Model of translation for training purposes

The translator formulates (mentally) a *Meaning Hypothesis* for the text segment s/he is processing as a Translation Unit, i.e. s/he temporarily assigns a meaning to it. To do this, s/he relies on knowledge of the source language, but also on the relevant part of his/her

World Knowledge. Both are contained in the *Knowledge Base*, represented as a box on the left side of Figure 5.1. The Knowledge Base may not provide the translator with all the knowledge required to formulate a Meaning Hypothesis, in which case s/he has to look for additional information in documentary sources, by asking human informants, etc. This part of the process is referred to in Figure 5.1 as *ad hoc Knowledge Acquisition*, and is dealt with extensively in Chapter 6.

Once the translator comes up with a tentative Meaning Hypothesis for the Translation Unit, s/he checks it for *plausibility* using his/her Knowledge Base, sometimes with further ad hoc Knowledge Acquisition. In other words, the translator looks at the idea or information s/he believes that the Translation Unit expresses and examines it critically in the light of other information available in his/her Knowledge Base, including information just added while reading the text, so as to detect potential contradictions.

Percival (1983: 94) stresses that "It is a mistake to become too committed to one's first understanding of a passage." One's first understanding of a text may well be erroneous, as demonstrated by countless errors made not only by students, but also by professionals who read source-language segments too fast or misunderstand even simple, relatively well written prose because of various linguistic and psychological mechanisms.

If, in the process of this Plausibility Test, the translator finds that his/her tentative Meaning Hypothesis is not plausible or not plausible enough, s/he tries to construct another Meaning Hypothesis and runs it through the same test. If the second Meaning Hypothesis is still not compatible with the information available in the Knowledge Base, a third Meaning Hypothesis is formulated, and so on.

Only when the translator reaches a Meaning Hypothesis which passes the Plausibility Test satisfactorily does s/he move on to the next phase, which is the *reformulation* of this Meaning Hypothesis in the target language.

The following is an example from a newspaper article given as a translation assignment to a translation class (this same text is discussed in the context of ad hoc Knowledge Acquisition in an appendix to Chapter 6):

> Zale's debt-reduction programme includes asset, sales, inventory reductions, store disposals, contracting out of some internal operations, and possibly a joint venture with one or more outside investors. (from the Canadian *Globe and Mail*, 1991)

In this particular case, a problem arises with respect to "... asset, sales, inventory reductions." Could the sentence possibly mean that there is a reduction of 'asset', of sales, and of inventory? From existing linguistic and extralinguistic knowledge, if there is a reduction in assets, the word should be in the plural. From extralinguistic knowledge, the idea of a debt-reduction programme which consists in reducing sales also fails to make sense. Thinking about another possible Meaning Hypothesis, one student came up with the idea that the comma after "asset" was a typo, in which case, after removal of the comma, "asset sales" becomes quite logical. It turned out that this was indeed the correct hypothesis: while preparing the translation assignment, the teacher had erroneously introduced a comma which did not appear in the original article.

2.2   The reformulation phase

Once the translator is reasonably sure of the meaning of a Translation Unit, s/he verbalizes it as a provisional Target-Text segment using knowledge of the target language as well as extralinguistic knowledge. For instance, in a conference, knowing that Norway is represented by a female delegate, s/he will translate into French a reference to the "Norwegian delegate" as "*la déléguée* norvé*gienne*" (with the appropriate gender markers). Similarly, if the required information about a "lawyer" referred to in an American text is available, s/he can choose to use in French either the word *juriste* (the generic term), or the word *avocat* (a lawyer qualified for court representation in France). If the translator's Knowledge Base does not include the required linguistic or extralinguistic information, s/he has to acquire it ad hoc.

The translator then makes sure that the target-language version of the Translation Unit complies with fidelity requirements by checking that none of the relevant information (the Message) in the Source Text has been omitted in the translation unless it is present elsewhere in the text or can be inferred easily from it, and that no *unwarranted* information not contained in the source-language Translation Unit has been added (as explained in Chapter 3, some changes in *Secondary Information* may be desirable or even necessary). If Fidelity Test results are not satisfactory, the translator writes a new target-language version of the Translation Unit and tests it again for fidelity. This recursive process continues until s/he feels that the result of the test is acceptable.

The translator also tests the target-language version of the Translation Unit for editorial acceptability; that is, s/he checks that it is editorially fit to serve its intended function in the target group in terms of clarity, language correctness, stylistic appropriateness, cultural/social adequacy and compliance with conventional terminological usage. If test results are not satisfactory, s/he rewrites the Translation Unit in the target language and tests it again. The process continues until results are acceptable. For instance, when translating a text from a language in which repetition of the same word is stylistically acceptable (Japanese is one such example), s/he may find that his/her first version of a sentence in a Western language contains repetitions; it may then be necessary to reword it using synonyms or paraphrases. If the Japanese text refers to a US president repeatedly, a corresponding English text may have to alternate between the name of the president with the title ("President So-and-So"), "the President" without a title, the name without a title, "the White House" etc. In isolation, these different words and groups of words are not equivalent, but in context, they will be interpreted by readers as pointing to the same information. Such tactics to ensure editorial acceptability in the target-language text obviously require extralinguistic knowledge from the Knowledge Base.

The editorial Acceptability Test should be conducted even for terms or phrases for which the practitioner has a "normal translation" (Percival 1983: 94), as the habitual target-language rendering of the segment may be stylistically inadequate, or even semantically wrong in the particular text at hand.

While testing the target-language reformulation of the relevant Translation Unit for acceptability, the translator should also check its plausibility again. This is a second opportunity to detect fidelity errors that may have escaped attention during the comprehension phase.

When the fidelity and Acceptability Tests for the first Translation Unit yield satisfactory results, the process starts all over again for the next Translation Unit, and follows iteratively with the subsequent ones until the end of the Text.

Periodically, the translator also conducts fidelity and Acceptability Tests on groups (*aggregates*) of Translation Units of various sizes (sentences, paragraphs, pages, etc.). There are three reasons for this:

1. After dealing with one Translation Unit, the translator may have skipped one or several of the subsequent Translation Units, or even a paragraph or a page. Such errors occur because contrary to ordinary readers, the translator does not read the Source Text in one continuous operation but moves back and forth from the Source Text to the Target Text. When returning to the Source Text, s/he may accidentally skip a segment and start working on another segment, further down, which could follow logically from the one s/he just read. Such gaps do not necessarily show up in the Fidelity Test performed on individual Translation Units. When checking a whole sequence of Translation Units, these omissions may be discovered either in the course of the comparison of source-language and target-language texts, or simply when reading the target-language text and finding that it does not read as it should and displays inconsistencies or other odd characteristics.

2. As translators advance in the translation of a text, they acquire more information and generally understand it better. Sometimes, a decision taken earlier about the relative plausibility of one interpretation of a Translation Unit over another is challenged by this new understanding. One might argue that reading the Source Text thoroughly before starting to translate it should help avoid such situations, but firstly, this is not always possible with long texts, and secondly, experience shows that pre-translation reading is never as thorough as reading in the course of translation, when every Translation Unit has to be understood well enough for reformulation (see Lagarde 2009).

3. The fact that the target-language version of a single source-language Translation Unit is acceptable does not ensure acceptability of the whole text. There may be

inconsistencies in terminological usage or stylistic drifts between the beginning and the end of a text which are not identified when Translation Units are tested individually. Only when reading larger units of text can such problems in its general flow be perceived.

3.   Comments

3.1   The Sequential Model and ordinary comprehension and production

Actually, the two phases of the Model are not specific to the translation process but also describe ordinary comprehension and production of Texts respectively: in language comprehension and production studies, recent models incorporate actions, tests and feedback reactions as an integral part of the comprehension and production processes (see for instance Clark & Clark 1977 or Matthei & Roeper 1985). This also implies that the much decried 'transcoding' or word-for-word method of translating, often presented as one in which there is *no* analysis, *does* involve some analysis as is indeed demonstrated by research in machine translation: even machines have to analyze textual input for translation purposes in spite of the very different 'sensory' reception and production means and processes involved. There are two important differences between the Translation situation and everyday comprehension and production. First, in Translation, comprehension and production follow each other systematically and act on the same message, whereas in everyday situations, comprehension may not be followed by production, and when production does follow comprehension, it is a reaction, with a different Message, not a reformulation of the same Message. Second, the action/test/action loops presented in the Sequential Model of translation differ from everyday language comprehension and production loops in that the tests are *systematic* and have Translation-specific targets. The Reformulation Loop aims at high-quality text production and the Comprehension Loop at a sufficiently clear and unambiguous understanding to meet the requirements of the reformulation phase that necessarily follows.

3.2   The Model and translation as it is practiced

As is the case of other models presented in this book, the Sequential Model is not designed to be an accurate description of the actual translation process. Rather, it represents an idealized process in which pedagogically important components are stressed.

3.2.1   *The processing of single vs. multiple Translation Units*
A rather important point in which the Model differs from advice often given to aspiring translators is that it describes translation as a recursive process followed Translation

Unit by Translation Unit, whereas many instructors tell students they have to read the whole text systematically before they start translating. Many translations are actually done in two phases: in the first, translators read the whole Source Text or at least some pages, try to identify difficulties, in particular terminological and linguistic problems, and attempt to solve most of them before starting the actual translation. In other words, some of the operations described in the Model, and in particular much ad hoc Knowledge Acquisition, take place partly or entirely during a preparatory phase which does not follow the sequence outlined in Figure 5.1.

Nevertheless, once actual translation work has started, for each Translation Unit, a Meaning Hypothesis has to be generated and checked before the translator moves on to reformulate the Unit in the target language and then checks the product for acceptability and fidelity. The fact that ad hoc Knowledge Acquisition operations may have taken place previously does not change the basic flow of operations.

3.2.2   Separation between comprehension and reformulation in the field and during training

The Model describes the reformulation phase as starting only after the comprehension phase has been completed. In actual practice, the translator is sometimes incapable of completing it, for instance when s/he does not manage to disambiguate fully a text segment, is not reasonably certain that the Meaning Hypothesis s/he developed is plausible, or cannot even construct a Meaning Hypothesis for the particular text segment concerned (as may happen when there are too many 'incomprehensible' terms and ambiguous structures). In such cases, which are not exceptional in the translator's daily practice, provisional target-language reformulations may be used as place-holders to allow the translator to progress.

If the Model were a descriptive one for scientific exploratory purposes, it would have to include this alternative translation route. As a tool to help guide beginning students towards best practices, it is probably better without it. Needless to say, the first translation exercises should be performed on texts for which the comprehension phase *can* be completed so that students can work their way through the Model to the completion of a satisfactory translation. When they reach a stage where they are given difficult texts in which they cannot complete the comprehension phase, they are told that they should follow the Comprehension Loop until they can progress no further and then make a decision. It is hoped that by that time action/test/action procedures have become systematic in their work.

3.2.3   Unsolved problems

More generally, in the field, some comprehension and reformulation problems may not be solved completely: translators may find out they do not have access to the necessary information or the time to access it (see Chapter 6). In such cases, it is not realistic to expect them to hand over the assignment to more qualified colleagues. Neither will they tell the Client at this late stage that they finally found out they could not accept it. Rather, they will try to find the best solution under the circumstances.

Professionals in both translation and interpreting try to avoid such situations and to only accept assignments which they feel they can handle. The code of professional ethics of the International Association of Conference Interpreters (AIIC) includes a clause according to which members of the Association should only accept assignments for which they are qualified. The problem is that it is impossible to predict all difficulties which may crop up in individual speeches. Similarly, translators tend to accept translation assignments only after they have enough information on the texts to be translated to decide they are qualified – that is, if they can afford to. Often, they ask to see the texts, or at least extracts, before they accept. However, many difficulties are only detected at the time of translation proper (see Lagarde 2009). Encountering problems which one cannot solve to one's full satisfaction is therefore a regular part of the Translator's professional life.

Again, during the initial part of translator training, when students are taught the basic concepts and approach, it makes sense to give them assignments in which the use of the 'right' method as outlined in the Model will lead them to satisfactory solutions to problems; otherwise they may be tempted to disregard it and take shortcuts, which can only be detrimental to translation quality as a whole. Later, at a point to be determined by the instructor, they should be introduced to more difficult assignments, with proper guidance on how to address difficulties which they cannot overcome completely.

3.2.4   *Decision-making, risks, gains and losses*

Basically, the appropriate response in such cases is a decision-making strategy: after collecting as much information as possible, translators must decide what they will write. These decisions involve expected gain and possible loss. Gain can take the form of increased clarity, more readable and convincing texts, a lower probability of misrepresenting the author's ideas etc. Loss may involve loss of information, lessened credibility because of inappropriate terminology, lower cultural acceptability because the Target Text says something or says it in a way which is not acceptable to Target-Text readers, etc.

From the viewpoint of professional ethics, consequences to be considered are those that will affect the Client, the author and the readers: loss of information, wrong information, loss of impact with respect to the author's aims (see Chapter 2), etc. In real-life situations, decisions are sometimes also weighed according to the expected impact of errors on the Translators themselves: loss of credibility, income, work, etc. (see Chapter 9 on 'laws' for the selection of 'coping tactics'). For instance, a Translator may be unwilling to ask the Client with insistence to provide him/her with a piece of information necessary to understand the Source Text fully or to reformulate it adequately in the target language for fear of irritating him/her and damaging the relationship, which would lead to loss of business. Ethically, such considerations are unjustified, but in real life, they are not infrequent. The temptation does not arise in the classroom, because of the setting and the close supervision available from the instructors. In the field, decisions depend on opportunities and on the Translator's personality.

Translators should try to aim for the best possible combination of Risk and Loss values for each situation. Some Errors are associated with such a small Loss that even a high probability of error is acceptable: for instance, the translator may select a technical term in the target language which is somewhat less frequently used than another term in the particular target group of readers for whom the translation is written but which is nevertheless semantically correct and not unacceptable. Some Losses may be so critical that the Risk of Error should be close to nil, for instance when translating user instructions for vital medical equipment.

In any case, translators have to *make decisions*. The Model provides a good opportunity to stress to the students that decision-making and risk-taking are an integral part of translation, as underscored by a number of authors (Levý 1967; Namy 1979; Mellen 1988; Sager 1992; Durieux 1992). This, plus the analysis and the knowledge acquisition components of the methodology, justify the claim that high-level translation is intellectual work. They also provide some justification for the profession's demands regarding social status and salary. Without them, translation cannot substantiate its claim that it is more than a secretarial job. Appendix B models the decision-making process graphically for instructors who wish to use such a model.

3.2.5   *The linearity of the sequential process*

Another difference between the model and actual translation practice is that in the latter there is not necessarily a regular linear flow of well-defined, clearly bounded Translation Units that follow each other in a smooth movement from comprehension to reformulation: there may be some interpenetration of Translation Units and some forward and backward movement between them – and between the comprehension and reformulation phases. In particular, oftentimes, the translator does not test a Meaning Hypothesis until after verbalizing it in the target language, if only mentally. Frequently, s/he only realizes there is a problem when trying to read the first target-language version of the relevant Translation Unit, in other words, when already in the reformulation phase.

3.2.6   *Tests on groups of Translation Units*

Acceptability and Fidelity Tests over more than one Translation Unit are represented in the Model only once. In a long text, several such tests are generally performed on different levels of aggregates of Translation Units. This should not pose a problem in the use of the Model: students can be made aware of the fact that in the flowchart, the aggregate testing procedure is sketched as a reminder that it is a necessary part of the process, because integrating it into the actual flow of translation steps accurately would have made the model too complicated.

More generally, these discrepancies between the Model and reality should not invalidate it for didactic use. What its structure makes visually salient is that each Translation Unit should be processed by way of an analysis toward a Meaning Hypothesis, followed by a testing procedure and then by correction, and that the target-language version produced for each Translation Unit should also be tested for fidelity and acceptability and corrected, often several times if necessary. These principles are important for training and remain valid in the field.

3.2.7   The Knowledge Base

The Translator's Knowledge Base, which is necessary for both comprehension and reformulation, comprises knowledge of the source and target languages (*linguistic knowledge*) on one hand, and *knowledge of the world* (*extralinguistic knowledge*) on the other. The relations between the two in discourse comprehension are discussed in Chapter 4. When knowledge acquisition takes place, either via the source-language text or through outside sources such as documentary texts, dictionaries, or experts – the whole procedure represented as a large box on the right side of Figure 5.1 and discussed further in Chapter 6 – the newly acquired knowledge is added to the Knowledge Base.

For each translation, the amount of new information acquired is obviously minute compared to any individual's total Knowledge Base, which is constructed from one's total life experience. However, the part of the Translator's Knowledge Base which is *relevant* to a given translation assignment can undergo extensive growth in the process, especially when working in a new field.

3.3   Revision

Revision, that is, the inspection and correction of a translation by a revisor after the translator has completed the task, is a repeat of the Reformulation Loop on groups of Translation Units (the lower part of the Model in Figure 5.1). The revisor starts the process with the Target Text, testing successive groups of Translation Units for editorial acceptability and fidelity, generally at the level of sentences and above. Ideally, s/he focuses on acceptability, on the assumption that the translator is conscientious enough to have checked thoroughly the fidelity of the text. When dealing with a translator previously unknown to the revisor or having the reputation of not being very competent, when the text itself is of critical importance, when the editorial quality of the target-language text is found to be poor or when there seem to be inconsistencies in the translation, the revisor must also focus on fidelity. This may at times lead back to the Comprehension Loop, for instance when s/he suspects that the translator may have chosen an unsatisfactory Meaning Hypothesis or omitted a segment which should have been rendered. For each group of Translation Units, then, revision can be said to follow in a way a process going in the direction opposite to that followed by the translation process itself.

4.   Interpreting vs. translation in the light of the Sequential Model

In certain programmes, especially those training both interpreters and translators and those in which training in translation is considered a possible gateway to training in interpreting, the Model can also be used to explain to the students some differences between interpreting and translation.

At the most basic level, the Model applies to both: in both cases, Translation Units are processed consecutively; in both cases, some degree of comprehension must be achieved before reformulation; and in both cases, testing and decision-making are part of the process.

Some important differences are found at more practical levels:

a.   Translators generally (but not always) have hours, days, or even weeks to complete the operations. Admittedly, they cannot afford to spend hours on each Translation Unit before moving on to the next, but progress at a speed of a few pages per day (generally from 6 to 15 pages or so, that is, about 2000 to 5000 words) in routine work is fairly common; they can therefore take at least some time to consult with experts, call colleagues and/or look for information documents, databases and dictionaries to solve individual problems. Interpreters work at speech delivery speed, that is, 100 to 200 words per minute on average. In 10 minutes to an hour or so they interpret a mass of words similar to that which is translated in writing in a whole day of work. In consecutive, they only have a few minutes to complete the processing of successive Translation Units as they are delivered by the speaker, and in simultaneous, they have a few seconds at most. An interpreter can consult a colleague sitting alongside in the booth or try to find the information in a document or glossary that is at hand (at a certain cost in terms of processing capacity and at a risk of 'losing' the next Translation Units – see Chapter 8) but cannot stop interpreting and leave the booth in order to find a solution to a problem.

It follows that in interpreting, a large part of the knowledge acquisition process must be completed *before* interpreting begins, while in translation it can take place *on-line*. This is not a minor difference, as knowledge requirements in interpreting are often unpredictable, with Bible quotations coming up at a data processing conference, mathematics being used at a medical conference and references to world politics being made at a conference on agriculture. Interpreters must therefore not only have a wider 'general culture' than translators, but also be able to take decisions more rapidly and be willing to take more risks (this concept of risk-taking is stressed by Claude Namy, of the University of Geneva – see Namy 1979: 53, 1988: 45).

b.   Translators can write a target-language text, then read it as the translation's reader would, then correct it, then read it again, and so forth. The interpreters' Reformulation Loop is contained in their own minds except for the final output. They cannot hear themselves as delegates would and then decide to change their speech, although they do correct themselves from time to time on a word or a faulty construction (for interesting studies of self-correction, see Petite 2005; Fellus 2005). Neither can they count on outside help while interpreting, except for the occasional technical term, name or number which either a delegate or a colleague can indicate to them (see Chapter 7). They are largely on their own as opposed to translators who may have a revisor review their work before it is delivered and shoulder part of the responsibility. Interpreting therefore requires a relatively high level of confidence in one's capacity to fulfil the task. Moreover, the interpreter's output is monitored and often assessed by colleagues or clients online. A good interpreter is never certain to be able to rise to the ideal performance level, which is to produce a clear and pleasant target-language speech 'perfectly' faithful to that in the source language. In fact, some clumsiness and some loss of information occur very frequently (see Gile 1989, Chapter 1, Alonso Bacigalupe 2006), and although their actual impact on quality perception and/or on communication outcomes is not necessarily large (see Chapter 3), interpreters are painfully aware of them. Working conditions are particularly stressful at conferences in which stakes are high and in which delegates really depend on interpreting, as well as in radio and TV interpreting, when interpreters are aware of the fact that hundreds of thousands or even millions of people are listening to them. In a case study, Kurz found that the level of stress of a conference interpreter was high at the beginning of a medical conference and then dropped, while it remained high throughout a TV interpreting assignment which was far less technical (Kurz 2002). Interpreters suffer from stage fright which they have to control as actors do, while translators are not subject to the same pressures, their main stress factor being deadlines for translation delivery (to which must be added – though this applies to both interpreting and translation when practiced as freelancers – the stress associated with market fluctuations and uncertainty concerning one's future work assignments and income).

On the other hand, the very fact that translators can go through the comprehension and Reformulation Loops several times and that their readers have all the time they need to look at the target-language text implies markedly different quality standards (see Chapter 2) and a different approach. Interpreters do their analysis and make decisions on the spot *as well as they can.* Generally speaking, once a target-language speech segment is out, it belongs to the past, although they may worry about its consequences if they feel they have performed poorly. In translation, a target-language text is not final until it is handed over to the client.

Until that moment, the translator has the opportunity, which some conscientious practitioners regard as a duty, to improve it as much as possible. Psychologically, interpreters are under stress while they work (and before the assignment starts) but can relax as soon as they are out of the booth, while translators tend to be under constant, albeit less intense pressure.

c.   Finally, another significant difference between interpreting and translation in the context of the Model presented here is that when testing the acceptability of aggregates of Translation Units (in the bottom part of Figure 5.1), interpreters can only do so on a very small number of units because of time and memory constraints (see Chapter 7). In simultaneous, they can operate on one, two, or possibly three Translation Units, but if they test the acceptability of more than one sentence before uttering it, they may not be able to keep in short-term memory the whole sentence plus the incoming source-language content. Moreover, the time lag associated with testing mentally more than one Translation Unit before rewording it in the target language may cause further problems. In consecutive, they have more time and could theoretically test many Translation Units for acceptability before actually uttering the relevant target-speech segments, but again, short-term memory limitations and speed and fluency requirements reduce the scope to a very small number of units tested in each aggregate of Translation Units, so that time and memory constraints turn out to be almost as severe as in simultaneous interpreting.

5.   Teaching the Model

5.1   Raising the students' awareness

This Model, like the Communication Models presented in Chapter 2, is practical, has little theoretical content and is designed to provide general methodological guidance rather than answers to specific problems. It will generally be taught at the instructor's initiative rather than as a response to students' questions. It can be introduced more naturally if it is presented as a tool for correcting errors found in students' translation assignments after such errors have been highlighted and questions as to what triggered them have been formulated in class.

For this purpose, the instructor can ask students to translate a non-technical source-language text containing a few ambiguities. Such texts generally provide a good fishing pond for errors associated with slack application of logical analysis. The instructor selects a short segment from a student's translation containing such errors, copies it onto the whiteboard, and asks students what they think of it – alternatively, for psychological reasons, it may be better to present anonymously a segment from an assignment done in previous years rather than one from the current group of students. Generally, it is easy to detect an error in a short, isolated text segment, and reactions from the class will be forthcoming. At that point, the instructor can point out that the source-language text contained no difficulty that could not be resolved by using logic. S/he may add that because of time pressure or for other reasons, the first reading of a Translation Unit may lead to an erroneous interpretation of its meaning, and that systematic testing of the plausibility of the Meaning Hypothesis is an effective way to reduce the number of translation errors. The ground is thus laid for presenting the Plausibility Test loop.

One example of such a text is given in Gile 1988a. The Source Text is Japanese, but regardless of the source language, there is something strange in the English translation of the first sentence, which reads as follows:

"There are countries that produce and sell computers and countries that produce and sell TV sets."

If a country has an electronics industry and manufactures computers, should it not also manufacture TV sets? The statement does not sound quite right and warrants a closer look at the Plausibility Test done by the student who wrote it. In this particular case, the problem stemmed not from the author's poor writing, but from general linguistic usage in Japanese: the text referred to a hypothetical situation, but this was not grammatically marked in the sentence, which read like a plain assertion. When such a sentence is found in a student's translation, chances are that it can be used for sensitization to the role of the Comprehension Loop.

Another example comes from the text of a French presentation read at a medical conference. The segment deals with the use of a particular substance called PGE1 for treatment of a pathological condition:

"… *Dans ces cas, la dose de PGE1 pourrait être réduite à 0 mg sans inconvénient.*"

Literally, the text says that the dose of PGE1 "could be reduced to 0 mg." Interpreters and translators may not have the necessary knowledge to judge whether it makes sense to do away with PGE1 altogether under the conditions discussed in the text. What they should be aware of is that this is a rather unusual way of formulating such an idea. It would be more natural to say something like

"… *Dans ces cas, on peut se passer de PGE1 sans inconvénient*" ('one could do without PGE1')

or

"… *Dans ces cas, on peut éliminer la PGE1 sans inconvénient*" ('one could do away with PGE1')

whereas "*pourrait être réduite à* …" ('could be reduced to') should normally be followed by a reference to some small value, but not zero. Such an unusual wording of this idea should raise doubts in the translator's or interpreter's mind. Is this not a mistake?

Is "0 mg" not an error? Other parts of the text or speech may show that indeed, the actual dose referred to in this sentence is not 0, and thanks to this Plausibility Test, the translator can identify the error, correct it and thus provide added value to the author and the readers/listeners.

While it may take some time and work to find good examples of source texts for the introduction of the Plausibility Test, opportunities to introduce the *Reformulation Loop* are rife, as they are provided regularly by linguistically deficient target-language texts handed in by students after a translation assignment: such a linguistically clumsy translation can be picked out, and its author can be asked whether s/he is satisfied with the translation. If the answer is no, the instructor can ask why the student did not improve it. The reply may be that s/he "did not have enough time," or found it difficult to re-express the Source Text's idea better, or did not dare deviate too much from the Source Text for fear of being "unfaithful". The instructor can remind the class of the translator's ethical obligation to produce a text that should serve the author, in particular through a linguistically acceptable target-language text (Chapter 2). This obligation means that the translator should strive to optimize the editorial quality of the product. A good way to do this is to scrutinize one's text, try out a change, scrutinize it again, correct it again, etc., which is precisely the procedure the Reformulation Loop describes. The instructor can also take this opportunity to present his/her own solution to the translation exercise to show to what extent *s/he* believes it is possible to deviate from the structures and words of the source-language text while remaining within the limits of fidelity. In line with the principles of process-oriented teaching (see Chapter 1), s/he can also stress that these criteria are at least partly personal, that they may not be shared by all other Translators and that they should not be taken as *the* reference model.

I believe it is a good thing to introduce the Comprehension and Reformulation Loops separately so as to show that problems in the latter are not necessarily linked to the former. It is then possible to move on and show the opposite case, which is indeed very frequent: an unresolved comprehension difficulty leads to problems in the reformulation stage, when the translator has to find a way to overcome or bypass the difficulty, sometimes by remaining vague so as not to betray the author's ideas (especially if the loss associated with potential error is large), at other times by taking bold decisions and accepting the associated risk.

5.2 Presenting the Model to students

Instructors can start introducing the Model by presenting either the Comprehension Loop or the Reformulation Loop with the action/test/action sequence. Then the Knowledge Base and ad hoc Knowledge Acquisition components are added. The second loop is then introduced, as well as its relations with the Knowledge Base and ad hoc Knowledge Acquisition. The testing of aggregates is presented last.

The following major points could be stressed:

a. Separation between the comprehension phase and the reformulation phase is important.

– Separation fosters *analysis,* as it forces Translators to *think* about what they *believe* they have understood. This is an important methodological point. When there is no separation, translators tend to view comprehension as less important, at best as a transient phase, only required at a superficial level to make reformulation possible. Therefore, they tend not to analyze Translation Units carefully. This leads to errors which could have been avoided.

– Separation between the two phases reduces the probability of *linguistic contamination* from source language to target language, which, otherwise, is likely – *and even inevitable* according to some authors (see for instance Percival 1983: 91).

There are two basic strategies for arriving at an editorially acceptable target-language text. One is to start with a *transcoded* translation and then work one's way up toward acceptable wording through the Reformulation Loop. Another is to start reformulation right away from a more or less deverbalized message, that is, from the *content* of the Translation Unit dissociated from its linguistic 'clothing' or 'packaging'. In interpreting, the latter is the natural way, because interpreters produce their output without being able to change it except for minor self-repair operations, which harm the quality of their delivery anyway. In written translation, rewording is possible, and there is no evidence to show a systematic difference between the two approaches as regards the quality of the final target-language text, but many professional translators who teach translation also seem to favour the same type of strategy as interpreters, which is the natural choice associated with the separation principle explained above.

b. In all cases, the role of the Knowledge Base is essential in both comprehension and reformulation. The extent of ad hoc Knowledge Acquisition operations in each Translation assignment depends on the degree to which the Translator's Knowledge Base provides the information or knowledge required to deal with the source-language text. Knowledge acquisition can be a lengthy process even if the number of information items required is small. Hours, days, or even weeks of research may be spent looking for a single item. In professional translation, productivity as measured by translation speed is of the essence (and has been found to be the main determinant of ad hoc Knowledge Acquisition among freelance translators in a recent empirical study – see Lagarde 2009). In order to achieve reasonable productivity, it is important to have limited knowledge acquisition requirements – or good access to the missing information. The former condition is met when Translators specialize, thus extending their Knowledge Base in the relevant fields as well as their knowledge of information sources, which reduces the time required for the acquisition of complementary information. The latter condition is met most often when they know an expert in the field who is willing to provide the information and/or when the Client provides it to them. Specialization is not a prerequisite in any absolute sense: theoretically, there is no reason why non-specialists should not be able to access the required information. The problem lies with the time this requires; Translators tend to specialize not because they *cannot* translate outside their specialty field, but because it takes too much time and effort to do so.

c.   The 'author-is-no-fool' principle: Authors can be poor writers; they may have to express their ideas in a language of which they have less than satisfactory mastery; they may have to write under time pressure. All these can result in source-language texts containing segments which do not seem to make sense. They are encountered frequently by translators. This is reflected in informal discussions between translators and in the literature (see for instance an empirical doctoral dissertation on the topic by Allignol, 1995; as well as Hönig 1988; Datta 1991; Lavault 1998; Schmitt 1999; Dahout & Quéniart 2000; Froeliger 2004). Frequent encounters with problematic source-text segments are one reason why the Comprehension Loop is particularly important, one which should be explained to students who tend to believe the printed word is almost by definition free from defects. When encountering them in a Source-Text segment, translators should assume that basically, *the author is not a fool* and does have a Message which makes sense even if the text is unclear or incorrect or seems to be illogical at first glance. On the basis of this assumption, translators should go through the Comprehension Loop again and again, trying out different interpretations of the text, until they reach a Meaning Hypothesis that makes sense or finally come to the conclusion that there is indeed a fundamental problem with the Message.

d.   Another difficulty arises when authors belong to cultures in which much leeway is allowed in the formulation of their ideas. A good case in point is Japanese culture, which tolerates and even encourages some vagueness in linguistic expression (see Condon & Saito 1977; Torikai 2009: 42). This is not necessarily a problem in intra-linguistic communication, but often causes severe problems in translation into languages in which more explicit information is required. In such a case, the Comprehension Loop is often associated with bold decisions, as explained in Gile 1988a, 1988c.

e.   In high-level translation as discussed here, ideally, the target-language text should contain no linguistically incorrect or clumsy structures, words, or technical terms. If the Sender-loyalty option is chosen, from the viewpoint of professional ethics in translation, editorial acceptability of the target-language text should be achieved regardless of the quality of the text being translated. And yet, only rarely do professional and conscientious translators write texts with which they are immediately happy. Most often, they have to go around the Reformulation Loop two or three times at least, stopping only when they feel they can really do no better. In earlier times, when translators could only handwrite, type or dictate their translation, have it typed and correct the typewritten version, then re-correct the corrected version, etc., the loop often stopped before the text had been fully optimized at the level of the translators' maximum writing skills: much work and much time were involved, and generally even the most conscientious professionals could only make corrections in their texts a few times. With the advent of word processing, the time and technical constraints associated with the reformulation loop have become less formidable. I believe the use of the word processor in regular high-level translation work has become virtually unavoidable in most markets. Moreover, word processors have increasingly sophisticated spelling checkers and even grammar checkers that analyze grammar and style, which helps detect many errors – though relying totally on such checkers would be a bad mistake.

5.3   The Sequential Model and error analysis

Once the Model has been presented and explained to students, its efficiency as a guiding framework can be reinforced throughout the translation course if whenever translation errors are found and whenever target-language texts are of mediocre editorial quality, instructors refer to it to locate the source of the problems and/or to make methodological points. This makes sense insofar as one of its main strengths lies in its use for error analysis. To my knowledge, it is the only conceptual framework for error analysis in translation that focuses on methodological issues rather than on linguistic or psycholinguistic aspects (regarding the latter, see for instance Dancette 1989).

The vast majority of errors found in translations can be ascribed to insufficient pre-existing linguistic or extralinguistic knowledge (a, e and c below), or to faulty implementation of a few translation steps (b and d below):

a.   Insufficient command of the source language

It has been stressed repeatedly by instructors from top-level professional Translator training programmes that full mastery of the source and target languages is a prerequisite for admission; theoretically, insufficient command of the source language should not be encountered in the classroom, at least in these selective programmes. However, it is a fact of life that the students' (or even the professional translators') knowledge of their passive working language(s) is sometimes deficient (see Chapter 9). In such a case, there are two possible remedies: consulting someone who does have good comprehension of that language, or compensating for linguistic weakness by ad hoc Knowledge Acquisition and/or analysis as suggested by the comprehension 'equation' of Chapter 4. The symptoms of insufficient comprehension of the source language are similar to those of insufficient analysis of the source-language text (see below), and remedial action to be taken by the instructor is also similar.

b.   Insufficient analysis in the comprehension phase

When the students' translations contain segments that run contrary to common sense or to what they are believed to know about the subject, chances are they did not read critically what they wrote; or if they did, they did not challenge deeply enough what the Translation Unit in the Source Text *seemed* to be saying.

When encountering such segments, instructors can first check whether this is the case (by asking the student, or by looking for comments on this segment in his/her IPDR – see Section 5.4). Perhaps the student did test the plausibility of his/her Meaning Hypothesis against his/her Knowledge Base and did find some justification – however weak it may appear to the instructor – for keeping it. When this is the case, in line with the principles of the process-oriented approach, it may be preferable at the beginning of the course to acknowledge the fact that the testing was done, and perhaps mention that the instructor's analysis is different – but without criticizing the student for his/her choice. As explained earlier, such a flexible attitude has the advantage of reducing the likelihood of a negative affective reaction by the students which may make them less receptive. Moreover, a tolerant attitude emphasizes the importance of the student's *approach* by ostensibly giving it more weight than to the actual results obtained. At a later stage, once the methodological principles are well established, individual translation solutions can be assessed on their merits as finished products (see Chapter 1).

If, however, it is found that the student *can* see that the text is not plausible, s/he should be urged to carry the analysis through to the end. In case there are several possibilities with roughly equal plausibility, s/he should be encouraged to take a risk and choose, depending on the potential Loss arising from an error. In professional life, minimizing the potential Loss may sometimes lead to the selection of an ambiguous target-language formulation, but students should be encouraged to make bold decisions while in training. This should help strengthen their methodological foundation.

c.   Weak extralinguistic knowledge

Even if a translator's command of his/her passive language is good and his/her analysis is systematic, the Plausibility Test may be inefficient if his/her Knowledge Base is too weak to allow detection of less than plausible meaning hypotheses.

In one (authentic) Source Text, the authors referred to a scientific study where a "significant difference" had been found "with $p>.05$". To anyone familiar to some extent with basic statistical procedures as found in scientific texts, there was obviously a contradiction, as 'significant' differences are sought at levels *below* certain thresholds, not above them. This inequality sign in the text was probably a typo. Students in class with no knowledge of statistics did not have any reason to doubt that the inequality sign was appropriate and translated the text with the uncorrected error. One student who had studied psychology and was familiar with statistical tests did correct it in his translation.

For reasons explained earlier, during the initial process-oriented phase of training, when errors in a student's translation are found to be due to a weak Knowledge Base rather than to the absence of plausibility testing, this weakness and its consequences need to be pointed out, but preferably without *blaming* the students for their lack of knowledge even if the instructor finds it disappointing. At a later stage, such weaknesses will influence assessment of the students' ability to start working professionally in the relevant fields.

d.   Insufficient efforts in ad hoc Knowledge Acquisition

Indeed, mistranslation is often linked to a lack of specialized knowledge, both linguistic and extralinguistic. Terminological errors are one symptom which reflects it, but so are most misinterpretations of the *information* conveyed by the source-language text. When such terminological errors, interpretation errors and deviations from appropriate editorial style are detected in the Target Text, instructors should examine the students' knowledge acquisition operations as carried out for the exercise and point out methodological weaknesses if they are the reason for the deficiencies in the Target Text (see Chapter 6). Knowledge acquisition can take much time and effort, and students are not necessarily motivated enough to do the work until its successful completion. This explains numerous weaknesses in their translations.

There is also little awareness among beginning students of possible traps, for instance those arising from the very specialized use of some words borrowed from everyday language in technical texts (see Lagarde 2009).

One striking example of carelessness in analysis comes from a student whose work in the classroom was generally good. In one translation on microcomputers from Japanese into French, she introduced the word *baignoire* (bathtub). The corresponding word in Japanese was "*basu*" which the general Japanese-French dictionary she used identified as a bus, a bath or a bathtub. The student thought that 'bathtub' could be a metaphor-based term (which indeed is the case of the appropriate term 'bus', which 'transports' electrical signal from one part of the computer to another), but she did not bother to check her hypothesis. The student cannot be blamed for not knowing about buses in microcomputers, but she should have checked through ad hoc Knowledge Acquisition that '*baignoire*' in French does indeed have a specific meaning in the context of computers.

e.   Insufficient efforts in the Reformulation Loop

The students' answers and the comments they make about problems they encountered (see below) may also reveal that knowledge acquisition was performed correctly and that the translation's weaknesses lie in the Reformulation Loop. Most of the time, problems can be attributed to one of three causes:

–   Students did not devote enough time and attention to the Reformulation Loop. In this case, instructors should stress professional ethics and professional pride, a major factor marking the difference between a true professional and an amateur, which makes it reasonable for the former to seek good social status and working conditions (see Section 5.5).

– Students may have spent much time and effort on the loop but nevertheless failed to find a good target-language wording for the Translation Unit at hand. This is often due to a general lack of confidence, and in particular to the fear of 'betraying the text'. When such an attitude is detected, it may help to recall the informational make-up of sentences and principles of fidelity as explained in Chapter 3, and to show the students at least one bold solution considered acceptable by the instructor as an illustration of their implementation.

– Students are often found to stick to one particular sentence structure in the target language in which they have trouble finding *the* appropriate noun, verb, or adjective. In such a case, it is frequently possible to break the deadlock by reconstructing the sentence in a totally different way or by merging sentences, sometimes with an associated change in the order of information.

In one translation exercise from Japanese, a word-for-word translation of the source-language text yielded the following French text:

> «Quels mots, dans quel ordre, combien doivent-ils être appris pour que l'on puisse dire qu'une méthode d'apprentissage des langues étrangères est efficace ? Ce sont des questions importantes dans la pédagogie des langues étrangères.»

An English version of the French text could read:

> "What words, in what order, how many should be learned in order for a foreign language learning method to be considered efficient? These are important issues in foreign language education."

In the classroom, this French sentence was perceived as very clumsy and required many changes before it became acceptable. None of the students found a satisfactory target-language solution until a suggestion was made to change the sentence structure markedly and turn it into:

> «Dans l'enseignement des langues étrangères, il est important, pour optimiser la progression, de pouvoir décider de la taille du vocabulaire à apprendre et déterminer ses éléments ainsi que l'ordre de leur apprentissage.»

Translated into English, this would read:

> "In foreign language teaching, it is important, in order to optimize progression, to be able to determine the size of the vocabulary to be learned, its elements, and the order in which they should be learned."

This is not necessarily the best translation solution for this case, but it was viewed by all students as acceptable, while all solutions suggested previously, which followed a structure similar to that of the Japanese sentence, were perceived as unsatisfactory. It should be easy for translation teachers to find similar examples in their respective working languages.

One important point to keep in mind besides the issue of linguistic interference is that as soon as the text to be translated departs from very general language and includes idioms which are part of a particular sociolect, be it an LSP or even the language of the news, the translator cannot rely solely on his/her native language proficiency to assess editorial acceptability and needs to check usage with appropriate sources. The World Wide Web has become a very convenient tool to check for the existence of collocations in reliable target language sources through the use of browsers (also see Chapter 9).

e.   Insufficient command of the target language

Poor reformulation can also be due to poor command of the target language, and in particular to poor writing skills (the assumption in this section is that students work into their native language – even if it is necessary to teach them translation into an acquired language, I believe that the most efficient guidance they can receive in the fundamental skills of translation requires classroom work into their native language). In a short training programme there is not much that can be done about such weaknesses except stress the importance of writing skills or tell students to take writing courses. In theory such problems should not arise, but in reality they do. If the curriculum is long enough, technical writing courses may bring students up to the required level.

A final important point regarding error analysis is that it can be performed to a large extent on the basis of the target-language text without having to look at the source-language text. When instructors are familiar enough with the subject, they can detect in the translation not only grammatical, stylistic, and terminological deviations from editorially acceptable language, but also many errors of substance even if they do not know the source language or the source-language text (see the appendix of Chapter 2). Using error analysis on the target-language text and the Sequential Model, it is possible to provide methodological guidance to trainees with a variety of working languages, including passive languages not known to the instructors.

5.4   IPDR – Problem reporting by the students

Another way of reinforcing the students' awareness of translation principles, and in particular of the principles incorporated into the Model, is to ask them to hand in with each translation assignment a report on problems they encountered and decisions they made (Integrated Problem and Decision Report). The idea is similar to the principle of translation diaries used elsewhere (see Fox 2000), but IPDRs are perhaps more specific in that they require the students to report systematically all the problems they encounter in the course of a translation and provide information about the options considered and the reasons for their final decisions (see Gile 2004). I have been using IPDRs systematically over 30 years and find they are very useful:

–   They force students to think about what they are doing and about problems they encounter, thereby raising their awareness of their nature and relative frequency.

–   They raise the students' awareness of the difference between comprehension problems and reformulation problems and thus help fight transcoding and foster meaning-based translation.

–   They help the instructor identify the causes of errors that could otherwise be attributed to more than one source (comprehension problem or careless reformulation, insufficient efforts in ad hoc Knowledge Acquisition or lack of access to information sources, etc.)

–   They help the instructor monitor the progress of the group's awareness of methodological issues (for a review of the relative advantages of different retrospection methods, see Hansen 2006a).

5.5   The Sequential Model and professionalism

Last but not least, the Sequential Model can be used to stress the importance of professionalism in translation. Basically, amateurs and mediocre translators perform the same operations as good translators: they read the source-language text, segment it into Translation Units and reformulate each of these in the source language, do some kind of plausibility and acceptability testing, use their Knowledge Base and acquire new knowledge. The difference between them and good translators lies not only in their relevant linguistic and extralinguistic knowledge and in their translation skills, but also to a large extent in their professionalism. In particular, as regards knowledge acquisition, a mediocre translator may simply look up a word in a bilingual dictionary or sometimes guess what the appropriate target-language equivalent should be, while a good translator will go to great pains to secure accurate and reliable information.

I believe that stressing the importance of professionalism in the classroom is good for each student's future career – and for the Translation professions as a whole. When students start working in the field, they come up against market pressures acting in a direction detrimental to quality, as clients are unfortunately likely to be "more concerned with the speed at which [a translation] arrives on [their] desk, its plausibility and its presentation" (Castellano 1983: 47) than with its intrinsic quality as a text and as a faithful reflection of the original source-language text as the carrier of a Message serving its author's intentions. If, in the course of their training, students acquire a sense of professional pride with respect to work well done, they may find themselves in a better position later to resist such pressures effectively.

Extending somewhat the comment made above, it can also be pointed out to students that the difference between a mediocre translator and a good translator lies not so much in the size of their existing Knowledge Base or in their talent for writing, but in their approach. Talent and extensive knowledge can increase productivity, but beyond these two parameters, if they have the basic qualifications, and in particular some aptitude for writing, conscientious translators who adhere systematically to sound methodology should produce better translations than less systematic and less conscientious practitioners.

Their Knowledge Base will necessarily expand over time even if they start with fairly limited extralinguistic knowledge. Translators can specialize in virtually any technical field by translating. The first steps may be slow and painful, but progress is possible, provided methodological principles, in particular those presented in the Sequential Model, are followed. By acquiring such specialized expertise and by being very systematic in quality control through regular tests and careful knowledge acquisition, translators can earn both professional pride and social status, both of which rate high in job satisfaction. They will also be more likely to keep their clients and find new ones by word of mouth, while talented but less conscientious translators are likely to lose demanding clients over time.

6.   What students need to remember

1.   Essentially (with some exceptions), translation involves comprehension followed by reformulation as opposed to language transcoding.
2.   Checking one's comprehension against one's Knowledge Base and against the context is important. If what the translator understands makes little sense, chances are that it is not what the author meant.
3.   Good translation involves decision-making under the translator's responsibility
4.   The translator's existing Knowledge Base is important, but ad hoc Knowledge Acquisition remains crucial and often takes up most of the time spent on a translation.
5.   Professionalism in translation is of the essence, both in terms of success in one's career and in terms of job satisfaction.

Appendix A

Examples of translation errors and weaknesses and of diagnosis using the Sequential Model

The following are examples from a translation trainers' seminar held in February 1992 in Lagos, Nigeria. The Source Text was translated from French into English in class. Target Texts 1 and 2 were handed in by two participants. Weaknesses as diagnosed by the instructor are indicated by numbers in their target-language versions and discussed in separate paragraphs.

Source text

Il y a des siècles que les peuples du nord et du sud de la Méditerranée vivent ensemble, se combattent, se conquièrent mutuellement, se courtisent et s'injurient; en bref coopèrent, au sens propre du terme.

Or, l'histoire – comme les avalanches – tend à s'écouler dans des couloirs traditionnels; c'est alors qu'elle prend sa force.

Possible translation (by the author):

Over centuries, peoples of the North and the South of the Mediterranean have been living together, fighting each other, conquering each other's territories, wooing each other, abusing each other. Yet, history – like avalanches – tends to always run its course in the same corridors. This is where it gains strength.

Target text 1:

Centuries ago (1), the peoples of the North and South Mediterranean lived together, got involved in internal wars from which they emerged as conquerors or losers, wooed and cursed one another; in short (2) cooperated in the real sens (3) of the word. But then, history – like a torrent – settles down (4) in the silent reservoir of tradition where it regains (5) its force.

Errors and problems spotted by the instructor, and tentative diagnoses:

1. The past tense is strange, as wars are still erupting in the area.
    Faulty or nonexistent Plausibility Test
2. missing pronoun?
    Faulty or nonexistent fidelity and Acceptability Test
3. missing 'e' at the end of the word 'sense'
    Faulty or nonexistent Acceptability Test
4. does a torrent "settle down"?
    Plausibility Test, Acceptability Test
5. "regains"? Why should a torrent which "settles down" regain its force in a "silent reservoir"?
    Plausibility, acceptability
6. Other problems:
    "torrent" for "*avalanche*" and "silent reservoir" for "*couloir*": Probably not due to faulty comprehension, because the lexicon in this source-language text is rather basic and the author of the translation has a rather good command of French. The problem probably lies mainly with his choice of a metaphor.

Immediate action in the classroom:

1. The translator was asked whether he thought wars in the Mediterranean area had been over for centuries, and spontaneously realized that there was something wrong with his translation in the past tense.
2. The translator was asked what he thought of the clause "in short cooperated in the real sens of the word"

    Having read it carefully, he found errors (2) and (3). The instructor then stressed again the importance of acceptability checking.

3.   The translator was asked about the acceptability of "history – like a torrent – settles down," and found no fault with the metaphor.

4.   The translator was asked to read the Source Text again and compare it with the Target Text. He then spotted the discrepancy between "*Il y a des siècles que … vivent ensemble*" ("have been living"), and his "Centuries ago … lived." The instructor took this opportunity to stress the importance of the Fidelity Test.

As regards "torrent" for "*avalanche*" and "silent reservoir" for "*couloir traditionnel*", the translator explained that he had deliberately chosen this metaphor. This meant that, as surmised, his understanding of French was not insufficient, but he needed to fine-tune reformulation strategies. Although the instructor thought the translator's choice exceeded the boundaries of acceptable changes, he did not insist at this stage, but made a note to come back to it at a later point, when procedures have been mastered and the attention is focused on the *product*.

The translator did not spot the discrepancy between "*prend sa force*" and his "regains its force." The instructor asked the other members of the group whether anything was wrong with the last sentence of the translation, and one of the participants identified the problem. The instructor then asked for explanations of the idea that history, like avalanches, gains strength when it flows in a traditional route, and pointed out that the error could have been avoided had the translator analyzed the idea in more depth and understood that avalanches becomes powerful when they are no longer scattered but converge into a great mass of snow flowing through the same gully. In this particular case, the participants being Nigerian, they did not know much about avalanches, and even the meaning of "*couloir*" in this particular context escaped them. The instructor pointed out the importance of knowledge acquisition in such a case.

Target text 2:

There are centuries (1) during which people of the Mediterranean (2) Sea live together with those south of it; they fight against each other, conquer, woo and abuse each other: in short they co-operate with each other in the real sense of the word. However, like an avalanche, history has a tendency of becoming (3) consigned (4) to tradition; it then assumes its full force.

Errors and problems spotted by the instructor and tentative diagnoses:

1.   French structure ("*Il y a des siècles que …*").
      Linguistic interference?
2.   "People of the Mediterranean" vs. "those south of it"
      Faulty Plausibility Test, insufficient Knowledge Base, or careless reformulation – see below.
3.   "a tendency of becoming"
      Faulty Acceptability Test or weak Knowledge Base as regards English grammar.

4. "consigned" – idea of restriction, rather than direction
   Faulty Acceptability Test, possibly general lexical weakness

In this particular case, the numerous linguistic problems indicate a possibly weak command of English, or insufficient separation between English and French resulting in strong interference.
Possibly insufficient understanding of French

Immediate action in the classroom:

1. The translator was asked whether "There are centuries during which people of the Mediterranean live together with those south of it … conquer, woo and abuse each other" made sense, thinking of who the people *south of the Mediterranean* could be, as opposed to "people of the Mediterranean." The answer could only be "Africans south of the Sahara," which led him to realize that his target-language text was incompatible with his knowledge of history: most of the conquering was done by people *around* the Mediterranean, none by people *south* of it. This should have led the translator to take a second look at the Source Text and discover that there was a deviation from fidelity. It seems that he did not check his text for plausibility at the aggregate level.
2. The translator was also asked whether this fighting, conquering, etc., had ceased centuries ago, and was reminded in particular of the Algerian war, which occurred in the middle of this century. Again, the importance of Plausibility Testing was stressed.
3. The translator was asked about the English acceptability of "a tendency of becoming" and acknowledged that he was suffering from interference from French. The instructor did not pursue the matter further, as this was a very basic problem outside the scope of the exercise, which focused on translation *methodology*.
4. The translator was asked about the meaning of "consigned" and its acceptability in English. Again, he acknowledged interference from French. Moreover, the instructor underlined that in French, the word carried connotations of constraints and limitations, and was incompatible with the idea of power that was stressed in the rest of the sentence, hence a further acceptability problem.

Appendix B

A model of decision-making in Translation

At any point where the Translator needs to make a decision any decision will entail a potential gain G, with an associated probability p_G of achieving it, and a certain loss L, with an associated probability p_L of incurring it. The best decision D_i among n possibilities (i = 1, 2, …., n) is the one with the combination which will yield the best balance between the expected gain and the possible loss taking into account the probability of each.

Best decision: $\max(p_{iG}G_i - p_{iL}L_i)$

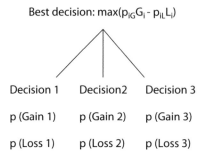

Decision 1	Decision2	Decision 3
p (Gain 1)	p (Gain 2)	p (Gain 3)
p (Loss 1)	p (Loss 2)	p (Loss 3)

This simple mathematical notation is convenient for students familiar with probability theory and statistics, but its presentation to other students is neither necessary nor always desirable. What is important is that they remember that any decision may have both positive and negative effects which they should think about before making their choice rather than reacting instinctively without thinking of the consequences.

Chapter 6

Ad hoc Knowledge Acquisition in interpreting and translation

1. Introduction

As explained in Chapter 4 with respect to comprehension and as shown in the Sequential Model introduced in Chapter 5, extralinguistic knowledge plays a major role in both the comprehension phase and the reformulation phase of translation. It soon becomes clear to students attempting to translate or interpret specialized texts or speeches in fields they are not thoroughly familiar with that as a rule, the Translator's pre-existing knowledge does not cover all Translation requirements. In fact, even in fields they do know, professionals often encounter comprehension and/or reformulation problems.

Much has been said about knowledge requirements in interpreting and translation. Some professionals and teachers take an ambitious view on the issue. In a paper on the teaching of technical translation, Barbara Folkart (1984) suggests that "the technical translator's stock in trade is an in-depth understanding of the referent" (p. 229), an ability to build up rapidly "a competence approaching that of the specialist reader for whom the Source Text was written in the first place." A similar position is taken by V. Kourganoff (1980). Such a requirement is in my opinion too strong. Many translations acknowledged as good by readers who are experts in the relevant subjects are written by translators whose knowledge of the field is limited. Other Translation instructors speak of a level of knowledge that is high enough for translation but not high enough to act as an expert in the field: the translator of a medical or engineering text does not have to know medicine or engineering well enough to practice medicine or build bridges. Such wording is probably a better reflection of reality, but beyond contradicting the previous position, it does not contribute much useful information.

The one point which does not seem to be challenged by practitioners and teachers of translation and interpreting is that the Knowledge Base of interpreters and translators of non-literary texts seldom contains all the information necessary for them to perform their work. It follows that ad hoc Knowledge Acquisition, defined here as the acquisition of information for a specific Translation task (as opposed to general ongoing knowledge acquisition during one's personal and professional life) is a regular and important part of Translation work. This chapter addresses fundamental issues in the use of information sources and in strategies for such ad hoc Knowledge Acquisition.

2.   Differences between interpreting and translation: A reminder

Essentially, the types of information required for interpreting and translation are similar in nature and in use:

a.   Linguistic information

–   *Lexical information* is necessary to understand more about source-language terms and to re-express referents in appropriate target-language terms. The ad hoc acquisition of terminological information is one of the most time-consuming tasks in translation – and probably the intellectually least gratifying to most people. This is why students tend to devote less painstaking effort to this part of the work than to others and to rely on dictionaries and glossaries without further analysis. It is important that instructors stress in class that correct terminological usage in translation can be an essential component of quality as viewed from the translation user's viewpoint. In Snell and Crampton's words (1983: 113):

> Although no one could fail to understand "front and back"/"left and right", the right note will be struck for a leaflet on a sailing boat by referring to "bow and stern", "port and starboard", etc., while for a text on equipment for horses, "fore and hind", "near and off" demonstrate knowledge of appropriate terminology.

When appropriate terminology is not found by the reader in a target-language text, this lowers the credibility of the translator and the translation and weakens its impact, hence a loss of communication effect from the author's or speaker's viewpoint (see Chapter 2).

Besides terminological information (*terms* will be defined here as lexical units with special meaning or usage in languages for special purposes), more generally, lexical information (about words in non-specialized language) is also frequently sought or checked by Translators, either because they are not sure about the meaning or usage of a word in the relevant field or target group or because they need to check that a likely candidate for re-expression which comes to their mind in the target language is not a 'false friend'.

–   *Stylistic and phraseological information* is required mainly for the purpose of reformulating the message in the target language along the same stylistic lines and phraseology as native authors writing the same type of text in the target language. For instance, in the commercial description of a microcomputer, the English "Includes math coprocessor socket" taken from an advertisement would translate literally into French as "*Comprend une embase pour coprocesseur mathématique,*" which is not a common sentence structure in French texts of the same type; a translation more in line with standard phraseology in French would be the simpler "*Embase pour coprocesseur mathématique*".

Again, if the style is wrong, the translation may lose much of its credibility and impact.

In this respect, references to Translation "into/from one's native language" (inter alia in discussions about directionality) is an oversimplified view of reality. Very often, Translators will be writing in a field and for a target group which use a sociolect (professional, scientific, technical, artistic etc.) closely related to general language but not identical to it. They will have to acquire and use expressions they are not familiar with in their daily language, but also, as already mentioned in Chapter 5, to beware of general-language terms which may have specific meanings and usages they are not aware of. Lagarde's findings (2009) suggest that such specialized terms in disguise can be a major trap in translation work.

b.   Extralinguistic information

Ad hoc acquisition of extralinguistic information on the topic, the Sender, the communication context etc. is required when the Translator's pre-existing knowledge and cues in the source-language Text are not sufficient for comprehension and/or reformulation. This may happen when the Text is editorially unclear, in particular when it is ambiguous, when it contains errors, when target-language and target-culture rules require explicit mention of information that is not explicit in the source language (for instance as regards titles, gender, the distinction between singular and plural etc., depending on the language – see Chapter 3 on Linguistically/Culturally Induced Information). More extralinguistic information is also necessary when the Translator is thinking of an alternative translation which involves paraphrasing, abstracting, implicitation or explicitation and needs to check equivalence.

$$\sim$$

One important difference between interpreting and translation should be recalled in the context of ad hoc Knowledge Acquisition: linguistic acceptability requirements are higher in written translation than in interpreting, especially with respect to grammar and style. Moreover, as explained later in this chapter, most of the ad hoc Knowledge Acquisition for a given translation task takes place *during* the translation work, whereas in interpreting, it takes place to a large extent *before* the relevant conference (at least under what conference interpreters consider 'normal' working conditions). Because of these differences, knowledge acquisition strategies taught to interpreters and translators differ to some extent.

3.   Information sources for ad hoc Knowledge Acquisition

3.1   Classification of information sources

Information sources for ad hoc Knowledge Acquisition can be classified in several ways. One is the convenient distinction between *documents* and *human* sources. Documents can be *hard-copy sources*, on paper (or films, microfiches etc.), or *electronic* sources, local (e.g. on a local computer disk or on a magnetic medium such as a CD-ROM) or remote (remote data bases, World Wide Web documents).

Documents can be divided further into *terminological* sources and *non-terminological* sources. The former – dictionaries, glossaries, terminological files, terminological data bases etc. – are essentially designed to provide information about the meaning of terms, their use to denote concepts and objects, as well as about translinguistic terminological correspondences. Non-terminological sources such as articles, books, catalogues, advertisements, official government documents, reports by intergovernmental and nongovernmental organizations, texts of law, contracts, patents, user manuals, powerpoint presentations, announcements etc. have different functions in their authors' minds – but as explained later in this chapter, they can be used and are often used to retrieve terminological information as well.

Incidentally, the terms *terminology* and *terminological* as used in the world of Translation are viewed by 'pure' terminologists as misnomers: *terminology* also denotes a scientific discipline devoted to the study of terms, and in particular of the way they are created, develop and interact (see for instance Maillot 1970, Dubuc 1978). In this text, I follow the translators' usage: 'terminology work' will be used as referring to the quest for information for the purpose of gaining better understanding of specialized terms and/or finding acceptable 'equivalents' in the target language in the context of Translation.

3.2   Fundamental variables in the characterization of information sources in Translation work

For professional Translators, the usefulness of sources for ad hoc Knowledge Acquisition revolves around five major variables:

1. *Existence*:

This variable seems trivial at first glance (a source either exists or does not exist), but is an important one, since certain types of sources are more or less likely to exist depending on the field and the circumstances, and knowing something about these probabilities has implications for knowledge acquisition strategies.

2. *External access*:

This variable refers to the *cost* of access to the information source in terms of time, financial outlay and effort (not least when the Translator is faced with the unwillingness of a gatekeeper – a librarian, shopkeeper or owner of a document – to allow access to it).

3. *Internal access*:

This variable is measured by the cost in time and effort required to retrieve the information sought 'in' the source once the source is accessed. Internal access is a function of the way information is organized in the source, of the source's editorial and visual or sound quality (handwriting, good or bad printing characteristics, layout of the text, quality of the voice in a voice recording etc.), of access channels to the information.

4. *Coverage*:

There appears to be a strong temptation to consider that the coverage of a source is strongly correlated with the volume of information it contains. Roughly, thick books are expected to provide better coverage than thin books, and in specialized dictionaries and glossaries, the larger the number of entries, the better the coverage is thought to be. This is not necessarily justified. First of all, a large proportion of the information carried by a documentary source, including a specialized dictionary or glossary, may be general rather than specialized, and the volume of specialized information may be a fraction of the total. Secondly, useful coverage depends on how much the Translator already knows, which will determine how much information and what type of information s/he will use the source for; the same source may offer effective and useful coverage to some and contribute little to others.

5. *Reliability*:

Information found in a source is more or less reliable. In many cases, a distinction can be made between *linguistic reliability*, which refers to terminology and phraseology, and *extralinguistic* reliability, which refers to information on substance. Sometimes, a source provides reliable information with inappropriate terms, and sometimes the terms are right but the substance is inaccurate.

3.3   Weaknesses and strengths of documents in the acquisition of terminological knowledge

1. *Existence*:

By definition, non-terminological documents always exist. The source-language Text is one; it provides both linguistic information (terminology and phraseology) and extralinguistic information on the subject it addresses. Beyond this trivial example, it should be pointed out that most often, Translation needs arise only after a theme or phenomenon has generated much thought and some writing. Bi- or multilingual terminological sources generally appear further down the road, when there has been enough interest in the subject to warrant the considerable work and cost involved in preparing them (see later in this chapter). In the past, looking for terminological sources was the prime strategy for Translators faced with an assignment in a field new to them. Over the past decade or so, there has been massive uploading of documents on the World Wide Web in many languages, and wondering about the existence of terminological documents and looking for them is no longer a high-priority option. The use of browsers and selection of appropriate keywords generally yield a rich crop of documents, including terminological sources.

2. *External access*:

External access to paper documents differs from the other variables discussed here in that it depends to a large extent on geographic and professional circumstances in the individual Translator's environment. When Translation requires the use of reference libraries, Translators who live in large urban centres are in a better position than others. If the source- or target-language country is far from the country where the Translator is working, external access is more difficult. In that respect, a Translator residing in France is in a better position when working from English into French than when working from Japanese into French. However, a large mass of documents can now be found online, not only in English and other Western languages, but also, increasingly, in other languages, which has reduced the Translator's dependence on paper documents and broken down geographic barriers as regards ad hoc Knowledge Acquisition. This is not yet universal, as the volume of documents available on the Web in some languages is still limited for some fields, but developments are fast. Access to sources is also limited by confidentiality considerations which do not depend on technology.

Another aspect of external access is contact between the Translator and the principals. Within the Translator's professional environment, when s/he has direct contact with the author of the Text and/or with the intended readers or listeners, access to sources (documents and/or the principals themselves) is better than when working through intermediaries. This is one major disadvantage of the professional intermediary system in Translation work.

3. *Internal access*:

In paper documents, internal access depends mainly on the internal organization and layout of the source. In this respect, terminological sources have the major advantage of alphabetic organization, which makes finding specific information easy, whereas in non terminological sources, this may require much navigation within the document. In electronic documents, internal access has become easy thanks to the 'search' function and only depends marginally on the internal structure of the document (information may take a fraction of a second longer to come on screen). The development of powerful browsers over the last decade also makes it possible to seek through keywords direct access to specific content in thousands of sources at once. Again, the exponential growth of the mass of Web documents has given a decisive advantage to non terminological sources in ad hoc Information Acquisition (the use of the Web in ad hoc Knowledge Acquisition is also discussed in Section 4.4 and in the appendix).

4. *Coverage*:

As explained earlier, the coverage of an information source is a highly subjective variable, in that it depends on the information sought and therefore on the Translator's pre-existing knowledge, meaning that the same source may offer a high return on queries to newcomers to the field and a low return on queries to others. Despite this variability, a number of general points about coverage can be made:

Often, a single terminological source will not cover all terminological needs for a Translation. The most obvious sources will meet basic requirements, but beyond them, finding a terminological document which offers the information sought may rapidly become difficult. This is due to a number of reasons:

- Firstly, the preparation of a terminological source requires much work which costs money, directly or indirectly. When it is produced by a commercial company such as a publisher, there is an obvious and legitimate concern about its profitability, which rules out frequent updates such as would be required in many fields with rapidly evolving technology and terminology. When the sources are not commercial, the issue is the availability of people and time to do the work rather than profitability, but the effects are similar, i.e. less frequent updates than evolution in the field would require.
- A second point relates to paper sources: if they were to cover *all* the terms likely to be used in a particular field, they would be very bulky and therefore difficult to handle physically; they would also be very expensive, which again would mean poor sales. This not a problem with electronic documents.
- Third, many terminological sources are at least slightly – and sometimes highly – selective in their choice of entries to include. From the terminologist's viewpoint, this is legitimate insofar as normalization can lead to clearer communication. On the other hand, in the field, terminological usage is not unified. Therefore, terminological norm-based selection of entries necessarily results in incomplete coverage, which, from the Translator's viewpoint, makes the source less useful.
- Fourth, because of the natural proliferation of terms, especially those used only in single companies or groups, no team of terminological experts has access to all the terms found in texts in a given field, meaning that 'proprietary' terms can generally not be accessed in terminological sources other than internal glossaries of the relevant organizations.
- Fifth, the production of terminological sources requires months if not years of collection work, editorial work, printing and distribution; in many fields, terminological innovation is so fast that lagging several months behind means missing much information, and, as explained by Claude Bédard in *La traduction technique* (1986), dictionaries can become outdated before they are even published. Bédard notes that the speed of innovation varies with the field involved, and that a dictionary on automotive mechanics from the 1930s may still be of some use, but in the field of data processing, it is desirable to use the latest edition of a dictionary (p. 34). In medicine, according to Nekrassoff (1977: 106–107), in the late 1920s, only about 3,000 syndromes were known, whereas in the late 1970s more than 30,000 could be found in the literature, with two or three new syndromes added every day. Electronic terminological sources such as databases can be updated

much faster than paper sources, but basically, they suffer from the same limitations and therefore cannot reach full, up-to-date coverage either.

5. *Reliability*:

The reliability of a source can be roughly viewed as a function of six sub-variables:

a.   *Its author's (or authors') command of the language(s) in which it is written.* As a rule, a source written in the author's mother tongue can be considered more reliable than one written in a non-native language, although it is possible to achieve good command of a specialized lexicon in one's specialty in a second language.

b.   *Its status as an original text as opposed to a secondary text* (based on another text), especially a translation. Generally, a text written directly in the language concerned is linguistically more reliable than a translation; this however is not an absolute rule, if only because some original texts are written by non-native speakers. As to the higher reliability of an original text as opposed to a secondary text (report, summary, synopsis etc. of an original text), it applies essentially when the author of the secondary text is not as knowledgeable in the field as the author of the original (see c below).

c.   *Its author's (or authors') knowledge of the field.* A journalist's text is generally less reliable than a specialist's (although it may be more clearly written and more readable). The better the match between the content of the text and the author's specialty or subspecialty, the greater its reliability. For instance, in the field of arrhythmias (a specialized sub-field of cardiology), there may be significant differences in reliability between texts written by general practitioners and cardiologists, and perhaps between cardiologists at large and cardiologists specializing in arrhythmias.

d.   *The match between the type of Text used as a source and the type of Text being translated.* The same subject is often dealt with differently with respect to style and terminology depending on the type of Text, the author and the target readers/ listeners. Authors writing for a large readership and attempting to explain developments in a given technology will tend to use standard and explicit terms, while technicians writing for specialists may use more jargon and acronyms. The same applies to speakers in a meeting.

e.   *Time:* As mentioned earlier, in many scientific and technical fields, developments are so fast that information, especially terminological information, becomes obsolete rapidly, sometimes within a year or so. When sources are not up-to-date, which is the general rule – Castellano goes so far as to say that "the time needed to compile and produce any printed dictionary means that it is at best five or ten years behind the times" (1983: 71) – some of their entries may no longer have the same meaning or usage.

f.   *The match between the source and the target-group sociolect:* A source may provide information which is reliable for the 'standard' or most common variety of the relevant sociolect, but not for the particular target-reader group, which may use organization-specific terms or phrases. This is conspicuously true for company-internal documents in the field of Information Technology.

Summing up, ideally sources should be:

- Written directly in the target language (translations should be avoided)
- Written by experts in the subject
- Recent
- Similar to the text to be translated with respect to text type (textbook, article in a journal, official report, catalogue, etc.) and to communication parameters (who writes for whom, for what purposes, under what circumstances).

4. Knowledge acquisition strategies in translation

4.1 Time considerations

As already mentioned, in interpreting, much of the specific knowledge required for task performance is acquired before beginning the task because there is no time for ad hoc Knowledge Acquisition while interpreting whereas in translation, specific knowledge can be acquired during the task as requirements arise. At first sight, it would appear that there is no scarcity of time for translators. And yet, the need to provide to their readers *finalized* texts which can withstand repeated, careful scrutiny in an environment where they are under constant pressure to deliver quickly brings them closer to the situation of interpreters than appears at first sight. This is where the World Wide Web, with the immediate access it provides to a huge mass of documents, has a considerable advantage over other types of documents (See 4.4 and the appendix).

4.2 Source selection

4.2.1 *Starting-point sources, Intermediate sources and End-point sources*
In written translation, the premise being that translation of high professional quality as defined in this book should ideally result in a publishable text, priority should be given to *reliability*. In this context, a useful distinction can be made between three stages in the ad hoc Knowledge Acquisition process and associated sources. The quest for information may first lead the Translator to a source whose reliability is uncertain such as a translated text or a multilingual dictionary. Information originating from this first source (*Starting-point source*) must be confirmed through a reliable *End-point source*. Sometimes, there are *Intermediate sources* as well.

In terminological knowledge acquisition, the starting-point can be (inter alia) a monolingual text in the source language which helps understand the problematic term or sentence, or a bilingual or multilingual terminological source of unknown reliability, and the End-point source can be a monolingual text in the target language which will be used for reformulation. In translation from or into *rare* languages (the term being relative to the particular environment at hand), going through an *intermediate language* may be an unavoidable route or the most practical one: for instance, when translating from Japanese into French, since there are few Japanese–French technical dictionaries, it is often necessary to use Japanese–English dictionaries, then English–French dictionaries as intermediate sources, with French documents serving as end-point sources.

Starting-point and intermediate sources may be texts of various kinds, written by natives or non-natives, in the source language, target language or a third language, with high, medium, or low reliability. What matters is that the end-point sources should be reliable.

4.2.2   *Access*

On the whole, the most severe problems arise with respect to external access to paper sources ('hard copy') and human sources. Internal access issues can be an obstacle in non terminological paper sources, but not in terminological sources and in electronic documents. Situations in the field are highly variable, but two general rules are widely applicable:

- *Specializing* helps. As mentioned in Chapter 5, specialized Translators know more about the field, but they also know more about information sources, their reliability and where and how to access them. On the other hand, beginners cannot always afford to specialize right away, and for some language combinations, there are few translators and specialization is not possible. In the past, this meant considerable investment in dictionaries and other paper documents. It would seem that in many working languages, thanks to the wealth of documents available on the World Wide Web, this is no longer necessary.
- *Direct contact* with the intended readers of a translation is generally a good way to access reliable sources in the target language and can enhance translation quality dramatically. Such contact also makes it possible to discuss and adopt consensus-based solutions to problems that cannot be solved entirely by the translator, including non-standard terminology.

4.2.3   *Initial source acquisition*

The more familiar translators are with the subject, the better they know where to find what, which eliminates much duplication and the purchase of unreliable, obsolete material. In the past, beginners often started by buying many dictionaries, which ended up on high shelves or in cardboard cartons after a short useful life. A recent study by Lagarde (2009) suggests that at least freelance translators in France have stopped such acquisition thanks to the availability of much material on the World

Wide Web, except for those working in languages where online material is still difficult to find.

To limit the extent of such unprofitable investment, it may be useful for teachers to make recommendations to students on purchase policy. Precise advice on specific sources is desirable whenever possible, but general recommendations are also called for: for instance, avoid multilingual dictionaries and old dictionaries (with the odd exception, which should be indicated by the instructor) and do not mistake a large number of entries for high coverage, as many of them may be irrelevant and belong to general language or to specialty fields other than the one under consideration.

4.2.4   *Library strategies*
Besides the purchase of documents likely to be used repeatedly and the development of personal sources (see Section 4.5), in many cases, libraries are important for knowledge acquisition. A thorough discussion of libraries is beyond the scope of this book and is left to individual instructors, but a few comments may be useful:

–   Only rarely will *one* non-human source meet all Information Acquisition requirements for any single translation task. Moreover, the law of diminishing returns applies to the acquisition of terminological information: while many sources naturally provide the basic lexicon in a given field, just as naturally, most of them will not provide those terms which occur less frequently in the relevant sociolect, and those items not found in the first few sources may require the translator to scan many other sources before the information is found – or not. When dealing with hard copy sources, it is therefore better to choose open-stack libraries whenever possible in order to facilitate external access.
–   In hard-copy non-terminological sources, the best internal access to information is found in books with detailed *tables of contents* and *indexes*.
–   When looking for terminological information in a library, it is a good idea to prepare an alphabetical list of items beforehand, so that pages of dictionaries and glossaries can always be turned in the same direction instead of the Translator having to shuffle back and forth. This is a simple strategy which is often forgotten but may save much time.
–   Last but not least, many textbooks contain glossaries, which are generally reliable and can offer field-specific information which is difficult to find elsewhere. Looking for books with such glossaries may prove to be a profitable strategy.

4.3   Bilingual and multilingual dictionaries

Because of the importance of reliability in source selection, bilingual and multilingual dictionaries, which are probably the best known and most widely used type of terminological source, "the first to which the translator will turn" (Castellano 1983), "often the first reference which students purchase" (Meyer 1988), "a tool which all translators use" (Mitchell 1988), deserve some attention here.

A first point to remember is that it is more difficult to bring together groups of experts in two languages than in one, and that it is even more difficult to organize common work between experts in three, four, or more languages. As a rule, the more languages a terminological source covers, the more its reliability may suffer from the complexity of the task. According to Castellano (1983: 72):

> The general but not universal rule with a specialized technical dictionary is that the greater the number of languages it covers the less reliable and the sketchier it will be found in practical use. ... The most useful is the monolingual technical dictionary or glossary, usually compiled by committees of specialists.

This does not mean that bilingual and multilingual sources should be banned: because of convenient internal access and sometimes good external access, they can be very useful as *starting points* for ad hoc Knowledge Acquisition. However, they should not be used as *end points* if at all possible. When they are, it is useful to keep in mind that generally, dictionaries are more reliable in one of the languages than in the others, depending on the native tongue of their author(s) and their place of publication. For instance, dictionaries prepared in Japan are generally more reliable in Japanese than in English or other languages.

4.4 Electronic sources

When they exist, electronic sources are superior to hard-paper documents in terms of internal access. Some translators still complain about not being able to find on the Internet specialized texts in some fields (see Lagarde 2009), but the number of documents posted online, including highly specialized documents, is increasing steadily and has already made surfing on the Web an obvious first step, and often a sufficient strategy in ad hoc Knowledge Acquisition for Translation purposes.

One major advantage of the Web over dictionaries is that it makes it possible for translators to check idioms and collocations in multiple contexts, whereas dictionaries generally have single-word entries, with a few idioms and examples at best. When working into one's B language, this is a particularly valuable asset.

The main concern in online knowledge acquisition is reliability. One problem is associated with the fact that there is little quality control for either language or information available on the Web, which means that texts written by genuine experts coexist with texts whose informational and linguistic quality may be poor (Wikipedia, a very popular online information source, is problematic in this respect). A second, related problem is that it is sometimes difficult to identify the author of a Web document and his/her qualifications as well as the date at which the document was written, which can make assessment of its reliability difficult. However, in many cases, the type of text, the identity of its authors, their institutional affiliation and their status as experts and native or non-native speakers of the language in which a Text is written or spoken (in audio- and video files) are indicated or can be guessed from names and/or the URL address of the relevant site (the full 'name' of the site which hosts the document).

Over the past decade, with the help of IPDRs (see Chapter 5), I have identified in the students' assignments a few major traps in the use of the Web for ad hoc Knowledge Acquisition. One is to consider that the best solution for a Translation problem (say a term or expression in the target language) is the one for which the largest number of hits has been found by the browser. This is misleading insofar as many hits can come from the same Web document; also, the reliability of each source cannot be ascertained before it is identified, and many hits can come from sources with low reliability. For example, when using browsers with French keywords, many hits turn out to be Canadian, but many French-Canadian terms and expressions are not used in France. Another frequent error is to reject the use in a Translation of a term, expression or collocation which is not found on the Web. It may be useful to point out to students that not all terms and expressions in use in real life are found on the Web, and sometimes innovation is the best solution. Yet another trap into which students tend to fall consists in reading sources superficially and picking up a term or expression which seems to fit without checking thoroughly enough whether the context and the meaning match those required for the Translation (examples are given in the appendix).

4.5 Individually developed sources

The value of hard-copy documentary sources may decrease steadily over time because of developments in the field and the associated aging of information and language usage. It does not make much financial sense to purchase every new edition of a dictionary or textbook because of the high cost involved and because only a small proportion of the content changes from one edition to the next. This, combined with other factors such as cost and storage problems, make it desirable for Translators to create and update their own sources, especially terminological sources.

A discussion of specific methods and formats for individual files and glossaries is beyond the scope of this text. Nevertheless, two observations fit the conceptual framework offered here:

– To ensure reliability, ideally, the *source of information* should be indicated for each entry, with a date and a reliability assessment ("reliable", "reliability uncertain" etc.). This is also a preventive step: when a client challenges the use of a term, in either good or bad faith (which can happen, when someone who has commissioned a translation has second thoughts, finds it is too expensive and looks for an excuse to withhold or reduce payment), the source can be quoted to establish authority or at least authentic use by experts. In practice, for obvious reasons, it seems that translators take the time to add these indications to their personal glossaries more often than interpreters.

–   In paper sources (including glossaries in the form of computer files which are printed out for use in interpreting), good internal access should be designed into the document from the start, for fear of losing information. Alphabetic sorting of the files is one possibility. More complex systems based on a semantic architecture of themes and sub-themes etc. are another option, but take time to plan and implement. When using electronic documents only (on computers, including portable computers, personal digital assistants and the like), good internal access is provided by the 'search' function regardless of such architecture.

According to Castellano (1983: 75), "A translator's most important glossary is the store of terminology he has built up for himself." I tend to agree, with the proviso that it applies in the medium and long term, not in the first few months of professional activity. Students should not be discouraged by the magnitude of the task when they see specialized dictionaries of 100,000 entries or more. Many include a high proportion of entries that are not relevant to the translator's needs or can be found easily elsewhere. Noting useful terms when they are found during Translation work can help the Translator build up a valuable terminology repository of several hundred to several thousand entries over several months to a few years.

4.6   Human sources

4.6.1   *Experts*

The human source is potentially the most powerful of all: an expert can provide reliable information more rapidly than any book or database, take on board the specific requirements of the Translator and present the information in the most appropriate way with the required clarifications. Native speakers of the source language can serve as Starting-point sources, and native speakers of the target language as End-point sources. When the same expert is a native speaker of the target language and understands the source language, the situation is ideal.

The main problem with human sources lies with external access: first, Translators do not necessarily know how to reach them, and second, experts cannot be counted on to devote much time and effort to helping Translators even when they are basically willing to. They can be very efficient in providing terminological information when they have it at their fingertips. They may also find pleasure in explaining to Translators unclear segments in texts, provided there are not too many. They are generally rather inefficient when correcting phraseology and suggesting improved wording of the Target Text, as the act of rewriting lies outside their field of expertise (they are knowledgeable in their field, but they are not necessarily good writers) and can be an arduous task.

From time to time, I find in translation assignments by students acknowledgements for the help given to them by experts… and gross mistakes. It is unlikely that experts did not know better. A more plausible explanation is a lack of attention to details on their part. Hence the idea of institutionalizing their services as *paid resource persons* (for written translation).

One possible option is to enter into professional *consultancy agreements* with the experts: a fee is offered for information, to be determined on the basis of time spent, the number of pages of Source Text read or the number of items (such as specialized terms) processed. Whatever the basis for such rates, the fee should be high enough to make it worth the expert's while and low enough to make the time gained by the translator profitable. In view of the speed at which experts can produce the required information, this is generally possible. Moreover, because of this speed, translation consultancies can be accommodated as a side activity without overloading the consultant's main professional schedule (but such consultancy could become a part-time or full-time job in itself). I had such an agreement for medical translation with a medical practitioner (see Gile 1986a), who found it interesting and profitable, as it provided him with an opportunity to read new medical texts while supplementing his income. It may be quite profitable for young engineers and scientists, as well as for advanced students in various disciplines. On the translator's side, such consultancy arrangements definitely increase productivity and reliability, and may also extend the range of fields in which assignments can be taken on. Financially, they are profitable if the translator has enough Translation offers to offset the cost of consulting. For instance, if the arrangement makes it possible for the translator to double his/her volume of work over a month, paying as much as 20% of one's fees to the consultant still results in an income gain of 60% for the translator.

This form of cooperation could also be institutionalized by translator associations and/or translation companies. Individuals could be approached and networks of resource persons could be set up. Such cooperation should perhaps not be implemented as part of initial translator training, as this would be counter-productive by allowing students to bypass plausibility testing and ad hoc Knowledge Acquisition, but student-translators can be made aware of the possibility for later action.

When human informants are not the Translator's regular partners in ad hoc Knowledge Acquisition in such a professional consultancy agreement, s/he should view them as valuable resources with limited access and limited motivation. It is therefore wise to spare their efforts by preparing one's questions carefully so as to allow them to provide the required answers immediately if they have them, without having to spend time explaining unnecessary information or trying to understand the Translator's specific needs (see Durieux 1990b for advice along these lines).

4.6.2   *Fellow Translators*

Besides experts, Translators can often count on inside help from fellow Translators. When working in teams, be it in translation or interpreting, the exchange of information is natural. Translators working alone on an assignment may call on the help of specialized colleagues they know. Translators' fora on the internet are another valuable resource. In all these cases, the main potential concern is reliability, unless such fellow Translators are experts themselves.

5.   Ad hoc Knowledge Acquisition in interpreting

5.1   The baseline

In conference interpreting, a considerable amount of relevant information is potentially available to interpreters from conference documents and from the presence of experts on the premises as well as from on-site communication during the exchanges. It follows that minimum knowledge requirements are partly lower for interpreting than for translation. While it is generally considered desirable for translators to be specialized, conference interpreters may define themselves as 'general practitioners' (see Schweda-Nicholson 1986, Feldweg 1990), although in the course of their career they tend to build up more knowledge in some fields in which they work frequently. On the other hand, as explained earlier, before starting to work at a conference, interpreters need to acquire as much specific information as possible, whereas translators can acquire knowledge while translating their text.

5.2   Strategies

5.2.1   *Three phases in ad hoc Knowledge Acquisition*

For the sake of the discussion, the preparation of conferences can be divided into three stages: advance preparation, last-minute preparation, and in-conference knowledge acquisition.

a. Advance preparation
Conference organizers are systematically asked by interpreters to provide them with full sets of conference documents in all the relevant working languages well before meetings are due to start. This is regarded as an important part of working conditions. The

documents requested include the conference programme, the list of participants, texts with background information about the conference, and, most important, documents on the content of the conference, including drafts of papers to be read or presented, abstracts, etc. These documents are by definition highly relevant to the conference and are used extensively by interpreters for preparation. Unfortunately, in the field, documents are not always provided to them, and when they are, they often turn out to be insufficient. In such a case, interpreters try to acquire relevant information by other means, and in particular by using the World Wide Web.

Briefings and rehearsals can be a very useful part of advance preparation. Briefings are short meetings organized for the interpreters, with the participation of the organizers of the conference and/or speakers. They may last up to a few hours. Sometimes interpreters are asked to participate in rehearsals, for instance in multilingual general assemblies of shareholders, when the management of the relevant company wants to make sure that the meeting will unfold under the best possible conditions. During briefings, general information is given to the interpreters, who can also ask specific questions which generally turn out to focus on concepts and terminology. Most briefings are held very close to the beginning of the conference, often just before the opening. Briefings are most useful when interpreters have had the time and opportunity to study documents in advance and have a set of questions to put to participants. When they do not, it is the organizers who take the initiative to think of the type of information which they think will be required by the interpreters, an exercise at which they are not necessarily adept.

b. Last-minute preparation

There are several reasons why conference documents are not always made available to interpreters in advance: papers are often finalized at the last moment, speakers are not always made aware of the interpreters' needs, they may not wish to disclose the content of their papers in advance, they may consider their papers confidential and are afraid of security breaches. Many documents are only available at the very last moment, on the premises. A relatively recent trend is to prepare powerpoint presentations which are brought to the conference venue on USB devices. Interpreters may be allowed to copy them onto their own USB keys and can study them on the spot if they have brought along their own laptops. A considerable amount of knowledge acquisition revolves around documents made available just before the beginning of the conference.

Unresolved issues can also be tackled minutes before the conference with the help of conference participants. Some speakers and organizers come to the booth of their own accord to give a copy of their paper to interpreters and to answer questions. Others have to be asked for help specifically.

c. In-conference knowledge acquisition

Finally, much information is gained during the conference itself, partly through documents which are handed out after it has started, partly through conversations with participants during breaks, and partly by listening to presentations and discussions, which may provide more information than do documents. New knowledge gained at any point during the conference is useful, because it improves conditions for interpreting subsequent presentations and statements. In particular, during the conference, information may be heard in languages for which no documents were available. Listening to the delegates in all languages is a good opportunity to build up relevant terminological and phraseological knowledge.

The same knowledge build-up occurs when listening to a colleague in the booth who has some experience in the field and knows the right terminology and phraseology – and when exchanging terms from glossaries other members of the team have prepared for the meeting. This type of in-conference knowledge acquisition can be very efficient.

5.2.2   *Issues in conference preparation*

There seems to be general agreement among conference interpreters on preparation methods except for one basic question relevant mainly to advance preparation: some believe that advance knowledge acquisition should focus on extralinguistic knowledge while others think priority should be given to terminological preparation. The difference in foci is generally not expressed explicitly, as proponents of both approaches agree that both extralinguistic and linguistic knowledge are necessary, but in prescriptive statements, proponents of the first approach are in favour of preparing for technical and scientific conferences by reading popularizing science books and articles as well as explanations in encyclopaedias, then moving on to more specialized articles, and studying conference documents as a last step. Proponents of the second approach recommend that interpreters focus on the study of specific *terms* likely to come up in the conference. Interestingly, the former position is advocated in the literature by theoreticians and teachers, while the latter seems to be more widespread among non-teaching practitioners. In the field, from personal observation, my impression is that even proponents of the first approach (focusing on general background information which is gradually narrowed down to the specific conference) act on terminology first.

A focus on extralinguistic knowledge is more in line with the intellectual image of interpreters which has traditionally been painted by pioneer trainers and academics. However, in view of the severe cognitive constraints which are part and parcel of interpreting work (see Chapters 7 to 9) and of the fact that many difficulties interpreters have to cope with online are lexical and terminological (see Chapter 4 and Chapters 7 to 9), it makes sense that terminological solutions should be given priority. Moreover, in view of the fact that online, the interpreter's focus and efforts are mostly concentrated at 'molecular' level (roughly at the level of a sentence, as opposed to individual words or whole texts), the contribution of extralinguistic knowledge is difficult to evaluate. Data from an experimental study by Anderson (1979) are not conclusive in this respect: she found no significant difference in simultaneous interpreting performance between interpreters who had either little or much knowledge of the content of the speeches beforehand and those who had none. The speeches were not highly technical, so it is difficult to assess the meaning and scope of the results, but they do challenge this part of the common wisdom of the profession. So do findings by Lamberger-Felber (1998) and Alonso Bacigalupe (1999), who found no clear-cut, spectacular effects of previous availability of written speeches to interpreters on simultaneous interpreting performance.

5.2.3   *Interpreter glossaries*

Interpreter glossaries are prepared more rapidly than translator glossaries because of time pressure: typically, a few hours are available for advance preparation during a crowded conference period, and entries are added or corrected during the conference itself, i.e. over one to a few days. In their glossaries, interpreters tend to list terminological indications appropriate for one particular occasion and to add little information regarding the reliability of the information, its source, the meaning or nature of the referents, etc. Because of their limited accuracy and reliability, such glossaries cannot always be depended on for use in conferences other than the one they were prepared for.

Glossaries are not very useful if their internal organization does not make internal access easy. Often, because of time pressure, interpreters just write down entries as they encounter them in documents or during the conference, sometimes on sheets of paper they happen to have on hand. They generally do not sort entries manually because of the time this would take. Until the mid 1980s, most interpreters either threw away a large proportion of their glossaries prepared for specific conferences or collected them in a disorganized way and lost access to much of the information. Microcomputers, text processing and spreadsheet software have changed the situation, in that it has become easy to enter terms in a computer and then do all the processing as many times as required, including sorting, updating and printing when a hard copy is needed. Information has become easy to store, maintain and access. In view of the value relevant glossaries have when interpreting at specialized conferences, this is an important change, the more so because the ease of glossary preparation makes it possible to go much further in one's preparation than in past years, when everything had to be done manually (see Section IV of Gile 1989).

5.2.4 *Reference documents*

Translators may purchase and keep reference documents, including textbooks, handbooks and dictionaries in their fields of specialty – though perhaps less so in recent years, with the advent of massive posting of online information on the Web (see Lagarde 2009). Conference interpreters may do the same for certain fields in which they work regularly, especially medicine and law, but on the whole, their attitude towards such reference documents seems to be different. This may be due to the fact that they generally work in a wider spectrum of fields jumping from one to the next from one day to the next, that they have little time to use these documents before meetings and even less so during the meetings. They also receive or collect (if only after searching and finding them on the Internet, printing them and taking them along to the booth) a large mass of documents which soon becomes too bulky to store and organize into useful archives. For all these reasons, they tend to purchase and use hard-copy (paper) reference documents less than translators.

6. Long-term Knowledge build-up in interpreters and translators

Interesting questions arise about long-term knowledge build-up in interpreters and translators. No research findings are available to date regarding knowledge accumulated by interpreters and translators in the course of their career, but a few hypotheses can be formulated. During written translation, knowledge can be acquired systematically, over rather long periods of time, often with reinforcement through multiple translation assignments in the same field – and through constant checking of information reliability, of fidelity and of editorial acceptability in the course of each assignment (see Chapter 5). In interpreting, each micro-task (such as trying to understand a sentence or a term or finding an appropriate term or expression to render it in the target language) is given consideration for a very short time (the order of magnitude is up to a few seconds for a sentence, and less than a second for individual terms), with virtually no repetition. Moreover, studies by Gerver (1974a) and Lambert (1988) suggest that the sharing of attention between listening and speaking during simultaneous interpreting may impair recall and recognition of the source speech, meaning that long-term retention of content may be low.

It therefore seems plausible that as regards extralinguistic knowledge, freelance interpreters acquire a wider but more superficial, more volatile and less structured knowledge than translators. This difference is probably less true of interpreters working mainly in one or a small number of fields, and in particular of staff interpreters in international organizations, but the distinction seems reasonable enough and could indeed be tested empirically. On the other hand, after repeated assignments in a given field, both translators and interpreters may acquire a solid knowledge of the relevant specialized terms and the associated phraseology.

The Translators' chronically low level of knowledge – and their subordinate status – sometimes breed frustration over time, perhaps more in conference interpreters, who work at conference sites where they are physically surrounded by 'real' experts and feel strongly that they lack autonomy. This issue is not often taken up in the literature, but see for example Torikai's account of pioneer Japanese interpreters' feelings about it (Torikai 2009, Chapter 5). Instructors may be able to reduce this frustration to some extent by warning their students about the possible onset of such feelings later in their career and by advising them to pursue some other activity, perhaps intellectual or artistic, or a hobby, in parallel. The situation may be markedly different in community interpreting, and – especially – in signed language interpreting, where interpreters may have more general and thematic knowledge and a higher social status than one of the parties, and can perhaps feel more often than conference interpreters that their action really matters.

7. Teaching suggestions

This chapter is another practical module with some conceptual guidance rather than full models. Practical teaching of the material is most efficiently carried out through exercises involving ad hoc Knowledge Acquisition.

Since knowledge acquisition naturally takes place during translation, one might wonder why it should be necessary to devote special exercises to this subject. The problem is that generally, in the course of translation assignments, both in the classroom and in professional practice, trainees and professional translators are primarily interested in the end-product, namely a completed Target Text, and do not have much time or motivation to step back and reflect on knowledge acquisition methods and their respective advantages and disadvantages. As a result, their learning curve may be less steep than it could be with more systematic analysis of their experience. This is why some specific action in the form of separate knowledge acquisition exercises and demonstrations (see the appendix) as well as permanent attention to the quality of ad hoc Knowledge Acquisition in the course of translation exercises are called for.

In keeping with the spirit of the process-oriented approach to Translator training, when commenting on translation assignments, instead of just approving some solutions found by students and criticizing others, instructors can discuss with them the choice of sources they used as well as their decisions, and highlight associated problems and phenomena as described in this chapter. For example, students will notice themselves that terminological sources they use do not cover all their needs and that they are not necessarily reliable, but explaining that this is an endemic problem rather than one associated with the sources they selected for a given assignment will help raise their awareness.

In-class demonstrations could include exercises whereby a Source Text in a specialized field is given to students who are asked to read it and identify all terminological problems they feel they will have to solve in order to translate it, and then to use a number of sources which are made available in the classroom to seek solutions. At the end of the exercise, which could last up to several hours depending on the length of the text, an analysis of the outcome can help highlight important points. This type of exercise could raise the efficiency of the learning process, since the whole time is spent on ad hoc Knowledge Acquisition without all the other operations involved in actual translation, the work is done on more sources than any individual student would probably use, and the effort is collective, thus representing the endeavours of a whole group of students and their outcome.

Other possibilities include controlling information sources, for instance by assigning different reference documents to students translating the same text and then comparing the results in the classroom.

In all these procedures, the main point is awareness-raising, making students experience the advantages and disadvantages of various types of sources and methods and *think* about them.

Integrated Problem and Decision Reports (see Chapter 5) are a good way of keeping track of the students' progress in ad hoc Knowledge Acquisition. By requiring them to report specifically on sources and decisions in dealing with terminological issues, they force them to maintain good knowledge acquisition quality and allow instructors to see whether they are on the right track and whether they still have individual and/ or collective weaknesses which call for remedial action.

The best time to teach the content of this chapter is probably at the stage where the basic principles of interpreting and translation have been taught and practiced on non-specialized texts and speeches and students are starting to work on specialized discourse. At that stage, they encounter the first difficulties in finding the additional information they need. Note however that the acquisition of phraseological information, or at least validation of the translators' intuitions as regards general-language usage on the Web, should come in very early on, when still translating non-specialized texts.

When training translators, simulating real-life situations is relatively easy: authentic source texts can be used, with appropriate briefs and reasonable deadlines. When training interpreters, classroom situations, including mock conferences, remain somewhat remote from actual working conditions, because 'authentic' speakers making statements live with genuine communication stakes are not available. In order to show the relevance of preparation to the interpreting task, it is advisable to use actual conference documents – and then play recordings from the actual conference in the classroom for the students to interpret. This ensures minimum ecological validity of the exercise in terms of preparation – if not overall ecological validity. Using recordings in the classroom as opposed to live speakers was rather controversial in some interpreter training programmes in the past, but is increasingly accepted and even popular (see for example de Manuel Jerez 2006).

In order to show the relative advantages of extralinguistic vs. terminological preparation as well as the strengths and weaknesses of different types of sources, comparative exercises can be organized, with half the class focusing on extralinguistic-knowledge oriented preparation, and the other half on terminology. Results can then be compared.

8. What students need to remember

1. Translation generally requires the acquisition of specific information for individual assignments. It is very useful in conference interpreting, and indispensable in written translation if the translator is to provide the Client with a publishable text.
2. In most cases, Translation involves reformulation of a Text in a sociolect (of the intended receivers of the Translation) which the Translator does not master as well as his/her (non-specialized) native language. In such cases, Translators need to check not only the terminology, but also the idiomaticity of their Texts systematically.
3. In order to ensure the reliability of information used for translation, knowledge acquisition can begin with a Starting-point source, then follow with an Intermediate source (both of which need not be very reliable), but information retrieved must be checked with the help of a reliable End-point source.
4. Online knowledge acquisition is convenient and can be a powerful tool, but requires caution with respect to reliability of the information and to its use in the Translation.
5. Human informants can be powerful information sources, and regular partnerships with experts can boost translation quality, productivity and profitability.
6. In interpreting, knowledge acquisition occurs ahead of the conference, during the last minutes before the conference, and after the conference has started. Specific terminological preparation is particularly helpful.
7. Personal glossaries prepared by Translators are very useful, sometimes more valuable than commercial dictionaries and glossaries.

Appendix

1. Classrooms demonstrations of terminological knowledge acquisition: A case study

The following is a summary report on a demonstration exercise conducted in the early 1990s at a professional translation workshop at the University of Montreal in order to increase the students' awareness of the limitations of terminological sources as discussed in Chapter 6. The exercise was done in collaboration with J. Dancette, who taught economic and business translation at the University of Montreal.

1. The following text, taken from the business section of a Canadian daily, was circulated among the students, who were asked to list the terms which they felt might cause them translation problems (the article was to be translated into French):

> Source text: People's unit – *Globe and Mail* – Report on Business (1991)
>
> Zale's debt-reduction programme includes asset, sales, inventory reductions, store disposals, contracting out of some internal operations, and possibly a joint venture with one or more outside investors. Mr. Gill has said the company is talking with six or seven interested parties, but no announcements are expected until next year. However, barring a spectacular Christmas season or a major equity infusion, analysts say Chapter 11 is becoming an ever more likely scenario.
>
> "Zale is in a precarious position. It's going to take quite an effort to pull it out," said George Hartman, an analyst with BBN James Cape Inc. in Toronto, adding that he thinks this will be the last Christmas season for Zale in its present form.
>
> Peoples acquired its Zale stake for $650-million in a leveraged buyout five years ago with the help of junk bond wizard Michael Milken, with Swarovski International Holding AG of Switzerland picking up the other half. Shortly after, Houston based Gordon Jewelry Corp. was added for $315-million.
>
> Today, the bonds used to finance the acquisitions are trading at a deep discount; and last week Moody Investors Service Inc. placed about $950-million in long-term debt on Zale, Gordon and Zale Credit Corp. on rating alert.

The identification of potential terminological difficulties was done collectively in class, and the terms perceived as problematic by at least some students (some are not really 'terms') were listed as follows:

1. People's unit
2. Debt reduction
3. Asset
4. Store disposals
5. Contracting out
6. Equity infusion
7. Chapter 11
8. Pull it out

9. Stake
10. Leveraged buyout
11. Junk bond wizard
12. Holding
13. Picking up the other half
14. Deep discount
15. Placed…in long term debt
16. rating alert

No comments were made to the students regarding the terms and word groups they collected, as this was not the purpose of the exercise at this stage. Had more time been available (the exercise was part of a four-session seminar), the following short comments could have been used for further sensitization to the types of problems they encounter (see also Chapter 4 on comprehension, and Chapter 5 on knowledge acquisition requirements):

- Of the 16 'terms', 14 are groups of two or more words rather than single words.
- Of the 35-odd single words that make up the 16 'terms', none is rare in general language. It is their combination and/or use in a specific context which turns them into part of 'specialized language'.
- One of the 'terms', *pull it out* is not a specialized term, but an idiom from general language. The student who identified this problem obviously had insufficient comprehension of English.
- The list includes one proper noun (People's unit), and one quasi-proper noun (Chapter 11, which refers to the Bankruptcy Reform Act). The first was probably not identified as a proper noun; otherwise, it would not have been listed as a problematic 'term' with respect to translation. As for the second, there was no time to check, but either it was not identified as a proper noun either, or the students who mentioned it put it on their list because they expected difficulties in explaining what it was to the reader of their French text.

2. About twenty terminological and non-terminological sources, which were provided by Dancette, were distributed to the students. They included bilingual dictionaries, monolingual glossaries of banking and business terms, a book in English explaining Wall Street, and newspaper articles in French on the same story. The sources were the ones that Dancette had in her possession and uses in her own translation work.
   One source was allocated to each student. Students were asked to use only the sources which were allotted to them individually, and to indicate:

   - when relevant, whether the term was *found* in the sources (to see the *coverage rate*)

- when relevant, what French 'equivalent' was given in the source
- what target-language rendition they intended to use for their translation of the text.

When they had finished with one source, they were given another source to process in the same way. The students had about an hour for the exercise.

Of the sources that had been brought to class, sixteen were used by the students during the working session. These included:

- Six specialized bilingual dictionaries on banking, business, and economics and law
- One general bilingual dictionary
- Five specialized monolingual dictionaries in English on accounting, banking, business, finance, and investment
- One book on Wall Street, in English
- One book on banking, in French
- Two newspaper articles in French on the same subject as the article in English used for the exercise

3.   Results indicate inter alia the following:

- The highest coverage rate in a single source was 10 of the 16 problematic 'terms'. The second highest was 9, the third was 6. That is, *most of the sources sampled had a coverage rate of less than 50%.*
- While the highest coverage rate was found in a specialized bilingual dictionary (*Le Robert et Collins du management*, 1992), the second and third highest coverage rates were found *in specialized monolingual dictionaries in English.*
- The second highest coverage rate was found in a dictionary *with only 3,000 entries*, which was published in 1985, and the third highest coverage rate was found in a dictionary with about 6,000 entries, published in 1987.
- The highest number of 'equivalents' in French given by a bilingual source which were suitable in the context was 8 (in *Le Robert et Collins du management*). Three other bilingual sources, one of which was a general (non-specialized). dictionary, gave 3 appropriate equivalents, one gave 1 appropriate equivalent, and one gave none.
- Even when appropriate 'equivalents' were indicated in the dictionaries, they were often one of several in a list, without sufficient information to allow the translator to determine which was *the* appropriate one.
- While time was too short to conduct an extensive analysis of the results, the findings made above could have been generalized into at least the following three points:

  - Bilingual dictionaries do not necessarily have the highest coverage rate, nor give reliable and sufficiently precise information.

- The size of a dictionary is not necessarily a good indicator of its coverage rate.
- The age of a dictionary is not necessarily a good indicator of its coverage rate.

Clearly, the results of the experiment have no 'scientific' value, because the situation was not controlled strictly and only represents one case study. However, I believe that the work carried out in class by the students made the instructor's subsequent comments more convincing, hence the value of the experiment as a didactic tool, in spite of the fact that it did not produce all the results that would have been necessary to illustrate all the points made in Chapter 6 regarding sources for knowledge acquisition. For a scientific investigation of sources, many replications of the experiment, with better control, would be necessary.

2. Browsing the Web for ad hoc Knowledge Acquisition: It looks like a duck...

As explained in Section 3.2.3, the Web is deceptively easy to use as a source for ad hoc Knowledge Acquisition, which misleads many students into adopting seemingly good solutions to their problems without checking rigorously enough whether they fit. A Wikipedia article on Renewable energies given to students to translate into French talks about Brazil, which has "one of the largest renewable energy programmes in the world, involving production of ethanol fuel from sugar cane...." One student translated this sentence as « *Le Brésil a mis en place l'un des plus importants programmes d'incitation aux énergies renouvelables du monde...* » (one of the largest programmes *of incentives in favour of* renewable energies) because she found in a website a reference to the World Wind Energy Award 2007 which was granted to the Brazilian government for the successful development and implementation of its Programme for Incentives for Alternative Energy Sources PROINFA. Indeed, this is the programme the text was referring to, but for some reason, the author did not talk about *incentives*. By adding what seemed to be a truthful clarification, the student changed (slightly, but unnecessarily) the focus of the sentence.

In the same text on renewable energies, the English text says "The Earth-Atmosphere system is in equilibrium such that heat radiation into space is equal to incoming solar radiation". One student who did very good ad hoc Knowledge Acquisition found in a scientific source that this equilibrium is precise, and wrote in her translation exactly that: "*la chaleur émise de la Terre vers l'espace compense exactement le rayonnement solaire qu'elle reçoit*". The problem is that though the fact is true, the author did not make this point, and the addition in the translation changes slightly the information and emphasis in the text, which is not in line with the Sender-loyalty principle. Another student found that the energy radiated from the Earth into space was mainly in the infra-red range and included this information in her translation, again, adding an element which was neither necessary for comprehension nor chosen by the author.

The same Wikipedia text also refers to "The World's largest geothermal power installation", the Geysers, "… with a rated capacity of 750 MW". A (generally very serious) student translated "rated capacity" as "*capacité évaluée à 750 MW*" (with a capacity assessed at 750 MW), because she found two websites talking about power plants with a "*capacité évaluée à 23 MW*" and a "*capacité actuelle évaluée à 7000 MW*" respectively, in which the figures refer to an assessed capacity. The context looked very similar, but the idea was not.

In matters of ad hoc Knowledge Acquisition, even if it looks like a duck and swims like a duck, it could be something else than a duck and rigorous checking needs to be done.

Chapter 7

The Effort Models of interpreting

1. Introduction

One of the most striking and challenging phenomena in simultaneous interpreting is the interpreters' persistent perception that it is fundamentally 'difficult'. This awareness may arise first during initial training, perhaps under the pressure of instructors who are felt by students to always find fault with their target speeches in interpreting exercises and to always demand better performance. And yet, even after graduation and after many years of experience, most interpreters feel that simultaneous interpreting requires intensive efforts to render all the information of the source speech in a good quality target speech and that they often fail to reach this objective to their satisfaction in spite of their best efforts.

Upon close scrutiny, it turns out that performance problems arise not only in fast, informationally dense or highly technical speeches, but also in clear, slow speech segments in which no particular obstacles are identified. Moreover, errors and omissions are found not only in the students' interpreting exercises, but also in the work of seasoned professionals. As an illustration, in a case study by Gile (1989, Chapter 4), over a segment of 70 seconds of speech, more than 10 incorrect and/or obviously clumsy target-language segments were identified in a slow, non-technical target-language speech made by an experienced professional interpreter with an excellent reputation. Similar observations can be made when looking at the data from most empirical studies, which involve several (up to ten, sometimes more) professionals and students who are given the same recorded speeches to interpret. For example, the following errors were noted in simultaneous French renderings of one English source speech produced by experienced interpreters:

> "that wasn't my fault" was interpreted into "*c'est ma faute*" ("it is my fault")
> "the Vietnamese government" was interpreted into "*les gouvernements*" ("the governments") by one interpreter, and into "*le gouvernement chinois*" ('the Chinese government') by another
> "and you think they think you're foolish" was interpreted into "*vous pensez qu'ils sont idiots*" ("you think they are stupid")

In view of the general level of mastery of English of these interpreters (all of them had English as an A or B language), insufficient understanding of the source language as an explanation of the errors must be ruled out. Moreover, since each source-speech segment was interpreted erroneously by only one or two of the 10 professional interpreters who had accepted to participate in the experiment, it is unlikely that the reason was technical, perhaps the poor quality of the recording at these points in the speech – otherwise, more interpreters would probably have had problems with the same segments. A third point is that some interpreters who interpreted the speech twice in a row (after a short break of a few minutes) made some errors the second time in segments which they had interpreted correctly the first time. This is an intriguing point: if they had overcome a difficulty when first interpreting a speech, why should they not be able to overcome it when interpreting it a second time, with the advantage of having become familiar with it and having had time to think about it? One possible explanation would be fatigue. However, the speech was less than 11 minutes long, and subjects were allowed to rest for a couple of minutes before starting to reinterpret it. In view of the fact that when interpreting in the field, the same subjects take turns of 30 minutes in the simultaneous interpreting booth, fatigue is also an unlikely explanation for the phenomenon. (Gile 1999a is a full report on this experiment – see also Section 9, which discusses this experiment again around the concept of 'Tightrope Hypothesis').

Observations of errors made by professionals in speech segments containing no apparent obstacle are intriguing, and trying to understand the reasons behind them seemed important, if only in order to help students understand why interpreting is so difficult and accept this as a fact of life rather than as a worrying sign of incompetence. Insight into the mechanisms leading to performance flaws was also sought in the hope of finding ideas and methods to help overcome the obstacles.

In this mindset, I developed an Effort Model for simultaneous interpreting, which was first sketched out in a paper on the relative difficulty of interpreting as a function of the specific pairs of languages involved (Gile 1983b). Ever since, I have been developing it and extending the analysis. This chapter is an up-to-date discussion of the Models (there are now several), which are central in my teaching of interpreting and have been adopted as a conceptual framework by many interpreting teachers – and, as it turned out, by researchers (see Gile 2008) – over the past 25 years. The Effort Models for simultaneous interpreting, for consecutive interpreting and for sight translation are introduced here as a simple set of constructs for explanatory purposes. Since in the literature, they are also discussed in the context of considerations from cognitive psychology, I have added some clarifications on how they relate to and differ from models and theories from mainstream cognitive psychology.

2.   Automatic operations, processing capacity and interpreting Efforts

2.1   Automatic and non-automatic operations

The development of the Models originated in two intuitive ideas based on observation and introspection:

- Interpreting requires some sort of 'mental energy' that is only available in limited supply.
- Interpreting takes up almost all of this mental energy, and sometimes requires more than is available, at which times performance deteriorates.

The idea that there is some association between the deterioration of the interpreter's performance and some kind of overload was not new. It had already been mentioned by Pinter (1969), as well as by several other authors, mainly in the context of discussions of the role of short-term memory in simultaneous interpreting (Fukuii & Asano 1961; Kade & Cartellieri 1971; Lederer 1978; Moser 1978; Wilss 1978). Subsequent reading in cognitive psychology provided useful information revolving around the concepts of *attention* and 'automatic' and 'non-automatic' operations, thus establishing a link between intuitive ideas from interpreting practice and some theoretical and empirical research.

Toward the end of the 1940s, Claude Shannon, an engineer working on communication, formulated the idea that any channel serving to transmit information had a finite transmission capacity beyond which information losses occurred (Shannon 1948). This idea, which had come out of studies on electric communication lines, was taken up by cognitive psychologists who adapted it to the case of the human mind (Broadbent 1958; Moray 1967; Kahneman 1973; Norman 1976). The idea is that some mental operations ('non-automatic operations') require attention (alternative names are 'attentional resources' and 'processing capacity'), and others ('automatic operations') do not. Such non-automatic operations also take time, whereas automatic operations are very fast. Non-automatic operations take processing capacity from a limited available supply (whether all of them take it from the same single reservoir or not is under debate). When the processing capacity available for a particular task is insufficient, performance deteriorates.

The distinction between automatic and non-automatic operations is sometimes difficult to make, as non-automatic operations vary in the processing capacity they require and may become automatic after enough repetition (see for instance Eysenck & Keane 1990). Gradual automation of cognitive operations is important in interpreting skills acquisition and will be discussed further in the next chapters.

Finding these concepts and theories in cognitive psychology was encouraging: if operations involved in interpreting were non-automatic, there was some basis for constructing an interpreting model around the ideas of processing capacity requirements and processing capacity limitations with prospects for good explanatory power as regards various phenomena experienced and observed while interpreting.

According to cognitive psychology, non-automatic operations are those which cannot be or are not automated, such as detecting a brief stimulus, identifying a non-familiar stimulus or a familiar stimulus presented under poor conditions, storing information in memory for later use, preparing for a non-automated response, controlling the accuracy of a movement or manipulating symbols in a person's cognitive system. Automatic operations include decoding a familiar stimulus presented under favourable conditions, triggering an automated response and operating a motor programme without control (Richard 1980: 149–150). Again, this distinction is a simplification of reality, if only because it may sometimes be difficult to discriminate between long and short stimuli or between familiar and unfamiliar stimuli. Nevertheless, it is shown in the next sections of this chapter that the operations making up interpreting as defined below clearly include components on the non-automatic side.

2.2   Interpreting Efforts

Drawing on my experience as a practitioner of simultaneous interpreting and as an instructor, I thought of attempting to analyze its operation with conceptual entities immediately familiar to interpreters and to students, namely a listening and analysis component, a speech production component, and a short-term memory component. I called these components 'Efforts' to stress their effortful nature, as they include deliberate action which requires decisions and resources.

2.2.1   *The Listening and analysis Effort*
The Listening and analysis Effort (or 'Listening Effort' for short) was defined as consisting of all comprehension-oriented operations, from the subconscious analysis of the sound waves carrying the source-language speech which reach the interpreter's ears through the identification of words to the final decisions about the 'meaning' of the utterance. In signed language interpreting, a parallel Viewing and Analysis Effort can be defined when the interpreter works from a signed language into a spoken language.

It is not yet clear how far the analysis of the meaning of the source-language speech must go before interpreting is possible. In the discussion of the interpreting and translation of specialized speeches and texts in Chapter 4, it is suggested that such comprehension goes at least as far as understanding the general underlying logic of each sentence. Even by the most conservative standards, one can say that except for some names which interpreters may simply try to imitate phonetically, interpreting requires at the very least the recognition of words in the source-language speech. This is enough to put the Listening and analysis component in the non-automatic category. The reason is that there is no one-to-one relation between the sound reaching one's ears and any single phoneme, word, or group of words pronounced by a speaker (the same applies to the visual flows perceived by one's eyes when interpreting from signed languages – a view which signed-language specialists Carol Patrie and Robert E. Johnson of Gallaudet University confirmed in a personal exchange). There is some variability in the way such words are pronounced, not only from one individual to another, but also in the same speaker repeating the same speech segment.

This is also why it is very difficult to recognize words on sonograms (graphic representations of sound). According to Guibert (1979), even human experts familiar with phonetics and with the lexical and syntactic rules of a language never manage to read correctly more than 75% of the phonetic segments on a sonogram. It is therefore not surprising that machines, which do not have at their disposal as much lexical and syntactic information, nor a level of knowledge of the world comparable to a human's, are unable to recognize natural chained (continuous) speech (as opposed to speech in which there are pauses between the words) with 100 percent reliability. This limitation persists even when they have gone through a 'learning process' with the voice of individual speakers (a necessary process when using dictation software).

In order for words to be recognized, acoustic features of the incoming sounds have to be analyzed and compared with patterns stored in the listener's long-term memory (or in the hard disk of a computer, in the case of speech recognition software). Following a complicated process involving knowledge of the probabilistic structure of the relevant language, the context and the situation, the listener decides that particular sound sequences correspond to particular words (see for example Hörmann 1972; Clark & Clark 1977; Costermans 1980; Noizet 1980; Matthei & Roeper 1985; Greene 1986). Undoubtedly, speech recognition as it occurs in interpreting has non-automatic components.

Actually, interpreters know that interpreting involves much more than speech recognition. Some kind of semantic representation of the content of source speeches is always present, which includes plausibility analyses (see Chapter 4, 5 and 6) and probably some anticipation. Chernov (1973) conducted an experiment in which he made students interpret sentences that seemed to be leading in a certain direction and then veered off to an unexpected ending. He found they were usually interpreted according to the direction they were taking initially, not as they finally turned out to end. His subjects not only identified words, but also made inferences about their meaning and anticipated on-line. Several studies by Gerver (1976), Lambert (1988) and others focused on comparisons of recall and recognition under various conditions and also led to results suggesting that when interpreting simultaneously, interpreters do achieve a level of comprehension much beyond the recognition of individual words.

No sophisticated research is necessary to ascertain that interpreting comprehension goes beyond word recognition: field observation provides ample evidence for the fact in practically any interpreted speech. As an illustration, below are French renditions by five professional interpreters of the same English speech segment. The material is taken from one experiment (Gile 1999b) involving in-laboratory interpreting of the same recordings of actual conference speeches.

Original English sentence (by speaker):

> "I was hoping to encourage the oil people to give a little bit back to the countries that they take the oil from"

French versions produced by five professional interpreters:

> «*Je voulais encourager les pétroliers à rendre un peu de leur butin aux pays où ils vont le prélever* » (Interpreter A)

> « *Je pensais pouvoir encourager les compagnies pétrolières à restituer un peu des profits aux pays qu'ils exploitent* » (Interpreter B)

> « *J'espérais que les compagnies pétrolières rendraient quelque chose à ceux dont ils prennent le pétrole* » (Interpreter C)

> « *Je voulais encourager les pétroliers entre guillemets à rendre un petit peu de ce qu'ils ponctionnent aux pays qui ont du pétrole* » (Interpreter D)

> « … *pour en quelque sorte sensibiliser les gens du secteur pétrolier afin qu'ils rendent un petit peu de ce qu'ils gagnent aux pays où ils prennent le pétrole* » (Interpreter E)

In this example, "oil people" was interpreted into "*pétroliers*", "*compagnies pétrolières*", "*gens qui font de la recherche pétrolière*" and "*gens du secteur pétrolier*". None of these rendering are word-for-word translations. In particular, *compagnies pétrolières* means 'oil companies' and shows that the English term was interpreted instead of being taken literally. As to the rest of the sentence, the word "*butin*" ('loot') used by interpreter A, the expression "*les profits*" used by interpreter B, "*sensibiliser*" ('raise the awareness') show the interpreters' understanding of the economic meaning of the situation and of the moral stance taken by the speaker. Many similar examples of the interpretive nature of comprehension during conference interpreting have been given by other authors, in particular by Seleskovitch and Lederer of ESIT. Such observations only confirm the difference between human interpreters and translators on the one hand, and machine translation programmes based on linguistic analysis on the other. The latter's failure can be attributed to their present inability to relate linguistic signs to knowledge of the world so as to disambiguate and solve other problems arising from the author's linguistic errors, mistakes in substance, and deviations from standard language and logic.

One might also add that the comprehension effort is probably more intense for interpreters than it is for conference delegates, i.e. the people to whom the speaker is talking (see also Chapter 8 and Chapter 9):

–   While they are interpreting, interpreters have to concentrate on everything the speaker says whereas delegates can select the information they are interested in.
–   The interpreters' relevant extralinguistic knowledge, and often the terminological part of their linguistic knowledge, are less comprehensive than the delegates'.

It follows that comprehension during interpreting is a non-automatic process. As will be explained later in this chapter, it is also critical in terms of processing capacity management.

2.2.2   *The Production Effort*

This is the name given here to the 'output part' of interpreting. In simultaneous inter-preting, it can be defined as the set of operations extending from the mental represen-tation of the message to be delivered to speech planning and the performance of the speech plan, including self-monitoring and self-correction when necessary.

As in speech comprehension, the impression of effortlessness in speech produc-tion is deceptive. Matthei and Roeper stress that (1985: 114),

> … the fact that virtually all people make many false starts, add ums and ahs, and often speak ungrammatically, suggests that production may be making quite a number of very substantial demands on our linguistic systems.

According to Holmes (1988: 324), "Speakers' efforts to realize their intentions are sel-dom completely fluent and error-free." For Clark and Clark (1977: 226), "Speaking is problem solving." Such problems become particularly salient in hesitations associated with the search for lexical units and with syntactic decision-making (Maclay & Osgood 1959): it often takes time to find the right word, and it often takes time to decide how to steer the sentence at a syntactic junction. Hesitations are the main symptom that makes speakers and their listeners aware of speech production difficulties. Hesitations are also the main factor that determines effective speech rate, i.e. the number of words actually uttered per unit of time, as opposed to the more mechanical articulation rate (Goldman-Eisler 1958; Clark & Clark 1977; Costermans 1980).

Speech production problems account for a number of interesting phenomena. One of them is that speakers tend to "be tempted and constrained to having recourse to ready made verbal sentences, phrases and clichés" (Goldman-Eisler 1958: 67–68). Cherry (1978: 79) explains that "We become prone to verbal habits. It is only too easy to use clichés, proverbs and slogans as a substitute for reasoned statements." Goldman-Eisler found that "Fluent speech was shown to consist of habitual combinations of words such as were shared by the language community and such as had become more or less automatic" (1958: 67), and concludes that meaning itself may be "guided through these channels and modified as a result" (1958: 68).

These observations suggest one reason why speech production under interpreting conditions may be difficult. People who speak on their own behalf are free to speak their own mind and bypass possible production difficulties by rearranging the sequence of information and ideas, or by dropping or modifying some of these or using standard phrases which are not necessarily quite in line with their initial message. In contrast, interpreters find themselves forced to follow rather closely the path chosen by another speaker, if only because waiting for a sentence to finish before starting to interpret it would cause excessive short-term memory load (see the discussion of memory load later in this chapter). In addition, "habitual combinations of words" generally differ from language to language, which makes the interpreter's speech production task more difficult than the speaker's – at least in this respect (see also the discussion of speech production in Chapter 9).

On the other hand, the very fact that lexical and syntactic choices are made by the speaker can in some cases help the interpreter, if s/he can make similar or 'parallel' choices in the target language, or at least use them in some way when retrieving words from his/her mental lexicon and making his/her own syntactic choices. Such verbal piggy-back riding is often done, at times consciously, and seems to help interpreters speak faster than they can when they have only their natural fluency to rely on – but entails risks, as explained below.

If an interpreter uses source-language words and structures to construct his/her own target-language speech, the speech production process becomes more vulnerable:

- Following the source-language structure and lexical choices in one's target-language speech is risky because the interpreter may get stuck because of syntactic and grammatical differences between the languages.

In a training session in the classroom, one student tried to interpret into French the following English sentence by following its structure and the speaker's lexical choices:

"This movement was shown by our team as consisting of three parts …"

The student started with: "*Ce mouvement a été montré par notre équipe …*", which mirrors the English sentence structure, and could not construct a natural, grammatical segment to complete the sentence, as French does not allow the passive of the verb *montrer* (to show) to be followed by a structure similar to "as consisting of." A natural translation of the sentence into French would have put "team" in the beginning of the target version, in something like:

Notre équipe a montré que ce mouvement se compose de trois parties …

("Our team showed that this movement consists of three parts")

- Besides the risk of getting stuck, when following the target-language structure and lexicon, interpreters may find themselves deprived of part of their own favourite productive linguistic resources as speakers (words and structures) which they might put to use if they were to produce a speech on the basis of meaning rather than on the basis of a linguistic structure borrowed from another speaker, in another language at that.
- Third, such transcoding is associated with great danger of linguistic interference between the two languages, be it gross interference resulting in grammatical errors, mispronunciations and false cognates, or more discrete interference that will make the interpreter's speech more hesitant, less idiomatic, less clear, less pleasant to listen to.

– Fourth, by focusing on language, the interpreter is in greater danger of processing the incoming speech more superficially than if s/he produced the speech from the meaning. This may generate more errors, because the interpreter will do less plausibility-testing (see Chapter 5).

For all these reasons, which they do not necessarily explain in so many words, interpreting instructors tend to say that the rule to be followed whenever possible is to produce the target-language speech on the basis of the meaning, not the words of the source-language speech (but see Chapter 9 on the role of Translinguistic Equivalences).

The fact that interpreting constraints force interpreters to deviate from their habitual speech production patterns may account for the poor quality of language output in students' interpreting exercises. In a naturalistic study conducted on five native speakers of French at ESIT, Paris, during a whole academic year (Gile 1987), the number of deviations from acceptable linguistic standards (as indicated by native informants) per sequence of 100 words was measured in three types of exercises: presentations by the students, exercises in consecutive and exercises in simultaneous interpreting. The target language was French in all cases. Deviations were found to be more numerous in consecutive than in presentations, and more numerous in simultaneous than in consecutive. Interestingly, most of these deviations did not seem to be due to interference between source and target language, at least not in any direct, visible way. No systematic comparison was done with the output quality of professional interpreters, but scrutiny of consecutive and simultaneous interpreting transcripts from other experiments seems to suggest that overall, linguistic deviation rates in professionals are much lower (however, see Alonso Bacigalupe 2006 for different findings). It appears that the effects of interpreting constraints on production are stronger in simultaneous than in consecutive, probably because of differences between the two modes, both in processing capacity management and in time constraints – the two are obviously linked.

A further difficulty, already mentioned for the Comprehension Effort in Section 2.1, arises from the fact that interpreters often have to produce speech in fields with which they are not necessarily familiar. Neither are they always familiar with the particular sociolect used by the relevant groups with respect to words, particularly technical terms, and phraseology – the same issue was highlighted in previous chapters when discussing written translation. Again, speech production in interpreting is clearly a non-automatic operation.

2.2.3   *The Memory Effort*

During interpreting, short-term memory operations (up to a few seconds) succeed each other without interruption. Some are due to the lag between the moment speech sounds are heard and the moment they are interpreted: phonetic segments may have to be added up in memory and analyzed until they allow identification of a word or phoneme.

To take only one example, when spelling a name and saying "D as in Denmark," phonetic features of the sound carrying 'D' may have to be held in memory until the word 'Denmark' is recognized, which makes it possible to recognize 'D' as opposed to 'T'.

Other short-term memory operations are associated with the time it takes to produce speech (selecting the appropriate words and syntactic structures and implementing the speech plan), during which interval the idea or information to be worded has to be maintained in memory.

Still others may be due to individual characteristics of a given speaker and/or his/her speech: if the speech is unclear because of its logic, information density, unusual linguistic structure or speaker's accent, the interpreter may wish to wait for a short while before reformulating it (in simultaneous) or taking notes (in consecutive) so as to have more time and a larger context to deal with comprehension and reformulation difficulties.

Language-specific factors may also require short-term memory operations. Inversions in determination sequences are one example, for instance in "System and application strategy" (from a Data Processing conference). The sequence was translated into French as "*stratégie en matière de systèmes et d'applications*." The sound and/or meaning of "System" and "application" had to be stored in short-term memory until after the interpreter heard the English word "strategy" and had said "*stratégies en matière de*".

Short-term memory operations fall under the category of non-automatic operations because they include the storage of information for later use (see Richard 1980, cited earlier). Furthermore, stored information changes both from one speech to another and during speeches as they unfold, and both stored information quantities and storage duration can vary from moment to moment, so that there is little chance for repetition of identical operations with sufficient frequency to allow automation of the processes.

3. Working memory

As explained in Chapter 1 and elsewhere in this book, in order to optimize the basic concepts and models for training purposes, they are kept simple and I have tried to avoid theoretical components to which students cannot relate in their daily interpreting experience. However, over time, the concept of working memory from cognitive psychology has come up again and again in the analyses of interpreting found in the literature. It also helps gain better understanding of the Effort Models presented later in this chapter and is useful in the analysis of some language issues (see Chapter 9). It is therefore briefly mentioned here.

Psychologists traditionally make a distinction between long-term memory (what we refer to as 'memory' in everyday life) and short-term memory, which is the ability to keep information and process it over a short period. A third type of memory, called sensory memory, as well as the interaction between the three, will be introduced in Chapter 9. Short-term memory has been investigated by many cognitive psychologists over the past decades. It is considered an important determinant of cognitive operations and is now sometimes referred to as 'working memory' (though 'short-term memory' is a fairly generic concept while 'working memory' is more specific). In 1974, Baddeley and Hitch developed a model of working memory with a specific structure and operational components, including a 'Central Executive', a modality-free cognitive mechanism which coordinates the operation of the other entities in the model, namely a 'phonological loop' which holds information in phonological form and a 'visuo-spatial sketch pad' specialized in spatial and/or visual information coding. Baddeley and Hitch's model is described in most introductory books on cognitive psychology – see for example Eysenck and Keane 1990. Further research in the field naturally led to tests of its ability to explain and predict cognitive phenomena and then to other models with further ideas about its components, including specialized verbal working memory (Caplan & Waters 1998), about its operation, about is relationship to long-term memory. According to Miyake and Shah (1999), several ideas and theories about the components and operation of working memory compete in cognitive psychology circles (for a recent review, see Timarová 2008), and some authors even doubt the usefulness of the concepts of working memory as a separate entity, but a consensus can be found with respect to the following points:

1. Working memory is a set of mechanisms or processes involved in the control, regulation and active maintenance of task-relevant information in the service of complex cognition; it operates primarily on currently 'activated' information from long-term memory.
2. Working memory requires processing capacity
3. Working memory has a small storage capacity

As explained in more detail in Chapter 9, working memory is necessarily part of the language-comprehension process and of the speech-production process. It is obviously part of the Memory Effort and perhaps conceptually very close to it, but the Memory Effort is explained here in such a way as to be intuitively recognizable by students and professional interpreters as a step in the interpreting process which involves memory and memory operations, not as a conceptual entity from cognitive psychology. Readers may consider the Memory Effort as corresponding to working memory if they wish, but for reasons explained in Section 13, I prefer to talk about short-term memory and about the Memory Effort when referring to the mechanisms of interpreting in general and to invoke working memory only in more technical considerations.

4. An Effort Model of simultaneous interpreting

4.1 A first view of the model

Using these definitions, simultaneous interpreting (SI) can be modelled as a process consisting of the three core Efforts described above, namely the Listening and Analysis

Effort L, the Short-term memory Effort M and the Speech production Effort P, plus a Coordination Effort C which corresponds to resources required to coordinate the three other Efforts (Eysenck & Keane 1990):

(1) $SI = L + P + M + C$

(In this formula, the 'equal' sign should be interpreted as meaning 'consists of', not as an equality in the usual mathematical sense, and the 'plus' sign as some kind of 'addition' in a very general sense, not as the usual arithmetic addition).

In a somewhat oversimplified form (see below), this model depicts simultaneous interpreting as a process which involves a set of operations on successive speech segments. Each of them is heard and analyzed (L), then stored in memory for a short while (M), and finally reformulated in the target language (P).

4.2   Simplifications in the model

Before going into further analysis of the Model, two major simplifications which it incorporates need to be highlighted.

4.2.1   *The sequential linearity simplification*

It is convenient to think of the Listening, Production and Memory Efforts as handling sequentially Translation Units or 'speech segments' (or 'chunks' as they would be called in the psycholinguistics literature), which can vary in length from one to several words forming a clause or even a sentence (see the discussion of Translation Units in written translation in Chapter 5), in the order in which they were uttered by the speaker: if the source speech consists of successive segments A, B, C, D, E, F etc., Production could focus on segment A while segment B has been analyzed and is waiting in short-term memory for its turn to be reformulated, and segment C is being analyzed by the Listening and Analysis Effort. Generally, with the exception of anticipated segments, source-speech segments can be reproduced in the Target Text (Effort P) only after they have been understood (Effort L).

Reality is more complex, if only because of syntactic differences between the source- and target language which naturally lead to information-order changes in the target speech. Other phenomena can lead to similar results. For instance, when the initial words in a speaker's sentence are not clear, the interpreter may need to keep them in memory until they are well understood. By that time, more than one Translation Unit is stored in short-term memory and it is not clear which will be rendered first. Finally, linguistic and semantic anticipation as alluded to earlier occur frequently in speech comprehension, and interpreters sometimes find themselves voicing in their target speech ideas or information which the speaker has not expressed verbally yet, at least not fully.

Nevertheless, the linearity assumption remains a useful simplification for the purpose of explaining strategies and tactics in the daily practice of interpreting, as discussed in Chapter 8.

4.2.2   *The additivity simplification*

As indicated in Section 4.1 above, the 'plus' sign in Formula (1) is a symbol referring to additivity in a very wide sense, not in a strictly arithmetic sense. Because of the complexity of the operations involved, including the sharing of the interpreter's working memory by speech comprehension and speech production (see Section 3 and Chapter 9), it is difficult to assess the added cognitive load which can be attributed to each Effort at each time. Inter alia, processing capacity requirements for each individual Effort are probably determined not only by their individual needs, but also by their interaction. One relevant factor is possible interference between the two languages in contact, the avoidance of which requires special attention. Indeed, some linguistic interference from source language to target language is often felt in the field (see for instance Alonso Bacigalupe 2006), and interpreters are taught to be aware of the danger and fight it, for instance by striving to avoid using words and sentence structures similar to those used in the source-language speech whenever possible.

In the Effort Model, additivity of cognitive load is assumed only in the sense that overall, the simultaneity of two Efforts is associated with heavier load than the operation of one (such as the Listening Effort only), and the simultaneity of three Efforts leads to higher cognitive pressure than the simultaneous operation of two.

5.   Processing capacity–related problems in simultaneous interpreting

5.1   Operational requirements

At any time, one, two, or three of the core Efforts are active: at one point, the interpreter may be producing a speech segment which has been planned beforehand while the speaker has paused, in which case only one Effort is active; at other times, s/he may be listening to speech and maintaining information from the speech in memory but is not speaking or preparing reformulation yet, in which case two of the Efforts are active; finally, there is now ample evidence that at least part of the time, interpreters do listen and speak simultaneously (see Gerver 1975; Čeňková 1988), and all three Efforts are simultaneously active. Operational processing capacity requirements during simultaneous interpreting can therefore be represented as follows:

(2) $TR = LR + MR + PR + CR$

    TR   Total processing capacity requirements
    LR   processing capacity requirements for L
    MR processing capacity requirements for M
    PR   processing capacity requirements for P
    CR   processing capacity requirements for C

In this 'equation', the equality sign can be interpreted in its usual mathematical meaning, but the plus signs refer to some additivity in a very wide sense.

In order for interpreting to proceed smoothly, the following five conditions have to be met at any time:

(3) $TR \leq TA$

TA   total available processing capacity

(Total processing capacity requirements should not exceed the interpreter's total available processing capacity.)

(4) $LR \leq LA$

LA   being the processing capacity available for L

(5) $MR \leq MA$

MA being the processing capacity available for M

(6) $PR \leq PA$

PA   being the processing capacity available for P

(7) $CR \leq CA$

CA   being the processing capacity available for C

The last four inequalities state that processing capacity available for each Effort should be sufficient to complete the task it is engaged in.

The difference between the two types of prerequisites defined by inequalities (3) on one hand and (4) to (7) on the other is an important one. Condition (3) refers to the availability of sufficient processing capacity to cover the needs of all active Efforts. When it is not met, a situation of saturation arises. For instance, a speaker's utterance may be fast and dense, therefore requiring the processing of more information per unit of time and raising capacity requirements beyond what is available to the interpreter (see Chapter 8).

Problems may also arise even if processing capacity requirements do not exceed total available capacity. Sometimes, it is inappropriate allocation of available processing capacity between Efforts which causes problems. For instance, the interpreter may direct too much attention to producing elegant reformulation of a previously heard segment of the source speech, and may therefore not have enough capacity left to complete a Listening task on an incoming segment. Had s/he been content with a simpler reformulation, enough capacity would have been left over for the L Effort. Inappropriate management of processing capacity results in individual processing capacity deficits ('individual deficits') in one or several Efforts, i.e. a situation where one or several of conditions (4) to (7) are not met.

Some students may be put off by a mathematical formulation of these conditions. A metaphor can also be used to illustrate the same ideas: interpreting can be likened to the management of manpower in a company 'SI' which has a service agreement with other companies 'A', 'M' and 'P' and assigns and despatches employees to their sites to cover their needs. Each of the three client-companies 'A', 'M' and 'P' is engaged in projects with variable manpower requirements. Firstly (condition (3)), 'SI' must have enough employees to cover all the needs of its clients 'A', 'M' and 'P' on their respective sites. Secondly (conditions 4 to 6), at any time, a sufficient number of employees from 'SI' must be assigned to 'A', to 'M' and to 'P' to cover their respective requirements. If the total number of employees in 'SI' is sufficient but they have not been assigned and sent to the site of the right client at the right time, work cannot proceed smoothly on the three sites. Finally, within 'SI', a team 'C' must coordinate the assignments, that is, receive requests from the clients, see who is available to be sent to 'A', 'M' and 'P' and make the necessary arrangements . If operations are to proceed smoothly, there must be enough employees in team 'C' as well.

5.2   Problem triggers

As explained in the introduction, a major objective of the Model is to explain interpreting difficulties, in particular recurrent problems which are well known to the interpreting community and often mentioned in the literature but which have not been analyzed in the past using a common conceptual framework (such triggers include names, numbers, enumerations, fast speeches, strong foreign or regional accents, poor speech logic, poor sound, etc.). In the Effort Models framework, problem triggers are seen as associated with increased processing capacity requirements which may exceed available capacity or cause attention management problems, or with vulnerability to a momentary lapse of attention of speech segments with certain features. These triggers, as well as the interpreters' common responses to the problems they generate, are discussed in Chapter 8.

5.3   Failure sequences

Problem triggers do not necessarily lead to actual problems. For instance, a long name may come up at the end of a sentence rather than in the middle and be followed by a long inter-sentence pause. In such a case, the requirements of the Listening and Analysis Effort are nil for a while right after the name has been pronounced by the speaker, and the interpreter can devote his/her full processing capacity to the Memory and Production components. If the same name is followed right away by a new sentence, it can cause more problems, because the three Efforts will have to be engaged in other tasks as well.

Quality deterioration, when it occurs, is not necessarily detected by observers. Processing capacity problems may result in deterioration of the content of the target-language speech (errors, omissions, etc.) and/or of its delivery (linguistic output, voice, intonation, etc.). As explained in Chapter 2, distortions of content are not always easy to identify (for some empirical evidence of the lack of sensitivity of listeners to errors and omissions, see Gile 1995). As for characteristics of delivery, unless there is a clear difference from one moment to the next, it may be difficult to judge that an acceptable rendition of a particular speech segment could have been better had there not been a problem.

Also note that, as explained below, it may be difficult to associate a particular quality deterioration phenomenon with the specific problem it originated in, because quality degradation may occur at a distance and affect a segment which poses no particular problem in itself. It is therefore not easy to identify all deterioration sequences from the trigger to the consequences or vice versa. However, some of the processes are perceived clearly enough by the interpreters themselves to be described, and theoretical models provide plausible explanations for phenomena observed in the field and help devise tactics and strategies for improved interpreting (see Chapter 8).

The simplest type of failure sequence can be exemplified by a momentary attention deficit affecting the Listening and Analysis Effort. This may result in the auditory loss of information in an incoming segment such as a name or number, which the interpreter fails to identify or understand and subsequently to reproduce in the target-language speech. In another simple failure sequence, an unexpectedly difficult segment comes up in the source-language speech, and because it is unexpected (a word in a foreign language, a name appearing out of the blue, a word which does not belong to the particular language register used, etc.), the interpreter has not allocated enough resources to the Listening and Analysis Effort and cannot complete the listening and comprehension task successfully; again, this results in his/her inability to render the information in the target speech.

Insufficient availability of processing capacity for an Effort may also be the consequence in a whole chain of events which can last several seconds: for instance, the interpreter may be devoting too much processing capacity to the Production Effort in an attempt to produce elegant wording in the target speech; this leaves him/her with insufficient processing capacity for the Listening and Analysis Effort, an ulterior speech segment is missed, and cannot be rendered. Alternatively, s/he may have engaged considerable resources in the Memory Effort, for instance in the translation of a long name such as "*Association internationale des villes francophones de congrès*" into English; some reordering of the informational sequence is needed in order to produce "International Association of Francophone Conference Cities", and this takes time and processing capacity at the expense of capacity left for analysis of succeeding incoming segments, which may therefore be missed. In this context, it is interesting to note that in her experiments on relay interpreting, Mackintosh (1983) observed that when numbers (a well known problem trigger – see also Mazza 2000) were rendered correctly, neighbouring segments were missed. Similar observations were made in more recent studies around other problem triggers (see also Section 9).

Following are two other possible scenarios:

–   A long name comes up in the source speech, and the interpreter chooses to interrupt or slow down the reformulation of a previous segment so as to concentrate on the name. S/he may then want to reproduce it as soon as possible in the target speech so as to unload memory and avoid saturation. By the time this is done, the previous segment may have been forgotten.
–   Bad pronunciation by a non-native speaker forces the interpreter to devote much processing capacity to the Listening and Analysis Effort, and therefore slows down production. This results in lag which in turn overloads the Memory Effort and results in loss of information from memory. Alternatively, memory is not overloaded, but production becomes very difficult because the interpreter has to accelerate in order to catch up with the speaker, which results in deterioration of output quality or decreased availability of processing capacity for the Listening and Analysis Effort and in the loss of a later segment.

Many other sequences are possible, resulting in the possible loss of segments that may not be difficult to understand or translate under normal circumstances but happen to be processed at the wrong moment, that is, at a time when not enough capacity is available to the relevant Effort for successful completion of the task at hand.

5.4   Anticipation

The usefulness of anticipation, often underscored by interpreters (see Chernov 1973, 2004; Moser 1978; Déjean Le Féal 1981; Cartellieri 1983), also becomes clear when analyzed through the Effort Model for simultaneous interpreting. Two types of anticipation are considered here: 'linguistic anticipation' and 'extralinguistic anticipation'.

5.4.1   *Linguistic anticipation*
The probabilistic nature of speech comprehension is widely accepted. In every language, words follow each other not at random, but with highly differentiated probabilities ('transitional probabilities'): for instance, in English, the probability that an article will be followed by a noun or an adjective is high and the probability that it will be followed by another article or a verb is low. Beyond general grammatical rules, collocations and standard phrases offer obviously high probabilities for specific word sequences. Knowledge of such rules, albeit unconscious, helps reduce uncertainty and thus also reduces processing capacity requirements in speech comprehension. Such 'linguistic anticipation' is viewed as very central in human language perception by Richaudeau (1973: 21). It appears, in particular in studies on reading, that subjects use transitional probabilities when identifying words (see Hörmann 1972: 97-101). All other things being equal, the more numerous and the higher transitional probabilities are in language as it is used and

the better they are known to the interpreter, the less processing capacity is required for speech comprehension. A high level of linguistic proficiency implies not only that one knows words and structures and can recognize them, but also that one has good knowledge of transitional probabilities and can use them in comprehension. Such high proficiency is difficult to assess in most everyday situations in which all or nearly all available processing capacity can be allocated to the listening task. In simultaneous interpreting, two other Efforts compete with the Listening and Analysis Effort for processing capacity, and mastery of transitional probabilities can become critical.

The potential importance of anticipation in interpreting can be seen very clearly in the case of Japanese. Japanese speeches offer many predictable sentence endings: from a certain point on, the informational content of the sentence is virtually ended. A naturalistic study of Japanese conference speeches reported in Gile 1992a suggests that they are numerous and can be rather long, up to more than 6 syllables and lasting more than one second. In the same paper, a theoretical analysis of potential implications is presented. In particular, Gile believes that interpreters working from Japanese may find considerable cognitive relief in such sentence endings. So far, it has been difficult to test this assumption directly due to methodological difficulties – as explained earlier, it is difficult to detect in the interpreter's online output the influence of any single factor – but modern brain imaging technology might open new avenues by making it possible to measure online cortex activation parameters at a high spatial and time resolution and perhaps detect changes when predictable sentence endings are identified by the interpreter.

5.4.2   *Extralinguistic anticipation*

Besides so-called 'linguistic anticipation', good knowledge of the conference situation, of the subject and of the speaker and good understanding of the unfolding statements often make it possible to anticipate ideas and information expressed in speeches. 'Anticipation' is defined here as some knowledge of the probability of the speaker reacting or speaking in a particular way in the context or situation at hand, not necessarily as the exact prediction of the speaker's world.

For instance, if during a debate on a problematic issue, a speaker starts his/her statement as a reaction to the opinion uttered by the previous speaker with the words: "No, Mister Chairman, I do not think that….", interpreters may anticipate that the statement will express disagreement. If in the course of a debate at a UN agency on the election of representatives to a committee, an African speaker says "Madam Chair, Europe, Asia and the Pacific as well as the Americas are represented in the committee, but there is no….", depending on the context, interpreters may expect words to the effect that there is no member from the African continent. Sometimes, a speaker refers to a diagram projected on screen and describes it. The interpreter, who can see the diagram as well, can see what part of it the speaker is referring to and anticipate with some accuracy what s/he is going to say.

Note that the distinction between 'linguistic' and 'extralinguistic' anticipation is made for didactic purposes, because of the practical implications, just as the distinction was made between 'linguistic' and 'extralinguistic' knowledge (Chapter 4), but depending on the type of analysis performed, one could well challenge the existence of a fundamental difference between the two.

~

Basically, the more anticipation reduces uncertainty, the more cognitive relief can be expected from it. This is where extralinguistic knowledge and conference preparation (see Chapter 6) become important. By using documents and preparatory briefings in order to acquire knowledge about a conference, that is, about relevant facts, names, ideas, terms and expressions likely to be referred to or used respectively during the conference, interpreters increase their ability to anticipate and therefore decrease processing capacity requirements for their Listening and Analysis Effort, and sometimes for their Production Effort. More capacity is left for tasks which require it, and risks of saturation can be reduced.

6.   An Effort Model of consecutive interpreting

The initial Effort Model was developed for simultaneous interpreting. Using the same principle, a similar Model was developed for consecutive interpreting. Note that this section deals with what AIIC members call 'true consecutive', in which the speakers' uninterrupted utterances are at least a few sentences long, as opposed to sentence-by-sentence consecutive in which there is no systematic note-taking.

Consecutive interpreting is performed in two phases, the comprehension phase (or listening and note-taking phase), and the speech production (or reformulation) phase.

Phase one: listening and note-taking

(8)   Interpreting = L + N + M + C

L   Listening and Analysis
N   Note-taking
M   Short-term Memory operations
C   Coordination

During this phase, L is the same Listening and Analysis Effort as in the simultaneous mode, and M is similar to the Memory Effort in simultaneous interpreting. In simultaneous, it is associated with the time which elapses between the moment a speech segment is heard and the moment its content is reformulated in the target language, deliberately omitted or lost from memory. In consecutive, it is associated with the time between the moment it is heard and the moment it is written down (if it is written down) or processed mentally and sent on to (long-term) memory. As to the Production Effort, during the first phase of consecutive interpreting, it is devoted to the production of notes, in contrast to the production of structured natural language as in simultaneous interpreting. The implications of this difference are discussed later in this section.

Phase two: target-speech production

(9)   Interpreting = Rem + Read + P + C

    Rem   Remembering
    Read   Note-reading
    P   Production

In phase two, the Rem component is the set of mental operations devoted to recalling the successive parts of the original speech from long-term memory and is therefore different from the short-term M component. At first sight, phase two may seem more difficult than phase one, with its long-term memory (Rem) and note-reading (Read) Efforts. However, if notes are good, they help perform Rem operations and may actually reduce Rem processing capacity requirements rather than increase them. Interpreters occasionally mention the role visual memory plays in recalling the speech: indeed, when notes are taken according to a few simple layout rules (see Rozan 1956), the layout itself can be hypothesized to act as a visual stimulator of memory regarding the logical structure of the speech. Furthermore, while phase one is paced by the speaker, in phase two the interpreter is free to perform the three Efforts and allocate processing capacity to each at his/her own pace, which also reduces pressure on the Coordination component.

In the reformulation phase, unlike the situation in the comprehension phase or in simultaneous interpreting, the interpreter does not have to share processing capacity between tasks under high cognitive load, and for competent interpreters with adequate mastery of their working languages, there are no problems arising from an accumulation of tasks under the pressure of time resulting in capacity requirement peaks. This is why, in terms of processing capacity, only phase one seems to generate potential threats of saturation. Operational requirements are defined as inequalities (10) to (14) as they were for simultaneous interpreting through inequalities (3) to (7) in Section 5.1. In consecutive, they apply to the comprehension phase, not to the reformulation phase.

Similarly to the case of the simultaneous interpreting model, the following conditions must be met at all times in order for consecutive interpreting to proceed smoothly:

(10) $LR + NR + MR + CR \leq TA$

(11) $LR \leq LA$

(12) $NR \leq NA$

(13) $MR \leq MA$

(14) $CR \leq CA$

When inequality (10) is not true, saturation may occur. When inequalities (11), (12), (13) or (14) are not true, failure may result in spite of the possibility of total available capacity being larger than total requirements.

Consecutive interpreting, processing capacity and note-taking

The fact that in consecutive, speech comprehension and speech production are separated in time is a major difference which distinguishes it from simultaneous. It lowers markedly the pressure on target speech production as well as short-term memory load arising from syntactic differences between the source language and the target language: interpreters can take down information in notes as it arrives, as opposed to simultaneous, where they have to keep it in short-term memory until it can be put together and reformulated into a succession of natural-sounding target language sentences. The fact that during the second phase of consecutive interpreting, more capacity and time are available for speech production than in simultaneous may explain why some interpreters who refuse to work into B in simultaneous are willing to do so in consecutive.

As for the first phase, which is paced by the speaker, it does not necessarily generate the same constraints as simultaneous, because note-taking allows more freedom than speech production. Note-taking is not governed by rules of linguistic acceptability – lexical, syntactic, stylistic, or otherwise. As explained below, notes can be taken with much latitude. When processing capacity requirements for the Listening and Analysis Effort become high, some resources can be freed by reducing the quantity of notes being taken. In simultaneous, slowing down speech production results in some lag, which has a cost in Memory Effort load and may have to be made up later at the expense of increased capacity requirements for Production. In consecutive, reducing the amount of information that is written down in notes does not necessarily result in much increase in information to be stored in short-term memory and reformulated in the target language at a later stage. Below are a segment from a speech and an approximate reproduction of one professional interpreter's notes (from an experiment reported in Gile 2001):
Source-language speech

> "... because every child has the same needs, and the right to a basic education, the right to food, the right to shelter, and the right to basic health and every child needs a friend ..."

Consecutive notes

```
    all same
    rights      ed.
                shelter
                health
    need friend
```

As can be seen, words such as 'because', 'every child', 'needs' and 'basic', as well as gram-matical words, were not written down by the interpreter, who nevertheless rendered faithfully the whole segment. This illustrates the latitude in note-taking mentioned above. Notes do not reproduce the speech; they are only written indications to help the interpreter remember it.

During the first phase of consecutive interpreting, problem triggers are similar to those found in simultaneous interpreting. The main difference between the two situ-ations is associated with the manual nature of note-taking: it requires more time than speech production because hand movements are slow, and therefore lead to some lag, hence to a higher pressure on short-term memory, which may in turn reduce the capac-ity available for the Listening and Analysis Effort. This has implications. For instance, single-word names which are recognized by the interpreter need not be problematic in simultaneous, but if they need to be written down and are long, they can trigger problems in consecutive.

It could be argued that note-taking requires less time than speech production in simultaneous, because notes can take the form of single words, abbreviations, draw-ings and symbols, whereas speech production in simultaneous requires the construc-tion of full sentences. Furthermore, as highlighted above, only part of the information is taken down while the rest is committed to (long-term) memory. This is true enough. However, for whatever information is written down, the time factor becomes important, especially when the interpreter does not have a readily available symbol or abbreviation for the information, and as shown by a number of empirical studies (see Section 5.3), lag at local level can impair the interpreter's ability to render the source speech suc-cessfully further down the road.

It follows that in terms of processing capacity, note-taking is critical, which explains and justifies the large volume of literature it has generated, from Rozan (1956) to Matyssek (1989) to a number of recent empirical studies (including Andres 2000; Gile 2001; Dam 2004a, b; Albl-Mikasa 2006 and several MA theses from China reported in various issues of the *CIRIN Bulletin* at www.cirinandgile.com). The criti-cal nature of note-taking is the focus of a classroom experiment (Gile 1991a) which demonstrates that students who have not yet mastered its principles and techniques tend to miss more names (used as an indicator – see Gile 1984b) when interpreting after taking notes than when they do not take notes (see a description of the experi-ment in Section 12).

In the interpreting community, there are differing opinions as to the desirable quantity of notes, the language in which they should be taken, the use of symbols, etc. Note-taking is an area in which the concept of processing capacity can be useful but has only recently been used extensively in performance analysis. The basic question is how to reduce processing capacity and time requirements of note-taking while main-taining the efficiency of notes as memory reinforcers.

Viewed from this angle, symbols and abbreviations are an attractive tool, provided they have been fully mastered by the interpreter – otherwise, retrieving them from one's memory when they are needed for writing may take up too much time and processing capacity. The much-decried idea of learning a large set of symbols rather than making them up when needed may therefore have distinct advantages.

The same line of reasoning can be applied when considering whether it is preferable to take notes in the source language or in the target language. Some interpreting instructors recommend taking notes in the target language, arguing that this fosters analysis during the comprehension phase and does away with the need to 'translate' in the reformulation phrase. On the other hand:

– Thinking of target-language 'equivalents' in the source language while listening takes up extra processing capacity,
– This is done during the listening phase, which is critical in terms of processing capacity, and may therefore increase risks of saturation,
– The extra time and processing capacity required in order to 'translate' source-language notes during the reformulation phase do not jeopardize the interpreter's performance, since reformulation is self-paced, with little risk of saturation.

A reasonable alternative would be taking notes in the target language when cognitive pressure is not too high and reverting to source-language notes when close to saturation. In an experiment, Dam (2004a,b) found that students tended to take notes in their A language when the going got rough irrespective of whether it was the source language or target language, but these data which reflect the performance of students are not enough to generalize. Until enough empirical evidence is available, it is difficult to say which position is of more practical value, but instructors do seem to agree on the need to save both time and processing capacity in note-taking.

7.   Efforts in sight translation

Sight translation is less frequent in conference interpreting than simultaneous or consecutive (but is very common in signed-language interpreting – according to a personal communication by Carol Patrie). It consists in 'reading' a source-language text aloud in the target language. It occurs when delegates receive a text and want to have it translated orally on the spot, or when a speech segment has been read from a text which is then handed over to the interpreter who is asked to translate it orally. It can be modelled as follows:

(15)   Sight translation = Reading Effort + Memory Effort + Speech Production Effort
       + Coordination

In sight translation, what was the Listening and Analysis Effort in simultaneous becomes a Reading Effort, and the Production Effort remains, but while short-term memory is necessary to identify and understand speech segments as it is in simultaneous or consecutive, longer-term retention of words and clauses until they are enlisted for target-speech production is less of a problem because of the continued availability of the information in the text.

Pressure on short-term memory therefore seems lighter in sight translation than in simultaneous or consecutive (as it is assumed by cognitive scientists to be lighter when reading than when listening to spoken discourse – see Michael *et al.* 2001: 240). Moreover, sight translation is self-paced, not paced by the source-language speaker. It would therefore be tempting to consider cognitive load less heavy in this particular translation modality than in interpreting.

On the other hand, in the Reading Effort, sight translators are not helped by vocal indications such as the speaker's intonation, hesitations or other pauses which are found in simultaneous and consecutive interpreting and which help them segment the text into Translation Units. Moreover, in contrast to consecutive, while reading, they cannot devote all their efforts to understanding the meaning of the text but must think of its translation as well in order for their target-language rendition to be smooth enough. This may pose little difficulty when the two languages are syntactically similar and when the source text is written in a style easy to segment, in particular when sentences are short and made up of independent clauses. When sentences are long and/or include embedded clauses, it may be necessary for the sight-translator to read much more than one Translation Unit before reformulating it, which involves more time and more effort, both in the reading component and in short-term Memory during production. This occurs inter alia when translating from languages such as German or Japanese into French or English. The same difficulty arises in consecutive and simultaneous interpreting, but, as noted above, in sight translation there is no help for segmentation from the speaker's voice.

When the text is given to interpreters in advance, they can take care of this particular difficulty partly or fully by reading sentences and preparing their segmentation mentally before sight translation, or by inserting handwritten slashes in the appropriate places. It is meaningful that many interpreters seem to perform this operation before they do anything else, including writing down target-language equivalents of source-language terms. Sight translators may also write numbers above words in a segment which will have to be reordered in the target language, as in:

2	4	3	1
Interamerican	Tropical	Tuna	Commission

To be translated into French as:

> *Commission* (1) *interaméricaine* (2) *du thon* (3) *tropical* (4)

When prior preparation is possible, Effort load can be reduced considerably.

Another major difficulty in sight translation is important in the initial training context: in interpreting, and especially in consecutive, the sounds of the source-language speech disappear rapidly from the interpreter's memory, permitting the reconstruction of the speech from its semantic content with little interference from source-language words and linguistic structures; in sight translation, these remain present before the practitioner's eyes throughout the operation (though the reader's gaze focuses only on a small text segment each time). This increases the risk of interference between the two languages and calls for more intense anti-interference efforts than in interpreting, making it a difficult exercise for beginners in spite of the facilitating factors described above.

8.   Simultaneous interpreting with text

Simultaneous interpreting with text is a very common interpreting modality, inter alia in speeches at international conferences, when speakers read a text which has also been given to interpreters.

Simultaneous interpreting with text is associated with the following Efforts:

(16)   Simultaneous Interpreting with text = Reading Effort + Listening Effort + Memory Effort + Production Effort + Coordination Effort

This combination of simultaneous interpreting and sight translation has the following features:

On the facilitating side:

–   The existence of vocal indications from the speaker, though these may not be as helpful as in ad-libbed speeches, because pause and intonation patterns when reading are not the same as when planning and producing speech online in ad-libbed statements (see an interesting analysis in Déjean Le Féal 1978).
–   The visual presence of all the information, which reduces memory problems and the effect of acoustic difficulties and unusual accents as well as the probability of failures due to insufficient processing capacity in the Listening and Analysis Effort. In other words, the Reading Effort and Listening Effort cooperate to a large extent – but they also compete, as explained below.

On the negative side:

–   The high density and peculiar linguistic constructions of written texts as opposed to oral discourse, which require more processing capacity in the analysis component (see Halliday 1985; Brown & Yule 1983).
–   Increased risks of linguistic interference, as explained above for sight translation.

–   The added cognitive load arising from the need to follow both the vocal speech
    and the written text. Two associated risks are noteworthy:

a.   Since all the information is present in the text, students often try to translate
     all of it even when delivery is too fast and they are being outdistanced.
     In such cases, saturation may occur and important speech segments may
     be lost.
b.   Speakers often deviate from the written text by adding comments, changing
     segments or skipping segments. When interpreters focus on the written text,
     they may miss these changes.

In conclusion, classroom experience shows that simultaneous interpreting with text is
a difficult exercise, but it does seem to make interpreting feasible under acoustic and
delivery conditions which would make it more difficult, and sometimes impossible
without the text.

Instructors insist that precedence should be given to the speech as it is heard from
the speaker, not to the text, but students generally feel a strong temptation to rely
on the text, which appears safer than the speech because its content remains available in 'solid' print whereas words disappear rapidly – and so does their memory. The
key to good simultaneous interpreting with text is good processing capacity management with the right balance between processing resources allocated to listening and
resources allocated to reading.

9.   The Tightrope Hypothesis

The full relevance of the Effort Models in explaining interpreting difficulties only appears
in conjunction with the 'Tightrope Hypothesis'. The Tightrope Hypothesis says that most
of the time, interpreters work close to saturation, be it in terms of total processing
capacity requirements or as regards individual Efforts because of high Effort-specific
requirements and/or sub-optimized allocation of resources to each of them. Without
the Tightrope Hypothesis, the natural assumption would be that available processing
capacity is sufficient to cover all the needs and that interpreting failures are due to
insufficient linguistic or extralinguistic knowledge or mistakes rather than to chronic
cognitive tension between processing capacity supply and demand.

Evidence for the Tightrope Hypothesis is mostly anecdotal, but it is massive:
many authors of texts on interpreting report that they or others experience frequent
interpreting failures not because they do not have the necessary knowledge at their
disposal, but because speeches are "too fast" or "too dense", in other words because
they do not have the capacity to process them rapidly enough. In many studies in the
literature, findings are explained explicitly or implicitly on the basis of the assumption

that interpreters work close to their maximum capacity (a Tightrope situation) even though the Tightrope Hypothesis is not necessarily named by the authors.

Evidence of a more 'scientific' nature (though indirect) comes from empirical studies. In one such study, Gile (1999a) had 10 professionals interpret simultaneously the same speech twice in a row. While many errors and omissions made during the first pass disappeared in the second pass, other segments which were interpreted correctly the first time were interpreted incorrectly the second time. In view of the fact that interpreting conditions were the same both times and that during the second pass, the interpreters had the advantage of previous familiarity with the speech, it is difficult to explain these new errors and omissions by factors other than processing-capacity limitations which left little room for sub-optimal allocation of attentional resources. This experiment was replicated by Matysiak (2001), who found similar results. Other evidence comes from a study (Gile 2001) which predicted specific difficulties in simultaneous interpreting vs. consecutive interpreting of the same speech on the basis of the Tightrope Hypothesis and which found errors and omissions consistent with the hypothesis. More indirect evidence comes from other studies in which problem triggers were found to affect adversely neighbouring segments (see inter alia Mazza 2000; Puková 2006; Cattaneo 2004 respectively on numbers, names and idiomatic expressions).

Note that no specific attempt at falsification has been carried out so far and that the evidence does not make it possible to identify the cognitive components which suffer most from limited capacity. Nevertheless, available evidence and the absence of criticism of the idea in interpreting circles and in the literature seem to grant reasonable credibility to the Hypothesis, which is central to the discussion of strategies and tactics in training and in the professional practice of interpreting.

10. The Effort Models and translation

Is processing-capacity saturation more frequent in the simultaneous mode or in the consecutive mode? Which of the Efforts require more capacity on average and under what specific conditions? What are the most frequent processing capacity-related errors in simultaneous and in consecutive interpreting? No answers are available to these questions yet because of the paucity of quantitative studies of processing capacity in interpreting.

One hypothesis that can probably be accepted as true even without such quantitative studies is that the risk of processing capacity saturation is far lower in written translation than in either mode of interpreting. In terms of Effort Models and for the purpose of the comparison between translation and interpreting, written translation can be modelled as:

(17)   Translation = Reading Effort + Writing Effort

In translation there is virtually no competition between Efforts, since all the available capacity can be devoted alternately to the Reading and analysis Effort and to the writing Effort. Moreover, as recalled elsewhere in this book, unlike interpreters, translators can generally read source-text clauses and sentences several times, and improve their target-language renderings iteratively.

This is an important but all too often forgotten point in the debate on the similarities and differences between interpreting and translation. Analysts tend to focus on linguistic differences between spoken and written language and point out that mastery of one does not imply mastery of the other. They also say that interpreters have to be faster than translators. These two conditions can be partially analyzed in terms of processing capacity, as shown above and as explained in Chapter 9.

Even when translators do have excellent mastery of spoken language in everyday communication conditions, it may not be adequate for simultaneous interpreting in view of the simultaneity and competitive relationship between the core Efforts in this interpreting mode. This could explain why translators who seem to understand and speak the two languages just as well as interpreters in everyday communication situations and who understand the basic principles and methods of interpreting and translation are sometimes found to be incapable of doing simultaneous interpreting (see also Chapter 9 on this issue). Processing capacity considerations could also explain why they can perform adequately in consecutive in fields they know well: because there is no overlapping of listening and speaking as in simultaneous interpreting, consecutive interpreting does not impose high pressure on speech production, and because of their familiarity with the subject, they anticipate much of the content of speeches and require little note-taking, both of which reduce markedly processing capacity requirements.

Finally, besides task-dependent processing capacity requirements, good processing capacity management (allocating and shifting processing capacity between the various Efforts) is important for interpreting. It takes some training to achieve good capacity management performance (see Pinter 1969), and expertise studies in cognitive psychology suggest that the improvement process continues over years. This is probably another reason why translators without specific training in interpreting find it particularly difficult to interpret in spite of their familiarity with the themes and mastery of the relevant languages.

These considerations suggest that possibly what separates interpreters from translators, besides the points already made in Section 4 of Chapter 5, is not so much a set of different personality patterns and professional attitudes or 'cultures' as a lack of oral production and comprehension practice and of attention-management training in translators – and perhaps a lack of training in editorial skills in interpreters.

11. Processing capacity and interpreting students

At the present time, little is known about the baseline status and possible changes over time of student interpreters' (and professional interpreters') total available capacity. Carroll (1978: 266) notes that:

> It is assumed that individuals vary not only in terms of their cognitive information, but also in the speed and facility with which they store, retrieve, and manipulate elements of information.

Just and Carpenter (1992) stress the existence of high inter-individual variability in working memory performance. An important question is whether it is possible to develop this capacity (and if so to what extent) through appropriate training or otherwise. Over the past decades, a number of empirical studies have focused on the interpreters' working memory performance by measuring memory span (see for example Padilla *et al.* 1995; Bajo *et al.* 2001) and the ability to perform certain tasks in interpreting (Liu 2001). Differences have been found between experienced interpreters and students, but these measured specific aspects of working memory performance rather than overall 'processing capacity'. Many other studies compared interpreting performance in beginning students, advanced students and professionals, but differences shown could be due to factors other than improved working memory performance, including knowledge acquired during training and work and higher availability of language for production and comprehension (see Chapter 9).

It is therefore difficult to say whether some kind of baseline processing capacity 'capital' increases during interpreter training, the term 'capacity' meaning storage capacity and/or computational efficiency of the interpreter's cognitive resources. What is likely is that over time, students learn to manage their available processing capacity (the Coordination Effort C) more efficiently and that processing-capacity requirements of the Listening and Analysis Effort and of the Production Effort decrease due to enhanced linguistic and extralinguistic knowledge and higher language availability for the relevant lexicon and language structures (see Chapter 9). It is generally difficult to identify the contribution of any of these factors in performance improvements, but there are some clear-cut cases: when students are told to construct simple sentences with simple words when interpreting into their B language, the aim is to reduce capacity requirements in the Production Effort by using highly available lexical units and by doing away with extra load arising from the planning and execution of complex speech plans; when they are advised to cut German sentences into small segments in German-to-French simultaneous interpreting (Ilg 1978: 88) or to try to stick closely to a fast speaker rather than lag behind (this lag is known as EVS or 'Ear-Voice Span'), they are given advice for capacity-management.

A small number of capacity-management tactics are taught in interpreting schools. Some attention-division exercises such as listening to a speech and counting backwards or shadowing are also advocated by some instructors as preparatory exercises before starting to study simultaneous interpreting (see for example Moser 1978; Lambert 1989, 1992; Watanabe 1991). Other teachers oppose shadowing, claiming that it is inefficient and dangerous because it allegedly fosters repetition with limited analysis (Thiéry 1989; Seleskovitch & Lederer 1989). At present, there is no experimental or other evidence supporting either of these views (but see de Groot's interesting observations on the relative efficiency of holistic exercises versus component exercises in de Groot 2000). Nevertheless, many if not most teachers do use some shadowing exercises in their interpreting classes, and many instructors consider them useful and important in preparing students for simultaneous, an opinion which is defended by Lambert (1992). In Japan, this is apparently the view of a large majority of interpreting teachers (see the first issue of *Kuootarii Tsuuyakurironkenkyuu*, reviewed in Gile 1992b).

Regardless of whether such component-skill training is used or not, much improvement seems to come from interpreting exercises held in the classroom and in practice groups, and later from the professional practice of interpreting – but how much is associated with increased processing capacity as opposed to better linguistic and extralinguistic knowledge, better language availability (see Chapter 9) or better processing capacity management remains unclear.

12. Teaching suggestions

Compared to most other chapters in this book, this chapter is definitely on the theoretical side. The concept of processing capacity and the Effort Models are central to the general conceptual framework offered to students and seem to be efficient in helping them understand many difficulties they experience as well as interpreting strategies and tactics advocated by teachers, including conference preparation, guidelines for work into one's B language, note-taking in consecutive and language skills enhancement (taken up in Chapter 9).

The concept of processing capacity can be introduced to interpreting students toward the beginning of the syllabus, for instance after the fundamental concepts and models around quality and fidelity (Chapters 2 and 3). The idea is to show them that listening for interpreting purposes requires more attention than listening in everyday life.

One way of demonstrating the fact it to make a short, informationally dense presentation, and then ask a student to repeat its content in the same language. In virtually every case, part of the information will have been missed. Other students are then asked what was omitted. Whenever one such piece of information is mentioned by one student, the class is asked who 'did not hear it'. It turns out that generally, some students will claim they did not hear particular words or ideas, at which point the instructor can point out that they did hear them, but did not register them because they were not listening with enough attention.

This can be used as a starting point to explain the basics of oral speech comprehension, including the fact that in most ordinary listening situations, listeners do not maintain a uniformly high level of concentration on the incoming speech, hence the 'listening losses'. The instructor can then move on, introduce the students to the role of processing capacity in speech production and explain the hesitations associated with the retrieval of words and with syntactic decision-making in speech production.

This will be facilitated by the students' new awareness of their own speech production problems, which is generally observed early on when they start studying interpreting (see Gile 1987). When they start exercises in consecutive with note-taking, the instructor can explain the Effort Model of consecutive, possibly using the following experiment for awareness-raising (already mentioned in Section 5):

Students are divided into two groups for an exercise in consecutive interpreting. One group is instructed to take notes and the other to refrain from doing so except as regards numbers, names, and technical terms if necessary. A short presentation containing several names is made, and a student is asked to interpret. Whenever s/he reaches a name, students are asked to indicate whether they heard the name properly. At the end of the exercise, the proportions of names 'heard' correctly among members of both groups are compared. In replications I have carried out in class, it turned out that students who did not take notes 'heard' the names better than the ones who did. The explanation, namely the idea that note-taking took away some of the processing capacity initially available for listening, can be a good starting point for the presentation of the whole model.

After they have been introduced, the Effort Models can be recalled whenever difficulties are analyzed and strategies and tactics are presented.

13. The Effort Models and cognitive psychology

Over the years, I have endeavoured to check the compatibility of the Effort Models with current theories in cognitive psychology, which I believe is the most relevant reference discipline since the phenomena under consideration come under the general framework of interpreting cognition. In informal talks, psychologists have told me that the principles on which the Effort Models are built are in line with current theories. Some, who are interested in simultaneous interpreting, cite them without criticizing them as they would probably criticize theories from within cognitive psychology. I believe they do so because these models are well known in the interpreting community, not because of their value for or in terms of cognitive psychology. For the sake of clarity, I should like to highlight some of the differences between their structure and underlying philosophy and models and theories in cognitive psychology.

Most importantly, the Effort Models were designed with a didactic purpose in mind, not for research purposes: they set out to explain well-known, recurrent difficulties in interpreting as well as advice given to students to overcome them, not to explore reality for the purpose of developing a theory which would explain and predict an increasing proportion of phenomena observed in the field until replaced by another theory which would explain and predict reality more accurately. In particular, they remain holistic, with no attempt to specify and test systematically the components of each Effort and their inter-relations. A comment by Eysenck and Keane (1990: 116) on the theory of attention as a central capacity (a general theory, which does not address interpreting) is relevant here:

"Perhaps the main argument against continuing to postulate the existence of attention of central capacity is that it has not proved fruitful in terms of deepening our understanding. For example, it is very easy to "explain" dual-task interference by claiming that the resources of some central capacity have been exceeded.... However, such reasoning singularly fails to provoke any further, and more searching, examination of what is happening."

This criticism, in line with the essential exploratory nature of scientific research, could well be applied to the Effort Models by cognitive psychologists. These models seem to work well as an explanatory framework, which is the very reason why they were developed in the interpreter training environment, but perhaps they "fail to provoke any further and more searching examination of what is happening".

Not unrelated to that is a clarification in response to some authors who write that the Effort Models have not been tested as a theory. Theories which require 'testing' in the sense of Popperian falsification are those which make claims. The Effort Models are basically a conceptual framework rather than a theory in the Popperian sense (i.e. one which should be formulated in such a way as to make it testable for the purpose of revealing its weaknesses if any so as to foster the development of alternative theories). What needs to be verified is the consistency of the concepts and principles on which it is based with current theories and findings in cognitive psychology. In this respect, the following points can be made:

1. The idea that human performance in cognitive tasks, including speech comprehension and speech production, relies on a limited amount of processing capacity, has been a mainstream idea in cognitive psychology and psycholinguistics since Kahneman's capacity theory of attention (1973) – as can be checked in virtually any textbook of cognitive psychology. Inter alia, Caplan and Waters (1998: 2) state that "Appeal to the notion of a limited capacity working memory system (or to equivalent concepts such as "processing resources") to account for features of human cognitive performance is widespread in cognitive psychology". The idea that maintaining information in short-term memory has

a cost in processing capacity is also in line with current thinking in cognitive psychology. So are the ideas that allocation of attention is at least partly deliberate and that coordinating several cognitive actions during the same time span also has a cost in processing capacity (see for example Gopher 1992; Newman *et al.* 2007).

2. What could be more problematic for cognitive psychologists is the definition of the 'Memory Effort'. If it is the same as working memory (WM), depending on the model of working memory chosen, one could argue that since working memory is a major component of both the Listening Effort and the Production Effort, it would be more logical to divide simultaneous interpreting into a Listening Effort, a Production Effort and a Coordination Effort while acknowledging that demands placed on WM are often heavier in interpreting than under ordinary conditions of speech comprehension and speech production.

    As recalled repeatedly in this chapter and elsewhere in this book, the Effort Models and other models presented here are essentially didactic and have been developed in such a way as to be immediately understood by student interpreters. Interpreters and students are aware of the fact that while interpreting, they need to store some information which they will later need to recover, and while some information storage and retrieval operations are subconscious (in the course of the Listening Effort and of the Production Effort), some are conscious and deliberate, with choices regarding what information to render immediately in the target language or take down as notes and what to store tactically while waiting for more information which will help understand it, confirm it and/or reformulate it into the target language. The 'Memory Effort' as defined in the Effort Models is what they experience consciously and can relate to both conceptually and in the choice of words. I feel that referring to specific working memory models as developed in cognitive psychology would be counterproductive both because teaching their architecture would be an inefficient overkill in view of the students' needs (understanding that short-term memory operations take up processing capacity and that they rely on a system with limited capacity) and because they tend to change rapidly.

    Nevertheless, the limited storage capacity of WM as well as its processing capacity requirements as demonstrated to be paramount in language comprehension and production (inter alia) by psychologists do play a central role in the Memory Effort.

3. The competition-between-Efforts principle is consistent with the theory of one central pool of processing capacity, not with the theory that there may be several pools that the Efforts can draw upon without there being interference between them. While the idea that working memory (or verbal working memory) is shared (see Caplan *et al.* 1998) can bridge the gap by explaining that all efforts need this central resource even if they also use processing capacity from other pools, the issue is not addressed specifically in the Models.

4.   Finally, as explained earlier in this chapter, while much anecdotal evidence cor-
roborates the Tightrope Hypothesis, it has not been submitted to precise empirical
tests in compliance with the criteria of empirical research in experimental psychology. Note, incidentally, the similarity of the concept with Just and Carpenter's
analysis and ideas about the 'total amount of activation' (1992).

It is encouraging for an author of models from the Interpreting Studies community to find
references to them in publications by psychologists (for instance in Shreve & Diamond
1997; de Groot 2000; Bajo *et al.* 2001; Christoffels 2004; de Groot & Christofffels 2007;
Ruiz *et al.* 2007) but some of these authors' translation of concepts used in the Effort
Models into the language of psychology, for instance the transposition of the Memory
Effort into working memory and of the Coordination Effort into the Central Executive in Baddeley and Hitch's working memory model, indirectly involves assumptions
which are not part of the Effort Models.

14. What students need to remember

1.   Simultaneous interpreting can be viewed as a set of three core Efforts, namely the Listening
and Analysis Effort, the Production Effort and the short-term Memory Effort, each of which
takes up part of a limited supply of processing capacity.
2.   Problems occur when total processing capacity requirements exceed available
processing capacity (saturation), and when processing capacity available for a given
Effort is not sufficient for the task it is engaged in at a given time (individual deficit).
Such problems are frequent because interpreters tend to work close to saturation level
(Tightrope Hypothesis).
3.   Consecutive interpreting consists of a listening phase, followed by a reformulation phase. In
terms of processing capacity, only the former is critical.
4.   Note-taking is a major processing capacity-consuming component of consecutive. Note-
taking management is an important aspect of failure prevention. There are many valid
systems for note-taking, and adapting them to the interpreter's personal 'style' or creat-
ing one's own note-taking system are valid strategies. The main point to remember is
that note-taking should take as little time and processing capacity as possible so that the
Listening Effort can remain efficient.
5.   In sight translation and simultaneous with text, some of the pressure on short-term
memory disappears, but texts often have a higher density than ad-libbed speeches, and
there is increased danger of linguistic interference. When interpreting simultaneously
with text, it is important to give precedence to the speaker's voice rather than to the
written text.
6.   Processing capacity constraints account for major differences between the skills required
for interpreting and translation.

Chapter 8

Facing and coping with online problems in interpreting

1. Introduction

In spite of good preparation and extensive experience in many fields, gaps in one's Knowledge Base are inevitable, and interpreters do find themselves in situations where they do not understand a term or a sentence in the source speech or do not know an appropriate term to express a concept in the target language. More fundamentally, even when such knowledge is not lacking, as explained in Chapter 7, cognitive load-related factors made critical by the Tightrope situation lead to numerous errors, omissions and otherwise sub-optimal rendering of the source speech through either total saturation or individual processing-capacity deficits in one or several Efforts. Such phenomena seem to be so common that they can be considered part and parcel of interpreting. Interpreting has been referred to by some professionals as (permanent) "crisis management," and in the light of the interpreters' daily experience, this may be a (painfully) appropriate expression to describe an aspect of interpreting which is unknown to the public at large.

Difficulties affect both comprehension and production, often through *failure sequences* as explained in Chapter 7. When interpreters are aware of actual or potential comprehension and/or reformulation problems, they tend to use a rather small set of 'coping tactics' to limit their impact.

Coping tactics are a fundamental practical skill in interpreting. Basically, they are taught within the framework of practical exercises. In most training programmes, this is done by *trial and correction*, with trial on the student's part and corrections from the instructor. Such corrections are generally prescriptive; instructors sometimes refer to the communication impact of the tactics in order to explain their preferences, but are not necessarily aware of other factors which influence them.

This chapter first looks at various factors and circumstances under which cognitive saturation is likely to occur. It then offers instructors illustrative lists of basic coping tactics for a general view of the issues (no claim of comprehensiveness is made, and other authors have discussed different sets of tactics). It also presents a conceptual framework which spells out the advantages and drawbacks of each tactic, and discusses a few norms and 'laws' which may help explain what makes interpreters prefer one tactic over the other beyond their individual merits.

2.   When do online problems arise?

2.1   Cognitive saturation and failure

2.1.1   *Chronic reasons*
The term 'chronic' is used here deliberately to refer to situations where an interpreter's cognitive skills and declarative knowledge (extralinguistic knowledge, knowledge of words and rules of grammar, etc.) are not sufficient to allow him/her to deal success-fully with the competing Efforts. This may reflect the particular cognitive potential of an individual, but also a provisional status of students or beginning interpreters who have not yet acquired the necessary cognitive skills (procedural knowledge). These include language skills, but also other skills, including rapid shifts in allocation of pro-cessing capacity (Liu 2001) and appropriate implementation of coping tactics (see later in this chapter). They are assumed to improve over time with practice and guidance from instructors. Practice will help automate whatever component processes can be auto-mated (see de Groot 2000) and reduce processing capacity requirements with increasing expertise, and guidance from instructors will direct students towards the best decisions.

2.1.2   *Occasional reasons*
The term 'occasional' is used here for cognitive saturation triggers which may be encoun-tered under specific circumstances in interpreters who have acquired operational-level expertise, as opposed to chronic weaknesses as referred to above.

Occasional reasons for cognitive saturation can be associated with objective fac-tors which have to do with linguistic, semantic and physical features of the source speech (problem triggers) as well as with the particular communication environment at hand (high stress, noisy environment, lack of specific background knowledge), or with subjective reasons such as an interpreter's momentary attention lapse or errors in processing capacity management.

2.2   Cognitive problem triggers

2.2.1   *Problems arising from an increase in processing capacity requirements*
a.   *High density of the source speech* increases processing capacity requirements, because more information must be processed per unit of time. This affects both the Listening and Analysis Effort and the Production Effort (speech production in simultaneous and note production in consecutive), as the interpreter's speech and note-taking are paced by the speaker. High speech density is probably the most frequent source of interpreting problems.

High speech density can be associated with:

   –   A *high rate of delivery* of the source speech. Note that some speakers produce rapid speech but provide little information, in which case speech density remains low.

- *High density of the information content* of the speech or of particular speech segments, even in rather slow speeches. In particular, *enumerations* are dense, as they consist of information elements put next to each other without grammatical or other words or word groups of low information density in-between. Prepared speeches that are *read* by the speaker are generally devoid of the hesitations, filled or unfilled, which characterize ad-libbed speech and lower density. Generally, they are also more densely formulated than spontaneous speech (see Halliday 1985 and Déjean Le Féal 1978).

b. *External factors* such as deterioration of the *quality of the sound* coming through the interpreter's earphones, a noisy channel, or other sources of sound interference also raise the Listening and Analysis Effort's processing capacity requirements (see Gerver 1974b for a study on the influence of 'white noise' in the interpreter's headset). *Strong accents* and *incorrect grammar* and *lexical usage* also increase the Listening and Analysis Effort's processing capacity requirements. So do *unusual linguistic style* and *reasoning style*.

c. *Unknown names* composed of several words increase capacity requirements for the *Memory Effort* unless they are very familiar to the interpreter in the target language. For example, the English name 'International Association of Conference Interpreters' translates in French into *Association internationale des interprètes de conférence*. If the interpreter does not know the French name, in order to translate the English name, s/he has to scan it mentally, decide that its second term should be translated first, then scan mentally the name again while keeping in (working) memory the information that the second term has already been translated, decide that the first term of the English name comes next, scan the name again and decide that 'of' is translated into *de*, scan the name a fourth and a fifth time and decide that the fourth term, and then the fifth term should be added to the French version, while keeping the decisions and their results in (working) memory. Such names are indeed very difficult to interpret, as illustrated by an experiment described in Gile 1984b (see below).

d. As explained in Section 3, *saturation* can occur through an increase in processing capacity requirements in the Short-term Memory Effort when the source language and target language are syntactically very different and force the interpreter to store a large amount of information for some time before being able to reformulate it in the target language. This is often the case in interpreting between German and English (see Wilss 1978; Kurz 1983) or Chinese and English or French (Dawrant 1996; Li 2001) to take just two examples – but there are many.

e. More generally, low anticipability of the source speech, which can be due to the speaker's personal style rather than to linguistic or cultural features or to flaws in his/her rationale, can have the same effect (see also Section 4).

2.2.2   *Problems associated with signal vulnerability*

Some speech segments do not necessarily require much processing capacity but are more vulnerable than others to a momentary processing capacity shortage because of their short duration and low redundancy and because consonants, vowels and syllables may sound very much alike. Such is the case of *numbers* and of short *names*, including *acronyms*. The briefest lapse of attention may cause information to be lost. In an experiment conducted with 15 professional interpreters who were asked to interpret a recorded speech containing 8 names, the ratio of correct rendering was very low even for very simple names such as "Jim Joseph" (Gile 1984b). This is the second type of problem-generation pattern referred to in Section 5 of Chapter 7, which results not from saturation, but from insufficient availability of processing capacity for one of the Efforts.

3.   Language-specificity related problems

Some theoreticians consider that interpreting is an intellectual task which, when working languages are well mastered, transcends them (Seleskovitch 1975). Some even claim that practitioners only rarely notice specific differences between languages while interpreting, since "ideas which are expressed clearly pose no comprehension or reformulation problems" (Seleskovitch 1977). Other authors hold a different opinion, when referring to the specificity of interpreting between German and French (Ilg 1978; Le Ny 1978), German and English (Will 1978) or Japanese and English (Fukuii & Asano 1961; Kunihiro, Nishiyama, & Kanayama 1969). Authors who deny that interpreting is language-specific are not always consistent in their assertions. For instance, Seleskovitch does advocate structuring the notes in consecutive as a function of the target language, which amounts to an acknowledgment of some language specificity of interpreting (Seleskovitch 1981: 40).

3.1   Possible language-specific differences in speech perception

Those who oppose the idea that interpreting is language-specific say that speech comprehension is the same in interpreting as it is in everyday conditions, and that it is the same in all languages (Lederer 1981; Seleskovitch 1981). While the fundamental mechanisms underlying speech comprehension in everyday life and in interpreting may be similar, the high cognitive pressure to which interpreters at work are submitted could make them sensitive and vulnerable to small language-specific differences that may not have significant implications under usual speech-comprehension conditions.

In studies of differences in reading performance between college-student readers of different working memory capacities, Just and Carpenter found small and often negligible differences when the comprehension task was easy, but large and systematic differences when it was demanding. They explain that limitations could affect performance only when the resource demands of the task exceed the available supply (Just & Carpenter 1992: 124). This could be the case in interpreting, as already explained in the context of the Tightrope Hypothesis in Chapter 7.

3.1.1   *Differences in the perception of words*

Content words, that is, mostly nouns, verbs, adjectives and adverbs, are important carriers of information in language. In terms of length and phonetic diversity, their distribution in different languages may differ statistically, and they may be on the whole more or less redundant morphologically and phonologically and more or less vulnerable to momentary lapses of attention.

Japanese *kango* (words written with Chinese characters) are probably more vulnerable than content words in most European languages, as they combine shortness with limited phonological variety (with a total of 50 syllables) as well as a high rate of homophony (a large percentage of words in Japanese vocabulary are pronounced identically). The findings of a study by Gile (1986a), in addition to the interpreters' own statements (see for instance Ito-Bergerot 2006: 227), seem to corroborate the idea that Japanese *kango* do pose at least occasional problems in speech comprehension which are far less frequent in languages such as English, French, German, or Spanish.

3.1.2   *Grammatical redundancies*

Grammatical redundancies decrease the information density of language and may offer a second, third, or fourth chance to recover information lost during its initial oral presentation.

For example, in 'Five dogs', the ending 's' provides a second time the information that there is more than one dog, and in '*La nouvelle directrice*', the information that the 'director' is a woman is provided three times: through '*la*' (as opposed to '*le*'), through the ending '*-elle*' in '*nouvelle*' (as opposed to '*nouveau*'), and in the ending '*-trice*' in '*directrice*' as opposed to '*directeur*'.

Grammatical redundancies are more numerous and frequent in some languages than in others. Again, in both Chinese and Japanese, they are much less frequent than in most European languages; as to the latter, some like Finnish, German, Greek, Slavic languages have kept them in complex declension systems, while in others (English, French, Spanish, Italian, Swedish etc.) they have practically disappeared.

3.1.3   *Syntactic structures*

It is a common view among psycholinguists that some syntactic structures facilitate comprehension and others make it more difficult by reducing the comprehender's ability to anticipate or by increasing processing capacity requirements, especially with respect to short-term memory (see for instance Richaudeau 1973, 1981; MacDonald 1997). Embedded structures, in particular, seem to impose increased pressure on the comprehender ("The man whose dog was chewing the bone that I had dropped a minute ago was reading a newspaper in German"). In some languages where determining elements tend to precede words and word groups that they determine, such as German and Japanese, there are many embedded sequences, which may make their comprehension more difficult under the high cognitive pressure of interpreting. The comprehension process of such sentences may even be qualitatively different from comprehension in languages where such sequences are few if analysis and short-term storage tactics differ in speech comprehenders. The issue is complex and I am not aware of studies that have tackled the problem in a comparative perspective, but there is no reason to rule out the possibility that such differences have significant implications in interpreting.

3.1.4   *Sociolinguistic aspects*

Besides each speaker's individual style, cultural factors also determine – to a varying extent – the way information is expressed in each language. In this respect, differences between the allegedly Cartesian style of the French; the formal, punctilious style of the Germans; and the more informal style of the Americans are sometimes mentioned in exchanges between interpreters. The alleged sociolinguistic characteristics of the Japanese seem to correspond more clearly to actual phenomena in the field. Some relevant principles of human communication between the Japanese are well known and have been documented extensively (see for instance Condon & Saito 1974, Mizutani 1981), and the analyses of two conference interpreters, Hara (1988) and Kondo (1988)). These include a certain unwillingness to take responsibility and to express personal opinions clearly; the Japanese also tend not to make very explicit statements about 'objective' information, and mutual understanding achieved without words is valued highly. All these are manifest in elliptic sentences, unfinished sentences, linguistically ambiguous structures. Lexical usage in Japanese also seems rather flexible (see for instance Gile 1984a). These features can produce comprehension difficulties, possibly more often than in French, English, or German, although no quantitative comparison seems to have been attempted to date (but see Ito-Bergerot 2006 and Kondo 2008).

Finally, a particularly interesting example of language specificity is that of predictable sentence endings, which, as explained in Section 5.4.1 of Chapter 7, may lower processing capacity load when interpreting sentence endings and could have further relief-affording effects on the beginning of sentences following them (Gile 2008). Sentence endings may be predictable in any language for semantic reasons, but at least as regards linguistic anticipation in conference speeches, they are more frequent in Japanese than in German, and more frequent in German than in English or French (Gile 1992a).

3.2   Possible language-specific differences in speech production

Possible language-specific differences in production are more difficult to pinpoint than possible difficulties in comprehension: production depends on the individual interpreter's selection of linguistic 'tools' (essentially lexical units and grammatical structures) most available to him/her, and less on the selection of linguistic components *by the speaker* being interpreted as in the case of comprehension – though the speaker's choice of lexical units and grammatical structures probably 'primes' cognate units and structures in the target language and therefore does influence the interpreter's production to a certain extent.

Besides speech-producer dependent factors, selecting lexical items and grammatical decision-making may be more difficult in some languages than in others because of differences in the variety of possible choices and in the flexibility of linguistic rules: a wide set of lexical items to choose from as opposed to a more restricted one, flexible or rigid lexical usage, the strength of collocations, the number of possible escape routes in sentence structuring in case the source language statement goes in an unexpected direction and forces one to reconsider one's options. The subjective impression of many interpreters is that English is more flexible than French and that Japanese is more flexible than English, with convenient escape routes up to the end of the sentence, but I am not aware of research which has demonstrated that such differences have practical implications. Nevertheless, the possibility that they matter cannot be ruled out at this time. There may also be differences in working memory load depending on grammatical agreement and other dependencies between various parts of the sentence which may require speakers to store grammatical information (such as gender or singular and plural or a particular verb tense) for a shorter or longer time when constructing sentences.

Another language-specific factor is the *similarity* or lack thereof between the source language and the target language in lexical, syntactic, and general informational terms. With respect to lexical units, phonetic or morphological similarity between the source-language word and a target-language word may accelerate the retrieval of an appropriate target-language word from long-term memory – even if it needs to be checked for interference (see Chapter 9). Syntactic similarity also means there may be less risk involved in anticipating and in shadowing the syntactic structures of the source speech. Such shadowing is associated with the risk of linguistic interference, but in critical cases such as very high delivery speed or informational density, it may become the best alternative. As for informational dissimilarity, as explained in Chapter 3, it is problematic inter alia when differences in Linguistically/Culturally Induced Information between the source language and the target language force the interpreter to:

- find roundabout ways to construct a meaningful, faithful and acceptable utterance in the target language when it requires information not provided in the source speech (for example, how do you express in Japanese an English utterance referring to one's brother without knowing whether he is younger or older than the speaker?),
- spend time and processing capacity deciding that it is acceptable to leave out some of the source-language information, or weigh the risks and make a decision based

on an educated guess (for instance, if a gender-bearing reference such as Mr/Mrs/Ms or s/he is required for a reference to a person and it is not known whether that person is male of female).

Another point regarding syntactic and informational similarities has to do with the *order of presentation of information* in the two languages involved. If it is different, this may involve higher workload for the short-term memory Effort, as information has to be stored for a while before it can be reformulated in the target language (see Section 2.2.1d above). Again, I am not aware of studies which have measured statistically the extent to which such factors change cognitive load during interpreting, but the existence and potential importance of these effects cannot be ruled out.

3.3   Culture-specific difficulties

Beyond linguistic parameters in the strict sense and linguistic/cultural parameters (such as differences in LCII), cultural differences associated with language communities may also be the source of online difficulties for interpreters. One example which is often cited in the literature on Japanese interpreting is that of deliberate ambiguity which characterizes Japanese speakers (see for example Ito-Bergerot 2006 and Kondo 2008). For cultural reasons, such speakers may tend to avoid clear answers, and in particular those which make commitments or express rejection of another person's ideas or requests. While such an attitude is acceptable and even favoured in some cultures, it may not be in other cultures, and the users of interpreting services may expect interpreters to provide them with 'clear' statements. Taking decisions related to such difficulties entails additional cognitive load and increases risk of saturation.

Note that the influence of such parameters can vary greatly across types of interpreted meetings. Typically, it may be insignificant in the utterances of speakers in specialized meetings where the relevant scientific or technical culture may be virtually uniform whatever the national background of the speakers, while its importance can be paramount in business and political negotiations.

3.4   Implications for training

While the relevance of language-specificity in interpreting has not been demonstrated empirically, arguments in favour of the hypothesis are strong, especially with respect to the implications of syntactic differences between the source language and the target language in simultaneous interpreting. For many practitioners and teachers of interpreting, language specificity has always been taken for granted in spite of counter-claims from a minority, albeit a vocal one, which were dominant in the literature from the early 1970s to the mid 1980s.

The non-specificity thesis has helped refocus the attention of interpreting teachers on issues such as attention, analysis, memory and communication variables rather than on linguistic issues, and can therefore be considered to have had some positive impact. However, I believe, as does Ilg (1980), that its proponents have gone too far and denied linguistic aspects of interpreting their rightful role.

The issue is by no means purely academic. Underestimating the importance of linguistic aspects of interpreting may lead to inappropriate strategies such as training students in part of their linguistic combination only under the assumption that the acquired skills will be transferred to their other language(s). Experience suggests that this is possible for the basics. It is possible to learn the basic mechanisms of consecutive interpreting even in monolingual programmes – that is, with exercises in which students interpret from one language *into the same language* (Feldweg 1980, 1989; Gile 1983a). The question remains whether teaching the basic mechanisms is enough to train *fully operational interpreters* in their specific language combinations. On the basis of conversations with interpreting instructors from numerous countries, I feel that most teachers believe that such basic mechanisms need to be fine-tuned in a language-specific context before they can be implemented effectively. When confronted with actual interpreting in their working languages, interpreters who have been trained in other language combinations often regress because of linguistic difficulties. A striking example is given in a paper by Karla Déjean Le Féal, who, after several decades of work as a conference interpreter with German, French and English, added Swedish to her language combination and found herself working as a beginner in many ways (Déjean Le Féal 2002). Such a situation forces one to retune processes in order to overcome new difficulties and take full advantage of new possibilities arising from the new linguistic combination. New language-specific tactics may have to be learned, as well as anti-interference strategies.

When considered from the gain-loss viewpoint, it seems that language-specific training is associated with much potential gain and little potential loss. The gain resides in the possibility of fine-tuning the implementation of principles and gaining *practical* experience during initial training. Beyond the implementation of methodological principles, language-specific training provides students with an opportunity to widen their vocabulary and increase availability of words and rules of languages they will need most often in professional practice (the issue of availability is discussed in detail in Chapter 9). The potential drawback lies in a possible loss of perspective, causing the student to focus on linguistic rather than methodological issues and to mistake the latter for the former. This risk is probably low if a solid consecutive interpreting foundation precedes training in simultaneous, as consecutive interpreting naturally promotes sound interpreting methods, away from excessive focusing on linguistic aspects. This is a strong argument in favour of having interpreter training start with consecutive.

Two further points should be made regarding these language-related and culture-related difficulties. Firstly, those mentioned in this section are examples which are often noticed in professional practice in the field. They are mentioned here because they have been under discussion in interpreting circles, but it is not claimed that the list is comprehensive. Secondly, the effect of these factors is presented as 'possible';

there is not enough empirical research to measure its actual magnitude in interpreting, and other factors, in particular the overall structure of the speech and its delivery (see below) may reduce their effective weight to a considerable extent.

4. The speaker factor

While features of language and culture are frequent sources of difficulties, a much stronger determinant of interpreting difficulty is the speaker factor, i.e. the way a particular speaker constructs and delivers his/her speech. Speeches are easier to interpret if constructed in a didactic, logically linear, coherent way, if the speaker has a good voice and clear pronunciation. Good prosody also helps. Relatively slow delivery of speeches can be said to reduce cognitive pressure on listening and production, but if it is too slow, information elements have to be kept longer in short-term memory before they can be integrated into target speech sentences, which may cause cognitive saturation. Perhaps more important than articulation rate is the relative length of intersentence pauses. Such pauses provide cognitive relief during which processing of the previous speech segments can be completed so that processing of the next segments is not hampered by imported load carried over from the previous sentence (see Gile 2008). The speaker factor can make all the difference in terms of interpreting difficulty.

~

All in all, besides the interpreter's knowledge and skills, numerous linguistic factors, cultural factors, environmental factors (such as the availability of documents, visual aids, overall redundancy of information in the meeting, quality of the sound etc.) and delivery-related factors interact in determining interpreting difficulty. This interaction is so complex that it is generally not easy to predict the overall difficulty of a given speech to a particular interpreter, though specific problems such as mentioned in Chapter 7 and earlier in this chapter can be anticipated.

5. Tactics in simultaneous interpreting

Many of the problems mentioned in this first part of the chapter are recurrent. Over time, interpreters have developed ways to deal with them. Scrutiny of the literature and discussions with conference interpreters from many countries, as well as visits to interpreting classrooms in various parts of the world, show that they are widely shared (language-specific tactics will not be dealt with here). In the second part of this chapter, the most frequent 'tactics' will be presented, explained and discussed. While in the

TS literature, such online decisions and actions are often called 'strategies', I prefer to reserve that term for planned action with specific objectives (for instance conference preparation strategies) and to opt for 'tactics' when referring to online decisions and actions. Also note that in contrast to usage in some other texts in the TS literature, my use of the terms 'tactics' and 'strategies' is restricted to *deliberate* decisions and actions aimed at preventing or solving problems, as opposed to spontaneous, perhaps unconscious reactions.

5.1   Comprehension tactics

The following are the main tactics used when comprehension problems arise or are perceived as threatening to arise under time-related or processing capacity-related pressure.

a. Delaying the response

When a comprehension difficulty arises in connection with a word or a sentence, interpreters may respond immediately with one of the other tactics presented below. However, they may also delay their response for a while (up to a few seconds), so as to have some time for thought while they receive more information from the source-language speech. After a while, they may have solved the problem entirely. If not, they may decide to resort to another tactic. Note that as explained in Chapter 7, some delay between the arrival of information into working memory and its integration into a target speech utterance is generally unavoidable. The delaying tactic referred to here is a deliberate decision arising in conjunction with a perceived difficulty.

Because of its very nature, the delaying tactic involves an accumulation of information in short-term memory, and is associated with the risk of losing speech segments in a failure sequence as outlined in Chapter 7.

b. Reconstructing the segment with the help of the context

When interpreters have not properly heard or understood a technical term, name, number, or other types of speech segment, they can try to reconstruct them in their mind using their knowledge of the language, the subject, and the situation (their *extra-linguistic knowledge*).

This reconstruction process is also an integral part of speech comprehension in everyday situations. It is defined as a tactic in the present context when it becomes a *conscious endeavour,* as opposed to an ordinary, subconscious process.

If successful, reconstruction can result in full recovery of the information. It may also entail some waiting until more information is available and therefore require time and additional processing capacity. Like the delaying tactic, it can therefore lead to saturation and/or individual deficits.

c.   Using the boothmate's help

In simultaneous interpreting, there are theoretically at least two interpreters in the booth at all times. One is *active* (producing a target-language speech), while the other is *passive* (listening, but not speaking). The passive colleague, who can devote his/her full attention to listening, has a better chance of understanding difficult speech segments than the active interpreter, whose processing capacity is shared by several Efforts most of the time. Moreover, on the production side, the passive interpreter can consult a glossary or another document, which takes up much time and processing capacity, and then give the information to the active colleague, generally in writing. The presence of a passive interpreter in the booth can therefore be a major asset for the active interpreter.

The active interpreter can ask for the passive colleague's help with a glance or a movement of the head. In teams that work well, the passive interpreter will sense a hesitation in the active colleague's speech and understand there is a problem. S/he can also anticipate problems and write down for his/her boothmate names, numbers, technical terms, etc. without even being asked for help.

When the problem is terminological, the boothmate may indicate to the active interpreter the *target-language term*, so that it can be used for reformulation. Alternatively, when the problem lies with a single word, name or number, the passive boothmate may write it down in the source language for the benefit of the active interpreter who did not hear it correctly. It is more difficult to explain *ideas* efficiently, because the active interpreter does not have time to read a long explanation, but body language sometimes does the job.

This tactic is a good one because it does not cost much in time and processing capacity, and pooling together the knowledge and intelligence of two persons, one of whom does not have to divide his/her attention under high cognitive pressure, provides a better chance of finding the information than using the resources of one person only.

In order for the tactic to work, the passive interpreter must be not only physically present in the booth, but also available and willing to make the effort to listen with attention and help the active colleague. This situation does not always occur:

–   Because of the intense effort involved in interpreting, interpreters feel strongly the need for rest. In teams composed of two members per target language, when conditions are difficult, interpreters may leave the booth when they have finished their active turn and only return shortly before they are on again, or else they may stay in the booth but shut themselves out and rest.

–   In conferences in which papers are to be read, documents are often given to the interpreters at the very last moment, and presentations are allocated individually to each member of the team. In such a case, all interpreters are busy reading their paper or interpreting, and no help is available to the active interpreter from other team members.

– For psychological and sociological reasons, including the awareness of one's weaknesses and some associated frustration, some interpreters do not like other colleagues to sit with them and listen while they are working.

It is important for instructors to point out the practical value of cooperation between interpreters as well as its importance in the framework of professional ethics aiming at offering clients better service. Practical aspects of such cooperation, involving in particular large and legible handwriting, should also be stressed.

d.   *Consulting resources in the booth*

When there is no passive colleague in the booth, interpreters can look for solutions in documents they have before them.

The efficiency of this tactic varies greatly: looking for a term in a commercial dictionary may require much time and processing capacity, but finding an important word in a document which was read and marked before the conference can be fast. This is why it is important to pay attention to both the preparation of documents and their management in the booth. Instructors should show students how to make important names and terms stand out for quick reference, using highlighters or other means. Writing important technical terms and names on a sheet of paper in front of the interpreter (beside the glossary prepared for the conference) is another way of making them readily available. Documents should be laid out in the booth, sorted and marked in such a way as to minimize the time needed to access them and to recognize their identification numbers or titles, possibly with different stacks for each language, sorted by numerical sequence, type of document, etc.

Over the past decade or so, the use of light portable computers in the booth has spread greatly. Such devices are a good alternative to paper documents: for a small volume and little weight they can carry the equivalent of numerous dictionaries, encyclopaedias and other reference books and documents. Moreover, with the spreading availability of Wireless connection to the Internet in conference centres, they often offer access to all internet resources. Finding information can be as simple as entering a word or part of a word in a 'search function menu', or a key word, perhaps with one or two more words to frame it, into the relevant box of an internet browser interface, thus requiring less time and attention than searching through multi-page paper documents. Nevertheless, consulting resources in the booth other than a one or two-page document containing just a few pieces of information remains a costly operation in terms of time and attention and should best be left to moments when the interpreter is not interpreting actively.

5.2   Preventive tactics

The following tactics are used when time or processing capacity pressure is such that the interpreter believes a problem may arise or is about to occur. The idea is to limit the risks of saturation or individual deficit (Chapter 7).

a.   Taking notes

When the speech contains figures and names that interpreters feel they may forget and that they cannot reformulate right away for syntactic reasons, they may take them down in notes rather than keep them in memory. While affording greater security as regards the items which are taken down, this tactic entails a cost in time because writing is slow. This increases the risk of losing other items of information that come before or after those written down (see Chapter 7). Again, this risk is reduced significantly when it is the passive colleague who writes down the information for the active colleague.

Interestingly, when translating in simultaneous from and into Japanese, some Japanese interpreters take down not only numbers and names, but also other information which 'Westerners' generally do not write (in this case, it is often the passive interpreter who takes down the information for the active colleague). The reason given by them is that syntactic structures differ greatly between Japanese and other (mostly Western) languages, which leads to much waiting before the reformulation of any specific part of a sentence, hence a possible overload of short-term memory and an increased risk of losing information. One is tempted to challenge the wisdom of this tactic because writing may increase lag and therefore working memory load as well, but the advantages may outweigh the disadvantages (the active interpreter does not *have* to read the notes taken for him/her by the passive colleague), something which only specific quantitative studies could determine if at all.

b.   Lengthening or shortening the Ear-Voice Span

By changing the Ear-Voice Span (EVS), that is, the time lag between the moment a speech segment is heard and its reformulation in the target language, interpreters can control to a certain extent processing capacity requirements for individual Efforts. By shortening the lag, they decrease short-term memory requirements; on the other hand, this deprives them of anticipation potential and increases the risk of misunderstanding an unfolding sentence and driving themselves into target-language sentences which will be difficult to complete if it turns out their anticipation was incorrect. By increasing the lag, interpreters improve comprehension potential, but may overload short-term memory.

Teachers sometimes advise students to try to lengthen or shorten their EVS in specific cases (for instance when encountering numbers), but I am not aware of a clear-cut, consistent theory or set of operational rules on the subject. It seems that EVS regulation is learned essentially through experience; I believe that this is one major benefit derived from *practice* in simultaneous interpreting during initial training, in addition to increased availability of relevant target-language elements (see Chapter 9) and automation of useful Translinguistic Equivalences (see Chapter 9).

c.   Segmentation and unloading of short-term memory

When faced with potential overload of memory, as with a source language and a target language that are syntactically very different, with embedded structures in the source language or with unclear sentence structures, interpreters may choose to reformulate speech segments earlier than they would normally, sometimes before they have a full picture of what the speaker wants to say. In such cases, they may resort to neutral sentence beginnings or segments in the target language that do not commit them one way or another (see Ilg 1978; Zhong 1984 quoted in Setton 1999). For instance, in a source-language sentence expressing a causal relationship such as:

> "Because of the complex character of equation (2) as shown above, compounded by the difficulty of finding a unique solution to equations (3) and (4) which correspond to a steady state system …"

the interpreter can say in the target-language something like:

> "Equation (2) as shown above is complex
> Equations (3) and (4) describe a steady system
> It is difficult to find a unique solution to them
> …"

While interpreting these segments, the interpreter will keep in mind the causal nature of the relationship, which will eventually be expressed by "Therefore …", "As a result…" etc.

Segmentation can save short-term memory capacity requirements by providing earlier relief to short-term memory. On the other hand, the very formulation of several grammatically complete short sentences instead of one may involve higher processing capacity requirements in the Production Effort. Recommendations can be given on a case-by-case basis.

d.   Changing the order of elements in an enumeration

Enumerations are high-density speech segments and impose a high load on short-term memory. One tactic often observed, related to the previous tactic, consists in reformulating the last elements first so as to free memory from the information, and then to move on to other elements. To my knowledge, no extensive analysis has yet been performed as to why this should reduce Memory Effort load. One possible explanation is that by reformulating the last elements first, it is possible to pick them up before they have been processed in depth and integrated fully into the semantic network, thus saving processing capacity. This tactic may work best with names, which can be reproduced from *echoic* memory (memory of the sound), or with terms which are easily transcoded; it may not be very effective if they cannot be transcoded or reproduced phonetically and require more processing capacity anyway.

5.3   Reformulation tactics

The following are tactics used frequently in reformulation. The first three are the same as those presented in Section 5.1 for comprehension.

a.   Delaying the response

This is the same tactic as used in comprehension, the idea being that the waiting period is used for a subconscious (or conscious) search for a missing term or sentence structure the interpreter cannot retrieve immediately from long-term memory, or for a socially/culturally appropriate way of rendering the message if rendering it as it was formulated initially is likely to cause problems. As was the case with comprehension, waiting entails a risk of short-term memory overload, as well as a possible increase in processing capacity requirements in the Production Effort when the information is eventually reformulated – because of the backlog that has accumulated in the meantime.

b.   Using the boothmate's help

As can be inferred from the descriptions in Section 5.1, the boothmate's help is more often given in the form of indications for *reformulation* than as explanations of what was said, which is reasonable in view of the strict time constraints involved.

c.   Consulting documents in the booth

Documents are often used in the booth for reformulation, in particular glossaries and dictionaries, with associated risks because looking for entries takes up time and processing capacity.

d.   Replacing a segment with a superordinate term or a more general speech segment

When interpreters find themselves momentarily incapable of understanding a speech segment or reformulating it in the target language, one possible solution is to reformulate the message in a less accurate manner by using a superordinate in the case of a single word, or by constructing a more general segment in the case of a whole clause or sentence: *"la streptokinase"* may be reformulated as 'the enzyme', *"Monsieur Stephen Wedgeworth"* as 'the speaker', *"deux cent trente trois millions"* as 'about two hundred and thirty million', *"DEC, IBM, Hewlett Packard et Texas Instruments"* as 'a number of computer vendors', etc.

This tactic, which requires little time, leads to loss of information in the target-language speech. This does not necessarily mean that the information is lost for the delegates; it may be repeated in another sentence in the speech, or be already known to them.

e. Explaining or paraphrasing

Interpreters may understand a term but not have available the appropriate equivalent in the target language, in which case they can *explain* it rather than translate it. In one conference in the early days of microcomputing, in the 1980s, the data processing term *tableur* (spreadsheet) was interpreted as "the programme which defines rows and columns and allows calculations to be made."

This tactic can be efficient informationally but has two drawbacks: one is the amount of time and processing capacity it requires, and the other is the fact that it may draw the delegates' attention to the fact that the interpreter does not know the appropriate term in the target language, possibly lowering his/her credibility and reducing the impact of the speech accordingly.

f. Reproducing the sound heard in the source-language speech

When encountering a name or technical term which s/he does not know or recognize, the interpreter may try to reproduce the *sound* as heard. This is not an 'intelligent' tactic insofar as it does not call for complex cognitive operations, but it can be efficient: if they know the name or term, delegates may 'hear' it as it *should* have been pronounced without even noticing that the interpreter has a problem. The approximation may also be detected and perceived as a distortion of the information, which may discredit the interpreter, especially if the name or term is well-known to the audience.

g. 'Instant naturalization'

When interpreters do not know the appropriate term in the target language, they may *naturalize* the source-language term, adapting it to the morphological and/or phonological rules of the target language. For instance, at a conference, the term *télédétection* (remote sensing) was rendered in English as "teledetection". At another conference, the English computer term 'driver', as applied to a software programme that helps operate a device such as a printer from a computer, was translated into French as "*driver*" (pronounced "dreevair").

This tactic may prove effective when the source-language and target-language lexicons are morphologically similar, as is the case of English and French medical terminology, and when there is much borrowing of terms into the target language in that particular field, for instance in information technology, where English is a loan language for most non-English speaking countries.

In these first two cases, the tactic often results in the interpreter 'inventing' terms that actually exist in the target language, as such naturalization may have been conducted previously by experts who needed the terms for their daily activity – the 'instantly naturalized' French versions of 'driver' cited above actually exist in the technolect of computer experts – there is also a French equivalent, the word *pilote*, which uses a slightly different metaphor. Also note that in some languages such as Japanese and Hebrew, borrowing lexical units (and even idioms in the case of Hebrew) from foreign languages, and in particular from English, is very frequent in daily life, and the interpreter's use of this tactic may not strike listeners as special in any way.

The instant naturalization tactic may also prove very effective when in their daily life, delegates read much written material in the source language. In such a case, they often recognize the 'naturalized' terms, which are likely to sound similar to the way they pronounce the words in the source language when reading.

h.   *Transcoding*

Transcoding consists in translating a source-language term or speech segment into the target language word for word. At a conference on accounting, the English term 'maturity date', the standard equivalent of which in the relevant context was *date d'échéance*, was interpreted as *"date de maturité"*.

For lexical problems, this tactic can be very efficient in the same cases as 'instant naturalization'. Like naturalization, it can also lead to existing target-language terms; in various fields, many terms have been created by such transcoding by experts, just as many terms have been created by phonetic naturalization. Even when transcoding does not lead to an existing target-language term, it may facilitate comprehension for the delegates because of the semantic indications the newly created term carries. At a dentists' conference, the English term 'mandibular block' (a type of anaesthesia) was interpreted as *"bloc mandibulaire"*, whereas the appropriate term was *tronculaire*. Delegates said afterward they had no trouble understanding *"bloc mandibulaire"*, even though it bore no similarity at all to the appropriate French term.

i.   *Form-based interpreting*

With respect to the transcoding tactic, it may be worth recalling that overall, for the reasons explained in Chapter 5 for translation, there seems to be agreement in the conference interpreting community that in order to optimize quality, interpreting should be done on the basis of meaning, not form: going through meaning instead of seeking direct linguistic correspondences allows better comprehension of the speaker's intentions and better reformulation in the target language with less linguistic interference and more idiomatic expression. Ideally, the transcoding tactic is only an occasional option when specific difficulties arise around a term or a small group of words. However, in case of fatigue or very fast speeches, when working in a cognate language pair, interpreters may give preference to what has been called in the literature 'form-based interpreting' (see for instance Dam 2001), relying essentially on source-speech words and syntax to guide them in producing the target speech. This mode of interpreting can lead to marked losses, especially in terms of idiomaticity and clarity, but some interpreters believe that at times it may salvage more information from the source speech than meaning-based interpreting. In a recent doctoral dissertation, Alonso Bacigalupe (2006) claims that form-based interpreting is perhaps more frequent than is suggested in the literature.

j.   Informing listeners of a problem

When interpreters believe they have missed an important piece of information, they may decide to inform the delegates of the loss by stepping out of their role as the speaker's *alter ego* and saying for instance "… and an author whose name the interpreter did not catch," or "… the interpreter is sorry, s/he missed the last number." When this happens, delegates may fail to react, but they can also ask the speaker to clarify or repeat the information, either on the spot or during a break.

This tactic is not used very often. It takes up time and processing capacity, and may therefore jeopardize the reformulation of other speech segments. Moreover, it draws the delegates' attention to the *interpreter's* problems. This has two drawbacks: first, delegates are interested in the speech, not in the interpreters and their problems; second, by drawing the delegates' attention to his/her problems, the interpreter may lose credibility, and therefore also indirectly weaken the impact of the speaker's message.

If important information is missed, conscientious interpreters consider it their ethical duty to inform delegates rather than gloss over it, but if the information is insignificant, or if informing the delegates may do more harm than good, they may decide to choose another tactic.

k.   Referring delegates to another information source

In specialized conferences, much of the information is given not only through the speakers' spoken words and body language, but also in written handouts and on screen, via slides, overhead transparencies and PowerPoint presentations. When encountering comprehension or reformulation difficulties, interpreters can refer delegates to "the figures/names/equation etc. on the screen/in your handout," etc.

This tactic is convenient and entails little loss and little cost in time and processing capacity.

l. *Omitting the content of a speech segment*

Interpreters may miss information without even noticing it because they did not have enough processing capacity available for the Listening and Analysis Effort when the speech segment carrying it was being uttered. They may also omit it because it disappears from short-term memory. The omission tactic discussed here refers to the case where an interpreter decides deliberately not to render in his/her target speech information present in the source speech. This can happen when a piece of information appears to have little value and other information with more value requires the interpreter's attention and may be lost if the unimportant part is rendered, for instance when the interpreter detects a high risk of saturation. In interpreted TV interviews, where synchronicity is essential, omitting the last part of a statement may be the best choice if the interpreter is a bit behind the speaker, especially when such a lag leads to some overlapping between the last part of an interpreter's rendering of a statement and the beginning of the next statement by another speaker.

Omission can also be the interpreter's choice if something grossly inappropriate was said and the interpreter feels strongly that if reproduced, it will cause major harm to the speaker's interests and/or jeopardize seriously the intended outcome of the meeting. An alternative to omission in this second case is attenuation of the offending words or ideas.

When information is omitted, it is not necessarily lost as far as the delegates are concerned – it may appear elsewhere or be already known to the delegates. This does not mean that the omission tactic can be selected lightly. It is unethical to omit deliberately important information without informing the listeners of the loss, and some interpreters (and clients) may challenge the legitimacy of the tactic in all cases and question the interpreter's ability to judge what is important and what isn't. However, situations of cognitive saturation where the only possibility of keeping interpreting and serving best the interests of the participants requires forced choices are rife in daily practice, especially with read speeches with dense passages, as are most speeches of important political personalities being interpreted live on TV.

When the decision to omit the content of a speech segment is taken by the interpreter because of its culturally or inter-personally inappropriate nature, the associated ethical problem is even more salient: what right does the interpreter have to play the gatekeeper? In court interpreting, such a decision is definitely unethical because of the particular norms involved. In personal and professional encounters between people from different cultural backgrounds where the stakes are diplomatic and/or interpersonal, the case for omission as a tactic is less difficult to defend, and many interpreters will admit that they have occasionally omitted or attenuated an inappropriate comment or joke in order to avoid a serious diplomatic incident (anecdotes can be found inter alia in Magalhaes 2007; Torikai 2009).

m. 'Parallel' reformulation

When working conditions are particularly bad and interpreters feel it is imperative to continue speaking despite their inability to understand and reformulate the source speech properly, they may *invent* a speech segment which is compatible with the rest of the speaker's statement.

This tactic is an extreme one, to be used exceptionally and with the uttermost caution, in cases where the content of the source speech is far less important than continuity in speech for the listeners' benefit (which may occur in some TV shows). I believe it should not be taught at the same time as other tactics. It is probably best left to the very end of training, when it is introduced very carefully, with explicit examples and strong emphasis on ethical considerations.

n. Switching off the microphone

This is another extreme tactic. In the 1960s and early 1970s, some purists advocated its use when working conditions are poor and interpreters feel they cannot do a decent job, perhaps in the hope that the resulting pressure would prompt organizers to provide interpreters with more documents. It is no longer taught in most training programmes and has become a rare choice in the field because it is now unacceptable to clients. It is probably safe to say that this tactic is only implemented when working conditions are so bad that interpreters believe they can do no useful work at all, meaning that *continuing to interpret would be worse than providing no interpreting* – and when they believe they can get away with it. Otherwise, they just continue interpreting, doing their best, perhaps after warning delegates that conditions are such that they cannot maintain good-quality interpreting.

6. 'Laws' in the selection of tactics in simultaneous interpreting

Interpreters do not choose tactics at random. They seem to follow 'laws' (the term is used here to name trends found in their behaviour, not in the sense of prescriptive rules), sometimes consciously, often unconsciously. Two of them correspond to norms which are corollaries of the fundamental Sender-loyalty norm (see Chapter 3), others do not.

Law 1: Maximizing information recovery (norm 1)

Interpreters generally consider it their duty to attempt to reformulate *all* of the speaker's Message in the target language (the Message being the intended information, as opposed to Secondary Information – see Chapters 2 and 3). Tactics leading to maximum information recovery such as reconstruction from the context, using the boothmate's help and consulting documents are favoured over replacing specific terms with superordinates, which entails a higher risk of immediate information loss in the target-language speech; this in turn is favoured over omission.

As stated earlier several times, the absence of information in the target-language speech segment does not necessarily imply that the information is lost to the delegates. The interpreter may decide to take the responsibility of deciding whether the information is already known to them or whether it may in fact be redundant, having been presented in another part of the speech or in an image on screen. Also note that information is not always at the centre of communication in exchanges interpreted simultaneously, a noteworthy example being TV shows (see below).

Law 2: Minimizing interference in information recovery

As explained in the framework of the Effort models in Chapter 7, because of time pressure, the way one segment is processed affects the availability of processing capacity for other segments. For that reason, maximizing the recovery of information in one segment may have a detrimental effect on the processing and transmission to the delegates of other information. The second law for the selection of tactics is based on this awareness by interpreters and on a view of information that rises above purely 'local' considerations: interpreters seek to recover as much information as possible on each segment without jeopardizing the recovery of other segments. On this basis, they favour tactics that require little time and processing capacity such as omission, naturalization and approximate repetition (tactic f) – over explanation, paraphrasing, and informing delegates of the problem.

Precedence is given to Law 1 or Law 2 depending on the importance of the relevant segments. When segment A is more important than its neighbouring segments B and C, the information-recovery maximization Law will prevail for segment A in spite of a high risk of interference. This is consistent with the idea, explained in Chapter 2, that the interpreter serves *communication* and keeps in mind the interests of the *participants in communication*, which implies prioritization of information carried by speeches. Again, doubts may arise as to the interpreter's ability and/or right to determine such priorities, but in the daily practice of interpreting, such decisions are numerous.

Law 3: Maximizing the communication impact of the speech (norm 2)

An act of communication, including interpreting, has an aim (or several – see Chapter 2), and the interpreter attempts to serve it according to certain loyalty principles. In specialized speeches in conference interpreting, maximizing the communication impact is often tantamount to maximizing information recovery. When interpreting interviews for TV shows, the communication impact sometimes depends more on the atmosphere and continuity of the flow of exchanges as well as on synchronicity (the interpreter is expected not to lag behind and make the interviewer and TV viewers wait) than on information – incidentally, synchronicity of simultaneous interpreting seems to rate rather high for delegates in general conferences as well, at least judging by a study by Moser (1997). This puts high on the priority list tactics which save time, perhaps at the detriment of information recovery.

As explained in Chapter 2, the communication impact of a statement or utterance depends not only on its information content, but also on its *packaging*. This general rule also applies to the interpreter's target-language speech, the impact of which depends on technical parameters such as fidelity to the source-language speech and delivery, but also on the interpreter's credibility. This is one of the factors that lead interpreters to favour or avoid particular tactics, beyond the informational aspect of their speech. For instance, if they feel they have not heard a name well enough and have reason to believe that pronouncing it inaccurately may generate adverse reactions in listeners, they may avoid trying to approximate the sound as heard. They may also feel that informing delegates of problems, especially when they are numerous, would take up too much time, dilute the speech, reduce their own credibility and weaken the impact of the speaker's statement more than the loss of information associated with the comprehension and production difficulties they encounter. In such a case, they may find it is better to cut the losses by refraining from informing the delegates (they may also take the same decision for less ethical reasons, if they think they can get away with it – see Law 5 below).

Law 4: The Law of least effort

This fourth law is not specifically related to interpreting tactics – it seems to prevail in all fields of human activity (Zipf 1949), including language (Miller 1962). This law tends to reinforce Law 2 on minimizing interference, as it favours tactics that require less time and processing capacity; but its rationale is different, and it tends to lead to tactics involving less effort even when processing capacity is available. Because of the intensity of interpreting in terms of nervous expenditure, it could be argued that it protects the interpreter from exhaustion, and therefore that in some contexts it can be justified. However, in the simultaneous mode, interpreters take turns in the booth and rest between them, so that they do not really need to save on energy while they are active. This law can therefore be considered an unwelcome intruder, which may generate loss of information and loss of impact without good reason.

Law 5: Self-protection

It is a fact of life that interpreters often fail to understand or reformulate speech segments in a way which *they* consider satisfactory. Thinking of the possible reactions of their listeners to what they regard as mediocre or poor performance, they may be tempted to give precedence to tactics that do not give away or highlight such problems. For example, they may avoid informing delegates of a problem, not with the legitimate aim of maximizing the impact of the speech (Law 3), but for the purpose of protecting themselves, sometimes running against Laws 1 and 3. It is difficult to establish in the field that any single tactic has been selected in the booth for the purpose of self-protection, but over time, interpreters do detect the presence of a self-protection trend in some colleagues.

The relative strength of these five laws depends on a number of personal and professional factors, and in particular on:

- Professional and personal ethics: If interpreters are conscientious, they will endeavour to maximize information recovery by giving priority to Laws 1 and 2 and by weighting them according to the relative importance of the relevant speech segments. If they are less conscientious, they may let themselves succumb to the law of least effort and the law of self-protection.
- Working conditions: When they are bad, with long working hours, insufficient manning strength in the booth, bad visibility of the conference room and the screen, lack of interest in the presentations on the part of the delegates, etc., the Law of least effort may gain more weight to the detriment of Laws 1 and 3. The potential effect of working conditions on the interpreters' motivation is one point to which the attention of conference organizers might be drawn (see Gile 1991b). This, however, is a double-edged sword, and could generate doubts regarding professional ethics in the interpreting community. Caution is of the essence.

7. Tactics in consecutive interpreting, sight translation and simultaneous with text

Most of the tactics listed above can also be used in consecutive interpreting, but there are a few differences.

- In consecutive, during the comprehension phase, the delaying tactic means leaving a blank space on paper, to be filled later – or not. In the reformulation phase, it may mean constructing the target speech or part of it without the information which the interpreter cannot remember and recover from the notes, in the hope of being able to recover it later.
- Generally, no passive colleagues ('boothmates' in simultaneous) are sitting beside the active interpreter in consecutive. Enlisting the colleague's help is obviously possible only in the rare cases when they are.
- In consecutive, the speaker and interpreter do not speak at the same time, and it may be possible for the interpreter to ask the speaker for clarification on an information element that has been missed. In most cases (the interpreter does not always have the possibility of talking directly to the speaker), informing the

delegates of the problem is not a relevant tactic. Note that asking the speaker for clarification once is all right, but doing so several times damages the interpreter's credibility – and results in loss of impact because the delivery of the statement is slowed down and becomes less smooth.

- Since in consecutive there is no immediate reformulation of the speech, changing the order of elements in an enumeration to alleviate memory load (Section 5.2 d) does not apply to the reformulation stage. It does apply to note-taking during the listening phase, where short-term memory load problems can be more severe locally than in simultaneous due to the relative slowness of note-taking as opposed to articulation rate in speech production.
- In consecutive, the segmentation tactic has a use in the *reformulation phase*. When threads of logic have escaped interpreters during the comprehension phase and when interpreters find it difficult to remember the logical links between information segments that appear in their notes, they can reformulate them in isolation one after the other, with the hope that the logic will come back to them while they speak, or that the delegates will be able to reconstruct the logical links themselves.
- Last but not least, as pointed out in Chapter 7, when processing capacity requirements become too high, the interpreter can stop taking notes and rely on memory for the relevant segment. This tactic is specific to consecutive interpreting.
- Other tactics for consecutive are part of note-taking skills. They are taught by instructors as practical techniques and are not discussed here as *coping tactics*. They include such actions as the use of abbreviations and/or drawings to save time, using pauses in the source-language speech to reread notes, noting in some detail the beginning and ending of speeches, etc. There are many publications on note-taking in the literature beyond the classic Rozan (1956) – see among many early examples Kade 1963, Henderson 1976, Ilg 1988, Allioni 1989, Garzone, Santulli and Damiani 1990, Lung 1999, Monacelli 1999. More recent references, including research reports, theses and even doctoral dissertations, can be found in the various issues of the *CIRIN Bulletin* posted online at www.cirinandgile.com.

In *sight translation*, most coping tactics requirements arise from non-comprehension of the source-language text, from problems in finding appropriate target-language terms and from processing capacity requirements associated with syntactic differences between the source language and the target language and with the need to fight linguistic interference between them. Several tactics listed above (using the boothmate's help, referring the delegates to another source, taking notes, changing the EVS, reformulating a parallel speech, and switching off the microphone) are irrelevant. Regarding the last two, while working conditions in the booth when no text is available can be so poor that no useful work can be done, with a written text it is exceedingly rare that the sight translator cannot extract *any* useful information from the text.

In simultaneous with text, as explained in Chapter 7, the fact that interpreters have the text of the speech before them has both positive and negative aspects. Specific tactics could perhaps be identified with respect to the allocation of more or less attention to the spoken speech versus the written text when encountering certain problems, but I am not aware of systematic reflection or rules on the subject.

8.   Handling speaker errors

When faced with an error made by the speaker, interpreters can react in one of three ways:

- They can reformulate the speech segment as it is, leaving the error uncorrected;
- They can correct the error in the target-language speech;
- They can draw the listeners' attention to the speaker's error.

Leaving the error uncorrected is in line with the Law of least effort, but may be detrimental to the impact of the speech. Error correction is in harmony with the aim of maximum information recovery and maximum impact, but entails three types of risk: one is that the speaker is right and the interpreter is wrong; secondly, a delegate listening to the source-language speech may pick up the speaker's error and make a comment on it, which will then force the interpreter to explain that s/he has already corrected it; thirdly, delegates may object to the interpreter's correcting the speaker (see Kopczynski 1994), which is understandable not only in courtroom situations where the actual words of witnesses and the accused can be just as important or more important than their Message (see Morris 1989), but also in other situations, in particular in debates when there are marked oppositions between participants. Informing the delegates of the speaker's error is in line with the Law of self-protection, but can reduce the impact of the speech by damaging the speaker's credibility.

9.   Coping tactics in translation

Of the tactics presented above for the case of interpreting, many also apply, at least in some related form, to written translation. In particular, reconstruction using the context, resorting to superordinate terms or more general text segments, informing the readers of a translation problem (generally by way of a footnote), explaining or paraphrasing, simplifying a text segment, instant naturalization, and transcoding yield similar results in translation and in interpreting.

The basic difference is that most often, coping tactics in interpreting are associated with recurrent problems resulting from processing capacity- and time constraints whose order of magnitude is measured in seconds or fractions of a second; in translation, they may result from the translator being unable to acquire all the required information over a longer period of time – that is, minutes in the case of extremely urgent translations and hours, days or weeks in most other cases. I believe that resorting to coping tactics, that is, performing crisis management in interpreting situations, is very much a part of the skills *interpreters* have to acquire in order to become operational. In translation, their use should be much less frequent. When training high-level translators, such tactics should perhaps not be introduced until the very last part of the syllabus, lest students succumb to the Law of least effort.

10. Teaching suggestions

Tactics are a practical component of interpreting skills and require no specific theoretical framework – though theoretical concepts and models can help grasp more fully their effects in terms of processing capacity and risks of local and more distant saturation and individual deficits as outlined in Chapter 7. They are essentially introduced during practical exercises, but I believe it is important that an explicit analysis of their advantages and drawbacks be made for the benefit of the students, lest the rationale underlying decisions be misunderstood as a flippant attitude toward the speaker, the delegates, or the very principle of fidelity.

In line with the process-oriented approach (see Chapter 1), during practical exercises, students should be encouraged to *explain* tactics they have chosen. However, since in this particular case, instructors wish not only to *explain* translation procedures, but also to establish certain ethical priorities, they cannot afford not to criticize tactics that follow the 'wrong' 'laws' (the Law of least effort and the Law of self-protection).

Last, when presenting tactics and 'Laws', instructors should stress the fact that these involve decisions, that is, personal choices with associated risks, for which the interpreter has to take responsibility as a participant in communication (see Chapter 2), albeit one with a subordinate role. In this respect, the interpreter's work converges with that of the translator, as described in the Sequential Model of translation explained in Chapter 5.

11. What students need to remember

1. In spite of their preparation and skills, interpreters do encounter difficulties online in both comprehension and reformulation.
2. The basic role of coping tactics is to prevent or limit damage resulting from interpreting difficulties.

3.   Tactics are generally selected so as to:

  –   Maximize information recovery for the delegates (a conference interpreting norm);
  –   Minimize interference between recovery of the affected speech segment and the rendering of neighbouring segments;
  –   Maximize the communication impact of the speech (another conference interpreting norm).

4.   In reality, two interfering phenomena are also active:

  –   The Law of least effort;
  –   Self-protection.

  Both should be avoided.

Chapter 9

Language availability and its implications in conference interpreting (and translation)

1. Introduction

The International Association of Conference Interpreters (AIIC) defines three categories of working languages for interpreters (AIIC 1982: 10):

–   *A languages*, in which interpreters possess native-like proficiency. When examining applicants for conference interpreting programmes, examiners look for the proficiency of *educated* natives. The same applies to B languages and C languages.
–   *B languages*, which interpreters are supposed to master both actively and passively *almost* as well as a native, and which are *active* working languages, meaning that they are supposed to work *into* them, at least in the consecutive mode.
–   *C languages*, which are *passive* languages. They are theoretically understood at native level, but interpreters do not work *into* them.

These formal definitions are explicit, but the actual status of working languages in the field is less clear. One of the problems lies in determining whether an interpreter's working language is an A or a B. Borderline cases are numerous, including so-called 'bilingual As' (are they *true* bilinguals? See Thiéry 1975), interpreters who have a vernacular language as their mother tongue (for instance in Africa) and whose official A language may have been acquired at a comparatively late age, interpreters who have been living in the country of their B language for many years, etc. Another problem is the very justification of the concept of A and B languages: some interpreters claim that if a B language is mastered well enough to be used as an active language, it should not be discriminated from an A language. Others say that if a B language is not used actively in simultaneous interpreting, its definition as an active language should be qualified, and there should be a new classification, with 'active languages for consecutive' and 'active languages for simultaneous' (see Reinert 1976; Keiser 1978).

   In the context of conference interpreter training, two major issues relating to language classification are the students' insufficient command of their working languages and questions about directionality. (Should interpreters work into their A language from their B and C language, or should they work into their B language from their A language?)

In translation, the problems are somewhat similar but with a few major differences:

- Insufficient command of a passive language in translation does not result in the same critical and sometimes catastrophic online situations, because translators have the possibility of doing further research or asking for help from colleagues or native speakers while interpreters have to react on the spot to all problems (see Chapters 7 and 8).
- For the same reason, while language-specific and language-pair specific features may have significant effects in interpreting and require specific tactics and methods because of cognitive constraints (see Chapter 7), their implications in translation are far less critical because translators tend not to work close to cognitive saturation.
- On the other hand, as already stressed earlier, in terms of grammar, stylistics and other editorial criteria, translators are required to have writing/editorial skills in their active language(s) which interpreters do not need because of their oral expression mode, where stylistic clumsiness and sometimes even agrammaticality may not be detected by listeners and, if detected, may not be considered a significant flaw.

This chapter focuses mostly on critical interpreting-related problems, but the concepts and models presented here also apply to translation, and a few comparative references are also made to translation.

2.   The students' command of their working languages

Theoretically, there seems to be a consensus among leading interpreting and translation schools in the West (in particular members of CIUTI – the International Permanent Conference of University Institutes of Translators and Interpreters) that at the time of admission into an interpreter training programme, students should already have a 'near-perfect' command of their working languages, and that at interpreter school, language skills enhancement should be limited to the acquisition and improvement of conference-specific and LSP-specific phraseology and terminology (Keiser 1970; see also Nilski 1967; Geleff 1971; Lederer 1975; Gravier 1978 on interpreting and translation, Seleskovitch 1981).

The basic position is clear: major interpreting schools in the West (but not in all parts of the world, and in particular not in China and Japan) wish to establish a strong distinction between interpreter training and language training. And yet, during entrance exams, it appears that linguistic prerequisites are not always met, with respect to both active languages (Carroll 1978: 12) and passive languages. In fact, many students fail their final professional examinations because of insufficient command of their working languages (Keiser 1978: 13, 18), not because of insufficient technical or cognitive skills. The situation in the field is therefore different from what it would be if theoretical linguistic prerequisites were met. Moreover, in many countries, including European countries, a large number of interpreter training programmes are part of or strongly associated with departments of modern languages where translator and interpreter training starts while language skills enhancement is still part of the curriculum. Finally, in spite of a clear norm adopted by many translators, interpreters, training programmes and professional organizations in favour of work into one's A language only, work into B languages is very widespread, and often in situations where the relevant interpreters' mastery of their B language is remote from the ideal B language as defined by AIIC (see Section 6).

Similar observations have been made as regards translation students (Delisle 1980; Harris 1981; Rainey 1988; Gémar 1990; Lang 1992; Snell-Hornby 1992; Viaggio 1992). Again, translation into one's non-native language is widespread, and in translation perhaps more than in interpreting, differences in the professional's A language and B language skills in terms of idiomaticity, style and even linguistic correctness can be strikingly manifest in the product of their work.

Some conference interpreting instructors are not willing to accept such a situation and should like to refuse admission to students whose command of the languages is not up to theoretical A, B and C-language standards. Such an option is problematic: Firstly, it is difficult to check language mastery at the required level, since relevant weaknesses may only be detectable under severe cognitive pressure encountered during interpreting – which the students have yet to learn. Secondly, much progress in one's language mastery can be achieved through hard work over a period of one to two years, and some talented students with insufficient language skills at admission are able to reach the required level by the time they take graduation examinations. Finally, in some programmes, economic constraints and strong market demand for some language combinations can tip the scales towards admission even when the prerequisites are not quite met. As a result, students do get admitted to interpreting and translation schools even when one or more of their working languages are weak. This can lead either to a high proportion of failures or, if training institutions keep their students despite their weaknesses, to loss of credibility for their diplomas, degrees or professional certificates.

Possible remedies are of two types. One consists in setting up language enhancement courses, as has been done in many schools. Another is to instruct students to improve their language skills on their own, by spending time in a country where their weak language is spoken (if their B or C language is found to be weak after the first year, they are often advised to spend a year in a relevant country before doing their second year of studies), by reading, listening to the radio and watching television, or performing specific exercises for enhancement of their linguistic skills. Déjean Le Féal of ESIT describes a set of exercises she recommends to her students in an interesting article published in 1976. These include:

- 'Complete reading', which consists in reading a text sentence by sentence, and then repeating each sentence without looking at the text
- 'Complete listening', which consists in repeating sentences and linguistic structures heard from a native speaker in a foreign language
- Careful listening to the way native speakers unwittingly correct non-native speakers when they use clumsy constructions
- Occasionally concentrating on function words rather than on content words so as to learn their proper use
- Learning structures and idioms by heart
- 'Shuttle exercises' in which student try to seek systematically appropriate wordings in one language for ideas they hear in another.

Many interpreting teachers include in their classes exercises that are partially or entirely aimed at language-skills enhancement. In his 'terminology class', Gérard Ilg of E.T.I. (University of Geneva) devoted much time to enriching and making more flexible the students' oral expression skills. His exercises include (Ilg 1978, 1980):

- *Paraphrasing*, which is a particularly popular exercise (Moser 1978; Lederer 1981)
- *Permutation exercises*, which consist of syntactic transformations such as inversions, conversion from active to passive or vice versa, addition or deletion of double negations, etc.
- *Summary exercises* and *expansion exercises*
- The search for *synonyms, hyponyms* and *hypernyms*.

Most instructors also give indirect language-enhancement training to student interpreters by commenting on their output and making suggestions for better wording. It does not seem reasonable to admit into high-level professional schools students whose command of their working languages is likely to remain too weak to allow them to graduate and become competent conference interpreters at the end of the programme. However, recognizing that some weaknesses can be and indeed have been successfully overcome by students over time should lead to more efficient strategies for the enhancement of language skills during training. The *Gravitational Model* presented later in this chapter is one tool for analyzing such strategies.

3. Language availability

Before introducing the Model, it is important to clarify the concept of *availability* in language comprehension and production, because to laypersons, including translation and interpreting students, the usual perception of language mastery is a binary one, in which an individual either 'knows' or 'does not know' words and rules of grammar, syntax, spelling etc. This binary view is too limited for an adequate insight into language mastery requirements for interpreting, and for simultaneous interpreting in particular: a major dimension of 'linguistic knowledge' is the *availability* of lexical units, including idioms and specialized terms on one hand and grammatical, stylistic, pragmatic and other language rules on the other. As will be explained, in many cases low availability has for all intents and purposes the same effect as lack of knowledge.

This section explains relevant phenomena with simple concepts, models and metaphors largely developed intuitively and later supported by theories and findings from cognitive psychology and psycholinguistics.

3.1   Language production and availability

Language production normally starts with information or another type of message which the speaker or writer wishes to express for communication purposes (see Chapter 2). It involves planning, i.e. the selection of syntactic structures and words available from long-term memory, and then execution of the speech plan through speaking, typing or writing manually, or signing. Availability issues arise essentially in the planning stage: it may take more or less processing capacity and time (see Chapter 7) for a statement-producer to retrieve the appropriate words and syntactic or other rules from long-term memory where the mental lexicon is stored and/or decide which syntactic structure to use when starting, continuing or completing a sentence. Availability issues in language production are easy to detect in everyday life: everyone is aware of hesitations when a particular word does not come to one's mind immediately or when some conscious recollection effort is necessary to decide how to continue and/or finish a sentence which has effectively been started. The main concrete manifestation of low availability in speech production is the hesitation pause, filled (by hesitations sounds such as 'um' or 'uh' or filler words) or unfilled.

In everyday life, low availability in speech production ('*speech production availability*') results mostly in pauses and hesitations which slow down the utterance and may make it unpleasant to listen to. It can also lead to lack of accuracy in expressing the initial idea if the speaker gives up on finding the right words and settles for others which are more available but do not reflect his/her message accurately. Other manifestations of low speech-production availability include false starts and various grammatical and other errors.

Low availability in written text production may slow down the writing of texts, but availability must be particularly poor for this effect to have practical consequences, because the mechanical act of handwriting or typing is much slower than the mental process of language production, and slowing down by a fraction of a second is hardly noticeable; moreover, in careful writing of translations or texts to be published, revision is important and takes up much time as well, so that ordinary delays in finding a word or making syntactic decisions due to low availability become virtually undetectable in everyday life (they can be measured with specialized software which monitors typing on the computer as well as pauses such as Translog – see Jakobsen 1999). Inaccuracies and errors due to low availability can also be corrected during self-revision.

3.2   Language comprehension and availability

Language comprehension can be modelled as a 3-step process. First, sound signals or visual signals (in the case of written texts and signed speeches) are perceived by sensory organs, namely the ears or eyes (and by receptors in one's fingers in the case of Braille readers), and linger in so-called 'sensory memory' or 'sensory stores' for a very short while, about a second or so. They are then forwarded to 'working memory' (see Chapter 7) where they are processed so as to yield meaning. In a third step, this meaning is used for an immediate reaction (such as a physical action) and/or sent to long-term memory for later use.

While the sensory perception phase is automatic, working memory processes are not. As explained in Chapter 7, non-automatic operations take up processing capacity, and more relevantly for the discussion which follows, they take up time. Processing sound signals or visual signals in order to extract meaning out of them is believed to involve comparisons between their perceived features and features of words or other linguistic units as stored in long-term memory. These comparisons are used to make choices between them as the likely candidates to which the signals correspond in the relevant context. As demonstrated by numerous experiments in psycholinguistics (many psycholinguistics textbooks provide further explanations and examples), this takes time. In everyday conversation in a well-mastered language, the process is generally very short, far less than a second for each incoming word (people read and communicate at speeds of more than 120 words per minute), and gives ordinary listeners the impression that comprehension is instantaneous. However, even in everyday exchanges, listeners occasionally take much longer to understand a word because it is unfamiliar or pronounced in an unusual way or is unexpected in the context (this slowing down shows that underlying analysis does take place), to the extent that they are aware of the delay between the time they perceive the sound and the time they reach understanding.

Dual-task experiments in psycholinguistics in which subjects are instructed to read or listen to statements and at the same time perform another task show that when part of one's processing capacity is engaged elsewhere, language comprehension is slower (see for instance Newman *et al.* 2007; Just *et al.* 2008). This is also the case in interpreting: as explained in Chapter 7, in the simultaneous mode, comprehension of the source speech takes place at the same time as target-speech production; in the consecutive mode, comprehension of the source speech takes place at the same time as the taking of notes. Processing-for-comprehension time, i.e. 'comprehension availability', therefore becomes a relevant parameter of the interpreter's mastery of his/her working languages.

Low *reading-comprehension availability* in fluent speakers of a language may be reflected in more efforts to understand texts, especially when reading syntactically complex sentences and sentences where an ambiguous word or expression and the downstream disambiguating context are remote from each other (Michael *et al.* 2001; Prat *et al.* 2007). This forces the reader to keep more information in working memory before being able to complete the processing of the ambiguous segment.

In speech comprehension, low availability often has more serious consequences, as illustrated by the following simplified scenario:

If an incoming speech consists of successive short speech segments S1, S2, S3, S4, S5 etc., under normal conditions, as the speech unfolds, working memory, which can store and process a limited amount of information (see Chapter 7), can analyze the corresponding sound signals and turn them into meaning with a slight lag, and sometimes without lag (when the hearer anticipates the coming segment). When comprehension availability is low, the speed of processing is slowed down and lag accumulates. As a result, the maximum storage capacity of working memory can be exceeded rapidly and if it is saturated at the time the speaker utters S3, either the incoming voice signal which carries S3 cannot be attended to, or it is attended to at the expense of previously heard segments such as S1 and/or S2, the processing of which cannot be completed. As a result, either previously heard sounds or incoming sounds cannot be fully processed to yield meaning, and the corresponding speech segments are not understood (see Fig. 9.1). In other words, while low production availability only slows down production, low comprehension availability can lead to non-comprehension. As explained later in this chapter, in interpreting, this has far-reaching implications.

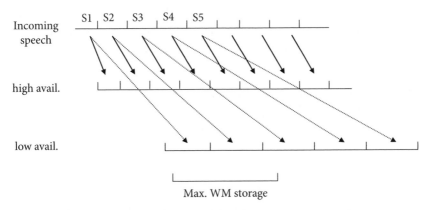

Figure 9.1 The effect of low availability on comprehension

In this scenario, while in a high comprehension availability situation, the listener's working memory can hold and process up to 4 segments of the incoming speech and keep up with the speaker, in a low comprehension availability situation, it is saturated after just a bit over 2 segments and non-comprehension occurs.

4.   The Gravitational Model of language availability

From the previous section it becomes clear that language availability in speech comprehension and production, and to a lesser extent in text comprehension and production, is of some importance in everyday communication. In interpreting, in view of existing competition for processing capacity between several Efforts which reduces the amount available for each, it is even more important, as insufficient availability may be a strong contributor to cognitive saturation and interpreting failures (Chapter 7). It is therefore critical for students and professionals to raise it to a maximum level. The Gravitational Model of language availability was developed to help explain to students both the concept and its implications.

4.1   Language constituents

For the purpose of this discussion, it is convenient to consider natural languages as composed of the following constituents:

Lexical units: These are 'words', including technical terms, as well as idioms. In this discussion the definition can be extended to set phrases which occur frequently; "Thank you Mister Chairman", "We will break for lunch", "the meeting is adjourned", "thank you for your attention", "the resolution is adopted" are examples found in everyday conference jargon, and other set phrases are frequent in other specialized areas of human activity. One's mental lexicon (i.e. the large set of such lexical units stored in a person's long-term memory) can vary greatly from one individual to the next. This is not surprising in view of the fact that an educated person's vocabulary consists of several tens of thousands to more than a hundred thousand different words (see Aitchison 1987: 5–8) and that people vary in their educational background, professional activities and other interests. In each of the languages or sociolects they use, a small fraction of this lexicon, perhaps a few thousand lexical units, is encountered daily, and a far larger proportion very rarely, depending on the individual's personal and professional environment (see Section 4.7).

Compositional rules of general (non-specialized) language: These are the rules that govern the way words are assembled (often with morphological changes induced by grammar such as declension and conjugation forms as well as grammatical agreements) in order to form linguistically correct and socially acceptable statements in oral, written or signed form in the relevant culture. They include grammatical rules, stylistic rules, pragmatic rules, social rules.

Rules of languages for special purposes: Beyond technical terms, LSPs sometimes have an important phraseological dimension, with stylistic and even grammatical preferences which may be different from those of general language – a case in point is the language of law which often includes grammatical rules no longer correct in modern non-legal language.

Collectively, these lexical units and language rules will be called *Language Constituents* (or LCs) in the following discussion. The set of all LCs known to an individual will be referred to as this individual's *LC system*. The mental lexicon is the lexical subset of the LC system.

4.2   The structure of the Gravitational Model of language availability

For every language used by a Speaker (in this chapter, the word 'Speaker' with an upper-case S will be used to encompass speakers, signers, listeners, readers and writers), his/her LC System is composed of LCs which have different levels of availability, ranging from what seems to be instantaneous and totally effortless retrieval from long-term memory to the tip-of-the tongue phenomenon in which a word (or perhaps some language rule) is known to be 'known' but is unavailable at a given moment.

The Gravitational Model represents the status of an individual's spoken, signed or written command of a language at a given time and in given circumstances by describing the relative *availability* of his/her LCs. To map this rather complex pattern graphically, a simple gravitational structure such as the one used by Bohr to describe the atom is used (Fig.9.2).

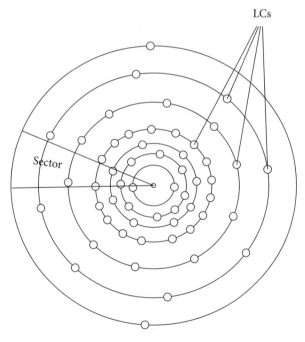

Figure 9.2 The Gravitational Model of Linguistic Availability

LCs are represented graphically as small circles gravitating on orbits around a nucleus. The distance between an orbit and the nucleus of the Model is an indication of availability: the closer the orbit is to the nucleus, the higher the availability.

Actually, at any time, for any LC, four distinct states of availability can be defined: availability for spoken speech or signed language *comprehension*, availability for spoken speech or signed language *production*, availability for *reading comprehension* and availability for *writing production*. While the four patterns are correlated, this correlation need not be strong for all LCs. People who do not read and write regularly may have lower availability for reading comprehension and writing production than for speech comprehension and production, and language learners who read a lot but do not practice speaking much may have higher writing and reading availability than speech comprehension- and production availability. An interesting case is that of Speakers of Chinese and Japanese who, with the advent of word processing, have started using electronic devices to write using keyboards with phonetic symbols which are then converted into more complex characters; while such Speakers still read characters regularly and maintain high reading availability of the relevant LCs, they may experience marked loss of written production availability when writing manually.

In other words, instead of one gravitational model, four would be needed to represent the status of language availability in any one Speaker for any language. For the sake of convenience, in view of the fact that the principles and dynamics are basically the same for all four dimensions, a single generic gravitational diagram is used here (and in the classroom) to serve as a visual aid for explanations.

Another issue arises from the fact that the model represents availabilities (of LCs) at a given time and in a given situation and context. When these change, so do probably availability levels in parts of the System. For instance, when taking part in a medical conference, speakers and delegates probably experience higher availability of medical language than when going skiing on a holiday. When they are skiing, they probably have higher availability or terms such as 'snow', 'ski lift', 'slope' etc. The assumption is that these parts of their System are '*primed*', i.e. made more available, both because of memory associations between these situations and the relevant LCs and because the LCs are stimulated by being used by them and/or around them – see Section 4.3. Since situations and contexts change, so can LC availability. One could therefore wonder about the usefulness of a model which provides only an instantaneous shot of an ever-changing system.

There are two answers to such an objection: firstly, part of one's LC system, that which is used very often, should be rather stable in terms of availability (see Section 4.4.1); secondly, besides the situation and context, availability depends to a large extent on dynamic rules which are assumed to be basically the same for all LC systems, and the focus of this chapter is on these dynamics and their implications.

Finally, the LCs represented in the Gravitational Model can be classified in different *Sectors* (subsets of the LCs in a Speaker's System), which, for any language, can be characterized in terms of languages for special purposes (LSPs) and of sociolects determined by social class, gender, age etc. Obviously, all Sectors share a rather large common set of general-language LCs, and many specialized Sectors also share other LCs (for instance, many scientific and technological fields and disciplines share a large number of specialized terms and set phrases). Again, in view of the didactic purposes of this model, Sectors will be discussed here as if they were distinct, but readers should keep in mind that this is a simplified view of reality adopted for the sake of convenience.

4.3   The dynamics of the Gravitational Model

One important fact about LC availability is that it is not static, but rises and drops at different rates, depending on circumstances. In the Gravitational Model, increasing availability is represented by 'centripetal' (inward) migration of the relevant LCs (moving from distant orbits to more central orbits), and decreasing availability by 'centrifugal' migration (moving to orbits more remote from the centre).

Some of these changes can be very fast. For instance, once an LC has been identified in speech signal and understood in a communication situation and/or used in speech or text production, it may become highly available for at least a few seconds regardless of its previous availability status. Other changes in availability are much slower – they may occur over months or years before they are detected by a Speaker. While attention has been devoted by psycholinguists to the 'priming' phenomenon (see Eysenck & Keane 1990: 183-184), I have not found precise measurements of long-term availability changes in normal adult language users in the literature (but see for example Tulving *et al.* (1982) for availability changes over a week for single words). The ideas and rules presented below were developed on the basis of field observation, introspection and informal discussions with translators and interpreters. They have also been quoted in the translation and interpreting literature as well as by a few linguists, which suggests they are not in contradiction with current thinking. However, fundamentally they should be viewed as assumptions, not scientifically verified laws.

> *Rule 1*: The Centrifugal Principle
> If not stimulated, LCs tend to drift outward (away from the centre of the system)

What is meant by *stimulation* here is either active use in speech or writing or passive exposure, when LCs are heard or read (or seen in sign language) *and* identified.

Rule 1 says that when LCs are not used, they tend to become progressively less available. Eventually their availability decreases to such an extent that they can be considered 'forgotten'. It is difficult to make precise quantitative assessments of the speed of such centrifugal drift, but the process seems to be rather slow. Under ordinary conditions (excluding phenomena such as psychological trauma), it may take months or years for an LC which had been 'learned' to the extent that it was a regular part of a Speaker's LC system (as opposed to, for example, a word encountered once in a specialized text and read aloud without further analysis) to be 'forgotten'.

> *Rule 2*: The Centripetal Effect of stimulation
> When stimulated, LCs tend to move inward

When an LC is heard or read (*passive stimulation*), or used by a Speaker in the production of an oral or signed speech or of a written text (*active stimulation*), it becomes more available for passive and/or active use. This migration is much faster than the centrifugal effect: under stimulation, a newly learned lexical unit can become highly available within seconds or minutes.

The sequence comprising a rapid centripetal progression followed by a slower centrifugal migration is often found in terminological preparation for conferences: interpreters achieve within hours or minutes high production and/or comprehension availability for technical terms they had never encountered before; this lasts for the duration of the conference, after which they may 'forget' these terms in a few days to a few weeks – but experience suggests that many of these apparently forgotten terms do not disappear fully from the LC system, because when they are encountered again later at another conference, they are recognized by the interpreter.

Rule 3: Stimulation frequency and the Centripetal Effect
The more frequently LCs are stimulated, the stronger the centripetal effect.

LCs used frequently tend to become more available than LCs used less frequently. The existence of a correlation between frequency of stimulation and ease of perception is well documented, with research-based statements to the effect that:

- frequently used words are perceived more easily and read more rapidly (Miller 1956: 272-273)
- word frequency plays an important role in coding and decoding (Leeson 1975: 116)
- rare words are "more difficult to process" (Clark & Clark 1977: 56)
- the more frequent an LC, the more "deeply it is rooted in the psyche of the individual and the community" (Mahmoudian 1982: 189)
- the frequency of occurrence of a word in a language affects the time it takes to gain access to that word in the mental lexicon (Matthei & Roeper 1985: 182).

Such frequency of occurrence is often a key parameter in speech comprehension and memory experiments (see for instance Keller *et al.* 2001; Prat *et al.* 2007).

- the frequency of word repetition was found to be a strong predictor of memorization in students (in a study by Biderman & Ravazzi, 1984).

Frequency of stimulation should not be regarded as the only important factor determining the strength of the Centripetal Effect. Automatic repetition without a context and without deeper cognitive processing does not appear to be very efficient in increasing availability. It seems that a minimum amount of depth of processing such as occurs in actual communication situations or in reading situations has to be involved for the Centripetal Effect to be effective.

Rule 4: The Centripetal Effects of active vs. passive stimulation
Active stimulation of an LC has a stronger centripetal effect than passive stimulation

Using an LC when speaking, signing or writing pushes it more strongly toward the Nucleus than reading or hearing and understanding it. This rule provides justification for the numerous active drill exercises in language classes.

Also, while active stimulation has a strong centripetal effect on both production and comprehension availability, passive stimulation acts more strongly on comprehension availability than on production availability.

Rule 5: The Escort Effect and the Interference Effect

Centripetal migration of an LC causes centripetal migration of other LCs associated with it

When an LC becomes more available, other LCs that sound or look similar, or that have been associated with it psychologically (through a learning situation, an emotional situation, etc.) also tend to become more available. This phenomenon is studied in the psycholinguistics literature for lexical units (see Costermans 1980: 20). It will be referred to here as the *Escort Effect*.

This rule is very important with respect to both lexical acquisition and lexicon maintenance: it suggests that while the initial acquisition of a particular word may take some time and repeated active or passive stimulation, the initial acquisition of other words closely related to it (for instance grammatical variations thereof, or other words having the same etymological roots and/or a similar morphology) will be faster; it also suggests that stimulation of a given word will not only stop its centrifugal drift and make it more available, but also have a similar effect on other words associated with it.

The Escort Effect is translinguistic. For instance, in a Speaker with French, English and German, if the French word *contrôleur* is stimulated through repeated encounters in context, one can expect to find increased availability of words such as the English 'control' and 'controller' and the German *Kontrolle* and *kontrollieren*. The Escort Effect could account for the comparative speed at which adults can learn cognate foreign languages, especially as regards scientific and technical terms, which often have common roots. It also explains why persons who have achieved a high level of proficiency in a cognate language in a very short time may struggle for years with a non-cognate language and show much slower progress (see Gile 1988b for the case of language enhancement efforts in Japanese by a Westerner).

The down side of the Escort Effect is *linguistic interference*, already mentioned several times in this volume: linguistic interference may cause the interpreter or translator to use a word incorrectly with respect to its meaning or connotation, to distort its sound when speaking or its spelling when writing, or even to use a word from the wrong language in the middle of a speech or text. For instance, because of interference from English, a French Speaker may use *contrôler* instead of *maîtriser* (which is often the best translation for 'control' in English whereas *contrôler* means 'check' in the sense of 'verify').

In the experiment mentioned in Section 1 of Chapter 7, one interpreter translated "They think you're stupid or you're foolish" (third example) into *"ils peuvent penser que vous êtes stupide ou fou"* ('stupid or insane'). The error is probably due to the phonetic similarity between 'foolish' and *fou* which was not countered by efficient monitoring and control.

Interference phenomena in interpreting and translation are not quite the same as in foreign language learning. Conference interpreters and professional high-level translators are well-educated individuals with a good command of their working languages. Furthermore, by training, they are aware of the risks of linguistic interference and constantly endeavour to avoid it (see for instance Thiéry 1975). Some gross interference is occasionally found in the booth or in translations nevertheless, but most of it is subtler and less salient. In particular, what might be called *silent interference* is frequent. Silent interference is interference not manifest through a visible, significant alteration of the lexical or syntactic output in the target language. It can involve some slowing down of speech production due to increased processing associated with the filtering out of possible intruders from the wrong language. It can also narrow the range of lexical units and syntactic rules used by Speakers, as they are eliminating those which they suspect may be due to interference. Silent interference is difficult to detect not only because its symptoms do not stand out, but also because other factors may induce similar symptoms. One such example is 'lexical restriction', which occurs under stress (Meier 1964, quoted by Hörmann 1972).

Finally, anti-interference control as it is practiced by professionals during interpreting can reasonably be assumed to increase processing capacity requirements in the Production Effort and may contribute to fatigue and to related effects that are difficult to diagnose as attributable to linguistic interference (see Chapter 7).

4.4   Further assumptions about the dynamics of the Gravitational Model

4.4.1   *The speed of availability changes*
Intuitively, some LCs lose availability more rapidly than others. Some terms learned during preparation for a conference and some words and phrases learned while travelling abroad seem to lose availability very fast. Others are more resilient in this respect. This can be due to frequent stimulation in the Speaker's environment, but also to emotional factors which may or may not leave a more lasting imprint in one's brain. Another possible explanation of availability resilience could be a long history of frequent use of the relevant LCs, which may also have left stronger traces in the Speaker's brain.

4.4.2   *Active and passive availability*
Another interesting aspect of LC availability is the relation between production and comprehension availability.

Previous published versions of the Gravitational Model included a central 'active' zone representing LCs available for production and a less central 'passive' zone where they were 'only available' for comprehension. This was obviously a simplification, as production availability is necessarily associated with at least some comprehension availability, and comprehension availability is necessarily associated with at least some production availability. The differentiation into two zones was done in order to stress that, when left without stimulation for a long time, LCs which were available for production gradually lost their availability until they could no longer be retrieved from long-term memory for production and could only be recognized when used by others in texts or speeches. After further reflection and observation of student reactions, I have come to believe this simplification could be misleading and prefer to do without it in this version of the Model. Nevertheless, I believe that it is important to point out to students that migration from high availability to low availability of LCs often means that production availability gradually declines even if they are still understood, which implies that in order to maintain availability, language maintenance is required.

4.4.3   *Oral and written availability*

As explained earlier, oral and written availability are correlated, but the correlation need not be strong.

This seems reasonable because there are clearly cases where people speak and understand spoken language but cannot write or write well, perhaps more so in languages with complex spelling rules and non-phonetic or partly phonetic characters than in languages where there are simple correspondence rules between phonology and signs for writing. A subtler analysis could invoke the fact that comprehension and production processes of written, spoken and signed language necessarily go through partly different physiological pathways, and that extensive use of one such pathway does not necessarily involve the use or similarly extensive use of another. For a general discussion of the issue, see Michael *et al.* 2001. For a more specific example, see Buchweitz *et al.* 2009, in which it was found that activation patterns in the brain were different when reading kanji words (written with 'Chinese' characters) and when reading in hiragana, a Japanese phonetic syllabary.

A corollary of this differentiation is that oral use of LCs probably tends to increase their availability for speech comprehension and production more than for reading comprehension and written text production, while written use of LCs probably increases their availability for reading and writing more than for listening comprehension and speech production. Again, these rules are tentative and their effect is difficult to quantify.

5.   The Gravitational Model and conference interpreting

5.1   The interpreter's LC system

Turning to the specific case of conference interpreters, an obvious requirement is that in all their working languages, their LC system should contain all the LCs needed to comprehend and produce speech in conference situations in which their services are used. With respect to standard general language, this condition is, at least theoretically, always met in competent interpreters. Problems may arise in nonstandard general language (regional dialects, slang, etc.), in literary language and in languages for special purposes. The latter category is particularly important, as it makes up much of the vocabulary of conferences and cannot be learned once and for all, both because of its extent (dozens to hundreds of thousands of lexical units in each LSP in the various scientific, technical, cultural, sports fields etc.) and because it is in constant evolution, at least as far as technology and many scientific disciplines go (see Chapter 6).

Second, since interpreting is performed under heavy time pressure, only highly available LCs are operationally relevant: LCs encountered occasionally and understood or available for speech production only after a comparatively large amount of processing (which may only take a second or a fraction of a second, but still involves a significantly longer process than the retrieval of highly available LCs) cannot be used in interpreting, as they may take up valuable processing capacity and time. This can lead to serious problems, especially in simultaneous interpreting (see Section 3.2 in this chapter and Chapter 7).

Interpreters in the booth tend to use regularly not all of their LC system, but only a sufficiently available subset thereof. For working languages other than the language of habitual use in the country and geographic area where they reside, such intensive use of this subset of one's LC system at the expense of less available LCs may in turn lead to further polarization between highly available LCs and other LCs. This could mean that interpreters who live in a country where their B language is spoken may find their A language impoverished over the years. This could happen at least with respect to some LCs which their colleagues who live in countries where their A language is spoken maintain at a high level of availability thanks to stimulation from their daily environment.

The *relevance* of LCs to the needs of interpreting is an important question in terms of both initial vocabulary acquisition and maintenance. Although there are countless glossaries of technical terms, I am not aware of lexicometric or other descriptive studies of the language of international conferences (besides studies of the specific jargon of conference procedure and standard formulas – though Gérard Ilg used to collect such expressions and formulas in several languages and distribute multilingual lists to his students at ETI and ESIT). Professional interpreters who generally have no trouble with their B and C languages in the booth (but situations can vary widely, especially when working for TV) can encounter words and idioms unknown to them but familiar to native speakers when reading novels, newspapers and magazines. On the other hand, after working for years in a wide range of conferences, they tend to know specialized lexical units and phraseology in many sociolects and technolects better than educated native speakers who are not experts in the relevant fields. This suggests that the wording "native-like proficiency" for the conference interpreter's mastery of working languages proposed by AIIC (1982) is inaccurate – though admittedly, it is difficult to find a better one for communication with the public at large, since long and detailed explanations could be counterproductive. In the context of this discussion, definitions based on concepts like "native-like proficiency" are highly demanding in some respects and insufficiently so in others: an *ordinary* native-like LC system (not specifically representing the case of conference interpreters) may contain a significant proportion of LCs which are not useful in interpreting, while useful LCs may be missing or not available enough.

5.2   The interpreter's and translator's multilingualism

The Effort Models and the Tightrope Hypothesis highlight the critical role of processing capacity limitations in the interpreting process. As explained in Chapter 7, it is assumed that interpreting, and in particular simultaneous interpreting, requires virtually all available processing capacity, which makes the interpreter vulnerable to phenomena such as increased short-term memory load arising from linguistic and communication phenomena which would have no practical consequence in everyday verbal interaction (including lexical or syntactic ambiguity, complex syntax, convoluted logic, slips of the tongue etc.). Under these circumstances, high language availability can make all the difference between success and failure in an interpreting task.

This, by the way, is one reason why it is difficult to assess accurately enough the level of language mastery of applicants to conference interpreter training programmes during entrance examinations. They may perform well in preliminary written examinations and in interviews in which they are required to show understanding of short speeches on general topics, to speak about themselves and to make short summaries of the content of articles read out to them – that is, under conditions which do not require attention division. When they start interpreting, competition between Efforts (Chapter 7) puts them under such cognitive pressure that sufficient availability becomes critical (see Gile 1987). It makes little sense to test their languages under interpreting conditions at a time when they have not started learning interpreting skills. Other means, such as testing them under dual task conditions, could do the job technically but are very unnatural, may require some practice and have a high cost in time – and might indicate the applicant's status at a certain time, but not his/her potential for development. Accepting some uncertainty about language availability at the time of admission may be the best option at this time.

In view of availability dynamics as outlined in Section 4.3, and in particular long-term LC use during the interpreters' and translators' career, the following observations and comments can be made about the interpreter's and translator's multilingualism:

Active languages and passive languages

In translators and interpreters, differences between mastery of active languages and mastery of passive languages can be very sharp: many translators and interpreters have excellent passive knowledge of their C languages, including passive knowledge of a rich set of words and idioms, but are not fluent in them. Generally, this reflects long-term evolution: initial acquisition of a foreign language normally addresses the four skills (speaking, writing, reading and understanding speech) in a relatively balanced pattern, though reading comprehension is often better than the three other skills. If over time translators and interpreters only use a language passively, the relative weakness of passive stimulation in terms of production availability enhancement (rule 4) results in centrifugal drift and loss of production availability as opposed to comprehension availability. Sometimes, working translators or interpreters wish to add another C language to their working language combination. In such a case, they may not bother to try to acquire production skills at all, an idiosyncratic position which foreign-language teachers may find surprising.

Oral and written availability

Interpreters work from speeches but also use much written material for reference and preparation and during conferences, when doing simultaneous with text and when using the texts which appear on screen. They therefore maintain both oral and written availability. Translators only work with written texts and may therefore have low listening-comprehension availability to the extent that they find it difficult to understand speeches in passive languages from which they translate (see Section 3.2).

Language interference

One of the most fundamental issues in language skills for interpreting is language 'separation', i.e. the ability to express oneself in one of the working languages without interference from another. Many applicants to interpreter training programmes who believe they are 'bilingual' turn out to be 'alingual' insofar as in their everyday speech production, they mix both languages unwittingly and therefore have no true A language in the sense of the AIIC definition. When such a situation is identified, these applicants are not admitted to the programmes, because their problem is deemed too fundamental to be solved during training.

Like other bilinguals who do manage to separate their languages in daily life, interpreters and translators still face the risk of interference throughout their career, especially in view of the disturbing presence of both languages in working memory at the same time during simultaneous interpreting, and what's more, under high cognitive pressure. Translators can check that their target-language renderings are free from interference in various ways, such as looking for collocations in reliable target-language sources on the World Wide Web (see Chapter 6) or consulting with native speakers, but interpreters have no such possibility and therefore need to be aware of the risk, be constantly vigilant about it and work on keeping their languages separate (see for instance Déjean Le Féal 1976; Thiéry 1975, 1976). One way of reducing the risk is to decide to limit oneself to one active language and one or several passive languages, since active availability is assumed to have higher interference potential than passive availability (Déjean Le Féal 1978). This is a further argument in favour of work into one's A language only whenever market conditions allow it (see below).

6. Directionality in interpreting and translation

One much-debated issue in translation and interpreting circles (see for instance Kelly *et al.* 2003; Godijns & Hinderdahl 2005) is that of directionality, i.e. the question whether interpreters and translators should preferably (or only) work into their A language or whether it is preferable or at least acceptable for them to work into their B language as well. In the 1980s, the prevailing position in the West was that high-quality expression was possible only in one's native language, hence the view that work into one's A language should be the norm. In East-European countries, the prevailing idea was that good comprehension of the source speech was only possible in one's native language, hence the need to work from one's A language into one's B language (see for instance Denissenko 1989). However, in some parts of the world, and in particular in Asian countries and in European countries with languages used by a small population, working both ways has always been a requirement because there were not enough translators and interpreters having major target languages such as English, Spanish, French or German as A languages and the local language as a B or C language. Recently, there has been increasing acknowledgment and acceptance of this fact even by representatives of institutions who have traditionally opposed work into B (see for example Donovan 2003).

The issue of native-language versus acquired-language mastery is complex and LC availability is only one of its aspects, but a highly relevant one because of the high cognitive pressure which interpreting involves. When a required LC is not available enough, be it into one's A, B or C language, there are significant risks of interpreting failure. It is not unreasonable to assume that on average, LC production availability is higher in one's native language and thus allows richer and perhaps more idiomatic speech production than in one's B language. However, setting aside those areas of activity in which an interpreter is engaged continuously over a relatively long period, LSPs are not 'native' in any of his/her working languages, and availability of their specific LCs probably depends on stimulation frequency, whatever the native or non-native status of the working language at hand. In view of the Tightrope Hypothesis (Chapter 7), it therefore seems reasonable to assume that in many cases, when the general linguistic proficiency of the interpreter is high, the distinction between his/her A language and B language may be less important than his/her familiarity with the relevant LSPs in each of the languages concerned.

In translation, language availability is not a strong determinant of performance, but editorial quality, and in particular the stylistic quality of the product, are important. For this reason, even in LSPs, it makes sense to foster translation into one's A language. On the other hand, if market conditions impose working into one's B language, this can be done both from one's A language and from one's C language. In interpreting, assuming that overall availability is lower in a B language than in an A language and that it is even lower in a C language, working from a C into a B entails higher risks of saturation and is avoided.

7. Availability and speech production tactics

7.1 High-availability preferences

As explained earlier against the background of cognitive saturation risks, LC availability status has major implications on interpreting performance, and therefore calls for certain strategic and tactical priorities. One advice given to interpreters working into a B language is to use simple words and constructions, because, as mentioned earlier, B-language LCs are presumably on the whole less available than A-language LCs and because simple words and constructions are assumed to be more available and therefore most likely to help avoid cognitive saturation. This advice applies to general language, not to specific LSP components and not to words and construction for which the interpreter has available Translinguistic Equivalences (see below). It also applies to work into one's A language when the going gets rough, essentially for the same reason.

Gravitational models similar to the one used here to represent language availability can be used for a variety of entities, perhaps for all types of information stored in long-term memory which need stimulation in order to remain available. Inter alia, they could be used to represent symbols and abbreviations for note-taking in consecutive. When they are used regularly, they become available for production and comprehension. If they are not, they become less available, and during the comprehension phase of consecutive, retrieving them may have an effect similar to that of trying to use words and structures with low availability in one's speech in simultaneous.

7.2   Translinguistic Equivalences

In the context of interpreting and language availability, it also makes sense to think of a Gravitational Model of *Translinguistic Equivalences* (TEs). Translinguistic Equivalences are defined here as regular associations or 'links' between particular LCs in two languages, essentially between lexical units and between set phrases.

At first sight, speaking of TEs may appear to be in contradiction with the position advocated throughout this book that Translation should preferably be meaning-based. As pointed out in Chapter 5 on the Sequential Model of translation and before that in Chapter 3 on fidelity, in order to be able to produce Target Texts without linguistic interference and with the help of all linguistic resources the Translator can muster in his/her active language, it is important to analyze the Source Text and grasp its meaning and the author's and clients intentions before reformulation – rather than do word-for-word translation ('transcoding'). The very idea of Translinguistic Equivalences could appear to mean that such analysis could be bypassed.

Meaning-based Translation remains the fundamental Translation approach advocated here. However, human speech includes a considerable amount of ready-made phrases (Goldman-Eisler 1958: 67-68; Cherry1978: 79). This is particularly true for the sociolects of international meetings. Moreover, in LSPs, there are often unique or quasi-unique names (technical terms) or phrases for the entities being discussed (objects, actions, ideas, feelings, objectives, functions, human agents, situations etc.). Due to the high risk of saturation during interpreting, once reference to such an entity is identified in a source speech through an analysis process, there are three possibilities: the interpreter can try to re-express the entity using his/her own words, 'deverbalize' and call up the corresponding LC in the target language from the semantic representation, or use a direct linguistic correspondence from source language to target language if available. In terms of cognitive economics, the first option is not desirable because of its cost in time and processing capacity. Moreover, it may well generate a target-language statement not in line with the standard sociolect familiar to the interpreters' listeners. The second option is linguistically acceptable but can take up valuable time and processing capacity. The third option, that of direct linguistic correspondence, is likely to save time and processing capacity which can be allotted to other parts of the source- and target speech for which no optimum ready-made solutions exist or are known to the interpreter or seem appropriate. From observation and introspection, I believe that whatever the theory, in their daily practice of interpreting, interpreters use direct linguistic correspondences very often without even thinking about it.

Even champions of meaning-based Translation mention the possibility of using such direct translinguistic links (see Seleskovitch 1976), and Gérard Ilg has always stressed in his interpreting classes and publications the advantages of using the high availability of translinguistic associations to free processing capacity for other tasks, but their importance has only been acknowledged in the literature recently through their incorporation into a number of interpreting models over the past decade years (see for example Mizuno 1997; Alonso Bacigalupe 2006; Ito-Bergerot 2006).

As is the case of LCs in production and comprehension, Translinguistic Equivalences are truly useful in interpreting only if they are highly available; if they are not, indirect paths can be more efficient, besides the fact that they entail a lesser risk of linguistic interference. As is the case of LCs, TEs become and remain highly available if they are stimulated often enough: According to de Groot and Christoffels (2006: 198), "Any translation act will become reflected in a memory trace that connects the two terms of the translation: the more often the same two terms (words or longer phrases) co-occur in a translation act, the stronger the memory connection between them will be."

In a 'natural' environment, this occurs when interpreters work frequently on the same themes and perhaps with the same groups of delegates. In a training environment, such TEs can be acquired through drills, perhaps using practice speeches from textbooks which students interpret several times or other recorded speeches. This by the way is one use of interpreting textbooks, which are popular in China (see Section 8.2).

In written translation, the use of Translinguistic Equivalences as opposed to the analysis and reformulation from the more or less deverbalized 'sense' is less attractive. The cognitive relief it affords is not necessary. Furthermore, the repetitions it may generate in the target text could be stylistically acceptable in oral speech but are inelegant in writing and may have to be removed during revision, in which case even the time gained by using TEs turns out to be a loss.

8. The Gravitational Model and language skills enhancement

8.1 The needs

As explained in Section 2, reality is somewhat remote from the ideal situation where students have an excellent mastery of their working languages and only need to work on specific skills. Many of them must invest intense efforts to bring them up to the required level, and in particular to extend their general vocabulary and knowledge of higher registers. Beyond that, they need to learn and improve both comprehension availability and production availability of LCs particularly relevant to their future work as interpreters. Depending on the market in which they intend to work (UN-type and EU-type intergovernmental organizations, non-governmental organizations or commercial companies specializing in health, statistics, economics and finance, legal issues, insurance, food, agriculture, telecommunications, satellites, medical issues etc.), this involves different LSPs and different LCs.

8.2 Methods

On the basis of availability dynamics as explained in Section 4, a few principles in language skills enhancement can be recommended:

1. Preferably, materials selected for training (texts, live speeches and recorded speeches) should have a high proportion of *relevant* LCs. In this respect, conference recordings and transcripts are ideal, as they are 100 percent relevant by definition. At the other extreme of the spectrum, poetry is not very relevant. Neither is discourse in very colloquial language. Though interpreters may encounter any type of sociolect during their working life, including poetry and slang, especially those who work for television, it makes sense to prioritize preparation for the type of language they are most likely to encounter when starting their career.

    Interestingly, Western and Asian attitudes differ towards learning materials. In the West, instructors tend to use mostly improvised or semi-improvised speeches (made out of notes, or 'oralized' from written texts) given live in the classroom by themselves, by students and by invited speakers. In Asia, and in particular in China, much use is made of textbooks which include relevant vocabulary, syntactic structures, standard phrases and sample speeches (see for example Feng 2002; Lin 2004; Zhong 2007; Zhuang & Qiu 2008; Komatsu 2005). Western instructors tend to reject the use of speeches not given live and not recent, and more generally the use of speeches which are not 'authentic' (note that this is apparently not the case in signed language interpreting – see for example Patrie 2000a, b, 2001, 2004, 2005). And yet, when the textbooks have been prepared carefully and on the basis of both experience with students and professional practice, they contain a large number of highly relevant LCs in typical speech contexts. Students can devote their attention to them until they have mastered them well, which is an advantage over random encounters which occur in live speeches given in the classroom.

2. Ideally, stimulation frequency should be high for the weakest relevant LCs, those which are in distant orbits, because they are the ones whose availability needs to be increased.

    This requirement runs contrary to a natural lexicometric distribution law: in any natural language, a small number of high-frequency LCs represent a very large proportion of LCs in texts or speeches, and as one moves away from these toward lower frequency LCs, their proportion in the texts or speeches drops steeply. This relationship between rank frequency of LCs and frequency of occurrence has been well documented for a long time (Kaeding 1897; Thorndike & Lorge 1944; Zipf 1949; Meier 1964). For instance, in a German corpus analyzed by Meier, the 30 most frequent words accounted for 30% of the total mass of words, and 50% of this total mass was made up of the 200 most frequent words, whereas 217,000 other words accounted for less than 4% of the total.

In practical terms, this means that common LCs, known even to individuals having a comparatively poor vocabulary in the language under consideration (perhaps a few thousand items), tend to be used repeatedly, while LCs with a lower frequency are encountered rarely. As a consequence, the most frequent LCs are likely to be the most available in a Speaker's mental lexicon because of their frequent use, whereas less frequent LCs are encountered much more rarely in daily language, to the extent that some may be forgotten and have to be learned anew at each encounter.

This is a particular instance of the law of diminishing returns. It explains why plain linguistic immersion can be highly profitable in the initial stages of the language learning process, when the core subset of LCs necessary for rudimentary communication needs to be strengthened, and suggests that it then becomes less and less effective for enhancing lexical command of a foreign language, as other LCs are encountered far less frequently.

In order to increase availability in the most effective way, it may be a good idea to use inter alia materials designed specifically for such purposes, in which LC frequency has been manipulated so as to provide more frequent encounters to the student than in authentic corpora. Such materials exist for elementary foreign language learning. With respect to conference language, again, there is something to say in favour of the Asian interpreting textbook system.

Also, in order to increase encounter frequency and make learning more efficient, it may make sense to have students interpret sample speeches several times. However, the exclusive use of textbook speeches is not a satisfactory solution. Firstly, it would necessarily be limited in terms of content and language – both of which evolve rapidly. Secondly, it may encourage students to move into 'automatic' form-based mode at the expense of analysis and creative meaning-based, context-base reformulation skills. A mixed method with some drills with textbook speeches and many interpreting exercises with live speeches and recordings of authentic speeches (as mentioned earlier, they are increasingly numerous on the World Wide Web) might be the most efficient – see for example the materials compiled by Dollerup (1996) and by Baigorri Jalón *et al.* (2004) for conference interpreting, as well as Patrie's *Effective Interpreting Series* publications listed in the references at the end of this book for signed language interpreting.

9. Teaching suggestions

Language availability is an aspect of working language mastery of which students are generally not aware when they consider enrolling in a conference interpreter training programme. Neither do they realize its critical importance in contributing to its successful completion. Language availability issues explain many difficulties they have as well as frequent failures, and active efforts to raise it over the training period may increase markedly their chances of success at graduation exams. Awareness-raising at an early stage – perhaps in the first weeks of training – is desirable, as it can help guide them in their practical work to enhance mastery of their working languages. Awareness-raising could even be useful earlier, when talking to language students and young translation students who consider seeking admission to a conference interpreter training programme later, so that they have a better idea of how to prepare for admission examinations. A more comprehensive discussion of issues around language availability can be conducted later in the programme, in conjunction with the presentation of the Effort Models (Chapter 7) and with coping tactics (Chapter 8).

The Gravitational Model and its dynamics can be taught in the lecture mode. The model is a convenient tool because of its visual nature. The dynamics of the model are the basis for recommendations. The crucial need to enhance and maintain availability should not be controversial, but potential implications about directionality, the use of textbooks or the use of Translinguistic Equivalences need not be mentioned if instructors have doubts about them.

10.   What students need to remember

1.   'Knowledge' of a language is more than a binary yes/no state for each lexical unit or rule. It includes availability, namely the time and effort required to retrieve the necessary knowledge for comprehension or production of Texts.
2.   High speech-comprehension availability is crucial in all interpreting modes.
3.   High speech-production availability is important in consecutive and crucial in simultaneous
4.   Availability is not static. It increases with repeated stimulation and decreases when LCs are not used. It is therefore possible to enhance availability when it is insufficient in a working language, and important to do maintenance work on one's working languages throughout one's career.
5.   For oral availability, and especially speech-comprehension availability, oral stimulation is important, while written stimulation is probably far less effective.
6.   In any language, increased availability, especially speech-production availability, entails a higher risk of linguistic interference with other languages. For this reason, it makes sense to work separately and differently on active languages and passive languages.

7. In everyday language, frequent words and expressions are encountered often and stimulation for maintenance is no problem. What is more problematic is stimulation for availability enhancement in less frequent words and expressions. Students should seek material and contexts where words and expressions relevant to conference speeches occur more frequently than in everyday language.

8. While meaning-based Translation is the rule in written translation and is important in interpreting, in the latter, the use of Translinguistic Equivalences can be helpful – but requires caution.

Chapter 10

Integrating more theory into training
The IDRC framework

1. Introduction: The advantages of a platform for introducing Translation theory to students

As explained in chapter 1, for Translator training proper, the most efficient aid from theory may be a limited set of concepts and simple models. In some training programmes, students are introduced into Translation *theory* more extensively: depending on the programmes, local academic rules may require a substantial theoretical input, especially at graduate level, or there is a local tradition of teaching theory, or course leaders decide to integrate more theory into the curriculum. In academic programmes teaching the academic discipline of Translation Studies as such as opposed to professional Translation skills, theory is obviously central.

Generally, when teaching theory in an academic discipline, several approaches are possible. One is to proceed thematically. Another is to follow a historical thread, start with the earliest ideas and/or findings and then describe further developments as they succeeded each other over time – or mix the two, as in Munday 2001. Yet another is to start with a presentation of the strongest current theory and then describe other theories by order of decreasing importance. All are rational, but at the same time problematic in the case of Translation Studies, especially when considering the needs and attitudes of translation and interpreting students:

One issue is associated with the diversity of translation and interpreting activities and with the diversity of existing Translation theories. Most Translation students are trained to become technical translators, audio-visual translators, subtitlers, conference interpreters *or* public service interpreters, some of them with signed-language interpreting working for the deaf. Their immediate interests therefore diverge to a considerable extent. At first sight, all of them could find concrete linguistic analyses of and solutions to their daily problems of some interest, but few of them would see the relevance of literary or philosophical theories, and while sociological analyses might be perceived as useful in reflection on public service interpreting, a cognitive approach seems more suited to address the conference interpreters' most salient concerns.

When a historical approach to the teaching of Translation theory is followed in the classroom, it naturally starts with ancient Greece and Rome and goes through the Middle Ages and Renaissance as in Robinson (1997), or with the early 1900s as in Venuti (2000), or perhaps with the 1970s, with the birth of Translation Studies as a discipline. In all these cases, the main approaches are historical, cultural, philosophical, religious or literary, and may be perceived as remote from the daily concerns of students and practitioners of Translation.

Andrew Chesterman (1997) adopts an original approach in analysing Translation Studies history through the concept of 'memes', units of culture which spread through populations (see Dawkins 1976). Snell-Hornby (2006) analyzes it through the concept of 'turns'. Both of these approaches are rather abstract, and again, can be perceived as remote from the student Translator's concerns.

This can breed some reluctance, and often resistance to Translation theory among students – and even among instructors. Many texts in the literature mention this problem (see for example Roberts 1988, Shuttleworth 2001, Lee 2006). Practitioners and would-be practitioners are not attracted to abstract analyses, which, to make things worse, are formulated in a language and with concepts which may require considerable efforts to grasp; neither do they perceive their usefulness. No attempt will be made here to join the debate (but, for arguments in favour of theory, see for instance Chesterman 2000, Lee 2006, Lederer 2008 as well as all the other references given in Section 6 of Chapter 1).

Nevertheless, once it is decided, for whatever reason, that a Translation theory course will be part of the requirements in a programme which basically trains students to become practitioners of translation and/or interpreting, it makes sense to look for a method which will make the theoretical content of the course more palatable to them.

One possible solution to facilitate their first steps in Translation theory is to start by introducing them to a general framework built on concepts which lie relatively close to their actual concerns. This framework can then be used as a platform for further exploration of the main theories and schools of thought, each being characterized by a certain 'position' with respect to the platform's components, and therefore with respect to the students' actual concerns.

This chapter presents such a framework, the IDRC framework, and explains its use in the classroom. As to the theories themselves, they are only characterized briefly (and partly) so as to show the relevance and potential of the framework. A few references are given for each in the next pages; full presentations and discussions are easy to find in the literature.

2.   The IDRC framework: Interpretation, decisions, resources and constraints

From the Translator's (and student's) viewpoint, Translation is essentially a form of *action* on a Text which leads to the *production* of another Text. Such action does not unfold at random and in a vacuum. It has a *direction* (or *skopos* in Vermeer's words), which is determined by the pursuit of certain *objectives* (generally communication objectives in a certain context), and is conducted with certain *resources* and under certain *constraints*.

2.1   Constraints and resources in Translation

The idea that Translation is done with some *resources* and under certain *constraints* is understood and accepted readily by students. Resources include most obviously existing words, idioms, rules of grammar, graphic forms, sounds, visual signs etc. as means to express information, ideas and intentions in the Translator's working languages. They also include the Translator's *knowledge* or *mastery* of these working languages, which, at any moment, does not cover all the existing linguistic resources. The Translator's *extra-linguistic knowledge* and Translation *knowhow*, including knowledge of the relevant *norms*, technical skills such as note-taking in consecutive interpreting or the use of Translation Memories in technical translation, relevant *strategies* and *coping tactics*, *ad hoc Knowledge Acquisition methods*, etc. can be added to the list of resources s/he can call on. The Translator's resources also include available *time*, *documents* and *tools* for ad hoc Knowledge Acquisition such as reference documents, dictionaries and glossaries, access to the Internet, equipment such as a computer and the necessary software, a table and a chair, space to work in, etc. Finally, the Translator's knowhow includes *social skills* in dealing with colleagues and clients, and for Translators who manage translation projects, *management skills* as well (see Gouadec 2002).

Constraints arise partly from *limitations in the Translator's resources*. Besides obvious limitations in the Translator's knowledge of his/working languages and extralinguistic knowledge, especially in specialized fields, the heaviest constraint may be the *lack of time*. For translators, according to a recent study by Lagarde (2009), the pressure generated by deadlines is a strong determinant of strategies and tactics. For interpreters, time constraints at cognitive scale (up to a few seconds) are strongly correlated with cognitive pressure in source speech comprehension, decision-making and target-speech production (Chapters 7 to 9). In translation, constraints are also determined by the Client's requirements with respect to page layout, type of language and terminology to be used etc., as well as, sometimes strongly so, by prevailing cultural and linguistic *norms* in the wider target environment. In interpreting, constraints are strongly determined by the speakers' 'style', including language, voice, accent, rhythm and other delivery parameters, but also by insufficient availability of documents for preparation and by the working environment, including the position of the interpreting booth (or seating arrangements at a table when doing consecutive, or seating arrangements and the speakers' and interpreters' position when doing signed language interpreting), the position and size of the screen if any etc. In public service interpreting and court interpreting, norms about the interpreter's role and latitude, but also *pressure* from one party to take sides and help rather than limit him/herself to the (increasingly challenged) neutral conduit role, are strong constraints. Note that while such norms have a constraining dimension, they also have a guiding dimension in that they help Translators decide how to act – they are constraints and resources at the same time.

2.2   Interpretation and decisions in Translation

Two other features of the Translator's action which students are well aware of are interpretation and decision-making.

2.1.1   *Interpretation*

In human translation Texts are not transcoded; they are analyzed and interpreted. Interpretation is obviously necessary when Source Texts are linguistically incorrect or clumsy, but the very transformation of visual and sound signals under which they are perceived by the Translator into meaningful words, sentences and speeches involves interpretation (Chapters 7 and 9).

2.1.2   *Decisions*

Decisions are necessarily part of the Translator's work, if only because words and grammatical structures to be used in the Target Text have to be selected by the translator or interpreter, but also because often, there are several possible interpretations of a Text or text segment, and the Translator has to decide which is the best under the circumstances (see Chapter 5 for translation). At a more fundamental and often subconscious level, decisions are involved when deciding that a visual or sound signal was produced as a physical representation of this or that word.

2.3   Structure of the IDRC framework

The IDRC view of the Translation process could therefore take the following visual form (note that contrary to the Sequential Model of written translation presented in Chapter 5, it is presented holistically, not Translation Unit by Translation Unit).

2.4   Features of the IDRC framework

As can be seen, the model is descriptive. It does not incorporate prescriptive ideas likely to be challenged by proponents of specific approaches to human Translation, as all schools of thought in the world of Translation theory can acknowledge the existence of resources and constraints in the Translator's environment, and all of them would accept the idea that interpretation and decisions are part of the Translator's work, though they would not necessarily agree on the extent, depth and latitude of interpretation-related and decision-related actions by individual Translators.

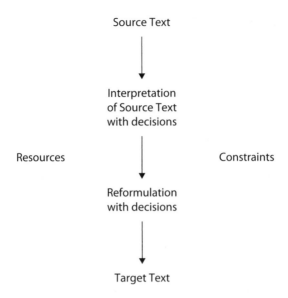

Figure 10.1 The IDRC model: Interpretation-Decisions-Resources-Constraints

Also note that the Model applies to all kinds of human Translation, from technical and legal translation to literary translation and from conference interpreting to public service interpreting through media interpreting.

Another central feature of the IDRC framework is that it *models the Translation process* and not the Translation product or the relationships between Source Texts and Target Texts as such. It is an *action-oriented model*, which, it is hoped, will appeal to students, because what they are asked to do in the classroom is act. Also note that as an action-centred model of Translation (in a more concrete way, perhaps, than the theoretical view adopted by German functionalists – see further down), IDRC places *responsibility* on the shoulders of individual Translators, who are expected to interpret and to decide rather than follow language-correspondence rules. In this respect, it presents a view of Translation rather remote from that of school translation (see Chapter 2).

3. IDRC as a framework for the introduction of Translation theories

IDRC is of little value as a standalone construct. As mentioned in Section 1, it was designed as a platform to facilitate students' access to Translation theories. The next sections explain in what way it can fulfil this function.

3.1 Viewing TS theories with IDRC

Over the past 30 years, Translation Studies (TS) has been developing at a steady pace in many directions, with paths influenced by literary theory, linguistics, including text linguistics (Hatim & Mason 1997), corpus linguistics (*Meta* 43: 4(1998)), relevance theory (Gutt 1991) and other cognitive disciplines, philosophy (Steiner 1975/1992, Stolze 2000), sociological and cultural approaches (Diriker 2004, Pym *et al.* 2006) – beyond these few examples, comprehensive accounts can be found inter alia in the 2nd edition of Routledge's *Encyclopaedia of Translation Studies* (Baker & Saldanha 2008). This represents a wealth of concepts, of theories, of research methods, to an extent which makes some people wonder whether TS has a legitimate existence as a discipline *per se*, but more importantly, which makes it difficult to find consistency in the mass of texts or to navigate among them.

The proposition that IDRC is a convenient framework to introduce Translation theories and schools of thought to Translation students rests on a number of ideas:

- Firstly, it is assumed that Translation students relate easily to the concepts 'resources', 'constraints', 'interpretation' and 'decisions'.
- Secondly, as will be explained later in this chapter, mainstream Translation theories can be at least partly characterized as a function of their approach to and treatment of resources, constraints, interpretation and decisions.
- Thirdly, such analysis makes it easier to integrate most major theories and schools of thoughts in TS into a coherent entity. Moreover, it shows that mainstream Translation theories are to a large extent complementary, each of them contributing something to awareness of and reflection on all or a subset of the relevant resources, constraints, interpretation activities and decisions.

The last two points are elaborated further in the next sections.

3.2 Translation theories viewed from the IDRC angle

The following is a thread which can be used to introduce different theories and schools of thought to students.

3.2.1 *The Translation's function and skopos theory*
When considering Translation as human action, a view which is incorporated into the IDRC platform and has been developed in theoretical terms by German functionalists (as "*Translatorisches Handeln*" or 'Translatorial action' in the words of Holz-Mäntärri 1984), a central question is whether such action has a 'direction' which could influence whatever choices Translators have when Translating. According to *skopos* theorists (see Reiss & Vermeer 1984/1991, Nord 1997), the function of the Translation, which is distinct and can be very different from the function of the original Text

(see Chapter 2), determines the Translator's action to a large extent. *Skopos* theory is therefore concerned with one determinant of the Translator's *decisions*. It is one of the two most popular theories in the Translator training environment and is especially present in German-speaking countries. It is an essentially theoretical view of Translation with prescriptive implications about the adequacy of target-oriented Translation strategies.

In terms of IDRC, *skopos* theory looks mostly at the decision components of Translation in the reformulation phase and says little about resources and constraints or about the interpretation part in the comprehension phase of the Translator's action.

3.2.2　*Prevailing norms and Toury's theory*

Once the function of a given Translation is determined, all other things being equal, the Translator is assumed to act in such as way as to serve it. According to Toury (1995), the way s/he will go about it will depend to a large extent on a set of norms which prevail in the target society, starting with a choice between target-oriented and source-oriented translation, but going further to determine what could be called 'social' choices beyond the Translator's individual choices. Toury's theory crystallized in the 1970s in the context of literary translation theory, and in particular of polysystem theory (see Even-Zohar 1990). It has developed into a popular research paradigm whereby norms in various periods of history and cultural groups are identified and discussed. While Toury's insights brought about considerable innovation in the world of Translation Studies (the 'Descriptive Translation Studies' approach is powerful in the TS community), they seem to have had little resonance in Translator training circles so far, but their relevance should not be neglected, since students, and later the professional Translators they will become, will necessarily be under some pressure to comply with norms dictated by the target society at large, but also by the Client, by readers of the translation or listeners to an interpreted speech, etc. Fidelity norms and language acceptability norms are perhaps the most conspicuous among them.

As a matter of fact, even before they become professionals, students are required to comply with classroom norms, which are defined by their instructors, and it could be useful for them to know that these are 'local' rules, not necessarily the same as those they will encounter later in the marketplace.

Like *skopos* theory, Toury's theory is positioned in the decision part of the Translator's action, with norms acting mostly as constraints, but also as resources giving the Translator some guidance (see Section 2.1).

3.2.3　*Domestication vs. Foreignization and Lawrence Venuti*

Finally, regarding the Translator's action, one major dilemma stemming from the fact that languages and cultures do not necessarily use similar words, linguistic constructions and information to describe reality, including people, feelings, actions, thoughts, social relations and physical positions, is that often a choice must be made between writing a target text which sounds like a 'native' text and losing some of the features of the source language and culture, or writing a text which keeps these features to a lesser or greater extent but sounds a bit (or more than a bit) foreign to the reader. Translation theorists and critics have been discussing this dilemma for centuries. As a matter of fact, Toury's 'initial norm' is about a choice between 'adequacy', which is source norms oriented, and 'acceptability', which is target oriented. Some innovation has been injected into the discussion by Lawrence Venuti (1995), who sees the problem not in terms of practical communication, but in ideological terms. For him, the choice of a 'domesticating strategy' (translating so as to make the text sound 'native') seems to imply ignoring or erasing to a certain extent the 'otherness' of the culture from which the Source Text is taken. The opposite choice, called 'foreignizing', is an ethical one (see Berman 1984).

This third school of thought, which is ideological in its approach, also focuses on the decision part of the Translator's action and says little about resources or constraints. It is not very relevant to the needs of non-literary Translators, whose approach is target-oriented.

3.2.4 Cognitive issues and Interpretive Theory

One of the first Translation theorists to become interested in the cognition of Translation was Danica Seleskovitch of ESIT, Paris. As a conference interpreter, she attempted to understand the mental mechanisms of interpreting, mostly through introspection and field observation – Seleskovitch 1975 is the published version of her doctoral dissertation. The theory she developed with other colleagues from ESIT, in particular Marianne Lederer (Interpretive Theory, formerly 'Theory of Sense'– *théorie du sens*), basically claims that interpreters and translators use their knowledge of languages as well as extralinguistic knowledge to extract the meaning or 'sense' from the Source Text, that this is followed by a 'deverbalization' stage in which the Translator forgets the linguistic form in which the 'sense' was conveyed in the Source Text, and then by the third and final stage, namely reformulation in the target language from the 'sense'. This theory became central to Translator training at ESIT in the 1970s and spread to other parts of the world in the form of a set of Translator training principles (see Seleskovitch 1977, 1981, Seleskovitch & Lederer 1989). It is still influential, especially in the training environment, in spite of criticism of its theoretical premises in the Interpreting Studies community (see inter alia Gile 1990, Pöchhacker 2004, Alonso Bacigalupe 2006) and even within ESIT (see Ito-Bergerot 2006).

In IDRC terms, the Interpretive Theory's main claim is that cognitive interpretation of the Source Text is central to Translation. It refers holistically to resources, essentially language mastery and extralinguistic knowledge, but does not say much about relevant constraints.

3.2.5   *Cognitive issues and Chernov's probabilistic prognosis theory*

While ESIT theorists were developing their Theory of Sense in France, in the USSR, Ghelly Chernov, a former UN interpreter, was developing his own model of simultaneous interpreting, which became and remained very influential throughout the 1980s and in the 1990s in Eastern Europe. Chernov's 'probabilistic prognosis theory' (see Chernov 2004) is based on the assumption that cognitive load on the simultaneous interpreter is very high, to such an extent that only online anticipation ("prognosis") of the speaker's statement makes it possible to interpret. This, by the way, could explain the Russian and East-European preference for work from one's A language into one's B language: anticipation is presumably easier when working from one's native language than it is when working from an acquired language because of better knowledge of transitional probabilities (see Section 5.4.1 in Chapter 7) and cultural patterns.

The focus of Chernov's theory lies clearly in (cognitive) constraints, and little is said about the direction of Translation and about non-cognitive resources and other types of constraints.

3.2.6   *Cognitive issues, cognitive psychology, Relevance Theory and the Information Processing approach*

While Interpretive Theory (IT) was developed by practitioners of conference interpreting from field observation and introspection, cognitive psychologists such as Henri Barik and David Gerver (see Gerver 1976) also became interested in the mental operations which allowed simultaneous interpreting to unfold. Their investigations followed the Information Processing approach, based on a view of cognitive operations as a series of parallel and sequential interactions between cognitive modules involving 'states'. They postulate in particular a flow of 'information' from the time the source speech is heard to the moment the target speech is uttered, representing various stages of processing with components where different kinds of memory and actions interact (see Setton 2003). Barbara Moser, a young graduate of the interpreter training programme at the University of Innsbruck, also developed a process model of interpreting on the basis of another model by cognitive psychologist Dominic Massaro (Moser 1978), and was thus the first interpreter to adopt this approach.

Concepts from cognitive psychology were absent from mainstream interpreting theory for a long time, but became popular again from the 1990s on (see Pöchhacker & Shlesinger 2002; Pöchhacker 2004). The concepts of processing capacity and working memory, as well as processing capacity limitations, have been central to reflection on interpreting over the past decade or so; they are only marginally present in research on written translation. The Effort Models presented and discussed in this book are constructed around the ideas of processing capacity and its limitations.

Also in the 1990s, another cognitive theory surfaced in Translation Studies. Following a book by Gutt (1991), translation theorists became interested in Relevance

Theory, which was developed by Dan Sperber & Deidre Wilson (1986). It claims that human communication is strongly influenced by the quest for optimal balance between the cognitive cost of (information) processing and expectations as to what one will gain from it. Relevance Theory is a strong component of Robin Setton's (1999) cognitive model of interpreting.

In IDRC terms, such cognitive theories focus on cognitive resources and constraints, and say little about the direction of the Translator's action.

Cognitive-psychological theories are only marginally present in translation research. Perhaps their strongest influence is found in Think-Aloud Protocol research done on the translation process, when analyzing the pros and cons of the method (Krings 1982/1986; Lörscher 1991; Englund-Dimitrova 2005).

3.2.7   Translation universals

Some theorists postulate the existence of so-called 'Translation universals', trends which Translators follow unwittingly. One of these 'universals', perhaps the best known, is the so-called Explicitation Hypothesis, first formulated by Shoshana Blum-Kulka (1986), according to which translations tend to be more explicit than Source Texts. Other universals are now being researched with the help of modern corpus analysis methods (see Mauranen & Kujamäki 2004). It seems that so far, research on Translation universals has focused on detecting them and on testing their existence rather than on theories about their genesis (but see below a counter-example). Such universals (or quasi-universals, if they prove to be robust in some local environments and not in others) could be associated indirectly with norms on how to perform Translation work, including *skopos*-related norms, in which case they could be considered part of a system of constraints. They can also be viewed as reflecting psychological mechanisms: for instance, Blum-Kulka believes that since Translators analyze Source Texts beyond the surface form, explicitation may be associated with a natural tendency to reflect in their own target-language wording the more comprehensive abstract representation of the text's content rather than its form. The Explicitation Hypothesis could also be explained by linguistically and culturally induced constraints, whereby Target languages may require more information than Source Texts provide explicitly in the relevant Source languages (see Chapter 3).

4.   Complementarity

When looking at Translation theories and schools of thought under the IDRC angle, one striking fact emerges: rather than direct competitors, most of these theories are complementary, each contributing insights or ideas about aspects of Translation the others have not addressed or processed in depth.

For instance, taking the two most influential theoretical paradigms in Translation didactics, *skopos* theory and Interpretive Theory, it is immediately apparent that one focuses on the direction of the Translator's act and the other on Translation cognition, but there is nothing in IT which contradicts the idea that the Translator's act depends on the *skopos* of the Translation and there is nothing in *skopos* theory which contradicts the idea that Translation is done from sense as opposed to words. Moreover, through different approaches, both theoretical paradigms support the idea that translators do not (or should not) *transcode* Source Texts into Target Texts: According to Interpretive Theory, the linguistic 'envelope' of the Source Text which carried the sense is forgotten through deverbalization and therefore becomes irrelevant, which rules out transcoding (though IT recognizes transcoding of some Text segments in particular cases); according to *skopos* theory, the Translation product depends on its *skopos*, which also means that it cannot be determined by transcoding, which is *skopos*-neutral. There does not seem to be any obvious reasons why instructors could not combine the two paradigms, and the fact that proponents from these two schools of thought seldom quote proponents of the other looks like a case of missed opportunities to use theoretical complementarity for student guidance.

To take another example, there can be little doubt that functionalists are aware of constraints in the Translator's work, but these are not their focus. On the other hand, Information Processing scholars work on cognitive constraints, but do not necessarily take the function of Translation into account. This can lead to inadequate analyses of Translation outputs and Translation strategies and tactics: some omissions and changes in the information or in the order of information found in the Translation product can be the result of deliberate action rather than secondary effects of cognitive overload, something which cognitive psychologists seem to have missed in their analyses of interpreting performance and which led to severe criticism by interpreters (see for instance Bros-Brann 1975 or Seleskovitch's reaction to an interdisciplinary symposium as reported in Widlund-Fantini 2007: 159). When training interpreters, proponents of Interpretive Theory and of functionalist theories could gain from incorporating cognitive constraints into their reflections, and followers of the Information Processing approach would gain better ecological validity and analytical accuracy when incorporating *skopos* and other communicational parameters into their experiments and analyses.

A similar analysis of schools of thought in TS leads to the conclusion that there is no contradiction between the idea that norms determine partly the Translators' choices (Toury's theories) and IT or *skopos* theory. As explained in Section 3.2.2, at micro-social level, these norms, as imposed by the Translator's Client with respect to language, layout, terminology, treatment of particular content etc. can be viewed as constraints under which the Translator has to act.

Cognitive theories can be seen as complementing IT, *skopos* theory and Toury's theory. *Skopos* theory and Toury say little about Translation cognition. IT does, but at a holistic level, when referring to Source Text comprehension on the basis of one's linguistic and extralinguistic knowledge, to deverbalization as a cognitive phenomenon and to reverbalization on the basis of 'sense'. Cognitive theories go into more detailed analysis of cognition. They seek to develop increasingly accurate models of reality with descriptive and predictive power. They therefore try to cover more and more ground and take on board new information elicited through experiments which explore various ideas and hypotheses. They are in competition with each other in the Popperian sense of scientific evolution, and far less stable than holistic theories or other theories which are not submitted to constant testing. However, progress in cognitive research has generated several ideas and concepts which have remained stable over a long period and can be incorporated into Translation theories. One of them is the idea of limitations in the human brain's attentional resources; another is the distinction between automatic and non-automatic operations; yet another is the working memory construct *per se*, though its precise architecture and operation are still subject to speculation and research, with various proposed models (Timarová 2008). These ideas have been integrated into recent models of interpreting, including Gile's Effort Models (see Chapter 7) and other models by Setton (1999) and Alonso Bacigalupe (2006).

All TS theories are not complementary, and some competition and oppositions can also be identified among them. For instance, it seems that ESIT's concept of deverbalization as a fading of language form from memory which occurs *after* comprehension may be in contradiction with the role and place of form-forgetting in language comprehension as analyzed by cognitive psychology. While it has been known for a long time (see Sachs 1967, or even Huey 1908, cited in Just and Carpenter 1992) that readers/listeners tend to forget the linguistic form of an utterance soon after they have heard/read it, this phenomenon should perhaps be viewed as *part of comprehension* rather than as an *ulterior* process, at least as regards continuous spontaneous speech: since comprehension of Text leads to a higher-level representation of its content which is sent to long-term memory, as soon as such a representation is achieved for a given Text 'chunk', there is no further need for information on its initial linguistic form in working memory which, being limited in resources, needs them to process the next incoming chunk – and therefore makes space by deleting (partly) linguistic information (see Just and Carpenter 1992: 123). In the case of the translation of single words or very short single-sentence statements, IT's view of deverbalization and this fading of information about form from memory may coincide, but in longer sentences and continuous speech, this is no longer the case.

Nevertheless, there is enough complementarity without oppositions between the theories to show the positive contribution of each in the Translation Studies landscape with the help of IDRC. It is clear from the emerging 'landscape' that teaching one theory and ignoring all others, as has been the practice in some institutions for many years, is counterproductive, as students quickly realize that no single theory provides answers, if only tentative, to questions arising from all the problems they encounter, which may be one reason for their loss of interest in things theoretical.

5. Using IDRC in the classroom

5.1 The role of IDRC – a reminder

IDRC is not a theory in itself. It was developed as an access ramp to Translation theories for students assumed to have little interest in them, with priority given to didactic efficiency. It was therefore designed to account mostly for the main theories found in the Translator training environment.

As such, the platform is not a very good tool to account for machine translation, or to help introduce linguistic theories in the classroom, except perhaps, to a limited extent, theories from pragmatics and cognitive linguistics. It does give instructors the possibility of introducing linguistic phenomena as resources on one hand, and constraints on the other, but does not take them much further in this direction. Neither has IDRC been conceived as a tool for the introduction of TS schools of thought with strong ideological components or implications such as post-colonialist theories, deconstructionism, feminism, Translation critique etc. It is probably most helpful when introducing to students the theories listed in Section 3.

5.2 IDRC in the classroom

The main potential advantages of IDRC as a tool for the classroom are the following:

- As a theoretical structure, it is a very simple one, with 4 components organized into one linear input-processing-output axis and two lateral components, one referring to resources and the other to constraints.
- All the components are close to the students' daily experience of Translation and do not require much assimilation of abstract concepts and terms.
- The whole structure can be easily accepted as reflecting the students' struggles with their Translation assignments. It is perhaps not unreasonable to assume that when the model is presented to them, they may welcome it as the prelude to a series of answers to their practical problems.
- Last but not least, IDRC is a good opportunity to hammer home some principles of human Translation as it is taught in most professional Translator training programmes throughout the world, in particular the idea that it is the Translator's duty to take decisions and the idea of the Translator's responsibility as a communicator.

To leverage these advantages, instructors can introduce the IDRC model and the teaching of theory by making the following points:

-   The practice of Translation has always been associated with difficulties such as the students themselves experience.
-   Over the centuries, translators, philosophers, theologians and others have been thinking about these difficulties and about how best to solve them.
-   More recently, these thoughts have been turned into academic and scientific theories. Basically, these theories seek to explore what Translators do, why they do it, and what they could do to solve problems and to Translate better.
-   Theories are conceptual constructs. Each is a tentative and provisional answer to questions, each has a slightly different angle and/or relies on different sets of data. Some may be formulated in somewhat abstract terms, and as students will see, they may go in different directions. In order to help understand what they are all about, they will be introduced within a framework which models Translation as a process involving interpretation and decisions in which the Translator operates with certain resources and under certain constraints. Each theory will be first characterized as focusing on one or several of these components and as highlighting some core ideas. Students are invited to keep these in mind so as to be able to navigate more easily among the theories.

After this short introduction, explanations about the theories themselves should be easier, especially if students are reminded periodically of the main thrust of each and of their respective positions in the IDRC framework.

Glossary

This glossary has been compiled to help readers understand some specialized terms used in this book, especially those which are used in a specific way here.

Active knowledge of a language   the ability to produce texts/speech in that language.

Active language   A language one works *into*. See *passive language*.

ad hoc Knowledge Acquisition   the acquisition of new knowledge for the purpose of preparing for or completing a Translation assignment.

Attentional resources   often used as a synonym for *processing capacity* available in the human brain for non-automatic operations.

Authentic text   An original text, as opposed to a translated text or a text inspired by another text, summarizing another text etc.

Availability   In this book, an abbreviation of *language availability*, which refers to the time and amount of processing capacity required to turn a visual or auditory signal into a language element such as a word, a syllable, a vowel or consonant etc. in comprehension, and the time and amount of processing capacity required to retrieve from long-term memory the appropriate words or linguistic structures which are necessary to express verbally an idea or piece of information.

Booth   When conference interpreters talk about 'the booth', they talk about the booth from which they do simultaneous interpreting. 'In the booth' refers to what happens during simultaneous interpreting.

Chunk   In the psycholinguistics literature, speech is assumed to be divided up into processing units or 'chunks'. In this book, similar concepts such as 'Translation Unit', 'Text segment' or 'speech segment' are used in the context of discussions of translation and interpreting, and the term 'chunk' is used in chapter 10 when discussing speech perception as such.

Conduit role   The representation of the Translator's role as that of a 'neutral' conduit which communicates contents without changing them. The 'conduit role' is associated with the image of the Translator's 'neutrality' and 'invisibility'.

Consecutive interpreting   a form of interpreting in which the speaker and interpreter alternate when speaking, in contrast to simultaneous interpreting, in which the speaker and interpreter speak at the same time. Conference interpreters make a distinction between 'true consecutive' and sentence-by-sentence consecutive (see *true consecutive*). When they refer to 'consecutive', they mean 'true consecutive' unless explicitly indicated otherwise.

Declarative knowledge   knowledge which can be described, such as facts known. It contrasts with *procedural knowledge*, which refers to know-how or knowing how to *do* things without necessarily being able to describe what one is doing.

Delegates   In the conference interpreters' jargon, the speakers and listeners at a conference, as opposed to interpreters, technicians and other service staff.

Depth of processing   In this book, the extent to which something has been analyzed.

Deverbalization   This concept, coined by Danica Seleskovitch of ESIT, Paris, has two meanings. One, which was Seleskovitch's initial use of the term, refers to the alleged stage during which a translator or interpreter who has understood a source-language statement forgets its linguistic structure and only keeps its non-verbal 'sense' in mind before reformulating it in the target language. The other one, which is used in this book unless explicitly indicated otherwise, refers to a deliberate attempt to Translate source-Texts with reference to their meaning and supposed *skopos* without interference from the source language.

Experts   In this book, the term refers to non-Translators who have specialized knowledge. Experts may be enlisted to cooperate with Translators in partnerships (see chapter 6).

Extralinguistic Knowledge, World Knowledges   Knowledge of 'reality' as opposed to knowledge of the language or *linguistic knowledge*.

Falsification   According to Karl Popper, an influential philosopher of science, a strong requirement from a scientific theory is that it be falsifiable, in other words, that it be formulated in such a way as to make it possible to show it is false if this is the case. Theories which are too general or formulated in such a way that it is impossible to demonstrate that the explanation they provide for the part of reality they describe does not hold are considered by Popper 'weak' scientific theories.

Information Acquisition   In the context of ad hoc Knowledge Acquisition (chapter 6), the acquisition of information for the specific purpose of preparing for or completing a specific Translation assignment (see also ad hoc Knowledge Acquisition).

Informational Texts   Texts with an essentially informational content, as opposed to an aesthetic content. Informational Texts include scientific, technical and other LSP texts, press articles, administrative texts, but also some advertisement texts which focus on facts, such as specifications of products. Other advertisement Texts may give priority to an aesthetic message. Literary works often include informational parts. Poems are not informational texts. Some TS scholars such as Jean Delisle use the term 'pragmatic texts' for 'informational texts' as they are defined here.

Intended Receiver   The reader or listener targeted by the Sender, as opposed to other readers or listeners.

Interpretation   this term is used here in the wide sense of assigning a meaning to an utterance or Text segment. The oral/signed form of Translation is referred to as *interpreting*.

Isomorphism   Two entities (in the case of this book, languages and cultural systems) are *isomorphic* when unique bi-directional correspondences between units (in this case, words, idioms, grammatical structures etc.) exist between them, for instance when for any word in one language there is one and only one corresponding word in another. Natural languages are close to isomorphic only in very restricted, specialized subsets.

I/T   Interpreting and translation. Also found as T/I and T&I. An alternative is *Translation* with a capital T.

Language availability   See *availability*.

Language Constituents (LCs)   In this book, the discrete components of a person's *declarative knowledge of a language:* General words, lexical terms, rules of grammar, style, spelling etc. Rules of grammar, style, spelling etc. are called *LC rules* in this book

Linguistic knowledge   See *extralinguistic knowledge.*

Mental lexicon   The set of lexical units, mostly 'words', which are stored in a person's (long-term) memory.

Message   In this book, not the statement as a whole, but part of its content, more precisely the part of its content which the Sender wishes to get across to the Receiver (as opposed to other parts of the content – see chapter 3). The Message is the 'Primary Information' in an informational statement.

Native environment of a Text   the origin of a Text: its initial author and the circumstances under which it was produced.

Oralize   Read a written text while changing its structure and wording and giving it the required prosody so that it becomes as close as possible to an ad-libbed speech. 'Oralizing' is one way of providing training material for interpreting exercises in the classroom on the basis of written texts.

Packaging   a synonym of 'form', referring to the choice of words, font, page layout and graphics in written translation, to features of the voice and delivery in spoken and signed utterances.

Passive knowledge of a language   the ability to understand texts/speeches in that language.

Passive language, Passive working language   a language *from which* one works into an *active language.*

Primary Information   The information which a Sender wants to send across to the Receiver. In informational Texts, the 'Message' and 'Primary Information' are synonymous.

Priming   In psychology, a phenomenon whereby if a stimulus has been presented to a person once, when it is presented next, reaction to it is faster. In the context of language availability (chapter 9), certain situations may prime certain language subsets (*Sectors*).

Principals   In a Translated communication situation, the Sender and Receiver(s). Other communication actors in professional Translation include the Client and the Translator.

Procedural knowledge   Knowing how to do things. See 'declarative knowledge'.

Public Service Interpreting   In this book, a synonym of community interpreting.

Receiver   reader or listener.

Referent   What a word or expression refers to (a person, object, idea, action, characteristic etc.)

Secondary Text   a text or speech which reports on an original text or speech (a summary, synopsis, criticism, translation of the original text or speech, etc.). The distinction is made when discussing the reliability of texts or speeches used as sources for ad hoc Knowledge Acquisition (chapter 6).

Sector   In the context of the Gravitational Model (chapter 9), a subset of words and rules pertaining to some specific activity (technical, artistic, relating to a sports activity, a hobby, etc.) or field of interest.

Segment (Text-segment, speech-segment)   A short part of a speech or text, as opposed to the whole speech or text. The concept of 'segment' is used when referring to 'local' analysis. In the Sequential Model of translation (chapter 5), segments become 'Translation Units'. In a discussion of psycholinguistic processing of speech, such segments are often referred to as 'chunks'.

Sender   author of a text to be translated or speaker whose utterances are being interpreted

Skopos   A term introduced by Hans Vermeer to refer to the 'function' or 'purpose' of a text, including a translation.

Sociolect   the language variant used by a social group as opposed to the wider national or supranational community (of French speakers, English speakers, German speakers etc.). Technolects and language variants used by lawyers, by scientists in various fields, by intergovernmental and non-governmental organizations etc. are all sociolects.

Strategies   In this book, strategies are planned actions, as opposed to 'tactics', which are online reactions to problems encountered or anticipated - see 'tactics'.

Tactics   actions taken by a Translator when encountering problems online. In the literature, they are often referred to as 'strategies', but here the distinction is made between online actions ('tactics') and action with a longer-term effect in mind ('strategies') – see 'strategies'.

Text (with a capital T)   written texts and oral/signed speeches.

Transcoding   word-for-word translation, as opposed to analysis and meaning-based translation. The French term *transcodage* seems to have been coined by Danica Seleskovitch of ESIT. Seleskovitch also used 'code-switching' for 'transcoding' in Seleskovitch 1976.

Translate (with a capital T)   translate or interpret.

Translation (with a capital T)   translation and interpreting. See also *I/T*.

Translation Studies (TS)   The academic discipline which studies translation and interpreting. The term was coined by James Holmes in the 1970s (see Holmes 1972/1987), and is often mistaken to mean the acquisition of Translation competence at school or at university.

Translation Unit   A short Source-Text segment on which a Translator's attention focuses while Translating. It can range from a single word to a short sentence, sometimes extending to medium-length sentences if they are simple to grasp. Translation Units are conceptually close to 'Processing Units' or *chunks*.

Translator (with a capital T)   Translator or interpreter.

Translinguistic Equivalences (TEs)   Regular correspondences between words, groups of words, idioms and utterances in two languages.

'true consecutive'   conference interpreters often distinguish between 'true consecutive', in which segments to be interpreted are generally a few minutes long and require note-taking, and sentence-by-sentence consecutive, which does not require the same skills.

World Knowledge   See Extralinguistic knowledge.

Bibliography

AIIC. 1982. *Practical Guide for Professional Interpreters*. Geneva: AIIC.

Aitchison, Jean. 1987. *Words in the Mind. An Introduction to the Mental Lexicon*. Cambridge, Massachussets: Basil Blackwell.

Albl-Mikasa, Michaela. 2006. "Reduction and expansion in notation texts." In Heine, Carmen, Klaus Schubert & Heidrun Gerzymisch-Arbogast (eds). *Text und Translation. Theory and Methodology of Translation. Jahrbuch Übersetzen und Dolmetschen*. DGÜD. Tübingen: Gunter Narr. 195–214.

Allignol, Claire. 1995. *Une difficulté de la traduction technique allemand-français: les déficits rédactionnels dans les textes de départ comme source d'erreurs en traduction*. Doctoral dissertation, Nanterre: Université de Paris X.

Allioni, Sergio. 1989. "Towards a grammar of consecutive interpretation." In Gran, Laura & John Dodds (eds). 191–197.

Alonso Bacigalupe, Luís. 1999. "Recepción del mensaje y preparación del texto: resultados de un estudio experimental en IS." In Lugrís, Alberto Álvarez & Anxo Fernández Ocampo (eds). *Anovar/Anosar Estudios de traducción e interpretación*. Universidade de Vigo, Servicio de Publicacións. Vol. 2. 11–25.

Alonso Bacigalupe, Luís. 2006. *Hacia un nuevo modelo de procesamiento de la información en interpretación simultánea: resultados de un estudio experimental*. Doctoral dissertation. Universidade de Vigo, Facultade de Filoloxia e Traducción, Departamento de Traducción e Lingüística.

Anderson, John. R. 1980. *Cognitive Psychology and Its Implications*. San Francisco: W.H. Freeman.

Anderson, Linda. 1979. *Simultaneous Interpretation: Contextual and Translation Aspects,* unpublished M.A. thesis. Montreal: Concordia University.

Andres, Dörte. 2000. *Konsekutivdolmetschen und Notation. Empirische Untersuchung mentaler Prozesse bei Anfängern in der Dolmetscherausbildung und professionellen Dolmetschern*. Unpublished doctoral dissertation, University of Vienna.

Angelleli, Claudia. 2004. *Revisiting the Interpreter's Role*. Amsterdam/Philadelphia: John Benjamins.

Baddeley, Alan D. & G. Hitch. 1974. "Working Memory". In Bower, G.A. (ed). *The Psychology of Learning and Motivation*. New York: Academic Press.

Baigorri Jalón (dir.), Jesús, Icíar Alonso Araguás & Marina Pascual Olaguíbel. 2004. *Materiales para interpretación consecutiva y simultánea (alemán, francés e inglés)*. Salamanca: Ediciones Universidad de Salamanca.

Bajo, María Teresa, Presentación Padilla, Ricardo Muñoz, Francisca Padilla, Carlos Gómez, María Carmen Puerta, Pilar Gonzalvo, Pedro Macizo. 2001. "Comprehension and memory processes in translation and interpreting." *Quaderns. Revista de traducció* n° 6. 27–31.

Baker, Mona & Gabriela Saldanha (eds). 2008. *Routledge Encyclopedia of Translation Studies*. Second Edition. London and New York: Routledge.

Bédard, Claude. 1986. *La traduction technique*. Montréal: Linguatech.

Bélanger, Danielle-Claude. 1995. «Les spécificités de l'interprétation en langue des signes québecoise. De l'analyse à la préservation de l'équilibre d'interprétation». Online paper, http://www.cvm.qc.ca/dcb/pages/effort.htm. Accessed on the 28th of December 1998.

Berman, Antoine. 1984. *L'épreuve de l'étranger*. Paris: Gallimard.

Bertone, Laura. 1989. "Teaching and Learning as Global Experiences", in Monterey Institute of International Studies, Division of Translation and Interpretation. *Proceedings of the Twentieth Anniversary Symposium on the Training of Teachers of Translation and Interpretation*. Pages not numbered.

Biderman, M.T.C. & N. Ravazzi. 1984. "Vocabulary Learning in the Mother Tongue", in den Hase, Jan & Jos Nivette (eds). *Proceedings of AILA Brussels 1984*. 518–521.

Blum-Kulka, Shoshana. 1986. "Shifts in Cohesion and Coherence in Translation", in House, Juliane & Shoshana Blum-Kulka (eds). *Interlingual and Intercultural Communication: Discourse and Cognition in Translation and Second Language Acquisition Studies*. Tübingen: Narr. 17–35.

Bonnet, Alain. 1984. *L'intelligence artificielle. Promesses et réalités*. Paris: Inter Editions.

Bossé Andrieu, Jacqueline. 1981. «L'admission des candidats aux écoles de traduction», in Delisle, Jean (ed). 163–174.

Bouderradji, Khadija. 2004. *Formation des traducteurs et réalité professionnelle: harmonie ou discordance ?* Mémoire de DEA, Université Lyon 2.

Broadbent, D.E. 1958. *Perception and Communication*. New York: Pergamon Press.

Bros-Brann, Eliane. 1975. "Critical comments on H.C. Barik's article: Interpreters talk a lot among other things". *Babel* 21:2. 93–94.

Brown, Gillian & George Yule. 1983. *Discourse analysis*. Cambridge University Press.

Bühler, Hildegund. 1986. "Linguistic (Semantic) and Extralinguistic (Pragmatic) Criteria for the Evaluation of Conference Interpretation and Interpreters". *Multilingua* 5:4. 231–236.

Buchweitz, Augusto, Robert A. Mason, Mihoko Hasegawa & Marcel Just. 2009. "Japanese and English sentence reading comprehension and writing systems: An fMRI study of first and second language effects on brain activation". *Bilingualism: Language and Cognition*. http://journals.cambridge.org. Accessed on February 5, 2009.

Caminade, Monique & Anthony Pym. 1995. *Les formations en traduction et interprétation. Essai de recensement mondial*. Special issue of *Traduire*, Paris: Société Française des Traducteurs.

Campagne, Louise. 1981. «Aptitudes, intérêts et réussite scolaire en traduction: étude longitudinale», in Delisle, Jean (ed). 175–192.

Caplan, David & Gloria Waters. 1998. "Verbal Working Memory and Sentence Comprehension." Draft of an article accepted for publication (Copyright 1998: Cambridge University Press), accessed on July 23, 2008   at *http://copgprints.org/623/0/bbscaplan.html*

Carroll, John B. 1978. "Linguistic Abilities in Translators and Interpreters", in Gerver, David & H. Wallace Sinaiko (eds). 119–129.

Cartellieri, Claus. 1983. "The Inescapable Dilemma: Quality and/or Quantity". *Babel* 29:4. 209–213.

Cary, Edmond. 1985. *Comment faut-il traduire ?* Lille: Presses Universitaires de Lille.

Castellano, Lanna. 1983. "The Practical Tools Employed", in Picken, Catriona (ed). 47–79.

Cattaneo, E. 2004. *Idiomatic expressions in conference interpreting*. Graduation thesis, SSLMIT, Università degli Studi di Bologna, Sede di Forlí.

Čeňková, Ivana. 1988. *Teoretické aspekty simultánního tlumočení*. Doctoral dissertation, Prague, Charles University.

Čeňková, Ivana a kolektiv (ed). 2001. *Teorie a didaktika tlumočení*. Praha: Univerzita Karlova Filozofická fakulta.

Chernov, Ghelly V. 1973. "Towards a Psycholinguistic Model of Simultaneous Interpretation" (in Russian). *Linguistische Arbeitsberichte* (Leipzig) n° 7. 225–260.

Chernov, Ghelly V. 2004. *Inference and Anticipation in Simultaneous Interpreting*. Amsterdam/Philadelphia: John Benjamins.

Cherry, Colin. 1978. *On Human Communication. A Review, a Survey and a Criticism*. Cambridge, Massachussets and London, England: The MIT Press.

Chesterman, Andrew. 1997. *Memes of Translation*. Amsterdam/Philadelphia: John Benjamins.

Chesterman, Andrew. 2000. "Teaching strategies for emancipatory translation." In Schäffner & Adab (eds). 77–89.

Christoffels, Ingrid. 2004. *Cognitive Studies in Simultaneous Interpreting*. University of Amsterdam: Experimenteel-psychologische onderzoekshool.

Clark, Herbert & Eve V. Clark. 1977. *Psychology and Language*. San Diego, New York, Chicago, Atlanta, Washington D.C., London, Sydney, Toronto: Harcourt Brace Jovanovitch, Publishers.

Collados Aís, Ángela & Manuela Fernández Sánchez (eds). 2001. *Manual de interpretación Bilateral*. Granada: Comares.

Collados Aís, Ángela, Manuela Fernández Sánchez, Daniel Gile (eds). 2003a. *La evaluación de la calidad en interpretación: investigación*. Granada: Comares.

Collados Aís, Ángela, Manuela Fernández Sánchez, E. Macarena Pradas Macías, Concepción Sánchez Adam, Elisabeth Stévaux (eds). 2003b. *La evaluación de la calidad en interpretación: docencia y profesión*. Granada: Comares.

Collados Aís, Ángela, E. Macarena Prada Macías, Elisabeth Stévaux & Olalla García Becerra (eds). 2007. *La evaluación de la calidad en interpretación simultánea: parámetros de incidencia*. Granada: Editorial Comares.

Condon, John & Mitsuko Saito (eds). 1974. *Intercultural Encounters with Japan*. Tokyo: The Simul Press.

Costermans, Jean. 1980. *Psychologie du langage*. Bruxelles: Pierre Mardaga.

Croker, Charlie. 2006. *Løst in Tränšlatioπ*. London: O'Mara Books Limited.

Dahout, J-C. & C. Quéniart. 2000. «De quoi un traducteur doit-il être capable ?», In Gouadec, Daniel (ed). *Formation des traducteurs. Actes du colloque international de Rennes 2 (24–25 septembre 1999)*. Paris: La Maison du dictionnaire.

Dam, Helle. 2001. "On the option between form-based and meaning-based interpreting: the effect of source text difficulty on lexical target text form in simultaneous interpreting." *The Interpreters' Newsletter* 11. 27–55.

Dam, Helle. 2004a. "Interpreters' notes: on the choice of language." *Interpreting* 6:1. 3–17.

Dam, Helle. 2004b. "Interpreters' notes. On the choice of form and language." In Hansen, Gyde, Kirsten Malmkjær & Daniel Gile (eds). *Claims, Changes and Challenges in Translation Studies*. Amsterdam/Philadelphia: John Benjamins. 251–261.

Dancette, Jeanne. 1989. «La faute de sens en traduction». *TTR* 2:2. 83–102.

Datta, J. 1991. "The role of judgement in translation." *Language International* 3:4. 15–18.

Dawkins, Richard. 1976. *The Selfish Gene*. Oxford: Oxford University Press.

Dawrant, Andrew. 1996. *Word Order in Chinese-English Simultaneous Interpretation: an Initial Exploration*. MA thesis, Fu Jen University, Taipei.

de Beaugrande, R. 1980. *Text, Discourse and Process. Towards a Multidisciplinary Science of Texts*. Vol. IV. New Jersey: Ablex Publications.

de Groot, A.M.B. 2000. "A Complex-skill Approach to Translation and Interpreting". In Tirkkonen-Condit, Sonja & Ritta Jääskeläinen (eds). 53–68.

de Groot, A.M.B. & Christoffels, I.K. 2006. "Language control in bilinguals: Monolingual tasks and simultaneous interpreting." *Bilingualism: Language and Cognition* 9:2. 189–201.

de Groot, A.M.B., & Christoffels, I.K. 2007. "Processes and mechanisms of bilingual control: insights from monolingual task performance extended to simultaneous interpretation." *Journal of Translation Studies: 10*. 17–41.

de Manuel Jerez, Jesús. 2006. *La incorporación de la realidad profesional a la formación de intérpretes de conferencia mediante las nuevas tecnologías y la investigación-acción. (Bringing Professional Reality into Conference Interpreter Training through New Technologies and Action Research)*. Doctoral dissertation, University of Granada.

Déjean Le Féal, Karla. 1976. «Le perfectionnement linguistique». *Etudes de Linguistique Appliquée* n° 24. 42–51.

Déjean Le Féal, Karla. 1978. *Lectures et improvisations - Incidences de la forme de l'énonciation sur la traduction simultanée,* unpublished doctoral dissertation. University Paris 3.

Déjean Le Féal, Karla. 1981. *L'enseignement des méthodes d'interprétation.* In Delisle, Jean (ed). 75–98.

Déjean Le Féal, Karla. 2002. «La "théorie du sens" au banc d'essai». In Israël, Fortunato (ed). *Identité, altérité, équivalence ? La traduction comme relation.* Paris/Caen: Lettres Modernes Minard. 145–156.

Delisle, Jean. 1980. *L'analyse du discours comme méthode de traduction.* Ottawa: Editions de l'université d'Ottawa.

Delisle, Jean (ed). 1981. *L'enseignement de l'interprétation et de la traduction.* Ottawa: Editions de l'université d'Ottawa.

Denissenko, Jurij. 1989. "Communicative and interpretative linguistics". In Gran & Dodds (eds). 155–160.

Dillinger, Michael. L. 1989. *Component Processes of Simultaneous Interpreting,* Ph.D. dissertation. McGill University, Montreal.

Diriker, Ebru. 2004. *De-/Re- Contextualizing Conference Interpreting.* Amsterdam/Philadelphia: John Benjamins.

Dollerup, Cay. 1996. *A corpus of consecutive interpreting.* Copenhagen, Studies in translation 5, Centre for Translation Studies and Lexicography, University of Copenhagen.

Dollerup, Cay. 2007. *Basics of Translation Studies.* Shanghai: Shanghai Foreign Language Education Press.

Dollerup, Cay & Anne Loddegaard (eds). 1992. *Teaching Translation and Interpreting: Training, Talent and Experience,* Amsterdam/Philadelphia: John Benjamins Publishing Company.

Dollerup, Cay & Annette Lindegaard (eds). 1994. *Teaching Translation and Interpreting 2: Insights, Aims and Visions.* Papers from the Second Language International Conference, Elsinore, 4–6 June 1993. (=Benjamins Translation Library 5). Amsterdam/Philadelphia: Benjamins.

Donovan-Cagigos, Clare. 1990. *La fidélité en interprétation.* Unpublished doctoral dissertation, Université Paris 3.

Donovan, Clare. 2003. "Teaching simultaneous interpretation into B". In Kelly *et al.* (eds). 367–380.

Dubuc, Robert. 1978. *Manuel pratique de terminologie.* Montréal: Linguatec.

Durieux, Christine. 1990a. «Le foisonnement en traduction technique d'anglais en français». *Meta* 35:1. 55–60.

Durieux, Christine. 1990b. «La recherche documentaire en traduction technique: conditions nécessaires et suffisantes». *Meta* 35:4. 669–675.

Durieux, Christine. 1992. «Transcodage et traduction». *Turjuman* 1:1. 15–22.

Englund-Dimitrova, Birgitta. 2005. *Expertise and Explicitation in the Translation Process.* Amsterdam/Philadelphia: John Benjamins.

Even-Zohar, Itamar. 1990. *Polysystem Studies.* Tel-Aviv: The Porter Institute for Poetics and Semiotics ; Durham, NC: Duke University Press, special issue of *Poetics Today* 11.1.

Eysenck, Michael W. & Mark T. Keane. 1990. *Cognitive Psychology A Student's Handbook.* Hove and London (UK), Hillsdale (USA): Lawrence Erlbaum Associates.

Feldweg, Erich. 1980. "Dolmetschen einsprachig lehren? Bericht über ein gelungenes Experiment". *Lebende Sprachen* 25:4.

Feldweg, Erich. 1989. "The Significance of Understanding in the Process of Interpreting", in Gran, Laura & John Dodds (eds). 139–140.

Feldweg, Erich. 1990. "Should conference interpreters specialize?" *The ATA Chronicle* 4:1. 161–167.

Fellus, Osnat. 2005. *Self-Corrections in Simultaneous Interpretation in the Language Pair Hebrew and English.* MA thesis, Bar Ilan University, The Department of Translation and Interpreting Studies. (in Hebrew)

Feng, Jason (Feng Jian Zhong). 2002. *A Practical Course in Interpretation*. Nanjing: Yilin. (in Chinese)

Folkart, Barbara. 1984. "A Thing-Bound Approach to the Practice of Technical Translation." *Meta* 29:3. 229–246.

Fox, Olivia. 2000. "The Use of Translation Diaries in a Process-Oriented Translation Teaching Methodology". In Schäffner & Adab (eds). 115–130.

Froeliger, Nicolas. 2004. «*Felix Culpa*: congruence et neutralité dans la traduction des textes de réalité». *Meta* 49:2. 236–246.

Fukuii, Haruhiro & Tasuke Asano. 1961. *Eigotsûyaku no jissai (An English Interpreter's Manual)*. Tokyo: Kenkyusha.

Fujimura, Katsumi. 1983. *Hanashikotoba to kakikotoba (Spoken Language and Written Language)*. Tokyo: Hiromatsushoten.

Garzone, Giuliana, Francesca Santulli & Daniela Damiani. 1990. *La terza lingua. Metodo di stesura degli appunti e traduzione consecutiva*. Milano: Cisalpino.

Geleff, P. 1971. «De deux mots, il faut choisir…le meilleur». *Meta* 26:1.

Gémar, Jean-Claude. 1983. «De la pratique à la théorie, l'apport des praticiens à la théorie générale de la traduction». *Meta* 28:4. 323–333.

Gémar, Jean-Claude. 1990. «Pour une méthode générale de traduction: traduire par l'interprétation du texte». *Meta* 35:4. 657–668.

Gentile, Adolfo. 1991. "The Application of Theoretical Constructs from a Number of Disciplines for the Development of a Methodology of Teaching in Interpreting and Translating." *Meta* 36:2. 344–351.

Gerver, David. 1974a. "Simultaneous Listening and Speaking and Retention of Prose." *Quarterly Journal of Experimental Psychology* 26. 337–342.

Gerver, David. 1974b. "The Effects of Noise on the Performance of Simultaneous Interpreters: Accuracy of Performance." *Acta Psychologica* 38. 159–167.

Gerver, David. 1976. "Empirical Studies of Simultaneous Interpretation: a Review and a Model". In Brislin, R. (ed). *Translation. Applications and Research*. New York: Gardner Press. 165–207.

Gerver, David & H. Wallace Sinaiko (eds). 1978. *Language Interpretation and Communication*. NewYork and London: Plenum Press.

Gile, Daniel. 1983a. «L'enseignement de l'interprétation: utilisation des exercices unilingues en début d'apprentissage». *Traduire* n°113. 7–12.

Gile, Daniel. 1983b. «Des difficultés de langue en interprétation simultanée». *Traduire* n°117. 2–8.

Gile, Daniel. 1984a. *La formation aux métiers de la traduction japonais-français: problèmes et méthodes*. Unpublished doctoral dissertation. INALCO, Université Paris 3.

Gile, Daniel. 1984b. «Les noms propres en interprétation simultanée». *Multilingua* 3–2. 79–85.

Gile, Daniel. 1985. «La sensibilité aux écarts de langue et la sélection d'informateurs dans l'analyse d'erreurs: une expérience». *The Incorporated Linguist* 24:1. 29–32.

Gile, Daniel. 1986a. «La reconnaissance des kango dans la perception du discours japonais». *Lingua* 70:2–3. 171–189.

Gile, Daniel. 1986b. «La traduction médicale doit-elle être réservée aux seuls médecins ?» *Meta* 31:1. 26–30.

Gile, Daniel. 1987. «Les exercices d'interprétation et la dégradation du français: une étude de cas». *Meta* 32:4. 420–428.

Gile, Daniel. 1988a. «L'enseignement de la traduction japonais-français: une formation à l'analyse». *Meta* 33:1. 13–21.

Gile, Daniel. 1988b. «Observations sur l'enrichissement lexical dans la progression vers un japonais langue passive pour l'interprétation de conférence». *Meta*. 33:1. 79–89.

Gile, Daniel. 1988c. "Japanese Logic and the Training of Translators", in Hammond, Deanna L. (ed). 257–264.

Gile, Daniel. 1989. *La communication linguistique en réunion multilingue Les difficultés de la transmission informationnelle en interprétation simultanée.* Unpublished doctoral dissertation. Université Paris 3.

Gile, Daniel. 1990. "Scientific Research vs. Personal Theories in the Investigation of Interpretation." In Gran, Laura and Christopher Taylor (eds). 28–41.

Gile, Daniel. 1991a. «Prise de notes et attention en début d'apprentissage de l'interprétation consécutive - une expérience-démonstration de sensibilisation». *Meta* 36:2. 431–439.

Gile, Daniel. 1991b. *Guide de l'interprétation à l'usage des organisateurs de conférences internationales.* Paris: Premier ministre – délégation générale à la langue française, Ministère des affaires étrangères - Ministère de la francophonie.

Gile, Daniel. 1992a. "Predictable Sentence Endings in Japanese and Conference Interpretation." *The Interpreters' Newsletter,* Special issue n°1. 12–23.

Gile, Daniel. 1992b. Review: "The Quarterly Journal of the Interpreting Association of Japan". *The Interpreters' Newsletter,* Special issue n°1. 71–72.

Gile, Daniel. 1994. "The Process-oriented Approach in the Training of Translators and Interpreters." In Dollerup, Cay & Annette Lindegaard (eds). 107–112.

Gile, Daniel. 1995. "Fidelity assessment in consecutive interpretation: an experiment." *Target* 7:1. 151–164.

Gile, Daniel. 1999a. "Testing the Effort Model's tightrope hypothesis in simultaneous interpreting – A contribution." *Hermes* 23. 153–172.

Gile, Daniel. 1999b. "Variability in the perception of fidelity in simultaneous interpretation." *Hermes* 22. 51–79.

Gile, Daniel. 2001. "Consecutive vs. Simultaneous: Which is more accurate?" *Tsuuyakukenkyuu – Interpreting Studies* 1:1. 8–20.

Gile, Daniel. 2004. "Integrated Problem and Decision Reporting as a translator training tool." *The Journal of Specialised Translation* 2. 2–20. www.jostrans.org

Gile, Daniel. 2005. *La traduction. La comprendre, l'apprendre.* Paris: PUF.

Gile, Daniel. 2008. "Local Cognitive Load in Simultaneous Interpreting and its Implications for Empirical Research." *Forum* 6:2. 59–77.

Godijns, R. & M. Hinderdahl (eds). 2005. *Directionality in Interpreting. The 'Retour' or the Native?* Gent: Communication and Cognition.

Goldman-Eisler, Frieda. 1958. "Speech Analysis and Mental Processes." *Language and Speech* Jan-March 1958. United Kingdom: Robert Draper.

Gopher, Daniel. 2002. "The Skill of Attention Control: Acquisition and Execution of Attention Strategies." In Meyer, D.E. & S. Kornblum (eds). *Synergies in Experimental Psychology, Artificial Intelligence and Cognitive Neuroscience. Attention and Performance.* Vol.9 Cambridge, Massachussets: MIT Press. 299–322.

Gouadec, Daniel. 1989. *Le traducteur, la traduction et l'entreprise.* Paris: AFNOR gestion.

Gouadec, Daniel. 2002. *Profession: traducteur.* Paris: La Maison du Dictionnaire.

Graham, John D. 1983. "Checking, Revision and Editing." In Picken, Catriona (ed). 99–105.

Gran, Laura & John Dodds (eds). 1989. *The Theoretical and Practical Aspects of Teaching Conference Interpretation.* Udine: Campanotto Editore.

Gran, Laura & Christopher Taylor (eds). 1990. *Aspects of Applied and Experimental Research on Conference Interpretation.* Udine: Campanotto Editore.

Gravier, Maurice. 1978. «Pédagogie de la traduction». In Lillebil Grahs (ed). Karlin, Gustav, Bertil Malmberg, *Theory and Practice of Translation (Proceedings of the Nobel Symposium 39, Stockholm).* Berne: Ed. Lang.

Greene, Judith. 1986. *Language Understanding: A Cognitive Approach*. Milton Keynes Philadelphia: Open University Press.

Guibert, Jean. 1979. *La parole. Compréhension et synthèse de la parole par les ordinateurs*. Paris: PUF.

Gutt, Ernst-August. 1991. *Translation and Relevance: Cognition and Context*. Oxford: Basil Blackwell.

Halliday, M.A.K. 1985. *Spoken and Written Language*. Victoria (Australia): Deakin University Press.

Hammond, Deanna L. (ed). 1988. *Languages at Crossroads, Proceedings of the 29th Annual Conference of the American Translators Association*. Medford, New Jersey: Learned Information Inc.

Hansen, Gyde. 1997. "Success in translation." *Perspectives: Studies in Translatology* 5:2. 201–210.

Hansen, Gyde. 2006a. "Retrospection methods in translator training and translation research." *Jostrans* n°.5, January. www.jostrans.org/archive.php?display=05

Hansen, Gyde. 2006b. *Erfoglreich Übersetzen. Entdecken und Beheben von Störquellen*. Tübingen: Gunter Narr.

Hansen, Gyde. 2009. "Linguistic sensitivity". In Laplace, Colette, Marianne Lederer & Daniel Gile (eds). *La traduction et ses métiers: Aspects théoriques et pratiques*. Paris: Minard.

Hara, Fujiko. 1988. "Understanding the Silent Culture of the Japanese". *Meta* 33:1. 22–24.

Harris, Brian. 1981. "Prolegomenon to a Study of the Differences Between Teaching Translation and Teaching Interpreting." In Delisle, Jean (ed). 153–162.

Hatim, Basil & Ian Mason. 1997. *The Translator as Communicator*. London & New York: Routledge.

Healey, F. 1978. "Translators Made, not Born?" *The Incorporated Linguist* 17:3. 54–58.

Henderson, J.A. 1976. "Note-taking for consecutive interpreting". *Babel* 22:3. 107–116.

Henderson, J.A. 1987. *Personality and the Linguist: A Comparison of the Personality Profiles of Professional Translators and Conference Interpreters*. University of Bradford Press.

Herbert, Jean. 1952. *Le manuel de l'interprète*. Genève: Georg.

Holmes, James. 1972/1987. "The name and nature of Translation Studies." In Toury, Gideon (ed). *Translation Across Cultures*. New Delhi: Bahri Publications.

Holmes, V.M. 1988. "Hesitations and Sentence Planning". *Language and Cognitive Processes* 3:4. 323–361.

Holz-Mäntärri, Justa. 1984. *Translatorisches Handeln: Theorie und Methode* (Annales Academiae Scientarium Fennicae B 226). Helsinki: Suomalainen Tiedeakatemia/Finnish Academy of Science.

Hönig, Hans. 1988. "Übersetzen lernt man nicht durch Übersetzen. Ein Plädoyer für eine Propädeutik des Übersetzens." *Fremdsprachen lehren und lernen. FLuL* n°17. 154–167.

Hönig, Hans. 1995. *Konstruktives Übersetzen*. Tübingen: Stauffenburg.

Hörmann, Hans. 1972. *Introduction à la psycholinguistique*. Paris: Larousse (translation of German version, Berlin-Heidelberg: Springer-Verlag, 1971).

Huey, E.B. 1908. *The psychology and pedagogy of reading*. New York: Macmillan.

Hung, Eva (ed). 2002. *Teaching Translation and Interpreting 4*. Amsterdam/Philadelphia: John Benjamins.

Ilg, Gérard. 1978. «L'apprentissage de l'interprétation simultanée de l'allemand vers le français.» *Parallèles* n°1, *Cahiers de l'E.T.I.*, université de Genève. 69–99.

Ilg, Gérard. 1980. «L'interprétation consécutive: les fondements». *Parallèles* n°3. 109–136, *Cahiers de l'E.T.I.*, Université de Genève.

Ilg, Gérard.1988. «La prise de notes en interprétation consécutive. Une orientation générale». *Parallèles* n°9. 9–13.

Ito-Bergerot, Hiromi. 2006. *Le processus cognitif de la compréhension en interprétation consécutive: acquisition des compétences chez les étudiants de la section japonaise*. Unpublished doctoral dissertation, ESIT, Université de la Sorbonne Nouvelle – Paris 3.

Jääskeläinen, Riitta. 1999. "Investigating Translation Strategies". In Tirkkonen-Condit, Sonja & John Laffling (eds). *Recent Trends in Empirical Translation Research*. Joensuu: University of Joensuu. 99–119.

Jääskeläinen, Riitta & Sonja Tirkkonen-Condit. 1991. "Automatised Processes in Professional vs. Non-Professional Translation: A Think-Aloud Protocol Study", in Tirkkonen-Condit, Sonja (ed). 89–110.

Jakobsen, A.L. 1999. "Translog documentation." *Copenhagen Studies in Language* 24. 9–20.

Jakobson, Roman. 1959. "On Linguistic Aspects of Translation." In R.A. Brower (ed). *On Translation.* Cambridge, Massachussets: Harvard University Press.

Janzen, Terry (ed). 2005. *Topics in Signed Language Interpreting*: Amsterdam/Philadelphia: John Benjamins.

Juhel, Denis. 1985. «La place de la réflexion théorique dans l'enseignement de la traduction». *Meta* 30:3. 292–295.

Just, Marcel Adam & Patricia A. Carpenter. 1992. "A Capacity Theory of Comprehension: Individual Differences in Working Memory." *Psychological Review* 99:1. 122–149.

Just, Marcel Adam, Timothy A. keller, Jacquelyn Cynkar. 2008. "A decrease in brain activation associated with driving when listening to someone speak." *Brain Research* 1205. 70–80. www.elsevier.com/locate/brainres

Kade, Otto. 1963. "Der Dolmetschvorgang und die Notation." *Fremdsprachen* 7:1. 12–20.

Kade, Otto & Claus Cartellieri. 1971. "Some Methodological Aspects of Simultaneous Interpreting." *Babel* 17:2. 12–16.

Kaeding, F.W. 1897. *Häufigkeitswörterbuch der deutschen Sprache.* Berlin: Selbstverlag des Herausgebers, Mittler Sohn.

Kahneman, D. 1973. *Attention and Effort.* Englewoods Cliffs, N.J.: Prentice Hall.

Katan, David. 2009. "Translation Theory and Professional Practice: A Global Survey of the Great Divide". *Hermes* n°42. 111–153.

Keiser, Walter. 1970. «Les écoles d'interprétation et de traduction répondent-elles à ce que la profession et les employeurs en attendent ?» *L'interprète* n°4.

Keiser, Walter. 1978. "Selection and Training of Conference Interpreters." In Gerver, David & H. Wallace Sinaiko (eds). 11–24.

Keller, Timothy, Patricia Carpenter & Marcel Adam Just. 2001. "The neural bases of sentence comprehension: A fMRI examination of syntactic and lexical processing." *Cerebral Cortex* 11. 223–237.

Kelly, Dorothy. 2005. *A Handbook for Translator Trainers.* Manchester, UK & Northampton, MA: StJerome.

Kelly, Dorothy, Anne Martin, Marie-Louise Nobs, Dolores Sánchez, Catherine Way (eds). 2003. *La direccionalidad en traducción e interpretación. Perspectivas teoréticas, profesionales y didácticas.* Granada: Atrio.

Kintsch, W. 1970. *Learning, Memory and Conceptual Processes.* New York, Chichester: Wiley.

Kintsch, W. 1974. *The Representation of Meaning in Memory.* Hillsdale, New Jersey: Lawrence Erlbaum Associates.

Kintsch, W. & T.A. Van Dijk. 1975. «Comment on rappelle et on résume des histoires». *Langages* 40. 98–116.

Kiraly, Donald. 1995. *Pathways to Translation. Pedagogy and Process.* Kent, Ohio & London, England: The Kent State University Press.

Kiraly, Donald. 2005. "Project-Based Learning: A Case for Situated Translation." *Meta* 50:4. 1098–1111.

Komatsu, Tatsuya. 2005. *Tsuuyaku no gijutsu (Interpreting Skills).* Tokyo: Kenkyusha.

Komissarov, Vilen. 1985. "The Practical Value of Translation Theory." *Babel* 31:4. 208–212.

Kondo, Masaomi. 1988. "Japanese Interpreters in Their Socio-Cultural Context". *Meta* 33:1. 70–78.

Kondo, Masaomi. 2008. "Multiple Layers of Meaning – Toward a Deepening of the "Sense" Theory of Interpreting." In WANG, Enmian & WANG, Dong Zhi (eds). *Towards Quality Interpretation in* the 21st Century. Proceedings of the 6th National Conference and International Forum on Interpreting. Beijing: Foreign Language Teaching and Research Press. 35–40.

Kopczynski, Andrzej. 1994. "Quality in conference interpreting: Some pragmatic problems." In Snell-Hornby, Mary, Franz Pöchhacker & Klaus Kaindl (eds). *Translation Studies An interdiscipline*. Amsterdam & Philadelphia: John Benjamins Publishing Company. 189–198.

Kourganoff, Vladimir. 1980. «Quelques traquenards du thème scientifique anglais». *Traduire* n°103. 4–6.

Krings, Hans P. 1982/1986. "Translation Problems and Translation Strategies of Advanced German Learners of French (L2)." In House, Juliane & Shoshana Blum-Kulka (eds). *Interlingual and Intercultural Communication*. Tübingen: Narr. 263–276.

Krings, Hans P. 1986. *Was in den Köpfen von Übersetzer vorgeht. Eine empirische Untersuchung der Struktur des Übersetzungsprozesses an fortgeschrittenen Französischlernern*. Tübingen: Gunter Narr.

Kunihiro, Masao, Sen Nishiyama & Nobuo Kanayama. 1969. *Tsûyaku Eigokaiwa kara doojitsuuyaku made (Interpreting: from English Conversation to Simultaneous Interpreting)*. Tokyo: Nihonhososhuppankyokai.

Kuootarii Tsuuyakurironkenkyuu (Quarterly Journal of the Interpreting Research Association of Japan), 1991.Vol.1, n°1.

Kurz, Ingrid. 1983. "'Der von uns…': Schwierigkeiten des Simultandolmetschens Deutsch-Englisch". In *Festschrift zum 40 Jährigen Bestehen des Instituts für Übersetzer- und Dolmetscherausbildung der Universität Wien*. Tulln: Dr. Ott Verlag. 91–98.

Kurz, Ingrid. 1988. "Conference Interpreters - Can They Afford not to Be Generalists?" in Hammond, Deanna L. (ed). 423–428.

Kurz, Ingrid. 1989. "Conference Interpreting: User Expectations", in ATA - *Proceedings of the 30th Annual Conference*. Medford, New Jersey: Learned Information Inc. 143–148.

Kurz, Ingrid. 2000. "Translators and interpreters: different learning styles?" *Across Languages and Cultures* 1:1. 71–83.

Kurz, Ingrid. 2002. "Physiological stress responses during media and conference interpreting." in Garzone & Viezzi (eds). *Interpreting in the 21 st Century*. Amsterdam/Philadelphia: John Benjamins. 195–202.

Lagarde, Laurent. 2009. *Le traducteur professionnel face aux textes techniques et à la recherche documentaire*. Doctoral dissertation, Université Paris 3 Sorbonne Nouvelle.

Lamberger-Felber, Heike. 1998. *Der Einfluss kontextueller Faktoren auf das Simultandolmetschen. Eine Fallstudie am Beispiel gelesene Reden*. Unpublished doctoral dissertation, Karl Franzens Universität Graz.

Lambert, Sylvie. 1988. "Information Processing among Conference Interpreters: A Test of the Depth of Processing Hypothesis." *Meta* 33:3. 377–387.

Lambert, Sylvie. 1989. «La formation d'interprète: méthode cognitive». *Meta* 34:4. 736–744.

Lambert, Sylvie. 1992. "Shadowing." *Meta* 37:2. 263–273.

Lang, Margaret F. 1992. "Common Ground in Teaching Translation and Interpreting: Discourse Analysis Techniques." In Dollerup, Cay & Anne Loddegaard (eds). 205–208.

Larose, Robert. 1985. «La théorie de la traduction: à quoi ça sert ?» *Meta* 30:4. 405–406.

Larose, Robert. 1989. *Théories contemporaines de la traduction*. Presses de l'université du Québec.

Lavault, Elisabeth. 1998 «La traduction comme négociation». In Delisle, Jean & Hannelore Lee-Jahnke (eds). *Enseignement de la traduction et traduction dans l'enseignement*. Ottawa: Les Presses de l'Université d'Ottawa. 79–95.

Lederer, Marianne. 1975. «Rapport sur le colloque sur les examens d'entrée aux écoles d'interprètes.» *Bulletin de l'AIIC* 3:2. 25–28.

Lederer, Marianne. 1978. *Les fondements théoriques de la traduction simultanée*. Doctoral dissertation. Université Paris 3.

Lederer, Marianne. 1981. «La pédagogie de la traduction simultanée.» In Delisle, Jean (ed). 47–74.

Lederer, Marianne. 2005. "What clues do the early studies of interpreting give us about translation, language and communication?" Online paper, www.hf.uio.no/ilos/forskning/forskning-sprosjekter/expertise/workshops/oslo2005/Lederer, last visited in December 2008.

Lederer, Marianne. 2008. "Can Theory Help Translators and Interpreter Trainers and Trainees?" In Wang, Enmian & Wang Dong Zhi (eds). *Toward Quality Interpretation in the 21st Century. Proceedings of the 6th National Conference and International Forum on Interpreting*. Beijing: Foreign Language Teaching and Research Press. 107–129.

Lee, Hyang. 2006. "Translator Training: Beyond the dichotomy of theory vs. practice." *Forum* 4:2. 41–51.

Leeson, Richard. 1975. *Fluency and Language Teaching*. London: Longman.

Le Ny, Jean-François. 1978. "Psychosemantics and Simultaneous Interpretation." In Gerver, David & H. Wallace Sinaiko (eds). 289–298.

Levý, Jiří. 1967. "Translation as a decision-making process." In *To Honour Roman Jakobson*, Vol.2. The Hague: Mouton. 1171–1182.

Li, Feng. 2001. *Etude de l'interprétation simultanée du chinois en français: spécificités linguistiques, solutions pratiques et retombées pédagogiques*. Doctoral dissertation, Paris, Université Paris 3.

Lin, Kevin. 2004. *Field Interpreting*. Beijing: Foreign Language Teaching and Research Press. (in Chinese)

Liu, Minhua. 2001. *Expertise in simultaneous interpreting: a Working Memory analysis*. Unpublished doctoral dissertation, University of Texas at Austin.

Lörscher, Wofgang. 1993. "Translation Process Analysis". In Gambier, Yves & Jorma Tommola (eds). *Translation and Knowledge, SSOTT IV*. Scandinavian Symposium on Translation Theory, Turku, June 4–6, 1992. Turku: University of Turku, Centre for Translation and Interpreting.

Lörscher, Wolfgang. 1991. "Thinking-aloud as a Method for Collecting Data on Translation Processes." In Tirkkonen-Condit (ed). *Empirical Research in Translation and Intercultural Studies: Selected Papers of the TRANS-SIF Seminar, Savonlinna 1988*. Tübingen: Narr. 67–77.

Lung, Rachel. 1999. "Note-taking skills and comprehension in consecutive interpretation." *Babel* 45:4. 311–317.

MacDonald, M.C. 1997. *Language and Cognitive Processes*, Special Issue on Lexical Representations and Sentence Processing 12. 121–399.

Mackintosh, Jennifer. 1983. *Relay Interpretation: an Exploratory Study*, M.A. thesis. University of London.

Maclay, H. & C. Osgood. 1959. "Hesitation Phenomena in Spontaneous English Speech." *Word* n°15.

Magalhães, Ewandro. 2007. *Sua majestade, o intérprete. O fascinante mundo da tradução simultânea*. São Paulo: Parábola Editorial.

Mahmoudian, Mortéza. 1982. *La linguistique*. Paris: Seghers.

Maillot, Jean. 1970. «Terminologie et traduction». *Meta* 16:1–2. 75–81.

Maillot, Jean. 1981. *La traduction scientifique et technique*, 2e édition. Paris: Technique et documentation.

Matthei, Edward & Thomas Roeper. 1985. *Understanding and Producing Speech*. New York: Universe Books.

Matysiak, Anna. 2001. *Controlled processing in simultaneous interpreting: A study based on Daniel Gile's Effort Models*. MA thesis, University of Poznan.

Matysek, Heinz. 1989. *Handbuch der Notizentechnik für Dolmetscher: ein Weg zur sprachunabhängigen Notation*. Heidelberg: J. Groos.

Mauranen, Anna & Pekka Kujamäki (eds). 2004. *Translation Universals. Do they exist?* Amsterdam/ Philadelphia: John Benjamins.

Mazza, C. 2000. *Numbers in Simultaneous Interpretation*. Unpublished Graduation thesis, SSLMIT, Università degli Studi di Bologna, Sede di Forlì.

Mellen, Donna. 1988. "The Translator: Translator or Editor?" in Hammond, Deanna L. (ed). 271–276.

Meier, H. 1964. *Deutsche Sprachstatistik*. Hildesheim: G. Olms.

Meta 43:4 (1998). Special issue on the corpus-based approach. http://www.erudit.org/revue/meta/1998/v43/n4/

Metzger, Melanie. 2002. *Sign Language Interpreting: Deconstructing the myth of neutrality*. Gallaudet University Press.

Meyer, Ingrid. 1988. "Pedagogical Lexicography and Translator Training: Teaching Cautious Use of Bilingual Dictionaries." In Hammond, Deanna L. (ed). 277–284.

Michael, Erica B., Timothy A. Keller, Patricia A. Carpeter & Marcel Adam Just. 2001. "fMRI Investigation of Sentence Comprehension by Eye and by Ear: Modality Fingerprints on Cognitive Processes." *Human Brain Mapping* 13. 239–252.

Miller, George A. 1956. *Langage et communication*. Paris: PUF.

Miller, George A. 1962. "Decision Units in the Perception of Speech", in *IRE Transactions on Information Theory*, IT-8:2. 81–83, reprinted in *Automatic Speech Recognition* Vol.2 Ha-79–81, University of Michigan: Ann Harbor, 1963.

Mitchell, AnnMarie. 1988. "Nontraditional Reference Sources." In Hammond, Deanna L. (ed). 285–289.

Miyake, A. & Shah, P (eds).1999. *Models of working memory: Mechanisms of active maintenance and executive control*. New York: Cambridge University Press.

Mizuno, Akira. 1997. "Imi no riron no hihan to tsuuyakumoderu" ("A criticism of the Theory of Sense and an alternative model"). *Tsuuyakurironkenkyuu - Interpreting Research* n°13(7:1). 53–67.

Mizutani, Osamu. 1981. *The Spoken Language in Japanese Life*. Tokyo: The Japanese Times.

Monacelli, Claudia. 1999. *Messagi in codice*. Milano: Franco Angelli.

Montani, Erica. 2003. *Il profilo psicologico dell'interprete*. Graduation thesis, SSLMIT, Università degli Studi di Bologna, Sede di Forlì.

Monterey Institute of International Studies, Division of Translation and Interpretation. 1989. *Proceedings of the Twentieth Anniversary Symposium on the Training of Teachers of Translation and Interpretation*. Monterey.

Moray, N. 1967. "Where is Capacity Limited? A Survey and a Model." *Acta Psychologica* n°27. 84–92.

Morris, Ruth. 1989. *The Impact of Court Interpretation on Legal Proceedings*. Unpublished M.A. thesis. Communications Institute, Hebrew University of Jerusalem.

Moser, Barbara. 1978. "Simultaneous Interpretation: A Hypothetical Model and its Practical Application." In Gerver, David & H. Wallace Sinaiko (eds). 353–368.

Moser, Peter. 1997. "Expectations of users of conference interpretation." *Interpreting* 1:2. 145–178.

Mounin, Georges. 1963. *Les problèmes théoriques de la traduction*. Paris: Gallimard.

Munday, Jeremy. 2001. *Introducing Translation Studies. Theories and Applications*. London and New York: Routledge.

Namy, Claude. 1979. «Du mot au message: réflexions sur l'interprétation simultanée». *Parallèles* n°2.

Namy, Claude. 1988. «Quinze ans d'entraînement dirigé à l'interprétation simultanée d'anglais et d'espagnol en français». *Parallèles* n°9.

Nekrassoff, Vladimir. 1977. "Translation, the Lifeblood of Medical Progress." In Horguelin, Paul E. (ed). *La traduction, une profession*, Proceedings of the 8th World Congress of FIT. Montréal.

Newman, Sharlene D., Timothy A. Keller, Marcel Adam Just. 2007. "Volitional Control of Attention and Brain Activation in Dual Task Performance." *Human Brain Mapping* 28. 109–117. Wiley-Liss.

Newmark, Peter. 1983. "An Introductory Survey." In Picken, Catriona (ed). 1–17.

Nida, Eugene. 1964. *Toward a Science of Translating*. Leiden: Brill.

Nida, Eugene. 1981. "Translators are Born and not Made." *The Bible Translator* 32:4. 401–405.

Nida, Eugene & Charles Taber. 1969. *The Theory and Practice of Translation.* Leiden, Brill.

Nilski, Thérèse. 1967. "Translators and Interpreters: Siblings or a Breed Apart?" *Meta* 12:2. 45–49.

Noizet, Georges. 1980. *De la perception à la compréhension du langage.* Paris: PUF.

Nolan, James. 2005. *Interpretation. Techniques and exercises.* Clevedon, Buffalo, Toronto: Multilingual Matters.

Nord, Christiane. 1991. *Text Analysis in Translation: Theory, Methodology and Didactic Application of a Model for Translation-Oriented Analysis.* Amsterdam: Rodopi.

Nord, Christiane. 1997. *Translation as a purposeful activity. Functionalist approaches explained.* Manchester: StJerome.

Norman, D.A. 1976. *Memory and Attention.* New York: Wiley.

Padilla, P., M.T. Bajo, J.J. Canas, F. Padilla. 1995. "Cognitive Processes of Memory in Simultaneous Interpretation." In Tommola, Jorma (ed). *Topics in Interpreting Research.* Turku: Centre for Translation and Interpreting, University of Turku. 61–71.

Patrie, Carol. 2000a. *English Skills Development*, Study Set on DVD by Carol J. Patrie. DawnSignPress.

Patrie, Carol. 2000b. *Cognitive Processing Skills in English*, Study Set on DVD by Carol J. Patrie. DawnSignPress.

Patrie, Carol. 2001. *Translating from English*, Study Set on DVD by Carol J. Patrie. DawnSignPress.

Patrie, Carol. 2004. *Consecutive Interpreting from English*, Study Set on DVD by Carol J. Patrie. DawnSignPress.

Patrie, Carol. 2005. *Simultaneous Interpreting from English*, Study Set on DVD by Carol J. Patrie. DawnSignPress.

Percival, Christopher. 1983. "Techniques and Presentation." In Picken, Catriona (ed). 89–97.

Petite, Christelle. 2005. "Evidence of repair mechanisms in simultaneous interpreting: A corpus-based analysis." *Interpreting* 7:1. 27–49.

Picken, Catriona (ed). 1983. *The Translator's Handbook.* London: Aslib.

Pinchuk, Isadore. 1977. *Scientific and Technical Translation.* London: André Deutsch.

Pinter, Ingrid. 1969. *Der Einfluss der Übung und Konzentration auf Simultanes Sprechen und Hören.* Unpublished doctoral dissertation, University of Vienna.

Pöchhacker, Franz. 1992. "The role of Theory in Simultaneous Interpreting." In Dollerup, Cay & Anne Loddegaard (eds). 211–220.

Pöchhacker, Franz. 1995. "Those Who do: A Profile or Research(ers) in Interpreting." *Target* 7:1. 47–64.

Pöchhacker, Franz. 2004. *Introducing Interpreting Studies.* London and New York: Routledge.

Pöchhacker, Franz & Miriam Shlesinger. 2001. *The Interpreting Studies Reader.* London and New York: Routledge.

Prat, Chantel S., Timothy Keller & Marcel Adam Just. 2007. "Individual Differences in Sentence Comprehension: A Functional Magnetic Resonance Imaging Investigation of Syntactic and Lexical Processing Demands." *Journal of Cognitive Neuroscience* 19:12. 1950–1963.

Puková, Z. 2006. *Daniel Gile's Effort Model and its application to simultaneous interpreting of texts with a high concentration of numerical data and enumerations* (in Czech). Master's thesis, Charles University, Prague.

Pym, Anthony, Carmina Fallada, José Ramón Biau, Jill Orenstein (eds). 2003. *Innovation and e-learning in translator training.* Tarragona: Intercultural Studies Group, Universitat Rovira I Virgili.

Pym, Anthony, Miriam Shlesinger & Zuzana Jettmarová (eds). 2006. *Sociocultural Aspects of Translating and Interpreting.* Amsterdam/Philadelphia: John Benjamins.

Rainey, Brian E. 1988. "Thoughts on the 'Language Crisis' and the Teaching of Translation." In Hammond, Deanna, L. (ed). 291–296.

Reinert, D. 1976. "Of Bs and Wasps...." *AIIC Bulletin* 4:2.

Reiss, Katharina. 1986. "Übersetzungstheorien und ihre Relevanz für die Praxis." *Lebende Sprachen* Heft 1. 1–5.

Reiss, Katharina & Hans Vermeer. 1984/1991. *Grundlegung einer allgemeinen Translationstheorie.* (Linguistische Arbeiten 147), 2nd edition. Tübingen: Niemeyer.

Rey, Alain. 1979. *La terminologie, noms et notions.* Paris: PUF.

Richard, Jean-François. 1980. *L'attention.* Paris: PUF.

Richaudeau, François. 1973. *Le langage efficace.* Paris: Denoël.

Richaudeau, François. 1981. *Linguistique pragmatique.* Paris: Retz.

Roberts, Rhoda. 1984. «Compétence du nouveau diplômé en traduction», in *Traduction et qualité de langue*, Actes du Colloque, Société des traducteurs du Québec / Conseil de la langue française, Québec, Editeur officiel du Québec. 172–184.

Roberts, Rhoda. 1988. "The role and teaching of theory in translator training programmes." *Meta* 33:2. 164–173.

Robinson, Douglas. 1997. *Becoming a Translator.* London & New York: Routledge.

Rozan, Jean-François. 1956. *La prise de notes en interprétation consécutive.* Genève: Georg.

Rubin, Eli H. 1948. *Diseases of the Chest,* Philadelphia and London: W.B. Saunders Company.

Ruiz, C., N. Paredes, P. Macizo, M.T. Bajo. 2007. "Activation of lexical and syntactic target language properties in translation." *Acta Psychologica.* doi:10.1016/j.actpsy.2007.08.004

Sabah, Gérard. 1988. *L'intelligence artificielle et le langage.* Paris: Hermès.

Sachs, J.S. 1967. "Recognition memory for syntactic and semantic aspects of connected discourse." *Perception and psychophysics* 2. 437–442.

Sager, Juan C. 1983. "Quality and Standards – the Evaluation of Translations." In Picken, Catriona (ed). 121–128.

Sager, Juan C. 1992. "The Translator as terminologist." In Dollerup, Cay & Anne Loddegaard (eds). 107–122.

Sawyer, David. 2004. *Fundamental Aspects of Interpreter Education.* Amsterdam/Philadelphia: John Benjamins.

Schäffner, Christina & Beverly Adab (eds). 2004. *Developing Translation Competence.* Amsterdam/Philadelphia: John Benjamins.

Schmitt, Peter. 1999. "Defekte im Ausgangstext." In Snell-Hornby *et al.* (eds). 147–151.

Schramm, Wilbur & William E. Porter. 1982. *Men, Women, Messages and Media.* New York: Harper and Row Publishers.

Schweda-Nicholson, Nancy. 1986. "A United Nations Interpreter Survey: The specialist/generalist controversy." *Multilingua* 5:2. 67–80.

Schweda-Nicholson, Nancy. 2005. "Personality characteristics of interpreter trainees: the Myers-Briggs Type Indicator (MBTI)." *The Interpreters' Newsletter* 13. 109–142.

Seleskovitch, Danica. 1975. *Langage, langues et mémoire.* Paris: Minard.

Seleskovitch, Danica. 1977. "Why Interpreting is not Tantamount to Translating Languages." *The Incorporated Linguist* 16:2.

Seleskovitch, Danica. 1981. «L'enseignement de l'interprétation». In Delisle, Jean (ed). 23–46.

Seleskovitch, Danica & Marianne Lederer. 1989. *Pédagogie raisonnée de l'interprétation.* Paris: Didier érudition.

Setton, Robin. 1999. *A cognitive-pragmatic analysis of simultaneous interpretation.* Amsterdam/Philadelphia: John Benjamins.

Setton, Robin. 2003. "Models of the Interpreting Process." In Collados Aís, Ángela, & José Antonio Sabio Pinilla (eds). *Avances en la investigación sobre interpretación.* Granada: Comares. 29–89.

Shannon, C.E. 1948. "A Mathematical Theory of Communication." *Bell Systems Technology Journal* 27:3. 379–423, 27:4. 623–656.

Shreve, Gregory & Bruce J. Diamond. 1997. "Cognitive Processes in Translation and Interpreting. Critical Issues." In Danks, Joseph H., Gregory M. Shreve, Stephen B. Fountain, Michael K. McBeath (eds). *Cognitive Processes in Translation and Interpretation.* Thousand Oaks, London and New Delhi: Sage Publications.

Shuttleworth, M. 2001. "The role of theory in translator training: Some observations about syllabus design." *Meta* 46:3. 497–506.

Snell, Barbara & Patricia Crampton. 1983. "Types of Translation." In Picken, Catriona (ed). 109–120.

Snell-Hornby, Mary. 1992. "The Professional Translator of Tomorrow: Language Specialist or All-round Expert?" In Dollerup, Cay & Anne Loddegaard (eds). 9–22.

Snell-Hornby, Mary. 2006. *The Turns of Translation Studies.* Amsterdam/Philadelphia: John Benjamins.

Snell-Hornby, Mary, Hans Hönig, Paul Kussmaul & Peter Schmitt (Hrsg). 1999. *Handbuch Translation.* Zweite, verbesserte Auflage. Tübingen: Stauffenburg.

Sperber, Dan & Deirdre Wilson. 1986. *Relevance: Communication and Cognition.* Oxford: Basil Blackwell.

Steiner, George. 1975/1992. *After Babel: Aspects of Language and Translation.* London, Oxford and New York: Oxford University Press.

Stolze, Radegundis. 2000. *Hermeneutik und Translation.* Tübingen: Gunter Narr.

Suzuki, Atsuko. 1988. "Aptitudes of Translators and Interpreters." *Meta* 33:1. 108–114.

Sykes, John B. 1983. "The Intellectuals Tools Employed." In Picken, Catriona (ed). 41–45.

Tennent, Martha (ed). 2005. *Training for the New Millenium.* Amsterdam/Philadelphia: John Benjamins.

Tetrault, Emery W. 1988. "On Generic Training." In Hammond, Deanna L. (ed). 323–338.

Thiéry, Christopher. 1975. *Le bilinguisme chez les interprètes de conférence professionnels.* Unpublished doctoral dissertation. Université Paris 3.

Thiéry, Christopher. 1976. «Le bilinguisme vrai». *Etudes de Linguistique Appliquée* n°24. 52–63.

Thiéry, Christopher. 1989. "Letter to the Editor." *The Interpreters' Newsletter* n°2. 3–5.

Thorndike, E.L. & I. Lorge. 1944. *The Teachers Wordbook of 30 000 Words.* New York: Bureau of Publications, Teacher's College, Columbia University.

Timarová, Šárka. 2008. "Working Memory and Simultaneous Interpreting." In Boulogne, Pieter (ed). *Translation and Its Others. Selected Papers of the CETRA Research Seminar in Translation Studies 2007.* http://www.kuleuven.be/cetra/papers/papers.html

Tirkkonen-Condit, Sonja. 1990. "Professional vs. Non-Professional Translation: a Think-Aloud Protocol Study." In Halliday, Michael, John Gibbons and Howard Nicholas (eds). *Learning, Keeping and Using Language. Selected Papers from the eighth World Congress of Applied Linguistics.* Sydney, 16–21 August 1987. Amsterdam/Philadelphia: John Benjamins. 381–394.

Tirkkonen-Condit, Sonja (ed). 1991. *Empirical Research in Translation and Intercultural Studies.* Tübingen: Gunter Narr Verlag.

Tirkkonen-Condit, Sonja & Riitta Jääskeläinen (eds). 2000. *Tapping and Maping the Processes of Translation and Interpreting. Outlooks on Empirical Research.* Amsterdam/Philadelphia: John Benjamins.

Torikai, Kumiko. 2009. *Voices of the Invisible Presence. Diplomatic interpreters in post-World War II Japan.* Amsterdam/Philadelphia: John Benjamins.

Toury, Gideon. 1991. "Experimentation in Translation Studies: Achievements, Prospects and some Pitfalls." In Sonja Tirkkonen-Condit (ed). 45–66.

Toury, Gideon. 1995. *Descriptive Translation Studies and Beyond*. Amsterdam/Philadelphia: John Benjamins.

Tulving, Endel, Daniel L Shacter & Heather A. Stark. 1982. "Priming Effects in Word-Fragment Completion are Independent of Recognition Memory." *Journal of Experimental Psychology: Learning, Memory and Cognition* 8:4. 336–342.

Venuti, Lawrence. 1995. *The Translator's Invisibility*. London & New York, Routledge.

Venuti, Lawrence. 2000. *The Translation Studies Reader*. London and New York: Routledge.

Viaggio, Sergio. 1988. "Teaching Interpretation to Beginners or How not to Scare Them to Death." In Hammond, Deanna L. (ed). 399–406.

Viaggo, Sergio. 1992. "Translators and Interpreters: Professionals or Shoemakers?" in Dollerup, Cay & Anne Loddegaard (eds). 307–312.

Vinay, Jean-Paul. 1983. "SCFA Revisited." *Meta* 28:4. 417–430.

Vinay, Jean-Paul & Jean Darbelnet. 1958. *Stylistique comparée du français et de l'anglais*. Paris: Didier.

Vinay, Jean-Paul & Jean Darbelnet. 1995. *Comparative Stylistics of French and English: A methodology for translation*. Translated and edited by J.C. Sager & M.J. Hamel. Amsterdam/Philadelphia: John Benjamins.

Watanabe, Shoichi ("Research Representative"). 1991. *Gaikokugokyôiku no ikkan toshite no tsûyakuyô-sei no tame no kyôikunaiyôhôhô ni kaihatsu ni kansuru sôgôkenkyû (Research on Interpretation Training Methodology as Part of Foreign Language Training)*, Report on a project funded by the Japanese Ministry of Education, published in March 1991 by the laboratory of Prof. Matsuo of Sophia University, Tokyo.

Weber, Wilhelm. 1984. *Training Translators and Conference Interpreters*. New York: Harcourt Brace Jovanovich, Inc.

Widlund-Fantini, Anne-Marie. 2007. *Danica Seleskovitch. Interprète et témoin du XXe siècle*. Lausanne: L'âge d'homme.

Wilss, Wolfram. 1978. "Syntactic Anticipation in German-English Simultaneous Interpreting." In Gerver, David & H. Wallace Sinaiko (eds). 343–352.

Winston, Patrick Henry. 1984. *Artificial Intelligence*. Cambridge, MA: Addison-Wesley. Second Edition.

Zhong, Shukong. 1984. *Shiyong kouyi shouce (A Practical Handbook of Interpretation)*. Beijing: Zhong-guo Duiwai Fanyi Chuban Gongsi [China Foreign Language Translation Publishing Co.]

Zhong, Weihe. 2007. *A Foundation Coursebook of Interpreting between English and Chinese*. Beijing: Higher education Press. (in Chinese)

Zipf, G.K. 1949. *Human Behavior and the Principle of Least Effort*. Cambridge, MA: Addison-Wesley.

Zhuang, Chenyuan & Yinchen Qiu. 2008. *Apprendre et pratiquer l'interprétation*. Beijing: Foreign Language Teaching and Research Press. (in Chinese)

CIRIN Bulletin www.cirinandgile.com

EST website   www.est-translationstudies.org

Name index

Concept index

Benjamins Translation Library

A complete list of titles in this series can be found on *www.benjamins.com*

61 HUNG, Eva (ed.): Translation and Cultural Change. Studies in history, norms and image-projection. 2005. xvi, 195 pp.

60 TENNENT, Martha (ed.): Training for the New Millennium. Pedagogies for translation and interpreting. 2005. xxvi, 276 pp.

59 MALMKJÆR, Kirsten (ed.): Translation in Undergraduate Degree Programmes. 2004. vi, 202 pp.

58 BRANCHADELL, Albert and Lovell Margaret WEST (eds.): Less Translated Languages. 2005. viii, 416 pp.

57 CHERNOV, Ghelly V.: Inference and Anticipation in Simultaneous Interpreting. A probability-prediction model. Edited with a critical foreword by Robin Setton and Adelina Hild. 2004. xxx, 268 pp. [EST Subseries 2]

56 ORERO, Pilar (ed.): Topics in Audiovisual Translation. 2004. xiv, 227 pp.

55 ANGELELLI, Claudia V.: Revisiting the Interpreter's Role. A study of conference, court, and medical interpreters in Canada, Mexico, and the United States. 2004. xvi, 127 pp.

54 GONZÁLEZ DAVIES, Maria: Multiple Voices in the Translation Classroom. Activities, tasks and projects. 2004. x, 262 pp.

53 DIRIKER, Ebru: De-/Re-Contextualizing Conference Interpreting. Interpreters in the Ivory Tower? 2004. x, 223 pp.

52 HALE, Sandra: The Discourse of Court Interpreting. Discourse practices of the law, the witness and the interpreter. 2004. xviii, 267 pp.

51 CHAN, Leo Tak-hung: Twentieth-Century Chinese Translation Theory. Modes, issues and debates. 2004. xvi, 277 pp.

50 HANSEN, Gyde, Kirsten MALMKJÆR and Daniel GILE (eds.): Claims, Changes and Challenges in Translation Studies. Selected contributions from the EST Congress, Copenhagen 2001. 2004. xiv, 320 pp. [EST Subseries 1]

49 PYM, Anthony: The Moving Text. Localization, translation, and distribution. 2004. xviii, 223 pp.

48 MAURANEN, Anna and Pekka KUJAMÄKI (eds.): Translation Universals. Do they exist? 2004. vi, 224 pp.

47 SAWYER, David B.: Fundamental Aspects of Interpreter Education. Curriculum and Assessment. 2004. xviii, 312 pp.

46 BRUNETTE, Louise, Georges L. BASTIN, Isabelle HEMLIN and Heather CLARKE (eds.): The Critical Link 3. Interpreters in the Community. Selected papers from the Third International Conference on Interpreting in Legal, Health and Social Service Settings, Montréal, Quebec, Canada 22–26 May 2001. 2003. xii, 359 pp.

45 ALVES, Fabio (ed.): Triangulating Translation. Perspectives in process oriented research. 2003. x, 165 pp.

44 SINGERMAN, Robert: Jewish Translation History. A bibliography of bibliographies and studies. With an introductory essay by Gideon Toury. 2002. xxxvi, 420 pp.

43 GARZONE, Giuliana and Maurizio VIEZZI (eds.): Interpreting in the 21st Century. Challenges and opportunities. 2002. x, 337 pp.

42 HUNG, Eva (ed.): Teaching Translation and Interpreting 4. Building bridges. 2002. xii, 243 pp.

41 NIDA, Eugene A.: Contexts in Translating. 2002. x, 127 pp.

40 ENGLUND DIMITROVA, Birgitta and Kenneth HYLTENSTAM (eds.): Language Processing and Simultaneous Interpreting. Interdisciplinary perspectives. 2000. xvi, 164 pp.

39 CHESTERMAN, Andrew, Natividad GALLARDO SAN SALVADOR and Yves GAMBIER (eds.): Translation in Context. Selected papers from the EST Congress, Granada 1998. 2000. x, 393 pp.

38 SCHÄFFNER, Christina and Beverly ADAB (eds.): Developing Translation Competence. 2000. xvi, 244 pp.

37 TIRKKONEN-CONDIT, Sonja and Riitta JÄÄSKELÄINEN (eds.): Tapping and Mapping the Processes of Translation and Interpreting. Outlooks on empirical research. 2000. x, 176 pp.

36 SCHMID, Monika S.: Translating the Elusive. Marked word order and subjectivity in English-German translation. 1999. xii, 174 pp.

35 SOMERS, Harold (ed.): Computers and Translation. A translator's guide. 2003. xvi, 351 pp.

34 GAMBIER, Yves and Henrik GOTTLIEB (eds.): (Multi) Media Translation. Concepts, practices, and research. 2001. xx, 300 pp.

33 GILE, Daniel, Helle V. DAM, Friedel DUBSLAFF, Bodil MARTINSEN and Anne SCHJOLDAGER (eds.): Getting Started in Interpreting Research. Methodological reflections, personal accounts and advice for beginners. 2001. xiv, 255 pp.

32 BEEBY, Allison, Doris ENSINGER and Marisa PRESAS (eds.): Investigating Translation. Selected papers from the 4th International Congress on Translation, Barcelona, 1998. 2000. xiv, 296 pp.

31 ROBERTS, Roda P., Silvana E. CARR, Diana ABRAHAM and Aideen DUFOUR (eds.): The Critical Link 2: Interpreters in the Community. Selected papers from the Second International Conference on Interpreting in legal, health and social service settings, Vancouver, BC, Canada, 19–23 May 1998. 2000. vii, 316 pp.

30 DOLLERUP, Cay: Tales and Translation. The Grimm Tales from Pan-Germanic narratives to shared international fairytales. 1999. xiv, 384 pp.

29 WILSS, Wolfram: Translation and Interpreting in the 20th Century. Focus on German. 1999. xiii, 256 pp.

28 SETTON, Robin: Simultaneous Interpretation. A cognitive-pragmatic analysis. 1999. xv, 397 pp.

27 BEYLARD-OZEROFF, Ann, Jana KRÁLOVÁ and Barbara MOSER-MERCER (eds.): Translators' Strategies and Creativity. Selected Papers from the 9th International Conference on Translation and Interpreting, Prague, September 1995. In honor of Jiří Levý and Anton Popovič. 1998. xiv, 230 pp.

26 TROSBORG, Anna (ed.): Text Typology and Translation. 1997. xvi, 342 pp.

25 POLLARD, David E. (ed.): Translation and Creation. Readings of Western Literature in Early Modern China, 1840–1918. 1998. vi, 336 pp.

24 ORERO, Pilar and Juan C. SAGER (eds.): The Translator's Dialogue. Giovanni Pontiero. 1997. xiv, 252 pp.

23 GAMBIER, Yves, Daniel GILE and Christopher TAYLOR (eds.): Conference Interpreting: Current Trends in Research. Proceedings of the International Conference on Interpreting: What do we know and how? 1997. iv, 246 pp.

22 CHESTERMAN, Andrew: Memes of Translation. The spread of ideas in translation theory. 1997. vii, 219 pp.

21 BUSH, Peter and Kirsten MALMKJÆR (eds.): Rimbaud's Rainbow. Literary translation in higher education. 1998. x, 200 pp.

20 SNELL-HORNBY, Mary, Zuzana JETTMAROVÁ and Klaus KAINDL (eds.): Translation as Intercultural Communication. Selected papers from the EST Congress, Prague 1995. 1997. x, 354 pp.

19 CARR, Silvana E., Roda P. ROBERTS, Aideen DUFOUR and Dini STEYN (eds.): The Critical Link: Interpreters in the Community. Papers from the 1st international conference on interpreting in legal, health and social service settings, Geneva Park, Canada, 1–4 June 1995. 1997. viii, 322 pp.

18 SOMERS, Harold (ed.): Terminology, LSP and Translation. Studies in language engineering in honour of Juan C. Sager. 1996. xii, 250 pp.

17 POYATOS, Fernando (ed.): Nonverbal Communication and Translation. New perspectives and challenges in literature, interpretation and the media. 1997. xii, 361 pp.

16 DOLLERUP, Cay and Vibeke APPEL (eds.): Teaching Translation and Interpreting 3. New Horizons. Papers from the Third Language International Conference, Elsinore, Denmark, 1995. 1996. viii, 338 pp.

15 WILSS, Wolfram: Knowledge and Skills in Translator Behavior. 1996. xiii, 259 pp.

14 MELBY, Alan K. and Terry WARNER: The Possibility of Language. A discussion of the nature of language, with implications for human and machine translation. 1995. xxvi, 276 pp.

13 DELISLE, Jean and Judith WOODSWORTH (eds.): Translators through History. 1995. xvi, 346 pp.

12 BERGENHOLTZ, Henning and Sven TARP (eds.): Manual of Specialised Lexicography. The preparation of specialised dictionaries. 1995. 256 pp.

11 VINAY, Jean-Paul and Jean DARBELNET: Comparative Stylistics of French and English. A methodology for translation. Translated and edited by Juan C. Sager and M.-J. Hamel. 1995. xx, 359 pp.

10 KUSSMAUL, Paul: Training the Translator. 1995. x, 178 pp.

9 REY, Alain: Essays on Terminology. Translated by Juan C. Sager. With an introduction by Bruno de Bessé. 1995. xiv, 223 pp.

8 GILE, Daniel: Basic Concepts and Models for Interpreter and Translator Training. Revised edition. 2009. xv, 283 pp.

7 BEAUGRANDE, Robert de, Abdullah SHUNNAQ and Mohamed Helmy HELIEL (eds.): Language, Discourse and Translation in the West and Middle East. 1994. xii, 256 pp.

6 EDWARDS, Alicia B.: The Practice of Court Interpreting. 1995. xiii, 192 pp.

5 DOLLERUP, Cay and Annette LINDEGAARD (eds.): Teaching Translation and Interpreting 2. Insights, aims and visions. Papers from the Second Language International Conference Elsinore, 1993. 1994. viii, 358 pp.

4 TOURY, Gideon: Descriptive Translation Studies – and beyond. 1995. viii, 312 pp.

3 LAMBERT, Sylvie and Barbara MOSER-MERCER (eds.): Bridging the Gap. Empirical research in simultaneous interpretation. 1994. 362 pp.

2 SNELL-HORNBY, Mary, Franz PÖCHHACKER and Klaus KAINDL (eds.): Translation Studies: An Interdiscipline. Selected papers from the Translation Studies Congress, Vienna, 1992. 1994. xii, 438 pp.

1 SAGER, Juan C.: Language Engineering and Translation. Consequences of automation. 1994. xx, 345 pp.